Delos White Beadle

Canadian Fruit, Flower, and Kitchen Gardener

A guide in all matters relating to the cultivation of fruits, flowers and vegetables,

and their value for cultivation in this climate

Delos White Beadle

Canadian Fruit, Flower, and Kitchen Gardener
A guide in all matters relating to the cultivation of fruits, flowers and vegetables, and their value for cultivation in this climate

ISBN/EAN: 9783337083151

Printed in Europe, USA, Canada, Australia, Japan

Cover: Foto ©Lupo / pixelio.de

More available books at **www.hansebooks.com**

CANADIAN

Fruit, Flower

AND

Kitchen Gardener.

1872.

CANADIAN
FRUIT, FLOWER,
AND
KITCHEN GARDENER.

BY

D. W. BEADLE, Esq.,

Secretary of the Fruit Growers' Association of Ontario, Editor of the Horticultural Department of the Canada Farmer, &c., &c.

A GUIDE IN ALL MATTERS RELATING TO THE CULTIVATION OF FRUITS, FLOWERS AND VEGETABLES, AND THEIR VALUE FOR CULTIVATION IN THIS CLIMATE.

TORONTO:
PUBLISHED BY JAMES CAMPBELL & SON.
1872.

GLOBE PRINTING COMPANY, KING ST., EAST, TORONTO.

Dedicated,

(By Permission,)

To the

President and Members

Of the

Fruit Growers' Association of Ontario.

By their most devoted humble Servant,

The Author.

CONTENTS.

SUBJECTS.
FRUIT GARDEN.

	PAGE
The Propagation of Fruit Trees—	
Grafting	5
How to Cleft Graft	6
How to Whip Graft	9
How to make Grafting Wax	7
To prepare Waxed Cloth	11
To Select Scions	11
Budding and when to Bud	12
How to Select Buds	14
When to Remove the Ligature and Head Back the Stock	16
The Pruning of Fruit-Trees—	
When to Prune and why	18
Where to Prune	20
Pruning to Produce Fruit	21
Transplanting Trees—	
The best Time to Transplant	23
Preparing the Ground	23
How to Plant	25
The best Trees for Transplanting	27
Mulching—	
What is Meant by Mulching	26
How to Mulch, and why it is done	26
Treatment of Young Orchards—	
To Protect from Mice	30
To Keep the Bark Clean and Healthy	31
Location of Orchard—	
Soil and Aspect	31
Hills and Valleys	32
Injurious Insects, and how to get rid of them—	
The Tent Caterpillar	35
The Two-striped Borer	38
The Buprestis Apple Tree Borer	40
The Codling Worm	42
The Plum Curculio	45

CONTENTS.

	PAGE
The Grape Vine Flea Beetle	49
The Green Grape Vine Sphinx	50
The Gooseberry Saw-fly	52

THE PRODUCTION OF NEW VARIETIES OF FRUIT—
How they are produced	53
Cross-fertilization	58
How to Cross-fertilize	59

THE APPLE—
Soil best Suited to Apples	61
How Propagated	62
Gathering and Sorting for Market	62
Packing and Marketing the Fruit	63
Best Kinds for Market	64
Dwarf and Half-standard Trees	65
Varieties of Apples, with description of each	66

THE APRICOT—
Climate and Soil Suitable	84
How Propagated	84
Varieties, with description	85

THE CHERRY—
Classes of Varieties and Soil best Suited	85
How Propagated and Stocks on which it is Grown	86
Varieties, with full description	87

THE NECTARINE—
| Cultivation and Varieties | 92 |

THE PEACH—
Soil best Adapted and Pruning	94
Manuring	95
Varieties, with description	95

THE PEAR—
Best Soil	97
Climate and Diseases	97
Manures and Propagation	98
Standard Trees	98
Dwarf Trees and how to Plant them	99
How to Prune them	100
Thinning Out and Gathering the Fruit	103
Growing for Market	105
Varieties, with full description	105

THE PLUM—
| Climate and Soil | 118 |

	PAGE
Best Fertilizers and Diseases	118
How Propagated	119
Varieties, with description	119

THE QUINCE—

Where it Can be Grown, and on What Soils	122
Best Manures and How Far Apart to Plant	123
How Propagated and Varieties	123

HARDY GRAPES—

Proper Soils	124
Preparing the Ground and Manuring	125
Distance Apart and Time and Method of Planting	125
Treatment of Young Vines and Pruning and Training	126
Trellis and Wire	127
Varieties and description	132
Mildew, &c.	138

GRAPES UNDER GLASS—

Shape and Size of Vinery	140
How to Build a Vinery	141
How to Heat it	142
How to Ventilate it	144
Best Form of Boiler	145
Best Size of Pipe	148
Border for the Vines	148
Soil for Border, Compost, and Drainage	149
Planting the Vines	150
Subsequent Treatment of the Vines	151
Temperature of Vinery by Day and Night	152
Quantity of Fruit that may be left on the Vines	153
Ripening the Fruit	154
Diseases of Vines—Shanking	155
Mildew	157
List of Vines most desirable for Vinery	157
List for Early Forcing	158

FRUITING EXOTIC VINES IN POTS 158

THE BLACKBERRY—

Soil	160
Cultivation and Propagation	161
Varieties, with description	161

THE STRAWBERRY—

Sexes	162
Soil and Manures	164

	PAGE
Best Time for Transplanting and Best Plants	165
Preparation of Ground and Planting	166
Production of New Varieties	167
Varieties, with full description	168

THE RASPBERRY—

How Propagated	171
Best Soils and How to Plant	172
To Cultivate	173
To Prune	174
To Protect in Winter	175
Varieties, and their description	175

THE CURRANT—

How to Propagate	180
How to Cultivate and Prune	180
Varieties, with full description	180

THE GOOSEBERRY—

The Mildew	181
How to Prune and Cultivate	182
Varieties	183

THE CRANBERRY—

Preparation of Soil	183
Planting and Cultivation	186
How to control the Water, so as to flood or drain off at pleasure	184
Varieties	187

THE HUCKLEBERRY—

Natural Soils	188

KITCHEN GARDEN.

ASPARAGUS—

How to Prepare the Soil	194
How to Plant and Cultivate	195
When and How to Cut and How to Cook	196
Varieties	196

BEANS—

Dwarf or Bush Varieties	197
Running or Pole Varieties and their Cultivation	199

BEETS—

How to Prepare the Soil and Cultivate	201
Gathering and Preserving in Winter	202
Varieties	203

CONTENTS.

BROCCOLI—
Culture and Varieties 204
BRUSSELS SPROUTS—
Cultivation and Use 205
CABBAGE—
Soil and Cultivation 206
Varieties 207
CARROTS—
How to Prepare the Ground and Cultivate 210
Uses and Varieties 211
CAULIFLOWER—
Soil and Manures 213
How to Cultivate and to Use 214
Best Varieties 214
CELERY—
How to Cultivate and Blanch 216
To Secure for Winter Use 218
Varieties 219
CRESS OR PEPPER GRASS—
Soil, Cultivation and Varieties 220
CUCUMBER—
Soil and Cultivation 221
Varieties 222
CORN—
Best Table Varieties 224
ENDIVE—
Cultivation 224
Blanching and Preservation during Winter 225
EGG PLANT—
Cultivation 225
Use and Varieties 226
GARLIC—
Cultivation and Use 226
HORSE RADISH—
Propagation, Cultivation and Use 227
KOHL-RABI—
Cultivation, Use and Varieties 228
LEEK—
Soil and Cultivation 228
Use and Sorts 228
LETTUCE—
Preparation of Soil and Cultivation 229
The Best Varieties 230

CONTENTS.

MELONS— PAGE
    How to Prepare the Soil.. 231
    How to Cultivate, and the Best Varieties............................ 232

ONION—
    How to Prepare the Soil and Cultivate............................ 234
    To Preserve during Winter, and the Best Varieties............... 237

PARSNIP—
    Preparation of Soil and Cultivation............................... 240
    Use and Varieties... 241

POTATO—
    Soil and Manures.. 241
    Planting... 242
    Cultivation and Forcing... 243
    Varieties.. 244

PEAS—
    Preparation of Soil and Sowing................................. 245
    Cultivation, Use and Varieties................................. 246

PEPPERS—
    Cultivation.. 247
    Use and Varieties... 248

RADISHES—
    Soil and Cultivation... 248
    Spring and Autumn Varieties................................... 249

RHUBARB OR PIE PLANT—
    Preparation of Soil.. 250
    Cultivation, Use and Varieties................................. 251

SALSIFY OR OYSTER PLANT—
    Soil... 251
    Cultivation and Use.. 252

SQUASH—
    Soil and Cultivation... 252
    Summer Varieties.. 253
    Autumn and Winter Kinds....................................... 254

SEA KALE—
    Preparation of the Ground..................................... 255
    Cultivation... 256
    Blanching, Cutting and Use.................................... 257

SPINACH—
    Soil and Cultivation... 257
    Use and Varieties... 258

CONTENTS.

TOMATOES—
    Cultivation.. 259
    Soil 262
    Varieties.. 263

TURNIPS—
    Soil and Cultivation....................................... 264
    Harvesting... 264
    Varieties.. 265

HOT-BEDS—
    Their Construction and Use............................. 265

COLD FRAMES—
    Their Construction and Use............................. 268

TOOLS—
    Steel Rake, Scuffle-Hoe and Digging Fork........ 268

FLOWER GARDEN.

HARDY FLOWERING SHRUBS—
    Berberry... 272
    Carolina Allspice **or** Calycanthus..................... 273
    Canadian Judas Tree..................................... 273
    Cornus Florida or Dogwood............................ 274
    Double Flowering Almonds............................ 274
    Deutzias, Single and Double-flowered.............. 276
    Filbert, Purple Leaved................................... 277
    Hawthorns, Scarlet, Rose-colored, **etc.**............. 277
    Honeysuckles, **Pink** and Red Flowering............ 278
    Lilacs, Persian White, etc., **etc.**....................... 278
    Prunus Triloba, Double **Flowered**.................... 279
    Purple **Fringe** or Smoke-bush......................... 279
    Rose Acacia... 279
    Rose of Sharon or Altheas............................. 280
    Japan Quince, Double and Single.................. 280
    Spireas—White and Rose, Single and Double... 281
    Siberian Pea-Tree.. 283
    Silver Bell... 283
    Syringa or Mock Orange............................... 283
    Snowball or Guelder Rose............................. 283
    Tamarix.. 284
    Weigelas, Rose-flowered, Variegated-leaved, etc.... 284
    White Fringe... 285

CONTENTS.

HARDY CLIMBING SHRUBS—   PAGE
- Ampelopsis or Virginia Creeper 286
- Bignonia or Trumpet Flower 286
- Birthwort or Dutchman's Pipe 286
- Clematis or Virgin's Bower, Various Sorts 286
- Honeysuckles, Various Sorts 287
- Wistaria or Glycine 288
- Ivy 289

HARDY HERBACEOUS FLOWERS—
- Achillea or Milfoil 290
- Aconite or Monkshood 290
- Aquilegia or Columbine 291
- Campanula or Bellflower 291
- Carnations 295
- Convallaria or Lily of the Valley 293
- Delphinium or Larkspur 293
- Dianthus, the Pink 294
- Dictamnus or Fraxinella 294
- Digitalis or Foxglove 296
- Dicentra or Bleeding Heart 297
- Funkia or Day Lily 297
- Helleborus Niger or Christmas Rose 297
- Iris, German, or Fleur-de-lis, &c. 298
- Lathyrus or Ever-blooming Pea 299
- Lychnis, Various Sorts 300
- Pansies 306
- Peonias, Herbaceous Sorts 300
- Phloxes, Tall and Short Varieties 302
- Spiræa or Meadow Sweet 304
- Sweet William, Dianthus Barbatus 296
- Tricyrtis (very fragrant, new, late-blooming) 305
- Violets 305
- Yucca, Filamentosa, or Adam's Needle 308

BULBOUS-ROOTED FLOWERS—
- General Observations 309
- Amaryllis 315
- Crocus 318
- Dahlias 318
- Fritillarias 320
- Gladiolus 320
- Hyacinths 312
- Iris, English, Spanish and Persian 323
- Lilies of Various Sorts 324

Narcissus	326
Snowdrops	327
Tigridias or Tiger Flower	327
Tuberose	328
Tulips	330

BEDDING PLANTS (Flowering through the Summer)—

Verbenas, and How to Care for them	332
Heliotropes and their Varieties	334
Bouvardia, Cultivation and Varieties	335
Coleus	334
Petunias	337
Lantanas	338
Lemon Verbenas	339
Zonale Geraniums	340
Variegated-Leaved Geraniums	343
Ivy-Leaved Geraniums	344

ANNUALS—

Asters	346
Balsams	347
Calliopsis	347
Drummond Phlox	348
Marigolds	348
Mignonette	349
Portulaca	349
Rocket Larkspur	350
Scabiosa or Mourning Bride	350
Salpiglossis	350
Stock, Ten Weeks'	351

ANNUALS—CLIMBING—

Convolvulus or Morning Glory	351
Dolichos or Hyacinth Bean	352
Gourds	352
Sweet Peas	352
Tropeolums	352

ANNUALS—EVERLASTING FLOWERS—

Acroclinum	353
Gomphrena, Globe Amaranth	353
Helichrysum	354
Helipterum	354
Rodanthe	354
Xeranthemum	354

CONTENTS.

ORNAMENTAL GRASSES—   PAGE
    Agrostis Nebulosa 355
    Briza Maxima 355
    Erianthus Ravennæ 355
    Pennisetum 355
    Stipa Pennata 355

WINDOW-GARDENING—
    Important Directions 355
    Plants suitable 359

ROSES—
    Cultivation in the Garden 361
    Climbing Roses, Choice **Varieties** 370
    Summer Roses, the Best Kinds 371
    Moss Roses 373
    Autumnal Roses, Blooming a Second Time 374
    Monthly Roses, for Window Gardening 377

CLIMATIC VARIATIONS—
    General Survey 379

HARDY EVERGREENS—
    American Arbor Vitæ 383
    American Yew 384
    Austrian Pine 384
    Balsam Fir 384
    Common **Juniper** 384
    Eastern Spruce 384
    Hemlock Spruce 385
    Lambert's Pine 385
    Lawson's Cypress 387
    Norway Spruce 385
    Nordmann's Fir 385
    Red Cedar 385
    Scotch Pine 386
    Siberian **Silver Fir** 386
    Siberian **Arbor Vitæ** 386
    Swedish **Juniper** 386
    Tartarian **Arbor Vitæ** 386
    White **Pine** 386
    White **Spruce** 387
    White **Cedar** 387

CONCLUSION 389
ACKNOWLEDGMENTS 390

ILLUSTRATIONS.

	PAGE
Figures **1 and 2,** showing the manner of cleft grafting; **figure 1** being **the scion** prepared for insertion in the stock, figure 2 the stock **with the** scions inserted..	6
Figures **3, 4,** 5, 6, 7, and 8, showing the method of whip grafting; figure 3 showing the bevelled surfaces of stock and scion, figure 4 the same tongued, figure 5 the graft and stock put together, figure 6 as tied together with a ligature, figure 7 as covered with grafting **wax,** and figure 8 as wound with a strip of waxed cotton	9, 10
Figure 9, a branch or scion prepared for budding........................	14
Figure 10, the best form of budding knife.................................	14
Figures 11, 12, 13, and 14 show the manner in which the operation of budding is performed; figure 11 is the bud when cut from the scion, figure 12 the stock with the bark loosened and prepared **to** receive the bud, figure 13 the bud inserted in the stock, and figure 14 the bud and stock bound with **its** ligature 14,	15, 16
Figure 15 represents the bud tied **to a portion of the stock,** in order to keep it upright during the **first weeks of its growth.** The broken white line across the **stock shows where the stock is to be cut** off when the bud has **grown sufficiently stout to stand erect without support.**	17
Figure **16 shows the place** at which a branch should be cut when **taken from** the tree...	20
Figures 17, 18, and 19 show where a small branch should be pruned; figure 17 representing it as cut too far from the bud, figure 18 as cut too close to the bud, and figure 19 when cut at the proper place...	20
Figures 20, 21, and 22 represent the proper and improper appearance of the roots of transplanted trees...............................	27
Figure **23** represents tent caterpillars, with their tent, the eggs from which they are hatched, and the cocoon into which they pass	35
Figures 24, 25, and 26 are the male and female **moths of the tent** caterpillar, and the chrysalis from which they are **hatched.......**	37
Figure 27 is a cut of the forest tent caterpillar............................	38
Figure 28 represents the two-lined apple tree **borer,** and the worm from which it is produced..	38
Figure 29 is the worm **and beetle** of the buprestis apple tree borer...	41
Figure 30 represents a piece of an apple that has been eaten by the codlin worm; the worm is crawling on the outside, and the moth is shown near the apple with the wings expanded, and on the apple with the wings folded. The cocoon is seen attached to a small piece of bark	42
Figure 32 shows the plum curculio in the beetle, worm and pupa state, magnified; and of the natural size, in the act **of** depositing its egg upon a cherry...	47
Figure 33 represents the grape **vine** flea beetle and the larva, both magnified, and the young larvæ feeding on **a** leaf of the vine..	49

ILLUSTRATIONS.

	PAGE
Figures 34, 35 and 36 represent the green **grape** vine sphinx in the moth, worm and chrysalis states...................................	50, 51
Figure 37 is a cherry blossom **cut open so as to show the** ovary, pistil, and stamens...	56
Figures 38, 39, 40 and 41 show **how the pollen enters the pistil,** descends to the ovary, enters it and comes in contact with the germ, so imparting to it the power of development................	57
Figure 42 represents an apple blossom cut open, showing the number of pistils..	57
Figure 43 shows **more distinctly the pistil and stamen**................	58
Figure 44, **a grape vine at the end of the third year**...................	128
Figure 45, **a grape vine in the autumn of the fourth year**...........	129
Figure 46, **section** of an astragal	142
Figure 47 represents a dwarf **pear tree at one season's growth from the bud**..	100
Figure 48, a dwarf pear **tree at two years from the bud**..............	100
Figure 49, the same tree at three years from the bud	101
Figure 50, the same tree at four years from the bud	101
Figure 47 shows the flow and return pipes, with the boiler and expansion tank in the vinery..	143
Figure 48 represents the method of admitting fresh air into the vinery without creating a cold draught...........................	144
Figure 49, a perfect strawberry blossom.....................................	163
Figure 50, a pistillate strawberry blossom	163
Figure 51, a blackcap raspberry plant, with the cane tips rooted in the soil	171
Figure 52, a cutting prepared **and planted**	180
Figure 53, the mode **of layering plants**......................................	182
Figure 54, **branch and fruit of the** cherry **cranberry**....................	188
Figure 55, **branch and fruit** of the huckleberry	189
Figure 56, early bassano beet...	203
Figure 57, Brussels sprouts...	205
Figure 58, green globe **Savoy cabbage**......................................	209
Figure 59, early horn **carrot**	211
Figure 60, egg-plant **and fruit**	225
Figure 61, kohl-rabi...	227
Figure 62, drumhead **lettuce**...	230
Figure 63, potato **onion**	239
Figure 64, tree onion	239
Figure 65, Chinese rose **winter radish**	250
Figure 66, autumnal marrow squash...	254
Figure 67, Hubbard squash	255
Figure 68, gladiolus flower	321
Figure 69, bouvardia bloom	335
Figure 70, lantana flower	338

INTRODUCTION.

The design of this book is to furnish the Canadian cultivator with a reliable guide in all matters relating to the cultivation of fruit, flowers and vegetables in our climate. It is the result of many years of experience and careful observation, in which the fruits that can be most generally grown in Canada have been the subject of special study. Many hundreds of varieties of the several kinds of fruits have been actually grown by the writer, and their value for cultivation in our climate thoroughly studied and tested. To this has been added the valuable information derived from a wide-spread correspondence with horticulturists in different parts of the Provinces, thus putting the writer in possession of the experience of others, in the several departments of horticulture, throughout the Dominion. Hitherto there has been no work devoted to these subjects which has been written by a Canadian, embodying his own actual experience and observation in these matters, and which Canadians could rely upon as adapted to their own peculiar necessities, and consult in all these interests of the fruit, flower and vegetable garden, with confidence, as embodying the experience of a practical man in these departments, who knows their peculiar position and wants from personal participation in their difficulties. In the hope of meeting these wants, and of helping some of my countrymen in their horticultural labors, these pages have been written, and are now offered to all who love good fruit, pretty flowers, and choice vegetables.

THE PROPAGATION OF FRUIT TREES.

It is now generally understood that the several varieties of our different fruit trees can not be propagated by planting the seeds of any particular sort, but that the only method of increasing the number of trees of any variety of fruit, is by propagating portions of that tree which we wish to multiply. Sometimes a small portion of a young branch, cut off from the tree, can be planted in the ground and made to take root, and grow, and increase in size, until it becomes as large as the parent tree. But this is not generally the case with apple, pear, plum, cherry or peach trees, and in the few instances of the varieties that will thus root from cuttings most freely, they grow slowly, and rarely make a strong, healthy and vigorous tree. To meet this difficulty, recourse is had to the operations known as grafting and budding. By this means one or more wood-producing buds are taken from the tree which we wish to multiply, and are so connected with a living root, that the bud is supplied by this root with the sap which nourishes it, and enables it to expand, and grow, and eventually form, according to the will of the cultivator, either a branch or an entire tree. In grafting, we take a young branch, having usually, three well developed wood buds, and insert this either into the body or branch of another tree; but in budding, we cut out only a single bud, and insert this under the bark of another tree, that we wish to make bear fruit of the sort borne by the tree from whence the bud was taken.

GRAFTING.—There are several methods of grafting, but for all practical purposes we may confine our attention to the two methods known as cleft-grafting and whip-grafting. Cleft-grafting is practised when the stock into which the grafts are to be inserted is much larger, that is, of much greater diameter than the scion. Whip-grafting, sometimes called splice-grafting, is performed when the graft and stock are nearly of the same size.

the wax, and then wax the whole. This will enable him to keep his hands clean and free from grease while he is putting in the scions.

In grafting a large tree, it is advisable not to cut off all the limbs in one season, even if it is intended eventually to graft them all. If they are all cut off and grafted at once, there will not be sufficient foliage formed by the grafts to elaborate the sap that will ascend from the roots, thereby causing an unhealthy condition, which often results in permanent disease and premature decay. The proper way is to graft not more than two-thirds of the branches the first season, and if the scions have made a good growth so as to furnish a good supply of foliage, then the remaining branches may be cut away and grafted the next year. If, however, the scions have made but a feeble growth, it is best to graft but a portion of the remaining branches, leaving a few to the subsequent season.

It is best to graft the top and upper branches first, so that the scions may not be shaded, and because the flow of sap is strongest towards the higher branches, and these, if left on the tree, would rob the scions set in the lower branches. If both the scions grow that were put into one branch of the tree, select the one that promises to be the more vigorous, and partly cut back the other during the month of August, or, if you prefer, at the next spring's pruning, so as to give the stronger one full room to grow, while you use the other to help heal over the stump, into which they were inserted, until such time as it can be cut away altogether. Do not be too anxious to remove all the sprouts that will start: if they seem to choke the graft, cut such back, but not wholly off; and only remove them entirely when the graft has become a branch.

For a better understanding of this mode of grafting, study the drawings on page 6. Figure 1 shows the graft ready for insertion; and Figure 2, the cleft stock with the scions in place.

The proper time for grafting large trees is in the spring, after the sap has begun to move and the buds to swell. If it be possible, choose a mild, cloudy day, with but little wind, for the wind and sun dry the fresh-cut wood of both stock and scion rapidly, which is to be avoided whenever practicable, and always as much as possible, by covering the wounds with grafting wax the more promptly in drying weather.

The tree to be grafted should be in a healthy and vigorous state; if not in such a condition the scion is less likely to live, and if it lives will make but a feeble growth. Such a tree should be prepared for grafting by thinning out the branches, and top dressing the roots with a liberal supply of manure; then, after it has exhibited signs of returning vigor in improved appearance of foliage and stronger shoots, it can be grafted with much better prospect of success.

WHIP-GRAFTING is performed when the scion and stock are nearly of the same size. This method is the one most commonly practised by nurserymen in growing trees for market, and will be used by the farmer or amateur only when grafting the small branches of young trees. To graft in this way, use a very sharp, thin-bladed knife, and with it make a smooth, sloping cut upwards on the stock and downwards on the scion, then form a tongue on each by making a thin upward cleft on the scion and downward on the stock. Now place these sloping cuts together and press the tongue of the scion into the cleft of the stock and the tongue of the stock into the cleft of the scion, taking care that the inner bark of the scion, on one side at least, exactly fits with the inner bark of the stock. If the scion have been well chosen with reference to the size of the stock, the bark can be made to fit on both sides, but though this is to be desired whenever practicable, it is not essential to success, for if the barks correspond on one side, circulation will be established through them between the stock and the scion, and the union between them be cemented. After thus uniting the graft and stock, it is

FIG. 3.

necessary to fasten them, by tying with bass-matting or cotton yarn, or a narrow strip of thin cotton cloth. This is usually done by carefully winding around both stock and scion, where united, a narrow strip of thin cotton cloth, or even thin paper or cotton yarn, which has been covered or saturated with grafting wax. When this is neatly done there is no need of any knot, the wax holding the ligature in its place. In grafting branches of trees in this way, care must be taken to exclude perfectly air and water from the wounded parts. When nurserymen propagate trees in this way, they select strong and vigorous seedlings, which they pack away in the cellar in moist sand before the ground freezes; these they graft with scions of any desired variety at their leisure, during the months of January, February or March, and as soon as grafted pack the grafts in boxes of sand or moist sawdust, and store them in the cellar until ready to plant them in the ground in the spring. When planted out, the place of union between the stock and scion is wholly under ground, and being in this way protected from the sun and air by the surrounding soil, it is not necessary to be so particular to cover the union with grafting wax as in the case of top grafting, where the whole is exposed to all the changes and influences of the atmosphere. It is a common practice with nurserymen to wind cotton yarn into medium sized balls and boil them in a composi-

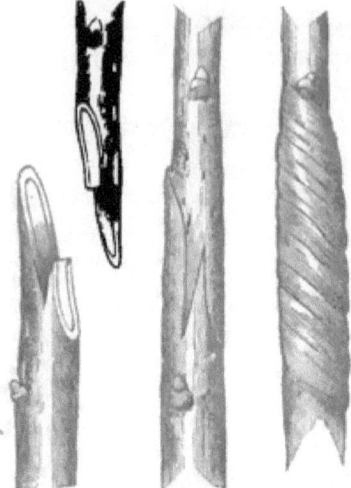

Fig. 4.   Fig. 5.   Fig. 3.

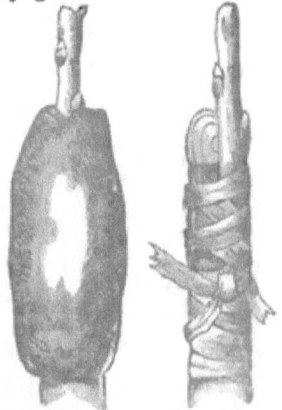

Fig. 7.   Fig. 6.

tion formed by melting together **three pounds of resin, a pound and** a quarter **of** lard and a pound and a half **of** beeswax. **The balls** are **taken out** while hot **and** allowed **to drain,** and when **cool** are ready for use. The graft is taken **in one** hand by the **root, with** the other the **end of the** string is **laid** on the lower end **of** the lap of the scion, **and** by twirling the graft in the fingers the thread is wound tightly **round** both stock and scion at the place of union sufficiently often to hold the parts together firmly, and then the thread is broken off. The wax holds the string in place without any tying, while it also preserves the thread from rotting until the union is perfected, and the expansion **of growth** causes it gradually to give way.

By consulting the engravings this method of grafting will **be** readily understood. Figure 3, page 9, shows the sloping cut made upon the **stock and scion. Figure 4, page 10, shows the cleft made** in them **to form the tongue. Figure 5 shows them** put together. Figure **6 shows the graft tied with a** strip of bass-matting or **cotton cloth.** Figure 7 shows the same covered with wax to protect the union from the weather, and Figure 8 shows the graft neatly wound with a strip of waxed cotton or paper.

THE WAXED CLOTH or paper is prepared by dipping the cloth or paper into the same preparation as that in which the balls of cotton **yarn** are boiled, when it is quite hot, **and then** drawing the sheet between a couple of sticks, so as to scrape off the superfluous wax, and when cold, cutting it into strips of the required width. Many use **these strips in cleft-grafting,** instead of the pure wax. Sometimes when the cloth or paper is too strong, it does not give way under the growth of the tree, and requires to **be cut** or removed, in order to prevent it from binding and injuring **the tree.**

SCIONS should be selected from healthy trees, and should be **cut from the** thrifty, well ripened shoots of the last season's **growth.** In this climate, it is safest **to cut** them in November, before the **severe frosts of winter. Sometimes the** cold of the winter is so severe **that the young wood is injured.** If not cut in November, it is better to wait until early in April, after the shoots have had an opportunity to recover from the severe freezing. They should never be cut from the tree when they are frozen. When cut, they should be packed in a box with damp moss, or sawdust placed in the bottom of the box and over them after they are put in. There should be enough moss or sawdust to prevent the scions from drying out or shrivelling. They should then be stored in the cellar, where they will be kept cool and damp, and free from frost. If there be plenty of moss or sawdust the scions will be preserved quite fresh without any further attention; and if, when taken out for use, they seem to be mouldy, there need be no cause for apprehension, if, on wiping it off, the bark looks bright and fresh. Experience has taught us that this mould does not injure scions. There is danger, however, of keeping scions too wet. The material in which they are packed should be damp only, not filled with water. A scion that has been soaked will not grow. They have been known to fail wholly, after standing for a few weeks with the butt-end in shallow water. The thing to be aimed at, is to keep the grafts as near as possible in the same condition as when first cut. In using the scions, reject the portion at the butt, as far as the buds seem small and imperfectly developed, and likewise the tip, as far as the wood seems soft and spongy.

BUDDING, or as it is sometimes called, inoculation, is the other method by which any given variety of fruit is perpetuated and multiplied, and in its effects and principles of operation is only another mode of grafting. In both cases, a bud of the variety we desire to propagate is brought into a living union with another root, and made to form the top and branches and fruit-producing portion of the tree. In grafting, we use a branch with several buds and considerable wood; but in budding we use only a single bud, with a very small portion of bark, and less wood.

There are some advantages in budding, as compared with grafting, when the stocks are small, as is the case in nurserymen's operations; but when the stocks have already become trees, as is usually the case with the farmer and amateur, grafting is the more convenient method, and generally more successful. When small stocks, **of one** or two seasons' growth, are used, budding is often more convenient, because the operation can be performed in midsummer, when the hurry of spring work has passed, and in case of failure, can, in many instances, be repeated the same **season.** Experience has also taught us that in our climate the grafting of stone fruits is attended with considerable uncertainty, and requires to be done with great nicety and skill, while budding is almost uniformly successful.

THE SEASON for budding is from July **to** September, **and yet** the best time, the time when the operation is most likely **to be successful, is variable.** The farmer does not **cut his grain because** a certain day of the month has **arrived, but when the grain has** reached **that state** of maturity which he **has learned by experience to be the time when** he **will secure the grain** in its best **condition.** So in budding, **the best time is** that in which the **bud will most** speedily and certainly unite with the stock, and **experience has** taught us that this is while the stock is in a growing state, so that the bark will separate freely from the wood, and yet when the activity of growth is somewhat diminished, which time is indicated by the formation **of** the terminal bud. At this stage also, the sap under the bark will have thickened and **become viscid** or sticky, **forming what botanists** term the **cambium. This** condition of **the stock is the most favorable time** for budding, and as **a rule it** will be found that **Plum stocks reach it the earliest** in the season, then follow Pear, Quince, **Apple, Cherry and** Peach stocks, in the order in which they are named. **It will be** readily understood that the time, when this condition of the stock will be attained, will be very materially influenced by **the** character of the season, the temperature, moisture, and the like. A cool, moist season, will protract the period of growth and postpone the period when the cambium begins to form, while a **hot** and dry season will shorten the growth and hasten maturity. A little experience will teach the operator the fitting moment, the general features of which only can be indicated in written directions.

14 THE PROPAGATION OF FRUIT TREES.

THE SELECTION OF SCIONS, from which the buds are to be taken, also requires the exercise of some judgment. Those are best that have formed their terminal bud, but as these are not always to be had, those which have begun to ripen their wood and have well developed buds should be selected, and the very green portion towards the extremity, where the buds are but partially formed, cut away. As soon as the scion has been cut from the tree, the leaves, with about half of the leaf-stalk, should be cut off, and the scion wrapped in a cloth of sufficient thickness to protect it from the sun and air. If the cloth be moistened it will be of advantage in keeping the scions cool, but they should never be soaked in a very wet cloth, much less in a vessel of water. Figure 9 represents a scion which has been cut from the tree, with the leaves and a part of the leaf stalk removed, and showing the buds which are to be used in budding.

FIG. 9.

THE OPERATION OF BUDDING is performed by selecting a smooth place in the stock, and with a sharp, thin-bladed budding-knife, (figure 10 shows the best form of budding knife, although any sharp thin-bladed knife may be used) make first a horizontal cut, just deep enough to cut through the bark, and then from the centre of this make a perpendicular cut of the same depth, the two cuts having the form of a T. Figure 12 shows the slits made in the bark. If the stock be small, that is, one or two years of age, the proper place for inserting the bud is as near the ground as can conveniently be done, and, if possible, the south side is to be avoided on account of its greater exposure to the sun. Could we have everything just the most favorable possible, we would select also a cool, cloudy day for the

FIG. 10.

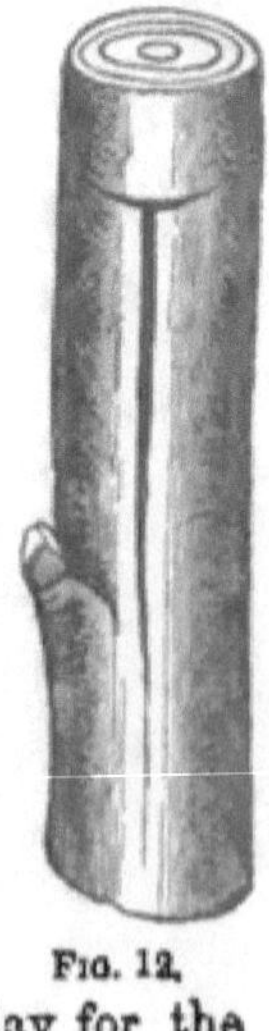

FIG. 12.

operation. After having made the incisions in the bark as just described, hold the scion or stick of buds in the left hand, and cut out one of the buds, together with a strip of the bark and a very thin slice of the wood, beginning to cut about half an inch above the bud, and bringing the knife out about half an inch below the bud. Figure 11 represents a bud cut from the scion and ready for insertion. If the wood be very ripe and hard, the slice of wood should be exceedingly thin indeed, but if the wood be green and soft, the thickness of the slice of wood may be increased in proportion to its greenness, but never to exceed one-third of the thickness of the stick or scion. Now with the rounded part of the blade of the budding knife gently raise the bark of the stock at the corners, and holding the bud by the leafstalk, insert the lower end under the bark, and slide it down the perpendicular slit, until the upper end of the bark of the bud coincides with the cross cut or horizontal cut of the T. If a little of the bark of the bud extends above the cross cut, it may be cut off with the budding knife, so as to form a square shoulder, exactly fitting to the bark of the stock above. In practice it is most convenient to hold the bud between the forefinger and thumb of the left hand, and at the same time that the corners of the bark are raised with the right hand, insert the lower end of the bark of the bud under the raised bark. Figure 13 shows the bud in place. After the bud has been inserted it should be tied in its place by winding around the stock a strip of bass-matting that has been previously moistened in water to make it soft or pliable, or woollen or cotton yarn will answer very well, taking care to cover all the wound, leaving only the bud with its foot stalk projecting. It is better to begin to wind at the lower end and proceed upwards, winding the ligature as smoothly and neatly as possible, yet firm and close, so that the bud may be kept in place and the bark smooth and snug to the stock. Figure 14 represents the

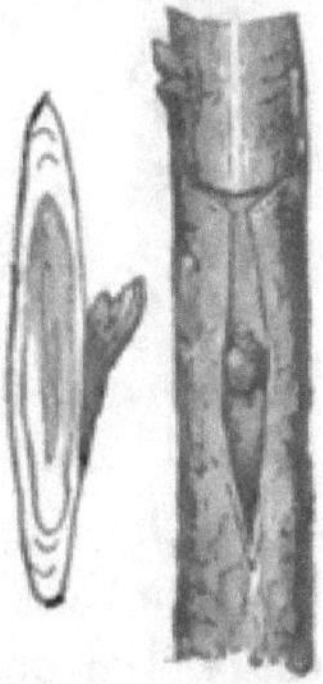

FIG. 11.   FIG. 13.

whole complete with the ligature tied around. Care should be had, in raising the bark of the stock, to avoid disturbing the cambium, the soft, mucilaginous secretion lying next to the wood of the stock.

Fig. 14.

The After Treatment of the bud consists in removing the ligature as soon as it begins to bind too tightly around the stock. In from twelve to fourteen days the bud should be examined, and if it appears plump and fresh it has probably begun to unite with the stock, but if it has shrivelled it is dead. If the stock will yet peel, it may be rebudded at once. If the stock has swelled much, so as to tighten the ligature, it may be loosened and re-tied, but, in common practice, where budding is done on an extended scale, the ligature is cut when the growth of the stock is such that the bark swells around the ligature. A little practice will enable the operator to decide when it is necessary to remove the string. Usually it is in about four weeks from the time the bud is put in, but the time will vary according to growth of the stock. Cherry and peach stocks usually swell more rapidly than apple or pear. Sometimes the strings are left on all winter, particularly if the budding has been done late in the season; but in our climate this practice is not to be recommended; the band retains moisture, and in cold weather gathers ice about the bud.

In the following spring the stock should be headed back to within about three inches of the bud as soon as the buds begin to start. This will cause all the buds remaining on the stock to push vigorously, and as soon as the inserted bud begins to grow all the natural buds must be rubbed off, and kept rubbed off from time to time, as often as they start. This is done so that all the sap may be thrown into the inserted bud, and its growth promoted. As soon as it has grown a few inches in length it will probably require tying to the stock, so as to keep it upright. In doing this the string or band should not be wound around the growing shoot, but merely passed round it and tied around the stock, forming **a loop** within which the growing shoot has **room** to expand, **the** string touching it only on one side, the side **of** the shoot farthest from the stock. Figure 15 represents a growing bud tied to the stock. **In the month** of **July the bud** will have acquired sufficient strength to enable it to stand erect without the aid of any support from the stock. **The** stock should now be cut back **down** to the bud. The pruning knife used for this should be both strong and sharp, and placing the edge against **the** stock on the **side** opposite the bud, with a sloping cut, drawing the knife upwards and towards the bud, the stock should be cut smoothly off in **such a way that** there shall be not a **particle of the stock left above the bud.** The **white line across the stock,** Figure 15, **shows the place where the cut should be made, thus taking off all that part of** the stock **above the white line.**

Fig. 15.

Budding may be performed in the spring, by keeping the scions in a cool place where the buds will not start, and inserting them in the stock after growth has commenced, but it is seldom practised in this country, because success is not as certain, and for want of time at a season **when so many** things require attention.

Some cultivators have found **it** advantageous in budding plums, in particular, in which the upper part of the bud frequently dies although the lower part **has** united with the stock, **to use** two separate ligatures in tying, covering the part below the bud with one bandage, and the part above with the other. As **soon as** the bud seems to have taken, the lower bandage is removed, but the other is allowed to remain for two or three weeks longer, which arrests the downward sap and perfects the union of the upper part of the bud with the stock.

PRUNING OF FRUIT TREES.

When is the BEST TIME for pruning fruit trees, is a question often asked, to which the reply of an old gardener was more appropriate than polite, who answered "whenever your knife is sharp." If fruit trees are properly attended to and pruned every year as much as is requisite, they will need but very little pruning at any time, and it is not of much moment when that little is done. The words of the lamented Downing should be graven upon the memory of every one who takes knife in hand against his fruit trees. He says, "A judicious pruning, to modify the form of our standard trees, is nearly all that is required in ordinary practice. Every fruit tree, grown in the open orchard or garden as a common standard, should be allowed to take its natural form, the whole efforts of the pruner going no further than to take out all weak and crowded branches, those which are filling uselessly the interior of the tree, where their leaves cannot be duly exposed to the light and sun, or those which interfere with the growth of others. *All pruning of large branches* in healthy trees *should be rendered unnecessary*, by examining them every season, and taking out superfluous shoots *while they are small*."

Yet there is a best time for pruning, and that time depends upon the object for which the pruning is done. The two purposes most commonly intended are all that it will be necessary here to speak of, namely, pruning to regulate the form of standard trees, and pruning to induce fruitfulness.

In PRUNING TO REGULATE THE FORM of standard trees, if the trees have been properly cared for every year, it will only be necessary to remove small branches, and this may be best done in our climate after the severe frosty weather of our winters is passed, and before the sap is in full flow. This will be in March or early in April, varying with the season and locality. If done at this time, the sap will not have fully ascended into the branch that is taken away, and will be directed into the remaining portions of the tree; if the pruning be done after the sap has ascended, it will be measurably lost to the tree. If the pruning be done before the severe winter frosts are over, experience has taught us that the frost so affects the tree through the wounds, especially if they be large and numerous, as to impair its health and vigor. But if the pruning has been neglected, and there are large branches to be removed, it is best done just after the trees have made their first growth and are taking what has been termed their midsummer rest, which is in July or August in our climate. It has been found that if large branches are taken off at this time the wood remains sound, whereas, if taken off in the spring, particularly if the sap is circulating freely, the wood is apt to decay, and though it may heal over, the part always remains unsound. Yet some caution is needed here, lest too many large branches be removed in one summer, and the vigor of the tree receive too severe a check. Summer pruning tends to lessen the vigor of a tree, and though we advise the removal of large branches at this season because it is better somewhat to check the growth of the tree than to risk the decay of the trunk, yet judgment should be used, lest this be carried too far. When large limbs are removed it is always advisable to use a fine saw, and after smoothing the cut with a sharp knife, to cover the wound with some preparation that will protect it from the weather. Common grafting wax, or a mixture of fresh cow dung and clay, may be used; but the most convenient preparation for this purpose is made by dissolving gum shellac in alcohol until the solution is of the consistence of ordinary paint. This may be applied with a common paint brush and kept in a wide-mouthed bottle, which should be kept well corked. Thus applied to the wounds, it soon hardens and forms a coating that is not affected by changes of weather, yet adheres closely and completely excludes air and moisture, and at the same time does not interfere with the growth of the bark over the wound.

There is also a right place at which to make the cut in removing entire branches; if cut farther from the tree than this point, a portion of the branch remains, which not only gives the tree an unsightly appearance, but which is very sure to throw out 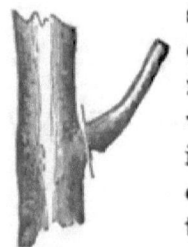 sprouts; and if cut closer to the tree, an unnecessarily larger wound is made, which requires more time to heal over. It may be noticed that where a branch unites with the main body there is a shoulder or slight enlargement. This shoulder is shown in Figure 16, and the line indicates the place at which the cut should be made. It

FIG. 16.   is at the point where the branch unites with this shoulder, so that the shoulder, or slight protuberance at the base of the branch, is left on the tree, and the wound made in 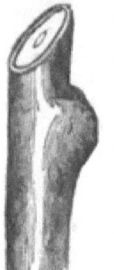 cutting is no larger than the diameter of the branch. Also in cutting back small branches care should be taken to cut them off just above the bud, not so close as to injure the bud, nor so far from it as to leave a long spur of wood. Figure 17 represents a branch cut back too far from the bud. Figure 18, a branch cut too close to the bud; and Figure 19, one that is cut as it should be. The cut should be made so that

FIG. 17.   the point of the bud will coincide with the edge of the cut. Such a cut will heal over sooner than any other, and the bud at the point will grow vigorously.

 The form of standard trees will need only such modification as may be requisite to admit a free circulation of air through the branches, and sufficient light and heat to ensure the fullest development of the fruit. If the top of a tree is permitted to become a thicket of branches, it is quite obvious that some parts will be too crowded, the air can circulate but

FIG. 18.   imperfectly, and the sunlight is wholly ex-   FIG. 19.
cluded. In consequence of this, much of the fruit will be below the normal size of the variety, but partially colored, and very deficient in flavor. This can be remedied by judicious pruning,

removing some of the branches from the interior, and keeping the head open to the light and air. On the other hand, pruning can be carried too far, especially by removing so much of the foliage as to leave the nearly horizontal limbs exposed to the full blaze of a nearly vertical sun. The evil effects of this are seen in the death of the bark on the upper side of the large branches thus exposed; the circulation is impeded, and the tree often assumes a stunted and sickly appearance. The pruner, then, must use his own judgment, and adapt his pruning to the special circumstances of his own case. An orchard that is exposed to the sweep of high winds will not suffer from want of circulation of air as one that is sheltered, and, if pruned as would be desirable for the sheltered orchard, might suffer for the want of that protection which the branches afford each other. So then, it is possible only to point out the objects to be sought, and leave to each one the carrying out of the particular amount of pruning, and the details of the work in his own orchard, in the exercise of those reasoning powers which will enable him to so shape his trees that foliage and fruit shall be fully developed in the greatest abundance. And in this exercise of the judgment lies the true secret of excellence.

Pruning to Induce Fruitfulness, is sometimes desirable in the case of trees of very vigorous habit, and that are tardy in coming into bearing. This pruning is applied not only to the branches, but also to the roots. The root-pruning simply consists in cutting off a portion of the roots, thereby lessening the quantity of nourishment derived from the soil. It is done in autumn, by digging a trench about eighteen inches deep around the tree, with a sharp spade, cutting off the roots that reach the trench. The distance that this trench should be from the trunk will vary according to the size of the tree, taking care that it be so far as not to cut off too many and too large roots. The digging of such a trench once will usually so check the wood growth that the tree will form fruit-buds, and set its fruit. After having thus thrown the tree into bearing, it is usually necessary to supply the tree with a little well-rotted manure, in order to keep it in sufficient health and vigor to perfect its fruit. The pruning of the branches for this purpose is performed in midsummer, and is not so much a cutting as a pinching off of the tender end of the shoots with thumb and finger. This checks the growth of the shoot, and concentrates the sap in the remaining part of the branch, thus inducing the formation of fruit buds. At least this is the tendency, and the operation usually produces, in a greater or less degree, the desired effect. But it sometimes happens that the tree is growing so vigorously that the buds will break and form shoots. When this is the case, recourse may be had to root-pruning; or by bending down the branches and fastening them in a perfectly horizontal position, or even curving them downwards, such a check will be given to the flow of sap that fruit buds will be formed. When a tree is growing rapidly it can not produce much fruit, and it is only when this wood-producing energy has expended itself by the completion of the growth of the tree, or has been checked artificially, that abundance of fruit will be produced. By this it will be seen that the formation of much wood is antagonistic to the formation of much fruit, and that whatever will lessen the wood growth, without injury to the health of the tree, will increase the production of fruit. A top-dressing of coarse salt, sown broadcast, at the rate of two bushels to the acre, has been found to increase the fruitfulness of some orchards.

TRANSPLANTING.

Deciduous trees can be best transplanted after the fall of the leaf in autumn, and before the putting forth of leaves in the spring. In mild climates and dry soils the autumn is the best season for transplanting. This gives an opportunity to the wounded roots to heal, and the soil to settle firmly about the tree during the early part of the winter, and the tree is ready at the first approach of warm weather to push out its rootlets into the soil and commence its **growth for the season.** But in those portions **of our** Dominion where **the ground** freezes early, **and** remains frozen all winter to as great or even greater depth than **the roots of the** newly planted tree extend, it is impossible that **any such** healing process should take place in the roots, and if **the soil** in which it is planted be of a very retentive character, water is apt to collect **about** the roots in the imperfectly settled earth, and in a greater or less degree prove injurious to the tree. Owing to these causes spring-planting has been found to be more generally successful **in** those parts of Canada, where the ground is not well protected with snow, than fall. Yet there are reasons which sometimes counterbalance all these difficulties, and make it **on the whole preferable** to transplant the trees in the fall. **There may be more leisure in the fall, or it may be more convenient to obtain the trees then, or the distance from the nurseries may be so great, that by the time trees can be procured in** the spring the **season is too far advanced.** From whatever cause the planter may decide to set his trees in the fall, if he will only take care that they do not suffer from water standing about the roots, and that in some way he protects the roots from severe freezing, they will usually pass the winter safely and grow well. This is very easily accomplished by raising a considerable mound of **earth** around the tree after it is planted, which serves to keep the tree from being rocked about by the **wind, sheds off the** rain and **melting snow, and in some measure** keeps out the frost. In the spring, before **the dry weather sets** in, this mound should be levelled off and the ground mulched as in spring planting.

PREPARING THE SOIL for **the** reception of trees does not receive that attention which its importance demands. If the ground has been well prepared, the growth of the trees will fully compensate for the labor. An excellent method of preparation is to summer-fallow the ground, giving it frequent ploughings and stirrings, so that it may be thoroughly pulverized. If it need manure, it should be put on in a well-rotted condition, as for a crop of grain, and thoroughly mixed and incorporated with the soil. If the whole ground be made thus mellow and rich before the trees are planted, they will live and make a good growth the first season; but if planted in hard soil, very often in a sod, no wonder that many of them die, and that those which live make a starved and sickly growth. Many persons, after preparing the ground in this way, think they cannot afford to lose so much labor just for an orchard, and so, as a matter of economy, they sow wheat or rye or some other grain, and plant their young trees in the grain. This is, beyond question, a false economy; but, if it must be done, let no grain grow within four feet of any tree. The grain will absorb the rains and dews and moisture that the young tree needs, and so rob the tree of its necessary nourishment, for trees can take up nourishment only in a liquid form. The writer was requested by a neighbor to examine his young orchard, which, he said, seemed to be all dying, and he was unable to account for it. The orchard had been planted the year before, in good rich soil, which was well drained, and had been made perfectly mellow, and the trees had not only lived but made a very fine growth. But this year, since the hot weather had set in, the leaves had begun to wilt and wither, and some of them to turn yellow, and the young shoots to shrivel and dry up. On arriving at the orchard, the trees were found standing in a field of most luxuriant rye, reaching, in many places, quite into the branches of the trees. It was at once recommended that the rye should be pulled up around the trees, so that there should be a circle of eight feet in diameter left clear around each tree, and that the rye so pulled up be spread on the ground around the trees as a mulch. This was done, and the trouble was at once arrested; many of the trees revived wholly, some lost only the ends of the young shoots that had become too much wilted to survive, while a few of the trees had already suffered so much that they were past all recovery.

Another thing that must not be overlooked in the preparation of the ground is drainage. Fruit trees cannot grow in water, and care must be taken to draw off all stagnant water not only from the surface soil, but from the subsoil. Much can be done to effect this by ploughing the ground into lands of the same width as the intended space between the rows of trees. By repeated ploughings, turning the furrow always towards the centre of the land, the ground may be thrown up to the required height, and the trees planted along the middle of each land. This method will be found particularly beneficial where the ground is naturally level, or the subsoil cold and sterile. A naturally rolling surface, with a porous subsoil, is to be preferred for fruit trees wherever it can be had.

In PLANTING, the trees should not be set into the cold and barren sub-soil, but if the surface soil be too shallow to receive the roots, it is better to throw the earth up around the tree so as to cover the roots to the proper depth and keep them in the mellow and fertile soil. Trees have been planted where the surface soil is thin, by spreading out the roots on the surface of the ground and covering them with earth, and they lived and grew well, whereas, if they had been planted in holes dug in the ordinary way they would never have been worth anything. It is a common error to plant trees too deep. They should not be set so as to stand any deeper after the ground has become settled than they stood in the nursery. The holes should be dug large enough in diameter to admit of the roots being spread out in their natural position, not coiled up or turned up at the ends, and the soil in the bottom of the hole should be loosened up and made crowning in the centre; upon this the tree should be set, and the roots spread out in a natural way. The rich and thoroughly pulverized surface soil should be carefully filled in, and worked with the fingers among the roots, and pressed down gently with the foot. When all is complete the surface should be left loose and friable, not trodden hard, as is often done, and should be made nearly level with the surrounding soil, if the planting be done in the spring; but if it be done in the fall, make a mound of earth over the roots and around the stem of the tree, as already recommended. In settling the earth about the roots of the tree, do not shake it up and down or swing it about, but let it be held firmly in place while the earth is being placed among and over the roots.

Mulching, by which is meant the spreading of coarse manure, half rotted straw, or any other litter on the ground over the **roots of the trees,** will be always found of great service in keeping the ground cool and moist, and promoting the growth of newly transplanted trees, particularly if the succeeding summer should be hot and dry. There is a substitute for mulching that **is perhaps better than a mulch,** but in the hurry of summer work it is so **sure to be neglected that the planter had better mulch his trees as soon after planting as possible.** If, however, he will keep the ground loose and friable around his trees by frequently stirring the surface, and never allow it to become baked and **hard,** he may safely dispense with mulching. But because it is recommended to spread coarse manure on the surface of the ground, let **it not be therefore inferred** that it is ever advisable to place fresh **manure in the soil about the roots of the trees.** It is very apt to **kill newly planted trees, and sure to do more** harm than good. **If it is thought necessary to enrich the soil, old** and perfectly **rotted manure** may be **thoroughly incorporated with it, but the** safer way is to place the manure on the surface, and let its fertilizing properties be gradually washed down by the rains. **It is** very seldom that trees which have been carefully taken up, care**fully** planted, and well mulched, will require any Watering **during the dry summer weather. If it should become necessary,** however, to give them water, it should be done thoroughly. **A mere moistening of the** surface of the ground is worse than none **at all.** Give enough to penetrate down to where the roots lie and to **soak the** ground about them thoroughly. And now, if the trees **have not** been mulched, it should be done immediately, in order to **prevent the evaporation of the water** that has been given, and the **baking** and cracking of the earth under the rays **of a** scorching sun. **If** no litter can be had with which to **mulch,** effect the same result **by stirring the** surface a few hours **after the water has been given, and before the sun** has baked the

TRANSPLANTING.

earth. If this be not attended to, better not to give any water at all, for the hot sun will only bake the earth the harder for your watering.

The TREES MOST SUITABLE FOR PLANTING are young, healthy **trees** of from two to four years' growth. It is difficult to transplant large trees successfully, on account of the impossibility of preserving the small fibrous roots, which are most numerous towards the extremities of the large roots, in sufficient quantity to support the tree. It is through the small fibrous roots that the tree derives its nourishment from the ground, and, therefore, the more numerous they are the more likely the tree is to thrive, and more of these can be taken up entire in removing **a small tree than** a large one. Young **trees, that have been grown in suitable** soil and properly taken **up, will be furnished with a good supply of roots. The best soil in which to grow young trees for transplanting is a good, sandy** loam. They will make **much better and more** fibrous roots **in** such a soil than when grown in stiff clay, and are consequently more likely to live and thrive well when transplanted. Some have entertained the opinion that trees from a sandy soil will not thrive when planted in clay, and that trees from a clay soil will not thrive when removed to sandy soil. This **is a great mistake.** A tree well supplied with fibrous roots will thrive in any soil, and the nurseryman who consults the best interests of his customers **will select** a rich, **sandy loam** in which to grow his young trees, experience having taught us that in such a soil they throw **out** an abundance of small and fibrous roots. In taking up a tree, it is impossible but that some of the roots will be cut off, but a tree that has been well taken up will have something of the appearance shown in Fig. 20;

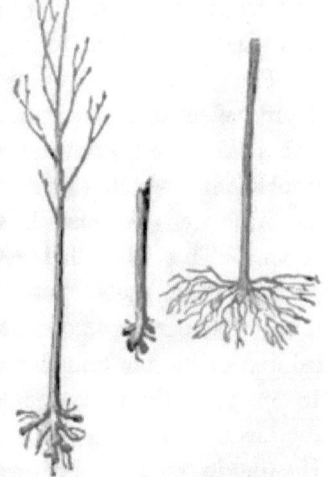

FIG. 21.   FIG. 22.   FIG. 20.

but trees that resemble Fig. 21 have been badly dug, and those are worse dug that look like Fig. 22.

It may be often of great advantage to procure the trees when they are two years old, plant them out in a nice piece of rich, loamy soil, in rows four feet apart and two feet apart in the row. Trees grown in this way, for a couple of years, make a splendid mass of roots, can be transplanted into orchard form at the owner's convenience, and are sure to live and dó well.

Low, stout-bodied trees are much better than those that are tall and slender. The diameter of the trunk of a tree is of much greater importance than its height. A tree that has a stout body is more surely healthy and well-rooted, and will be able to support a top and keep erect, while a tall, slender tree is apt to have slender, tapering roots, and is often too weak-bodied to sustain the top without being tied to a stake. Besides all this, in some parts of the country where the cold is severe, it has been ascertained by actual trial that stout trees, with low heads, are much better able to resist the cold than those which are trained high, with long, exposed trunks. We strongly urge upon planters living in the colder sections of the country to select stout, low-headed trees, and keep them branched low, being assured they will be more healthy and live longer, and yield more and finer fruit than when trained high.

Trees, when received by the planter, should be kept from the drying effect of the sun and wind until he is ready to plant them out. The most convenient and effectual method is to dig a trench, into which the roots are placed and covered with soil. Here the trees can remain safely until it is convenient to plant them. This is called *heeling-in*. On taking them out for planting the roots should be examined, and any bruised or mutilated parts pared smoothly with a sharp knife, and any injured or broken branches pruned smoothly, or entirely removed. In planting, the roots should be covered with a mat or old bit of rug, or anything, indeed, that will keep them from getting dry. Heeling in may be also practised where it is not desired to plant the trees in the autumn, and it is not practicable or convenient to obtain the trees direct from the nursery in the spring. But in such cases the roots must be well secured from frost, and the tops also should be covered with branches of evergreens. Shortening the side branches and a portion of the top of the tree at the time of transplanting in the spring is advisable, in order to restore the proportions between the root and the top. Judgment must be exercised in this operation, keeping in mind that the object is to lessen the amount of foliage somewhat, because the quantity of roots have been lessened. As a rule, about one-third of the top, including the side branches, may be removed. In cutting away the side branches, it is better merely to cut them back, leaving three or four buds, instead of cutting them off close to the body of the tree. The circulation through the trunk of the tree is kept up by the foliage that will form on these spurs, whereas, if cut off close to the trunk, the exposed wood seasons back into the trunk, and if there be many of them, seriously interferes with the circulation of the sap. For this reason do not cut off the small spurs and leaf-buds which may be on the body of the tree. They materially aid in keeping the body fresh and sound, and the sap in free and healthy circulation. After the tree has become established they may be removed, and then the slight wound will rapidly heal over.

The AFTER-TREATMENT of young orchards consists in keeping the ground mellow and in good heart. Doubtless the very best thing for the trees is to keep the ground thoroughly cultivated, the surface loose and friable, and free from weeds, without attempting to raise any crop; but this is not to be expected of the most of our planters, who hardly feel able to till the soil so thoroughly for so many years without any return. Hoed crops are the best to raise in an orchard, treating each tree as a part of the crop, giving it the same manuring and cultivation as the rest. Cereals, as rye, wheat, barley and oats, are not so suitable, and there can be nothing worse for a young orchard than to seed it down and let it lie in grass to be mown or pastured. If put down in grass, let it never be cut, or if cut, left to decay on the ground where it grew. A top dressing of lime at the rate of twenty bushels to the acre may be applied with benefit, especially about the time the trees come into bearing, to be renewed every three or four years. Ashes, leached or unleached, crushed or ground bones, gypsum or plaster, chip manure from the old wood pile, horn shavings, wool waste, and occasionally a light coating of well rotted barn-yard manure, will all be found beneficial to the orchard, applying these in such quantities, and at such intervals, as will keep the orchard in a healthy condition, but not induce an excessive wood growth. After the trees have become so large as to shade most of the ground, it will no longer be profitable to grow crops of any kind in the orchard. It may now be seeded down to grass, which should not be removed from the orchard, but suffered to remain and decay on the ground. This will serve as an excellent protection to the roots, and by its decomposition enrich the soil. A dressing of ashes, bone dust or plaster, should not be neglected; it will be amply returned in the increased beauty, size and quantity of fruit.

To Protect the Trees from Mice, which are often very destructive to young trees by gnawing off the bark at the surface of the ground, and, when they become numerous, injure even bearing trees, the trees may be painted with the following mixture, which is recommended by Downing. Take one spadeful of hot slaked lime, one of clean, fresh cow dung, half a spadeful of soot, and a handful of flour of sulphur; mix the whole together with sufficient water to bring it to the consistence of thick paint. In the autumn paint the trees with this mixture from the ground to the highest snow line, choosing dry weather in which to apply it. This is a perfectly safe application, and has been proved by repeated trial to be entirely harmless to the tree. In those parts of the country where the snow is seldom deep, it has been found that a mound of earth raised around the tree to the height of a foot or so, enough to be above the ordinary level of the snow, will fully preserve the trees from their ravages, for they always-work under the snow, never in open daylight. Coarse paper may be tied **around** the tree, and smeared with coal tar; and **some use** strips of roofing-felt fastened around the tree; others, **old stove pipe**—in short, anything that will keep the mice **from gnawing the bark.**

A WASH FOR THE TRUNKS AND BRANCHES is made by dissolving one pound of potash in two gallons of water. If this be applied with a brush or swab to the bark of the trunk and larger branches before the buds burst in spring, it will make it smooth and glossy, and is sure death to the bark-louse and all insects and their eggs which **harbor** in the crevices and under the scales of the **bark.** It is **also a great** preservative from **the attacks of insects, and seems to promote** the health of the tree, giving **a fresh and lively** appearance **to the bark.** Soft **soap—that which is ropy is** preferable **to that which is like jelly**—is also an excellent preservative from **insects, and may be applied by rubbing it on** with a **coarse cloth.** If the bark of the tree has become very rough, it **is necessary to** scrape off the loose pieces before applying the **wash.** This can be readily done by cutting a piece, in shape like a new moon, out of the edge of an old hoe, which will shape the edge of the hoe so as to fit very nearly to the trunk of the tree. The soft soap is preferable to the **potash wash for old trees with such thick and rough bark.**

SOIL AND ASPECT.

It is essentially necessary to the health and longevity of fruit trees, and the perfect development of the fruit, that the soil in which they are planted should be perfectly drained; and by this should be understood not only the entire removal of all stagnant surface water, **but of** all stagnant water in the soil. If such a condition does not naturally exist, it should be secured by artificial means. To plant fruit trees where the roots must be soaked with excess of water during any long-continued period, can only be productive of disappointment and loss. This having been secured, all other questions concerning the soil are, comparatively, of little moment. Soils that will produce good crops of grain will be found well adapted to fruit. The soils best suited to the several fruits will be mentioned when we come to treat of the different fruits separately, but for most of the fruits of our climate, strong calcareous loams, that is, loams in which there is just enough sand to make them easily worked, and which are abundantly supplied with limestone, are the best suited to the raising of fruit.

Deep valleys, with only small streams of water, are bad situations for fruit trees, for the reason that, in calm nights, the cold air settles down in these valleys, frequently killing buds and blossoms, while on the adjacent hill-tops they entirely escape. Usually hill-sides, sloping to the west, are the best for fruit trees, protecting them from the rays of a bright sun after a clear frosty night. The borders of large rivers and lakes are favorable situations, large bodies of water having an ameliorating effect upon the temperature. Sometimes a slight mist rising from the water in the morning, after a frosty night, so softens the rays of the sun that the frost is drawn out very gradually, and the injurious effect of sudden thawing prevented. An aspect that is sheltered from the sweep of the prevailing winds by a belt of woodland, and particularly of evergreens, enjoys an immunity from extremes of cold which often prove injurious to more exposed orchards. As our forests fall before the axe, and the country is laid bare to the frost-laden winds of our Canadian winters, and the climate thereby becomes more harsh, the most successful fruit growers will be those who have sheltered their orchards by planting belts of evergreens, and, as strongly advised by Mr. Elliott, occasional evergreen trees, or clumps of them, scattered with judgment here and there through the orchard, and always so disposed as that their ameliorating effect shall be most beneficially felt by the adjacent fruit trees. Much might be written on the value of such belts and clumps of trees to every farmer; on the great benefits accruing, not only to the orchard, but to the farm crops, to the stock, and to his own house — concerning their ameliorating influences on the temperature, on the purity and healthfulness of the atmosphere, on the electrical conditions favorable to animal and vegetable life, on the amount of rain and dew; but, alas, in this age of haste, an enlarged and enlightened policy, which takes into consideration the wants of a life-time, and plans with reference to the needs and comforts of years yet in the distance, is almost wholly lost in thoughts of immediate advantage. "Oh, I shall never live to reap the benefits of all this outlay and care," is a sufficient answer to all such suggestions, just as though man lived for himself alone. Is it nothing to have left behind you the impress of your enlarged views upon the acres your children shall till? Is it nothing to have laid foundations broad and deep, upon which those who come after you may build, and bless the forethought and wisdom with which you provided for their comfort and health? Is there not a pleasure more rich and sweet than that which centres in self? But enough. Some coming generation may plant and plan with reference to the permanent value of farms and homesteads; we are too busy.

INSECTS.

Every cultivator of the soil has need to study carefully the character and habits of insects. Not a farmer but has suffered more or less from their ravages, and the losses of the farmers of our Dominion from the destructive habits of these little creatures can only be counted in millions of dollars. Indeed, that General Superintendent of Education will deserve the lasting gratitude of his countrymen who shall make the habits of insects one of the branches of Common School education.

There are many insects which prey upon the foliage of our fruit trees, and some upon the fruit. Only those can be described here which are most widely distributed throughout the country, and whose ravages are most serious. The Entomological Society of Canada has undertaken the labor of giving a complete account of the noxious insects of the Province of Ontario, and in doing this must necessarily describe the most, if not all, of those which are to be found in the other Provinces. This task will be accomplished in a series of Reports, in which will be described in turn the insects injurious to the several fruits and crops, and as incidental to this, those insects also will be described which are of service to the cultivator, by reason of their habit of feeding upon those that are injurious; so that, in time, every fruit grower, gardener and farmer will be made acquainted with the habits of their insect friends and foes, and with the best known methods of combating the enemies. The Reports which relate to insects affecting fruits will be incorporated with the Reports of the Fruit Growers' Association, and placed in the hands of all its members, and those who wish to possess the fullest information on this subject should carefully study these reports.

In the earlier history of fruit raising in Canada, no serious inconvenience was felt from the depredations of insects, and very possibly in most of the newer settlements the same immunity may now exist. But in all the older settled parts of the land, and especially in those parts where the climate is most favorable to fruit-growing, insects have been suffered to continue their labors without any interference of man, and so to multiply their numbers that the injury they inflict is becoming, indeed has already become, matter of serious moment. Yet most of our fruit growers content themselves with complaining, and put forth no active efforts to lessen the evil. This arises partly from the habit, so long indulged, of letting them alone, partly from another habit in which they have been educated, of regarding the fruit crop as of secondary importance, but largely from want of acquaintance with their tiny foe, and of the weapons with which to fight it, and the vulnerable spot at which to aim. Achilles, dipped by his mother in the Styx, was made invulnerable in all his body, save the heel by which she held him, and only he who had his secret knew how to aim the arrow by which he fell. By the study of the life and habits of these insects will we gain the knowledge of their secret, and find out how to aim our efforts so as to accomplish their destruction. In this there is much yet to be learned. Let each, then, avail himself of the information we now possess, and give to these robbers of our orchards and gardens such diligent attention, that our means of fighting them may be improved, and their numbers largely diminished.

The growing and marketing of fruit is already assuming considerable importance in some parts of the country, and fruit is becoming one of our commercial products. They who would reap from their orchards the surest and largest golden harvest, must send to market the finest and fairest fruit, and this can only be done by him who most perseveringly and most intelligently wages war upon these tiny insect foes, which accomplish by dint of numbers a work of destruction to which, regarded as individuals, they seem to be wholly inadequate.

THE TENT CATERPILLARS.—These caterpillars are widely distributed throughout the country, and are sometimes so numerous as to strip the leaves from entire orchards. There are two species; they are called the American and Forest Tent Caterpillars, and get their name from their habit of making themselves tents to dwell in. Fig. 23, *c*, is a representation of a cluster or bracelet of eggs from which these caterpillars are hatched. They are fastened, as shown in the engraving, around some small twig of the tree, conveniently near the buds from which the leaves are to grow upon which the young caterpillars are to feed. As the buds burst and the tender leaves put forth, on some day when the air is warm and full of moisture, the young caterpillars are hatched. If the leaves be not yet

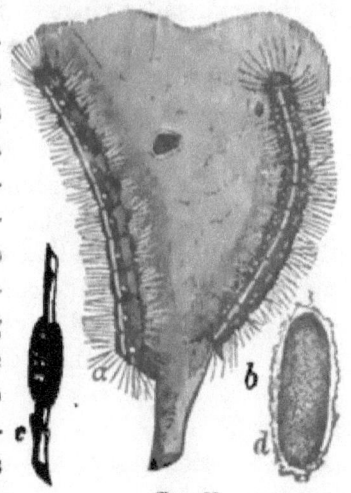

FIG. 23.

sufficiently grown to **supply them with** food, there is no **danger** of their perishing with hunger, for they will feed upon the soft glutinous substance which covers the eggs, and has served to shield them from the wet. Selecting some convenient fork in **the branches, they spin in it a** web, which they enlarge as they **increase in size.** This **web** or tent is their place of abode, from which they go in **search of** food, and to which they **return when their hunger is satisfied, all** going out and returning together in **regular procession. When full grown** they are about two inches **in length, colour deep black with a white** stripe extending along **the back, and on each side of this stripe are numerous irregular** yellow **lines and a row of pale blue oval spots.** The Forest Tent Caterpillar has a row of white spots **along the back instead of a stripe.** When they have attained to this size they leave their **tents and** become scattered about, seeking secure places in which **to spin their** cocoons, such as the crevices of fences and the loose **bark of old trees,** or any neglected rubbish. The cocoons are **oval, pale yellow, loosely** woven, and the meshes filled with a fine **powder resembling sulphur.** Having wrapped himself in **this cocoon, the caterpillar changes to the pupa state, remaining in this** condition about three weeks, when the moth **comes forth,** working its **way** out at one end of the cocoon. **The moth is of a** dull, reddish buff colour, with two parallel, nearly white stripes **or bands running** obliquely across the fore-wings. These moths are **most abundant** in **July, live** but a few days, in which the females lay their eggs upon **the twigs of the trees in a** broad belt, usually encircling the **twig, and cover them** with a thick coating of glutinous matter, **which gives the bracelet the** appearance of having been varnished, **and serves to protect the** eggs until the young caterpillars **are hatched,** and then becomes their first food.

The Forest **Tent** Caterpillar does not make so large a tent nor place it **in** the forks of the branches, but merely makes a slight web **on** the side of the trunk or large branches. **When** nearly **grown** they congregate **upon the** trunk of the tree or **some large branch** when not feeding, and may then be killed by **the thousand.**

The best method of destroying these insects is to search the orchard carefully in the spring, before the buds are much swollen, and cut off the belts of eggs on the twigs and burn them. These bracelets will be found from one inch to twelve inches from the end of the shoots, and a little practice will enable one to discern them readily. It is best to search for them on a cloudy day, thus avoiding the glare of a bright sun. As each belt contains some three hundred eggs, this is a rapid and convenient way of destroying this pest. But, as some may escape notice, it will be necessary to go through the orchard just as the young leaves make their appearance, and search for the webs or tents in the forks of the branches. These may be cut off and the worms crushed under the foot, or with a light ladder ascend the tree and destroy them with the hand, which may be covered with a stout buckskin mitten.

There is no need of our orchards being overrun with these caterpillars, a little attention in the way already pointed out will enable every one to keep them in subjection. He who suffers from this cause may thank his own carelessness and indolence, and deserves, in addition to losing his apple crop, to be compelled to pay into the treasury of the municipality a handsome fine. Fig. 23 represents one of the tents of the American Tent Caterpillar, with two of the larvæ, *a* and *b*, on it, showing the side and back view, and *d* represents the cocoon. Fig. 24 is the male moth, and Fig. 25 the female moth, and Fig. 26 the pupa which is found inside of the cocoon. Fig. 27 shows the Forest Tent Caterpillar, distinguished from the other by the row of white spots on the back instead of a white line.

These caterpillars are found most abundantly in our apple orchards, but they feed also upon the cherry, and have been found

FIG. 24.

FIG. 25.   FIG. 26.

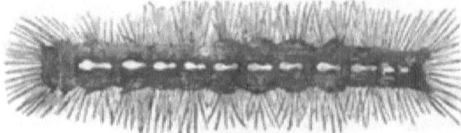

FIG. 27.

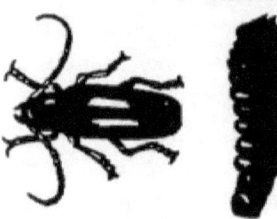

FIG. 28.

on the peach. The writer cannot remember ever having seen them upon the pear.

THE TWO-STRIPED BORER. *Saperda bivittata*. This beetle is very destructive to young apple trees, and sometimes attacks the pear and quince. It does its work so silently, and removed from observation, that fine orchards have been entirely ruined before suspicion was entertained that any danger threatened. Fig. 28 represents the beetle or perfect insect and the grub from which it is produced, or the same insect in the larva state. The perfect insect is light brown on the upper side, marked with two chalky-white stripes, running lengthwise of the body; the under side, the face, the antennæ, and the legs are white. It is usually about three quarters of an inch long, moving about at night and remaining concealed by day. During the months of June and July the females deposit their eggs upon the bark of the tree, near the root, at that part known as the collar of the tree. Here the bark is softer than at any other place on the trunk. From the eggs are hatched little fleshy whitish grubs without feet, which cut through the bark, and, on reaching the sap-wood, excavate a round, smooth cavity, about the size of a silver dollar, immediately under the bark. At the bottom of this cavity it makes a hole, out of which it casts its excrements, which appear like very fine sawdust. At this stage of its existence its presence can be readily ascertained by searching for this dust on the ground, just around the trunk of the tree. When the larva has become about half grown it ceases to cast the dust out of this hole, but proceeds to fill up the cavity it had made, at the same time boring a passage or gallery upward into the heart of the tree. This gallery is continued upwards, of variable length, sometimes not more than two inches, and sometimes twelve **inches,** and is gradually brought outwards **again to the bark of the tree,** but not through it. When the grub has completed this gallery it turns around and returns to that part of it which **is nearest to the heart of the tree; this part it now enlarges by** tearing off the **fibre from the walls, and with this** fibre carefully and securely closes the entrance, **so that if some insect** enemy should find its **way into** the chamber where it passed the first part **of** its life, that enemy could not enter the gallery to its present abode. At the same time it crowds **its** sawdust-like excrements into the upper extremity **of the** gallery, **against the bark, thus diminishing the** danger **of attack from that quarter, and, at the same time, keeping its new chamber tidy. Having thus** perfected its **arrangements,** it again **turns around so as to have its head upwards, passes the winter in a torpid state, and in the spring casts off its skin and becomes a pupa, from which, in June, the perfect insect hatches,** climbs **to the upper end of the gallery,** tears away the fine sawdust, gnaws **a** hole through the bark, and creeps forth.

The larva, when full grown, is about an inch long, and less than a quarter of an inch thick, of a pale yellow colour, with a brown head and black jaws. When there are several of these borers in one tree, they often **completely girdle it, thus causing its death. They are distributed more or less numerously** throughout the country, and will probably extend in **time to** those localities **that now seem to** be exempt, **so that no orchard,** particularly no young orchard—for young and thrifty trees are the favourite resort of this beetle—can be considered safe from their ravages. It is very important that the trees should be carefully examined three or four times every year, lest these borers effect a lodgment unawares.

There is a simple method of keeping them out of the **trees,** and, if **this** be faithfully employed, they will never effect a **lodgment.** It has been found **that strong alkalies will** destroy the vitality of the egg, and, indeed, it is believed that the presence of such an alkali prevents the parent beetle from depositing her eggs, either because the odour is offensive to her, or because her instincts teach her that the eggs will only perish if she places them where they will come in contact with it. The most efficient method of applying this alkali is in the form of a ropy soft soap, which may be rubbed upon the body of the tree with a swab, particularly at the collar, and a handful deposited in the forks of the tree, where the branches separate from the main trunk, to be dissolved and washed down by the rains. A solution of potash, at the rate of a pound of potash to two gallons of water, will be found to answer the purpose in the absence of soft soap, but will need to be oftener applied.

But if the grub has already got into the tree, the easiest and simplest method is to hunt him out and kill him. This can be done with a stout-bladed knife or a narrow carpenter's gouge. Sometimes the newly-hatched grubs may be found in the month of August, while yet in the bark, their presence being indicated by small black spots in the bark about the collar of the tree. Washing this part of the tree with strong lye, or the above solution of potash, will often be effectual in destroying any of the young larvæ that may have escaped detection. At the same time search carefully for the fine sawdust castings, which indicate a larger grub within; and, if these are seen, find the excavation in the sapwood, and hunt him out. If the grub have made his gallery into the heart of the tree, the upper opening may be found, usually from three to six inches above the chamber in the sapwood, by sticking a pin into the bark until, by the ready sinking of the pin, the exact spot is known; then, with the point of the knife, cut away the bark and pour some of the lye or potash solution down the gallery until, by its soaking through into the chamber below, you know that it has accomplished its work. By renewing the search for these sawdust castings at intervals through the fall, winter and early spring, they may be effectually routed.

THE BUPRESTIS APPLE-TREE BORER. *Chrysobothris femorata.* This beetle is more universally distributed than the two-striped borer just described, and, like it, injures and often destroys young apple-trees by eating the sapwood so as frequently to girdle the trees. Fig. 29, *a*, shows this insect in the grub or larva state, *b* in the perfect or winged-beetle state. The grub is yellowish white, soft and footless, broad and flattened near the head, rapidly tapering toward the other extremity. Its jaws are a deep black, and highly polished. The head is blackish brown, and nearly concealed by the second segment or ring. The beetle has a rough, uneven surface, of a blackish brown colour, with something of a coppery lustre, but the under side looks like burnished copper, extending down the legs to the feet, which are of a deep, shining green. The eggs are deposited in the crevices of the bark, on the trunk and larger branches; from these the grubs are hatched, and eat their way through the bark to the sapwood. Here it makes an excavation in the wood directly under the bark, increasing the size of the chamber with its age. When fully grown it bores into the solid heart of the tree, where it remains during its quiescent state, and comes out, in the end of June or early in July, a perfect beetle. This one loves to bask in the sun, and may be found on the trunks of the trees when the sun is hottest.

FIG. 29.

The application of soft soap to the trunk and larger branches, or of the solution of potash mentioned before, will be effectual to prevent these borers from getting into the trees. Alkaline solutions destroy the eggs and kill the young grubs while yet in the bark. But, if the grubs have reached the sapwood, the only way of making sure of their destruction is to hunt them out with a knife and put them to death. Their presence can be readily detected by the discoloration of the bark, that portion directly over their burrow being both flattened and dead. Young orchards should be thoroughly examined two or three times a year, and well rubbed with soft soap or washed with the potash solution.

THE CODLING-WORM. *Carpocapsa pomonella.* This insect is in every orchard in the land, and does more injury to the apple crop than any of the others; yes, probably more than all

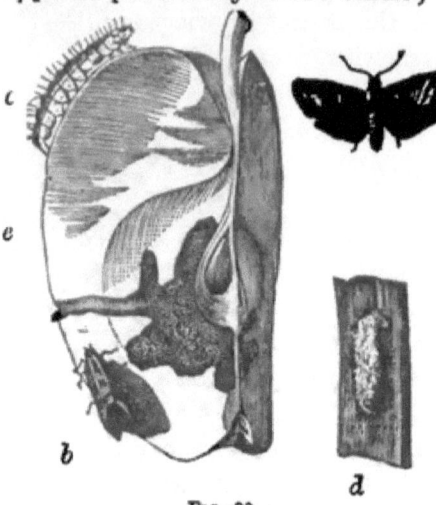

FIG. 30.

the others combined. It is a tiny creature, so very small that it has never been seen in its winged state by the great majority of fruit raisers, whom it has robbed of tens, if not of hundreds of dollars. In some seasons, fully one-half of the fruit is so marred and eaten out by this worm that it is not fit to be sent to market. It is an European insect that has crossed the ocean and taken possession of the orchards of the new world, an invader not so easily driven out. At Fig. 30, *a* represents the moth, with its wings expanded, as when flying, and *b* the moth when at rest. It is a beautiful little moth, the expanded wings not extending over three quarters of an inch, but the fore-wings are crossed with numerous grey and brown lines, giving them the appearance of a watered silk, and near the hind angle of each of the fore wings is a dark brown, oval spot, edged with a bright copper colour. The hind wings are a light yellowish brown, as lustrous as satin. These moths, during the month of July, deposit their eggs on the young apple, in the cavity at the blossom end of the fruit, and, as if to destroy the value of as many apples as possible, they take care to lay but one egg on each apple. There are occasional exceptions to these rules; they do sometimes deposit a second egg in the cavity where the stem is inserted, but these exceptions are met with just often enough to prove that the parent moth intends to deposit only one egg on each apple.

In a few days these eggs are hatched, and each little **worm** begins to eat its way down to the core, which is readily reached from this **point**. Arrived at the core, it gradually excavates for itself a chamber, feeding upon the pulp **of** the apple, and increasing in size until it has reached maturity. This is done in **about four** weeks, when it is scarce half an inch long, of a delicate **pink** colour, and thinly covered with very delicate white hairs. Fig. 30, c, represents the worm of full size. When its growth is completed, it eats its way through the side of **the** apple and crawls out. If the apple has not dropped from the tree, it can let itself down very gently by a silken thread which it spins, and **seek** a secure retreat. The worm does *not crawl into the ground*, as many have supposed, but seeks a hiding place in any **crevice,** under the rough bark, between dried **blades of grass,** in the folds **of an old rag, in** short, anywhere that a safe retreat can be found. Hidden **away in this hiding place, it spins around itself a thin,** silken **cocoon, like very fine tissue** paper, and, inside of this cocoon, throws off its skin and becomes a pupa. The cocoon is shown at Fig. 30, d, and e represents a portion of an apple cut open so as to show the chamber made by the worm around the core, and the channel reaching to the side, by which the worm makes his way out. In due time the pupa, or chrysalis, as it is also called, works its way out of one end of the cocoon, and the moth, now fully formed within the chrysalis, breaks the shell of the pupa, and **comes out.**

There are two broods of these little codling-worms in each summer. Some, at least, and probably only a part of them, come out in the moth state in August, and proceed to deposit their eggs **on** the sound apples, apparently selecting the winter fruit. Hence we sometimes meet with these worms in the fruit that has been stored for winter use.

The effect upon the fruit is, as a rule, to cause it to ripen prematurely and fall to the ground. No doubt, sometimes, the worm has escaped from the fruit before it falls, but usually the **worm** may yet be found within the freshly-fallen fruit. However, it does not remain long in the fruit after it has fallen, but proceeds to make its way out, and seek its hiding place, very soon after the fruit comes to the ground. For this reason it is important that the fruit should not be permitted to remain on the ground, but be gathered up regularly every day. If it be possible to keep a litter of small pigs in the orchard, with sharp appetites, they will consume the apples as fast as they fall, and thus destroy a great many of the worms. But it will not do to depend upon this method of destroying them alone. Many will escape from the apples before they drop, or creep out soon enough thereafter to escape the pigs. In order to catch these, a rope of straw may be twisted around the trunk of the tree near the ground, and another just below the branches, or, if convenient, strips of woollen rags, lightly twisted together, may be tied around the trees, and a handful of woollen rags laid in the fork of the branches. The worms will seek these as hiding places, and spin their cocoons there. These bands may be examined, and when the worms or cocoons are found to have become numerous, those that are of straw may be taken off and burned, and new bands put in their places. The woollen bands or rags may be searched, and the codling-worms killed, or they may be dipped in hot water, or placed on a board and pounded with a mallet so as to crush the insects concealed within the folds, and then replaced. Dr. Trimble, of New Jersey, recommends this plan, and it is said that as many as a thousand have been taken in this way, from one tree, in a single season. In addition to these methods of destroying them, great advantage will be derived from building numerous small fires in the orchard at night, with chips and shavings, during the month of June. These codling-worm moths, and the moths of a great many other injurious insects, attracted by the light, fly into the blaze and are burned.

It is not possible sufficiently to impress upon the mind of each one who has an orchard the importance of using every one of these methods for the destruction of the codling-worm. So rapidly do they multiply, so destructive are their ravages, so sure

are some of them to escape—their very insignificance and little-
ness shielding them—that it will be only by the use of every one
of these means of destroying them that we shall so succeed in
keeping them in subjection as to secure a portion of sound fruit.
If the labor be too great, then do cut down your orchards, and
not leave them to be breeding places for these pests, from which
to spread into the orchards of your neighbors who are trying to
secure some fruit that shall be sound and fit for market.

THE PLUM CURCULIO. *Conotrachelus nenuphar.* This
insect is the pest of all our stone fruits. It is to be found in
nearly all parts of the Dominion, and wherever it has become
numerous it wholly destroys the plum crop, and renders the
cherry crop useless. Nearly every fruit grower has been made
to suffer from its ravages, and unless energetic efforts are made to
keep it in subjection, we may bid farewell to all our choice
plums, cherries and other stone fruits. But there is no necessity
for this. It has been repeatedly shown that it is quite within
our power to so lessen their numbers that we can secure a fine
crop of these delicious fruits. Should any have doubts of the
possibility of accomplishing this very desirable result, they will
be much gratified by the perusal of the Report on the Plum
Curculio, made to the Fruit Growers' Association of Ontario, by
W. Saunders, Esq., of London; Ont., and printed at page 50 of
the Report of the Association for the year 1870. It will there
be seen that many succeeded in saving their plums by devoting
a little time every day for about a fortnight to the business of
catching them.

The simplest and, under ordinary circumstances, the best
method of catching the curculio is to spread a cloth under the
tree, and jar it by a smart blow. If the trees are of some
size, it is recommended to bore a small hole into the trunk of
the tree, just below the branches, to the depth of about one-
third of the thickness of the tree. Into this slip an iron bolt that
will just fit into the hole. The bolt should be cut off square at
both ends. A piece of common cotton sheeting, long enough to

reach as far as the branches extend, and made wide enough by sewing, if necessary, two breadths together, may be fastened at each end to a strip of lath, or any light stick that will serve to keep the cloth extended. By using two of these sheets, spreading one on each side of the tree so as to cover the ground under the branches, and having a place cut out of that side of the sheets next to the tree, in order to receive the trunk of the tree, all the insects that fall from the tree will drop on the sheets, and can be readily seen and gathered up. After spreading the sheets on the ground, a smart blow should be struck on the end of the iron bolt with a heavy hammer. This will jar the tree to the extremities of the branches, and cause the curculios that are in the tree to drop down and feign themselves dead. Having provided a vial, with some alcohol or strong whiskey in it, the curculios may be picked up and put into the phial for safe keeping. Or a wide-mouthed bottle may be used, filled with saw-dust, which is kept moist with alcohol. Shaking the tree will not answer the purpose; that will not bring the curculio down, it is necessary to jar the tree, and if a bolt of iron is not let into the trunk, upon which to strike, care must be taken not to bruize the tree by striking on the bark. It may be often convenient to saw off a stout limb, leaving a few inches projecting from the trunk, and to strike the blow on the end of this stump of the limb. This will answer the purpose of the iron bolt, and save the bark from being bruised.

The best time of the day for catching the curculio is before seven o'clock in the morning, and after seven in the evening. Both morning and evening should be tried, for in some seasons the curculio will be found to be more numerous in the evening, and in other seasons more numerous in the morning. The season of the year for catching them is as soon as the blossoms fall, which is usually about the twenty-fifth of May, and should be continued as long as the curculio are found. They will be usually very abundant upon the plum trees, both wild and cultivated, and upon the cherry trees, especially the sweet varieties.

In addition to the use of sheets and jarring the curculio from the trees, it is recommended to place bits of bark, with the concave side down, on the ground under the trees, as soon as the spring opens. The curculio will take shelter on the under side of these pieces of bark, and by turning them over every day and gathering the curculio that will be found clinging to the under side, their numbers may be very rapidly diminished. The number that will be found under these chips will be much greater in some seasons than others, varying with the state of the weather. If cold, wet, and storm prevail, they will seek shelter under the chips, but if it be warm and pleasant weather they will be found in the trees.

Another mode of destroying these insects, which should be employed in addition to both of the foregoing, is the gathering of the injured and fallen fruit, regularly every day, before the curculio grub or larva has time to crawl out of the fruit. Some have fenced in their plum and cherry trees and turned the pigs in to devour the fallen fruit, but when this cannot be done, the fruit should be carefully and regularly picked up, and either fed to the pigs or cooked so as to kill the insects within.

But now for the insect itself. In Figure 32, *c* is a magnified representation of the perfect insect, the line underneath it indicating its natural length; *d* shows it, of the natural size, at work on a cherry, on which may be seen the crescent mark, and a dot indicating the position of the egg; *a* is the grub or larva, and *b* the pupa, both magnified.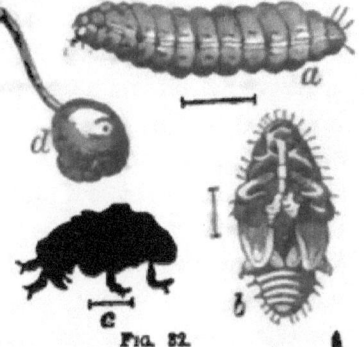

Fig. 32.

The adjacent lines are intended to show the actual length of the several forms of the curculio. The curculio is a rough, hump-backed beetle, of a brownish gray color, about a fifth of an inch in length, with a short snout. When alarmed, this snout is drawn close up to the body, and the legs folded up, so that the insect looks like a dried bud, or a little bit of bark or dirt. In this way it escapes detection, lying perfectly still for a long time as though dead. A sudden jar of the tree upon which it is at work frightens it, and folding up its legs it drops to the ground. By spreading a white sheet under the tree to receive the curculio when it falls, it is easily seen and gathered up. It has wings, however, and in warm weather will fly both during the day and night. The mouth is placed at the extremity of the snout, and with this the female bites the fruit and prepares a place for the egg. C. V. Riley, State Entomologist of Missouri, says that the operation of depositing an egg occupies about five minutes. "Having taken a strong hold on the fruit, the female makes a minute cut with her jaws, just through the skin of the fruit, and then runs her snout under the skin to the depth of one-sixteenth of an inch, and moves it back and forth until the cavity is large enough to receive the egg it is to retain; she then changes her position and drops an egg into the mouth of the cut; then turning around again, she pushes it by means of her snout to the end of the passage, and afterwards cuts the crescent in front of the hole, so as to undermine the egg and leave it in a sort of flap."

In a few days there is hatched from this egg a small white grub, which eats its way towards the centre of the fruit, where it remains feeding upon the pulp until it has attained its full growth. In the case of the plum, the natural development of the fruit is brought to a premature conclusion by the presence of this curculio grub, and the plums fall to the ground before they have completed their growth. This is not the case, however, with the cherry, which remains on the tree until maturity, and the eater is often disgusted at finding the fruit that looked so tempting, tenanted and half-eaten by this grub. It would seem that all this was arranged just in this way to secure the perpetuation of this pest, for the curculio grub attains its full growth with the ripening of the cherry, but as it completes its growth before the ripening of the plum, this drops off at about the time the curculio grub has finished its growth, so that it may find its way just at that time into the ground. Shortly after the plums drop, the grubs eat their way out of the fruit, crawl into the ground a short distance, and then make for themselves a small cavity, in which they change into the pupa state. During this stage they are inactive, and remain confined in their subterranean cell some three or four weeks, by which time they have become developed into perfect beetles, and crawl forth to lay more eggs and destroy more fruit.

Annoying and destructive as the curculio has been, there is notwithstanding no reason for allowing it to deprive us of our fruit, for with the knowledge we now have of its habits and of the means of capturing it, none but the lazy and careless will go without an abundance of cherries and plums.

THE GRAPE VINE FLEA BEETLE.—*Haltica chalybea.*—This insect feeds on the grape vine both in the beetle and larva state, and is often very destructive to the grape crop. It is very small, of a bright steel-blue color, though sometimes it is quite green, and jumps, when one tries to catch it, with the agility of a flea. Fig. 33, *d*, is a representation of this beetle, and *b* shows it in the larva state; both are magnified, the true size being indicated by the hair line at the side of each. *a* is a leaf, perforated by these larvæ, which are shown at work upon it, and *c* is a representation of the pupa.

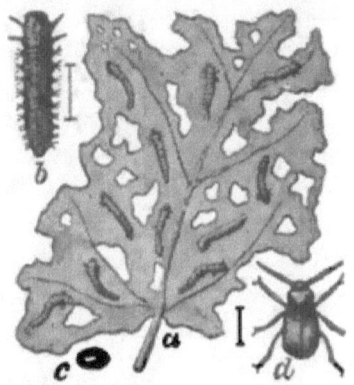

Fig. 33.

It does the greatest injury in the beetle state. Just as the buds are bursting in the spring, these little fellows, who have been fasting all the winter, and are too impatient to wait until the leaves are expanded, begin to feed on the opening buds, eating up leaves, stems, grapes and all, as they lie enfolded in the bud. In this way they make sad havoc, destroying the entire crop of fruit and sadly mutilating the vines.

These beetles deposit clusters of orange-colored eggs on the under side of the vine leaves, from which the larvæ are hatched; these are small, dark-brown worms, with black heads, which feed usually on the upper side of the leaves, but are sometimes to be found on the under side. In this stage they are very easily gathered and destroyed. They attain their full size in from three to four weeks, when they crawl into the ground and pass into the chrysalis state, from which they emerge in due time, as little, blue or green, jumping flea-beetles.

In the beetle state it is difficult to catch them, they verify the saying "that when you put your finger on them they are not there." We have no confidence in any dusting of them with air-slaked lime or sprinkling of them with soap suds; they are not so easily killed. White hellibore sprinkled on the opening buds may poison them. But the sure way of destroying them is to make thorough search among the young leaves for the eggs and the larvæ, and carefully pick them off and crush them.

THE GREEN GRAPE VINE SPHINX. *Chœrocampa pampinatrix.* This insect belongs to the family of Hawkmoths, which remain concealed during the day, but may often be seen of a warm summer's evening hovering over the flowers in the garden, much after the manner of a humming bird, and thrusting their long proboscis into the nectaries of the flowers.

In the moth state it is a very pretty insect. The upper side of the fore wings is of a dark olive green, banded with greenish grey, and the hinder wings are dull red. Fig. 34 is a very good representation of this moth. Fig. 35

Fig. 34.

shows the chrysalis, and Fig. 36 the caterpillar. The moth lays her eggs on the under side of the vine leaves, from which the caterpillar is hatched in a few days, at first only one-fifth of an inch long, and having a long black horn on the last segment of the body. It is a great eater and rapidly increases in size, undergoing some changes in appearance during its growth, until it reaches a length of two inches, when it is usually of a light green color, dotted along the back and striped on each side as shown in Fig. 36. It is during this caterpillar state that it commits its depredations, consuming the foliage, and when numerous, stripping the vine quite bare.

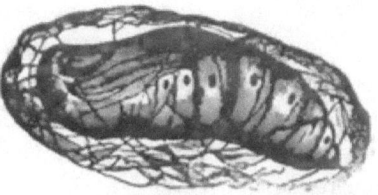

Fig. 35.

After attaining its full growth, the caterpillar descends to the ground, gathers some leaves together with a few silken threads, and passes into the chrysalis state. Those that pass into this state early in the season soon hatch out as winged moths, lay more eggs, which soon produce more caterpillars; but those which go into the chrysalis state late in the season, remain in the chrysalis state all winter.

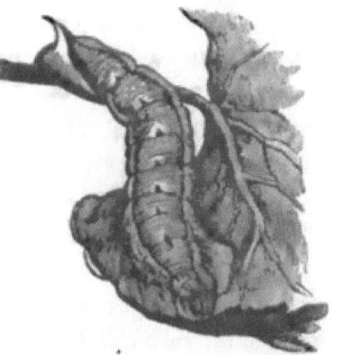

Fig. 36.

There is but one way of getting rid of this vine-leaf eater, that of searching for them on the vines, picking them off and killing them. Fortunately it is an easy matter to find them, for they usually make clean work as they go, eating the entire leaf and leaving only the foot stalk standing. Only a careless and slovenly cultivator need ever suffer very materially from the ravages of this insect.

THE GOOSEBERRY SAW-FLY.—*Nematus ventricosus.*—This insect feeds, when in the worm state, on the currant and gooseberry, and these usually make their appearance in such numbers that they soon strip the plants of their leaves. The perfect insect is a small, four-winged fly, about as large as the common house fly. About the first of May the female fly deposits her eggs along the ribs on the under side of the leaf. She is provided with a delicate saw, with which she cuts slits in the leaf ribs to hold the eggs. The eggs are very small and white, distinctly visible without the help of a microscope. These hatch in a few days, and the little worms immediately begin their work of devouring the leaves. They are of a pale green color, dotted with black. As soon as they acquire a little size and strength, they may be found on the edges of the leaves, holding on by the fore legs, in such a position as to bring the edge of the leaf to their mouths, thus enabling them to consume it with the greatest facility. The worms attain to a length of about three-quarters of an inch, and when fully grown, descend to the ground, burrow a short distance into the soil, and there change into the chrysalis state. About the first of July, the flies come out of the chrysalis, crawl out of the ground, and deposit a second supply of eggs, from which a second brood of worms is hatched. These do as their predecessors had done, making fearful havoc with the leaves of currant and gooseberry, and descending into the ground, pass into the chrysalis state. This second brood, however, remains in the ground all winter, awaiting the return of spring and the putting forth of the young leaves before the flies come out to deposit their eggs. Besides these two regular armies of saw-fly worms which invade our currants and gooseberries every summer, there are occasional raids from irregular squadrons, which do mischief in proportion to their numbers, and make it necessary to keep continual watch and ward. Fortunately, we have, in powdered white hellebore, a cheap and perfect instrument of destruction. It can be procured of the druggists at from forty to fifty cents per pound, and an ounce of this mixed with about a pailful of water will be sufficient for twenty plants. The best way of using the hellebore is to put it in water in the proportion of an ounce of powdered white hellebore (the white hellebore, not black) to a pailful of water, and with a common watering pot, with not too fine a rose, sprinkle it thoroughly over the leaves, being careful to thrust the rose into the bush so as to sprinkle the lower leaves on which the early brood while yet young will be found. It will be necessary to keep a careful and constant look-out for these worms, examining with care the leaves on the lower branches and in the interior of the bush, and use the hellebore whenever they are discovered. A couple of days' delay after they are once discovered will usually give them time to strip all the leaves from the plants, but a timely and thorough application of hellebore will kill the worms and save the plants. This hellebore is poisonous, and should be cared for accordingly, though not as virulent as many, and requiring to be taken in larger doses than most other poisons to produce serious consequences.

THE PRODUCTION OF NEW VARIETIES.

The method by which varieties are perpetuated, and trees of any given sort are multiplied by grafting and budding, has been already fully explained; now we propose to shew how new varieties of good qualities can be produced. It is true that very many, perhaps the most, of our valuable varieties of fruit have been accidental productions, in which the hand of man played no other part than that of sowing the seed, and oftentimes not even that; but study and experiment have shown that there are certain laws which govern the processes of reproduction in the vegetable as well as the animal world, and that it is in the power of man to so direct these processes of vegetable reproduction as to secure definite results. The stock-breeder makes himself acquainted with the laws of animal reproduction, and by skilful direction so uses them as to produce an animal having the desired qualities or combination of qualities. In like manner the producer of new varieties of fruits studies the laws of vegetable reproduction, and by skilfully directing their operations produces a new variety of fruit combining certain desired qualities.

This is a most fascinating field of study and experiment, one that has as yet been but very partially explored, and that offers to the Canadian fruit grower the opportunity of producing varieties of fruit adapted to our own peculiar climate that shall far surpass the majority of those now in cultivation. Hardy apples that shall thrive in the harsh climate of our colder sections and yield fruit of high flavor, are yet sought after, not only by the fruit planters of our Dominion, but by the dwellers in all the north-western United States. The present boundaries of successful pear culture are yet to be greatly enlarged by the production of new varieties of superior hardihood. Wild grape vines are found growing in far colder parts of our land than are now thought to be available for the production of our cultivated varieties, but needing the touch of no magician's wand to change their austere fruit into a luxury for the table. The blackberry, raspberry, blueberry, whortleberry, cranberry, and all the host of small fruits, only await the skilful employment of nature's own laws to be changed into new forms, with new characters, properties and flavors.

It is true that there are causes which influence the production of new varieties of fruit, more subtle, and perhaps therefore less easily directed and controlled by man, than those which affect the production of choice breeds of animals; but this is only saying that the labyrinths of vegetable reproduction have not yet been all threaded, and that there are discoveries still to be made, and great rewards to crown the patient student. Nature loves to unfold her mysteries to those who will take the pains to watch her operations; and while availing ourselves of what we know, we may confidently expect to attain to such fuller knowledge as shall enable us to produce at will the qualities we desire. As it

PRODUCTION OF NEW VARIETIES.

now stands, it **is** possible to make very near approximations to the attainment **of** the desired result, and the labors of the painstaking operator are always crowned with gratifying results, often even richer and better than his most sanguine expectations. **Sometimes the** results of his labors are very different from his intentions, as though nature would say to him, you have not yet fathomed the depths of my secret places; study me more carefully, consider more fully all the conditions which influence results, and conduct your operations with greater nicety, then will you find me a willing servant to do your bidding.

New varieties are, as a rule, produced from seed; and **so far** as the hand of man can control results, **in** the present state **of** our knowledge, they are always produced from seed. Sometimes trees and plants produce what are termed sports. A branch of a Spitzenburgh apple tree, operated upon by forces whose modes of action are as yet to us unknown, will produce russet apples, whose appearance, texture and flavor even, differ more or less widely from all the other apples on the tree. A branch of a tree will assume a drooping habit, or put forth variegated foliage, or leaves curiously cut or curled in a ringlet. These unusual developments man is able to perpetuate by grafting, and **so** to increase their number **that every** man can **ornament his** lawn with the ring-leaved willow, or **the variegated-leaved ash**, or the **cut-leaved** birch. **But no one has yet penetrated** so far into the hidden things of **nature as to be able to unfold to** us the laws which govern their production, **or teach** us how we may at will **produce** like variations. **Some** physiologists, with wise looks and high-sounding phrases, will tell **us** that somewhere, away back **in the** ages of long ago, an atom became impressed with the tendency **to** assume such an abnormal form, and by slow degrees **has** communicated this tendency to its fellow atoms, until favorable conditions having arisen, this tendency has been able to give expression to itself in the form in which we see it developed. But what is an atom? What is such a tendency, **and by** whom impressed? Can atoms arrange themselves as they please? Are they not moved by forces outside of themselves, and arranged by these forces according to definite laws? These variations are doubtless produced according to fixed laws, and when we shall have learned these laws, then we may be able to use them in the production of such variations. In the mean time, we can avail ourselves of what we know of the laws which govern the production of varieties by seed, and by directing them, secure new and valuable fruit.

In order to know how to produce, from seed, varieties of fruit having certain desired qualities, it will be necessary to examine the structure of a flower, and learn how nature works in the formation of seeds. By looking at Fig. 37, which is a representation of a cherry blossom cut in two, it will be seen that there are several organs brought to view. Those which more particularly concern us just now are those which are called the seed vessel or ovary, the pistil, and the stamen. The pistil, with the ovary at its base, is indicated by the letter *c*, the knob at the top is called the stigma, and the portion between the stigma and the ovary is called the style. Around the pistil stand the stamens; the upper part, divided into two lobes, is called the anther, and from the anther proceeds a fine yellow powder, called the pollen. The seed is formed in the ovary only when the pollen fertilizes the germ. Should this fertilization not take place, the germs that are in the seed vessel never become developed into seeds, but perish. At Fig. 38 the reader will see a single grain of pollen highly magnified, and will notice that it is not very unlike a tadpole in appearance, only that the part which corresponds to the tail of the tadpole is, in the pollen-grain, a little rootlet. This pollen-grain falling on the stigma, throws out its little rootlet, which runs down into and through the entire length of the style, as will be seen by examining Fig. 39. On reaching

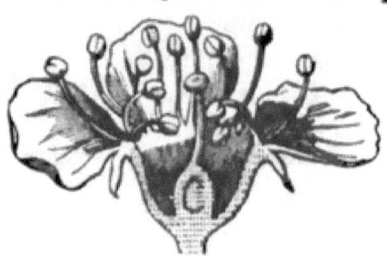

Fig. 37.

the ovary it penetrates it, and coming in contact with the germs that are in the ovary, fertilizes them, or in other words, imparts

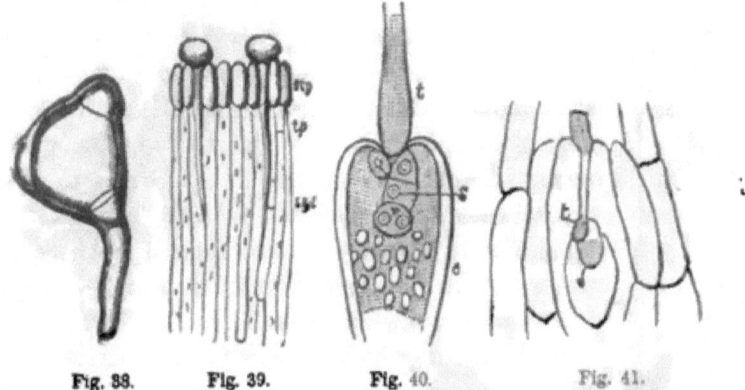

Fig. 38.   Fig. 39.   Fig. 40.   Fig. 41.

to them the power of growth and development into perfect seeds. In Fig. 40, *t* represents the lower end of this pollen rootlet entering the ovary, and in Fig. 41 it is seen after it has entered the ovary and come in contact with the germ *e*. Fig. 42 represents an apple blossom cut in two, and by comparing this with Fig. 37, it will be seen that the apple blossom has three pistils, while the cherry blossom has but one. This diversity exists in a yet

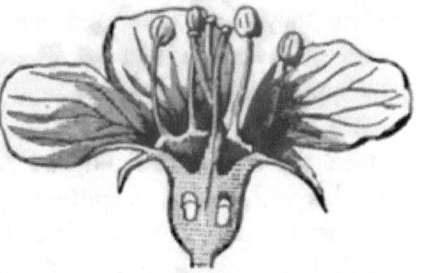

Fig. 42.

greater degree in the strawberry blossom, which has a very great number of pistils; but whatever the number of pistils, the process is ever the same, the pollen must reach the germ through the pistil or pistils, or the germ will perish, and in the case of numerous pistils, it will be seen that each pistil supplies its own division of the seed vessel or ovary with the needed pollen. That these organs may be the more readily recognized, they are shown separate from the flower. Figure 43 shows, at the left hand, the stamen, with the anther on the top, from which

PRODUCTION OF NEW VARIETIES.

the pollen dust is falling; and on the right hand a pistil, the knob on the top being the stigma, and the oval swelling at the base the ovary.

Fig. 43.

The art of producing new varieties from seed consists in taking the pollen of one variety of the fruit and applying it to the stigma of the pistil in the flower of another variety. The mode of doing this is very simple. When the flowers begin to open, you will select a variety, say of apple, having certain qualities which you wish to combine with the qualities which are possessed by another variety of apple, and so to have an apple which unites in itself the several qualities which are now found separate, a part of them in one apple and a part in another. As soon as the flowers begin to expand, you will select some of the flowers upon which to operate, and will cut away the anthers, which are on the ends of the stamens, before they burst open and let out their pollen. This can be most easily done with a pair of small sharp-pointed scissors. As the apple and pear usually produce their flowers in clusters, it will be necessary to cut away all the flowers except those from which the anthers are clipped off; and after cutting away the anthers, with a good magnifying glass examine the stigma to see if there be any grain of pollen fallen upon it; if there be, the whole flower should be cut off. You will procure pollen from the tree of the other variety by carefully cutting off some of the flowers whose anthers have recently burst and are covered with pollen, and taking them with you to the flowers whose anthers you have removed, you will apply the anther laden with pollen to the stigma of these flowers. Sometimes the tree which bears the pollen you wish to use comes into blossom some time before the tree that you wish to use as the seed-producing parent. In that case, the pollen can be shaken into a sheet of smooth writing paper, and put into a small vial, closely corked up, and laid away in a drawer, or other dark place, that is also dry and cool, and kept until the other tree comes into flower, and may then be applied by means of a fine camel's hair pencil. When the pollen has been applied to the pistil of these flowers, they should be enclosed in a piece of gauze or thin book muslin, to prevent anything from interfering with your work. It is advisable to repeat the application of the pollen on each day for a few successive days, as it may be that at the first application the stigma had not reached that stage which was favorable to the reception of the pollen and its growth. This operation can only be well done in dry weather, for it is only then that the pollen will be dry and dust-like. If gathered in this state, and kept as already directed, it will preserve its vitality for a considerable time, thus rendering it an easy matter to procure pollen from trees at some distance from those upon which you desire to operate. Care must be taken to deprive the flower which you wish to fertilize of all its anthers, before they have burst and thrown out their pollen upon the pistils, for if the pollen has fertilized the germs at the base of the pistils, no subsequent application of other pollen will be of any avail.

This work of cross-fertilization can be performed with all our fruits, and the excellences of one variety of apple be combined with those of another, or of one variety of pear with another, or of plum or cherry, strawberry, raspberry, grape, &c., &c.; but seed-bearing fruits, such as the apple, pear and quince, cannot be crossed with the stone-bearing fruits, as the cherry and plum. What are the precise limits within which this cross-fertilization can be effected have not yet been fully ascertained, and a very interesting field of discovery lies opened here before the careful experimenter. If it shall be found that the apple can be crossed with the pear, or the pear with the apple, as some facts seem to indicate, or the plum and cherry can be made to unite in cross-fertilization, or the strawberry with the raspberry, what new creations lie open before the experimenter. But even within the already ascertained field of cross-fertilization, there is plenty of scope for experiment, and much that is valuable as well as interesting will reward our labors.

In the case of some of our well-known varieties which have been perpetuated and multiplied by grafting and budding, there is more difficulty in securing the desired combination of qualities, than in those which have never been grafted, but are growing on their natural stock. Precisely what are the influences of the stock upon the graft, it is not possible to state; but it is quite possible that they come in to affect the operations of the cross-fertilizer.

In performing this operation, it should be borne in mind that the constitution of the seed-bearing parent is apt to be transmitted to the progeny. It will be necessary, therefore, to remember that unless this parent be healthy, hardy and productive, the seedlings raised from it will be very likely to be deficient in these qualities. On the other hand, it is thought that the form and color and qualities of the fruit will partake largely of the male, that is, the parent from which the pollen was taken. There is constant inquiry for very hardy apple trees, yielding fruit of fine quality; and indeed this is true of all the fruits; and while it may be necessary to sacrifice size of fruit on account of the shortness of the season and quality of soil, yet it may be quite possible to produce an apple tree that shall have the hardihood of the Siberian crab, and yet yield a fruit as large and perhaps as good as the famed English golden pippin. We commend this pleasant task of producing new varieties of fruits by cross-fertilization to the attention of our Canadian lovers of good fruit, in the confident expectation that every patient worker in this interesting field will be most abundantly rewarded.

If the pollen that you have applied to the stigma fertilizes the germs in the seed vessel, the fruit will grow and come to maturity, containing within itself the seeds which have been developed from those germs, and which you are to preserve and plant with jealous care, watching and waiting until they grow up and become trees and yield their fruit, the fruit possessing the qualities you hoped to combine, when you dusted the pollen on the pistil of the parent fruit. Of course, in the case of apples and pears, the results of this labor can only be known **after the** lapse of several years, something shorter in the plum and **cherry,** and considerably **less** in the grape, or raspberry, or currant, or strawberry. But if these experiments are continued, and every year some new cross-fertilizations are effected, soon every year will bring its pleasure in the testing of new fruits, called into existence by your skill, beginning with the small fruits that come earliest into bearing, and extending eventually to the **appearance of the** new apples and pears.

THE APPLE.

This fruit can be grown with some **degree of** success in all parts of the **Dominion,** and in some **parts it can be grown to as** high a degree **of** perfection, in **all the requisites of quantity,** quality and appearance, as in **any part of the world.** Already Canadian apples **are attaining a favorable position in the markets** of Great **Britain, and the attentive cultivator** finds the orchard the most remunerative part of the farm.

The soil most favorable to the growth of the apple tree, and the production of fine apples, is a strong calcareous loam, **yet it** will thrive and yield good fruit on all soils. Any soil of sufficient fertility to produce good farm crops will be suited to the apple, yet a clayey loam **is preferable** to light sand, and a rolling, uneven surface to level ground. But it is of the greatest moment, and essentially requisite to the **health** and longevity of the tree **and** the perfect development of the fruit, that the soil be perfectly **drained.**

The pruning of an apple orchard is simply for the purpose of keeping the head of the tree open, so **as to give** the leaves ample exposure **to the sun** and air. If done regularly every year, but little cutting will be needed at any one time, and that chiefly of small branches. No rules can be laid down other than the suggestions already given on the subject of pruning, and each grower must learn to use his judgment, and adapt his pruning to the habit of growth of the tree in hand.

Apple trees can be propagated both by budding and grafting, each method being usually quite successful, if only the stock be in a healthy and vigorous condition.

It is very desirable that a little more care should be bestowed upon the gathering and putting up of apples intended for market. Of course the fruit should be all carefully gathered by hand, so that none of it shall be bruised, and be judiciously sorted. Much of the fruit now sent to market has been handled too roughly, and not been sorted at all. It will usually be found most profitable to assort the fruit into three grades: the first composed of fair, full sized, perfect fruit; the second of the sound, well-formed, but smaller sized apples; the third of the inferior sized, knotty, scabby, wormy and imperfect specimens. In the city markets, the first grade will bring the very highest price; the second grade may be kept for home consumption, or if sold, will bring as much, often more, per barrel, than could have been obtained for the whole lot unsorted. Indeed, in some markets, especially in those of Great Britain, the whole question of profit or loss depends upon the proper sorting of the fruit; and a reputation once obtained there for putting up fruit according to quality, will cause that brand to be sought after, and secure the sale of those apples at the best rates. Every fruit grower who sends fruit to market should brand or mark every barrel or package with his own name, or some distinctive mark, so that he may secure the advantages that are sure to accrue to a judicious sorting of his fruit.

It is also important that the apples should be so put up that they will be perfectly tight, and not shake about in the barrel. A little practice will enable any one to pack apples securely. The usual method is, to pave the bottom of the barrel with apples, placing the stem down, as closely as they can be packed without bruising; then put in a market basketful at a time, introducing the basket into the barrel and pouring the fruit out gently, not allowing the apples to fall, but roll out and on to those already in the barrel. As each basketful is emptied, the barrel is gently shaken, so that the apples shall be well settled to their places. The barrel is filled full, even with the top, the head placed on, and by means of a screw packer, pressed down into its place. If this is not roughly done, the apples will be pressed just enough to keep them tight, so that when the barrel is rolled about, the apples will not be shaken in the barrel. As soon as the head is in place, the hoops should be put on, driven home, and securely nailed, and the heading at both ends secured by nailing cleats on the inside of the chime. Mark the barrel on the end which was the bottom when putting the apples in, so that it may be opened and the fruit taken out from that end. After the barrel has been fully secured and marked, it should be laid on the side and kept in a cool place, under cover from sun and rain, until sent to market or removed to the cellar. A dry cellar that can be kept at a temperature just above freezing, is an excellent place in which to keep apples in a fresh and sound condition.

How to market the fruit, after it is gathered, is a question of considerable importance, and one that deserves much more consideration from the grower than it usually receives. As it now stands, our fruit raisers wait until some travelling fruit buyer comes along, and drive the best bargain they can. Sometimes he comes again to get the apples he has bought, and perhaps as often he is never seen again. Sometimes the grower agrees to barrel the fruit and deliver it at some Railway Station or wharf, and after taking it there, can find nothing of his purchaser. We have not space to discuss this subject fully, but suggest that the fruit growers in any given neighborhood might unite, and select the best business man of their number to proceed to the city which affords the best market for their apples, and there establish such business relations with some responsible and honorable house as will secure the sale of their fruit. We have heard parties complain that they could not find a market for their fruit, because no one had been round to buy, while their neighbors within a dozen miles of them, who had established business connections in the city, found ready sale at good prices.

The best varieties of apples for market purposes are not usually those of the highest flavor. Many things are required in an apple to make it a profitable variety, and foremost among these requisites is a showy appearance. This attractive appearance is the result of good size, uniformity of shape, and bright color. A red apple is more attractive and more saleable than a green or yellow one. But it is also important that the tree should be decidedly prolific, setting its fruit regularly throughout the tree, and that the fruit should be of a uniform size. It is much better that all the apples on the tree should be of one medium size, than that there should be some very large and many very small.

In the descriptions of different varieties of apples which follow, care will be taken to indicate those which have been found to be profitable for market. Descriptions will be given only of those varieties which have been found to be among the most desirable for cultivation in the Dominion. Many of these are fruits of the highest excellence, while some of them, though not attaining to the rank of "best" in flavor, possess, nevertheless, such qualities of hardihood of tree, or productiveness, or beauty of appearance, combined with agreeable flavor, as to make them worthy of attention.

Dwarf apple trees are often desirable in small gardens, more as an object of ornament than profit. They are very attractive, both when covered with blossoms and when laden with fruit. They come into bearing a little earlier than standard trees, and may be of any desired variety. A truly dwarf apple tree is produced by budding or grafting a scion of such a variety as you may wish upon the Paradise apple stock. This is a very dwarf-growing variety of apple, rarely becoming much larger than a black currant bush, and the variety of apple that is grafted upon it is unable to attain its customary size of tree, but becomes instead a mere shrub. Another stock has been used for dwarfing the apple tree, known as the Doucin, but it does not lessen the size of the tree nearly as much as the Paradise stock.

Half-standard apple trees is a term used to designate those which have been so pruned as to form the head of the tree much nearer the ground than is usually done. This method of forming low-headed trees is the true one in all the colder parts of the Dominion. The trees suffer much less from the severity of the climate, are healthier, longer lived, and yield more fruit than if pruned up with long, naked trunks. Those who have made trial of both methods report, that "trees *allowed to branch out low,* say about three feet from the ground, *are generally healthy;* but those that have a long trunk are sure to get black on the southwest side, and soon die off."

VARIETIES OF APPLE.

It is not the purpose of this work to give a list of the names of all the varieties that are in cultivation, much less to give a description of them. Those only are described which are known to be valuable, and adapted to the climate of some part of the Dominion, possessing sufficient points of excellence to make them worthy of the attention of the Canadian cultivator. The alphabetical arrangement has been adopted as being the most simple and convenient.

ALEXANDER. — *Emperor Alexander.* — *Russian Emperor.* — This is an exceedingly hardy variety, which originated in Russia; has now been widely disseminated throughout the Dominion, and has been found to be one of our most hardy sorts, almost as hardy as the Siberian crabs. It is reported to succeed well in the Ottawa region, and in Nova Scotia. The fruit is very large and showy, greenish yellow, faintly streaked with red on the shaded side; but on the exposed side, rich orange, very brilliantly marked and streaked with bright red. The flesh is tender, juicy, and of "good" flavor. The apples ripen in October, and will keep into December. The tree grows vigorously, forming a spreading head, and bears abundant crops. Such is the fine size and handsome appearance of the fruit, and the prolific character of the tree, that it may safely be planted, in limited quantity, for market; for as it is not a long keeper, it is not safe to attempt to handle a very large number of barrels.

BALDWIN.—*Steele's Red Winter.—Woodpecker.*—This very popular variety originated in the State of Massachusetts, and is well deserving of the high estimation in which it is held. In rich alluvial soils which are deficient in lime, the fruit is not as finely colored, nor as high flavored, as in limestone soils, and is subject to spots of bitter or dry rot; and in such soils, especially if there be a cold, wet subsoil, the tree suffers, becomes diseased, and in cold winters is badly injured, and sometimes destroyed. The tree is not sufficiently hardy to withstand well the cold of our more severe latitudes; yet in dry soils, abounding in lime, it will withstand, unharmed, quite severe cold, as may be inferred from the fact that it is successfully cultivated in the apple region of Nova Scotia. In the Ottawa and St. Lawrence districts of Ontario, the Baldwin is reported as tender, though it succeeds in Frontenac and westward, through the greater part of the Province.

The tree is a vigorous, upright grower, forming a spreading head, and exceedingly productive. The fruit is large, roundish, but narrowing towards the eye, yellow in the shade, but nearly covered with red in the sun. The flesh is yellowish white, crisp, sub-acid, ranking in quality as " very good." It ripens in December, but is usually in its best condition in March, and will keep in a cool cellar until the middle of May. This is one of the most profitable varieties for market with which we are acquainted, when grown in favorable soil and climate. Combining early fruiting with great productiveness, good size, handsome appearance, very good flavor, and long keeping, with a toughness of skin and firmness of texture which admit of being handled and transported without injury, it stands in the front rank of profitable varieties for the orchardist.

BENONI.—This apple also originated in the State of Massachusetts, and is worthy of more attention than it seems to have received from Canadian planters. **It flourishes well on the rich alluvial soils of** the western prairies, and withstands the severity of that climate; hence we infer that it will be found sufficiently hardy **to endure** the climate throughout a very large portion of our Dominion, and so far as it has been tried here, we have not **heard** of any lack of **hardihood.**

The tree is a vigorous, upright grower, forming a handsome spreading head, and an early and abundant bearer. The fruit is of medium size, rather below than above; roundish, striped and marbled with dark crimson, on a rich yellow ground; having a yellow flesh, which is tender and juicy, with a pleasant sub-acid flavor, in **quality "very good."** It is in use **here during the** latter part of August and **the most of September.**

DUCHESS OF OLDENBURGH.—We **can heartily commend this variety to every fruit grower in the Dominion, to those in the most favored fruit growing sections, and to** him who has his **dwelling where the** winter is long and fierce. Originated in Russia, **one** might suppose on **the very** confines of Siberia, it **endures the** cold of Canada and **of the** far North-west most triumphantly. The tree is quite vigorous, upright in habit, and forming a rounded head, which has a very pleasing appearance when covered with its large, glossy, dark green leaves. **It bears** fruit when quite young, and most abundantly, **which is very uniform in size, and remarkably fair and free from** blemish.

The fruit is of full medium size, sometimes large, very regularly **formed, and of a very attractive,** showy appearance; always **commanding a ready sale in** the markets, as it is especially **valuable for cooking, being for this** purpose without a rival **in its season.** The skin is smooth, with **a** yellow ground, most **handsomely** streaked **and washed** with **red, and covered** with a light **blue bloom. The flesh is** yellowish white, tender, juicy, with a brisk sub-acid **flavor. The fruit ripens** here during the first **half of** September, and will not keep long. It is not usually ranked very high in flavor; but as grown in our climate, it should **stand** at least **as "good," and** in those sections where but few varieties can be grown, it will stand high on the list as a very valuable fruit. Those favorably situated for disposing quickly of a considerable quantity of September apples, will find this a very profitable market variety.

EARLY HARVEST.—*Yellow Harvest.—Early French Reinette.* This excellent summer variety cannot be grown with the same results in all parts of the country. To be grown in its full perfection, it requires a soil abounding in lime and potash, and these seem to be essential to both the vigor and longevity of the tree and the full development of size and flavor in the fruit. Where such soil can be had, the tree does not seem to be very tender, growing in nearly all parts of Ontario, and in Nova Scotia. But when grown in rich alluvial soils, deficient in lime, and particularly if not thoroughly and deeply drained, the tree is tender, the fruit often very badly spotted, cracking and dropping off without attaining its full size; and those specimens which may be measurably fair are usually deficient in flavor. But when a suitable soil can be supplied, the tree seems healthy, and the fruit fair, smooth and of excellent quality.

The tree is upright, a moderate grower, forming a spreading head, bearing early and abundantly. The fruit is of medium size, roundish, smooth, of a bright straw color; the flesh white, tender, juicy and rich, with a pleasant, sprightly sub-acid flavor; in quality, "very good;" ripe the end of July and first of August. It is excellent both for cooking and as a dessert fruit, and well deserving a place in every collection where it can be grown, and in case of doubt, well worth a trial.

EARLY JOE.—Without question this is the richest, most delightfully flavored, and best of all the summer dessert apples. It flourishes best in rich soil, and seems to be nearly, if not quite, as hardy as the Red Astrachan. Unfortunately the tree is a very slow grower when young, and consequently nurserymen grow as few as they possibly can, and never send them out to customers without expecting, and usually they receive it, a considerable scolding on account of the insignificant appearance of the tree. On this account it has not been very widely disseminated. To grow the tree to the size of a Baldwin at three or four years from the bud, would require a lengthened period of cultivation, which would fully double the cost of the tree. Notwithstanding this habit of its early life, the tree seems to make some amends as it acquires age, and attains to a fair size, bearing early and abundantly.

The apple is below medium, yellow, washed and striped with red, and overspread with a thin bloom. The flesh is yellowish, fine grained, tender, juicy, with a delicate, aromatic, pear-like flavor, quality, "best." Ripe the latter part of August and first of September.

This variety does remarkably well as a dwarf tree, and can be so grown in grounds of limited extent, where its delicious, and at the same time handsome fruit can be gathered fresh from the tree, which is requisite if it is to be enjoyed in the perfection of its flavor.

ESOPUS SPITZENBURGH.—We have in this another of those excellent varieties which attain their full development only in soils that abound in lime and potash, and in such soils, it is a fruit of the very highest excellence, and the tree a very abundant bearer. Yet in most soils this apple is well worthy of a place in any collection, on account of the very fine quality of the fruit, which, in our opinion, in its combination of excellence for the dessert and for cooking, is unsurpassed by any other apple, if, indeed, there be any that can equal it.

It originated at Esopus, on the Hudson River, in the State of New York, a district famous for the excellence of its apples, whence it has been widely disseminated. The tree is a slender and slow grower, with long and drooping branches, and except in soils abounding in lime, is but a moderate bearer. The fruit is large and oblong, in color bright red, profusely dotted with yellow russet dots, with a yellow flesh, fine grained, firm, crisp, juicy and rich, with a peculiarly delicious flavor; quality, "best." It is in use from December to March, and is everywhere, and in every form in which apples are served, particularly acceptable.

Yet we cannot recommend the planting of this tree extensively for market. Only the fortunate possessor of the peculiar soil requisite to the full development of tree and fruit may venture beyond what will supply the wants of his own family. There are other sorts less fastidious in their choice of soils, which can be better trusted to yield remunerative crops. In point of hardihood, it is about equal to the Baldwin, capable of enduring a very considerable degree of cold, when planted on deep, dry soil.

With the exception of the Ottawa and St. Lawrence districts, it is grown generally throughout Ontario; and we are informed that it is much esteemed in the apple-growing region of Nova Scotia.

FAMEUSE.—*Pomme de Neige.—Snow Apple.*—The precise origin of this favorite apple is unknown, and whether it was long ago introduced from France, or had its birth-place in the Province of Quebec, it has most emphatically made Canada its home. Here it is grown in a perfection seldom elsewhere seen; here its fine qualities are fully brought out, and here its ruddy fruit is admired and appreciated by those of every age and every rank.

The tree is hardy, very hardy; standing in the next rank to the Siberian crabs, and thriving in any properly drained soil, in well nigh every part of the Dominion. It is a moderate grower, with large, glossy green leaves and dark shoots, and bears abundantly and early. The fruit is deep dark red in the sun, growing lighter in the shade, where it is sometimes a pale greenish yellow; the flesh is snow white, very tender, breaking, juicy, almost melting, with a delicate aroma, and most agreeable mild flavor; quality, "very good." To be used only for the dessert. Ripe in December and January. The fruit is sometimes kept until April, but usually at the expense of more or less of its flavor.

In some parts of Western Ontario, the Snow Apple is subject to the attacks, in some seasons, of a parasitic fungus, which grows on the skin of the fruit, producing black spots, which are sometimes so numerous as very materially to disfigure and injure the fruit, dwarfing its growth, impairing its flavor and causing premature decay. This fungus seems to be more prevalent in hot and dry seasons and in the warmer parts of the Province. Those who reside where the fruit is exempt from these black spots, and consequently always fair and of fine flavor and appearance, could **make an** orchard of this **variety very** valuable by shipping the fruit to the Chicago or New York market, where it will command ready sale at the best prices.

GOLDEN RUSSET.—*English Golden Russet.—Golden Russet of Western New York.*—This is a very valuable market fruit, and has given great satisfaction to those who have planted it for market purposes. The tree is sufficiently hardy to thrive well in most of Ontario, and in the apple region of Nova Scotia; it **is** even more hardy than the Baldwin, and is said to flourish along the St. **Lawrence, in the Counties** of Stormont and Glengarry. It **comes into bearing early, yields** abundant crops of very even **sized fruit,** and seems to flourish in all soils, especially in the rich **alluvial soils of the** West. Considerable confusion exists in regard **to** the variety; there are so many Russets, and Golden Russets, and English Russets, and American Russets, that it is difficult to decide upon the precise kind intended; but this **one,** which is so valuable and profitable for market, may readily be distinguished from all others by the very numerous white dots upon the young shoots, which give them a decided speckled **appearance. The trees** grow vigorously upright, forming spreading and somewhat irregular **heads.**

The fruit is of medium size, roundish, very uniform, covered with a dull yellowish russet, somewhat bronzed on the exposed side; the flesh is often greenish white, always fine grained, firm, crisp, juicy, and of a high, mildly sub-acid, flavor; quality, "very good." **It is ripe** in January, and keeps well until May; and bears handling and transportation remarkably well.

GRAVENSTEIN.—We must thank Germany for having produced this most excellent autumn apple, beautiful in appearance **and** superior in quality. It has been widely disseminated, and is as valuable in Canada as in the north of Europe. The tree grows upright and stout in the nursery, and forms a fine, large, spreading head in the orchard. It thrives well in Nova Scotia, and in the greater part of Ontario, bearing fruit at Arnprior, in the County of Renfrew. It comes into bearing early, and is very productive.

The fruit is large, bright yellow at maturity, and beautifully striped with various shades of red and orange; flesh tender, crisp, juicy, and of a high aromatic flavor; quality, "best." It ripens in October, and will keep through November. Valuable both as a cooking and dessert apple, and always commanding the highest price of any apple, of its season, in the markets. To those who will attend to the gathering and shipping of this apple in the early part of October, and are not too remote from the large markets, this variety will be a very valuable one to plant in moderate quantity.

GRIMES' GOLDEN PIPPIN.—We describe this apple here because of its great excellence, and because we believe it will thrive well in a large part of the Dominion. At present it has been planted in Canada only to a very limited extent, but it is well worthy of a most extensive trial. Wherever it has been tried it is much esteemed for the hardihood of the tree, and its uniform productiveness every year. So far as our observation extends, we have found the tree moderately vigorous, upright habit, with peculiarly large knobs at the base of the branches where they join the main stem or limb. The fruit is medium, roundish, of a rich golden yellow, slightly netted with russet; flesh yellow, firm, fine grained, crisp, juicy, rich, with a peculiar spicy sub-acid flavor, which is certainly "very good;" and we are inclined to believe, that after a more full acquaintance, it will rank as "best."

HUBBARDSTON NONSUCH.—This fine, large apple originated in the State of Massachusetts, and thrives well in all the apple region of the Dominion. The tree is a vigorous grower, forms a large, spreading head, and yields abundant crops of fair, beautifully formed, even **sized** fruit, and **is well worthy of a** place in every orchard.

The apples **are** large, roundish, narrowing towards the eye, so regular **in outline** that they could hardly be more symmetrical had they been turned with a lathe. **The ground color** is yellowish, **irregularly** striped with various shades of red, and often thinly overspread with russet on the **shaded side.** The flesh is yellowish, juicy, tender, blended sweet and acid, producing a very agreeable flavor; quality, "very good." It ripens towards the end of October, and keeps until January. This variety commands a ready sale in the city markets, and we believe **it** would be profitable as a **market** variety, bearing in mind that **it is not a late** keeper.

JERSEY SWEETING.—This is a very good sweet autumn variety, **and we are disposed to give it the preference over the other sweet varieties ripening at that season. The tree** is a vigorous, erect **grower in the nursery, but comes into** bearing young, and does **not seem** to become a large tree in the orchard. It is not sufficiently hardy to be classed with the Snow Apple, Red Astrachan and Duchess of Oldenburgh in that respect; but it flourishes well in all soils, and bears immense crops.

The fruit is of medium size, with a thin, greenish yellow **skin,** which is streaked **with red, and in exposed specimens** nearly covered with **a dull red. The** flesh is yellowish white, **very** fine grained and tender, abounding in juice, which is very **sweet, yet** of a sprightly flavor; quality, "very good." It ripens **gradually** from **the early part** of September till the middle or **end of October.** It is valuable for all purposes of a sweet apple.

KING OF TOMPKINS COUNTY.—Not ranking with our most hardy **sorts,** it nevertheless thrives well in the apple growing sections of **all the** Provinces. It is **a** vigorous growing variety, forming a large, spreading **head, and bears** good crops of fruit **every year.** The fruit is large, yellowish, shaded with red and **striped with crimson;** flesh yellow, somewhat coarse grained, but **tender, juicy, with** a very agreeable rich vinous flavor; quality, "very good." In use from January to March. This variety has been very highly recommended as a market fruit, but we notice in it a tendency to drop from the tree, especially during the high winds of September, which materially lessens its value as a profitable market fruit. We therefore advise market orchardists to plant it in sheltered positions, and not too freely at first.

KESWICK CODLIN.—This variety is valuable in some of the colder parts of the Dominion, though not sufficiently hardy to endure as great severity of climate as the Snow Apple, St. Lawrence and Alexander. In the County of Renfrew the tree lives and bears fruit, but it is not healthy. In the milder parts, where most varieties succeed well, it is quite superseded by higher flavored sorts. It is valued chiefly as a cooking apple, being used for that purpose before the fruit is fully grown; but to our taste the Early Harvest is much to be preferred to it for all purposes.

The tree is moderately vigorous, upright in habit, and forming a small, round head. It comes into bearing very early, and is enormously productive; flourishing finely on rich alluvial soils. The fruit is very variable in size, running from small to large; conical in form, with one or two raised lines from the stem to the eye; greenish yellow in color, with sometimes a faint blush on the sunny side; the flesh yellowish white, juicy, with a brisk acid flavor; quality not above "good." Ripe last of September to middle of October. We have never seen this apple attacked by that parasitic fungus which is sometimes so injurious to the Early Harvest, and on this account it will be valuable where that suffers frequently from this cause.

LARGE YELLOW BOUGH.—*Sweet Bough.*—*Early Sweet Bough. Sweet Harvest.*—This is the best early sweet apple, ripening in harvest, not all at once, but gradually, from the middle of July to the end of August. The fruit is usually large, somewhat conical in form; color a very light greenish yellow; flesh white, tender, juicy and sweet. It is very good when baked, or as a dessert fruit.

The tree grows stout, moderately vigorous, **forming a fine round head, and** is a regular and abundant bearer every year. The tree is **sufficiently hardy to** thrive well **in most parts of the country, only the extremely cold parts need be excepted, and does well** on all dry soils.

LATE STRAWBERRY.—*Autumn Strawberry.*—A very handsome and excellent variety, which originated in Western New York, and has been very generally disseminated. The tree is reputed to be hardy, enduring the western climate as far north, **at least,** as Iowa, and will, beyond doubt, be sufficiently so **to thrive in** the greater **part of** Canada. **It is deserving of more attention from our fruit growers** than it **has yet received, especially as a** dessert **fruit, for it combines with excellence of quality, a very attractive appearance, while the tree is a constant and abundant bearer.** The apple is full medium size, roundish conical, red, striped **with darker red, beautifully shaded** according **to the** exposure **to light, and covered with a** thin bloom; flesh yellowish **white, juicy and tender, with** a very pleasant vinous flavor; quality "very good;" indeed, none better in its season, which **is** all the month of November.

MONMOUTH PIPPIN.—*Red-cheek Pippin.*—Considerable **interest** seems to have been **manifested within a few years past by planters, in** some sections, in the cultivation **of this variety. It derives its name from the county in the State of New Jersey in which it originated, and has been successfully grown** in the more **southern New England States;** but from all we can at present **learn of the tree, we do not** believe that it possesses that degree **of hardihood which will** make it valuable to those not residing in the **most favored apple districts of Canada.** The tree has an erect habit **of growth, is** moderately vigorous, and a good bearer. The apples **are large, pale greenish yellow,** with a ruddy cheek; flesh yellowish white, **juicy, sub-acid, with** considerable perfume; quality "very good." **In use from December to** March.

MOTHER.—We desire **to call** attention to this variety, on **account of** the **hardihood of the tree and** excellence of the fruit, believing that it will be very valuable in some of our colder districts. The tree has been found to be perfectly hardy in the State of Maine and the Territory of Nebraska, hence we have good reason to expect that it will be a very desirable addition to our varieties. It has an upright habit of growth, is moderately vigorous, and a good bearer. The fruit is large, color clear rich red, handsomely splashed and marbled with darker red, flesh yellow, juicy, very tender, highly aromatic, of a rich sub-acid flavor; quality "best." In use from December to February.

NORTHERN SPY—This is one of our more hardy sorts, mentioned in the valuable report of the Fruit Growers' Association of Ontario, as succeeding in all parts of that Province, even in the Ottawa and St. Lawrence districts, and classed in point of hardiness with the Fameuse and St. Lawrence. Yet we notice that an enthusiastic amateur, residing near Arnprior, in the County of Renfrew, says that it fails with him. It is possible that Arnprior, which lies on a parallel some one hundred and twenty miles north of Toronto, is beyond the limit of the successful culture of this variety, though the Fameuse and St. Lawrence have been in successful bearing at that place for many years.

The tree grows naturally very erect, forming a close, compact head, which requires careful thinning out in order to admit sufficient air and light to perfect the fruit. It is slow in coming into bearing, but when once arrived at the bearing state, it yields large crops. The buds put forth late, usually ten days later than on most of the trees in the orchard, and on this account the fruit sometimes escapes late frosts which destroy the earlier blooming sorts. It requires a soil rich in phosphate of lime, or made so by the application of a plentiful supply of bone dust, else a large portion of the fruit will be undersized and flavorless.

The fruit, when well grown, is large, handsomely striped with light and dark purplish red, and covered with a thin bloom; flesh white, very fine grained, crisp, with a delicious, mild, sub-acid flavor. But such fruit can only be grown with good cultivation, and a full exposure of the fruit to light and air, and then it will rank in quality as "best." But if the tree be neglected, the top over-crowded, the fruit grown in shade, and the soil poor, there will very likely be a great abundance of small, half-colored, flavorless apples, not even worthy of being called good. In use from January to June, and to the last retains its fine, sprightly, refreshing flavor.

POMME GRISE.—This is a favorite dessert apple throughout Canada, generally supposed to have originated in the Province of Quebec, and is sufficiently hardy to endure considerable severity of climate. The tree grows but moderately, usually erect in the nursery, and forming in the orchard a small rounded head; comes early into bearing, and yields large crops. The fruit is usually below medium size, flattened in form, color greenish gray russet, with a little red on the sunny side in exposed specimens; flesh yellowish, fine grained, tender, rich and agreeable flavor; quality "very good."

POMME GRISE D'OR.—*Swayzie Pomme Grise.*—We are inclined to believe that this variety originated on what is known as the Swayzie farm, a few miles above Niagara, on the Niagara River. The original tree was blown down during the summer of 1870, and was standing in an irregular clump of apple trees, having the appearance of being the original seedling nursery, from which were raised the first apple trees planted out in orchard form on the farm. From this place, certainly, the variety has been disseminated through western New York and a considerable part of western Ontario; and as we have never seen any description of this apple in any work on Pomology, nor heard of any trees not derived from the above named source, we have no doubt but that it originated on the Swayzie farm.

The tree is a moderately vigorous, upright grower, forming in the orchard a medium-sized tree, with a rounded head. It has proved to be hardy in localities some distance north of Toronto; but we are not aware that it has yet been tried in the Ottawa

7

and St. Lawrence districts. It comes soon into bearing and yields good crops of fruit, though not as abundant as the Baldwin or R. I. Greening.

The fruit is of medium size, usually a little larger than the Pomme Grise, roundish oblong; **color a bright** cinnamon russet, **with a golden glow on the side next the sun;** flesh white, crisp, breaking, juicy, with a peculiar aromatic, pear-like flavor; quality "best." In use from January to May and June. It is pre-eminently a dessert apple, and in its season has **very few** equals, none superior.

RED ASTRACHAN.—This very valuable and handsome apple was introduced into England from Sweden in 1816, and from thence has found its way into Canada, where it is very much at home, ranking among our best and most hardy sorts. We had supposed that it would thrive where any apple tree would live, **short of a Siberian Crab;** but we have recently learned that at **Arnprior, in the County of** Renfrew, it has not succeeded in the hands of at least one most zealous cultivator of fruits. Yet it thrives in Maine and Minnesota, and is usually hardy.

The tree is a vigorous, upright grower, forming a rounded head, comes very **early into bearing, and yields** abundant crops. The fruit is full medium size, roundish, **color deep crimson,** covered with a light **bloom; the** flesh is white, crisp and juicy, with a rich acid flavor; quality "very good." Ripe about the first of August. A very popular variety in the market, selling **readily; excellent for cooking.** A few trees of this apple might be profitably planted for market purposes by those living near **large towns.** It does not keep long, and therefore must soon be in the hands of consumers.

RHODE ISLAND GREENING.—Would that this valuable apple were only a little more hardy, then it might be recommended **without reserve; but it suffers too** much from the climate in all the colder sections, such as the region of the St. Lawrence and **Ottawa in** Ontario, the most of Quebec and New Brunswick. It **thrives** best in warm, well-drained soils, abounding in lime, requires good cultivation, and is much benefited by an occasional dressing of wood ashes.

The tree is **a** vigorous, but very crooked grower in the nursery, and forms a large, spreading head in the orchard. It soon comes into bearing, and is exceedingly productive, yielding fair, even-sized fruit. On this account it is very extensively planted for market purposes, being one of the most profitable sorts.

The fruit is large, roundish, green at first, but gradually changing to a greenish yellow at maturity, with sometimes a dull red cheek; flesh yellow, fine grained, very juicy, with a lively, pleasant acid flavor; quality "very good." In use from December to March.

RIBSTON PIPPIN.—This is truly a splendid apple with us, and though **our cousins** over the border do not esteem it as highly as they do **the Baldwin, Swaar, and some others, yet** in our climate it is one **of** the very best. The tree is sufficiently hardy to **thrive** throughout a large part of the Dominion, though it is not **able to endure** a climate like that of the Ottawa district in **Ontario**. It flourishes in the apple regions of Nova Scotia and New Brunswick, where it maintains fully its high character.

The fruit is full medium in size, sometimes large, especially on young trees; color yellow, mingled with russet, shaded and splashed with red on the exposed side; flesh deep yellow, crisp, with a rich, peculiarly aromatic, sub-acid flavor; quality "best." The tree is moderately vigorous, and bears young and abundantly.

This apple commands a ready sale, at the very highest prices, in the markets of Great Britain, and might be advantageously and profitably planted in considerable quantities by the orchardist who will carefully gather the fruit early in October, sort it properly, and ship it at once by steamer to the trans-Atlantic markets, where its reputation is fully equal to that of the famous Green Newtown Pippin.

ROXBURY RUSSET.—*Boston Russet.*—*Putnam Russet.*—This variety has been largely planted for market purposes, for which it is particularly valuable, on account of its long-keeping qualities, and ability to endure handling and transportation without injury. The fruit is a little above medium size,—when under good cultivation, large; color dull greenish russet when gathered, gradually changing to yellow russet at maturity, occasionally flushed with reddish brown in the sun; flesh greenish white, not very juicy, with a pleasant, mild, sub-acid flavor; quality "good." Ripens up in February and will keep until July.

The tree, when young, has the perverse, crooked habit of the Greening, and forms in the orchard a spreading, somewhat straggling head. It is as hardy as the Rhode Island Greening, and about as prolific.

SAINT LAWRENCE.—*Springle.*—This is one of our very hardy varieties, bearing fruit even in the Ottawa district of Ontario, in the Province of Quebec, in Nova Scotia and New Brunswick. It originated in Montreal, as we are kindly informed by J. H. Springle, Esq., about fifty years ago, in the garden of the late Henry Schroden, from the seeds of some decayed apples thrown on a heap of refuse. The original tree was still alive and healthy a few years ago. The tree is a vigorous, upright grower, forming in the orchard a fine spreading head, and is abundantly productive. The fruit is large, handsomely striped with various shades of purplish red on a yellow ground; flesh almost as white as the Fameuse, sometimes stained with red; crisp, juicy, with a pleasant, somewhat aromatic, vinous flavor; quality of fruit grown in the colder sections "very good," in the warmer portions, only "good."

At the Provincial Exhibition of 1870, there was exhibited by Mr. Shuttleworth an apple much resembling the St. Lawrence, which, however, seemed to ripen later and possess a more sprightly and spicy flavor. We believe it to be well worthy of a trial.

SWAAR.—Originated in the same region whence came the Esopus Spitzenburgh. This variety has been widely disseminated, and in certain sections is much esteemed. In the milder sections, on stony, rich soil, it flourishes well, and the fruit is of excellent flavor; but in the colder portions the trees suffer from the severity of the winter, and eventually perish. It is but a moderately vigorous grower, very apt **to be** crooked in the nursery, and requires **good** cultivation. We cannot recommend it for general cultivation, though those who **are so** fortunate **as to** possess a **favorable** soil and climate, will **find it a** fruit of great **excellence; deep** rich golden yellow when ripe, with an exceedingly **rich,** spicy flavor and perfume. **In use** in February and March.

TALMAN'S SWEET.—This **is the** best sweet winter apple for Canada that has been brought to our notice. The tree is very hardy, thriving and fruiting in the colder, **we** had almost said coldest, parts of the **Dominion,** keeping company with the **Snow** Apple and the **St. Lawrence.** It is an upright, vigorous grower, forms a large **spreading head,** and bears large **crops. The fruit** is of medium size, **greenish** white **in autumn, becoming pale straw** color **at maturity, flesh white, fine grained, juicy, rich and** very sweet. A most valuable variety for baking, surpassing for this **purpose all** other sweet winter apples that we have tried. May be used from December to April. There is but a limited demand for sweet apples in market; consequently, notwithstanding the hardihood of this tree, and its great productiveness, we do not advise orchardists to plant it largely for market purposes.

TETOFSKY.—It is to be expected that this apple, **which originated** in Russia, should be **hardy in this climate, and** such is the case so far as it has been tested; **and it has been found** to flourish in the equally cold climate of Northern **Minnesota.** We strongly advise residents **of the coldest sections to** give this variety a careful trial, in **the** expectation **that** it will prove **to** be more hardy than the Red Astrachan, and equally as valuable for summer use. The tree grows erect and forms a spreading head, begins to bear at two **years from the** bud, and produces large crops every year. The leaves are very large, of a light glossy green, giving the tree a very pleasing appearance. **Where the** climate is too cold to admit of the tree being grown as a standard, we believe it would **answer** admirably grown either as a half-standard or dwarf.

The fruit is of medium size, roundish, beautifully striped with red on a yellow ground, and covered with a light bloom; flesh white and juicy, with a pleasant, sprightly acid flavor; quality "good." In use the last of July to middle of August. The very attractive appearance of the fruit would no doubt give it a ready sale in market, and those favorably situated for disposing of summer fruit might plant a limited quantity for market purposes with profit.

TWENTY OUNCE.—*Twenty Ounce Apple.—Cayuga Red Streak.* This is a very popular variety in market on account of its large size, handsome appearance, and cooking qualities; and no doubt in suitable soil and climate it is a profitable variety, in moderate quantity, to the orchardist. The tree is tolerably hardy, not equaling the Red Astrachan in this respect, but more hardy than the Rhode Island Greening. It is a moderately vigorous, erect grower, and forms a neat, compact head, and bears good crops. The fruit is large, always fair and showy, being handsomely marbled and splashed with red on a yellow or greenish-yellow ground; flesh is yellowish, coarse-grained, of a sprightly sub-acid flavor; quality "good." May be used in October, and will keep through January.

WAGENER.—Under proper cultivation this will prove to be a very valuable apple. It has not been sufficiently tried in the various parts of our Dominion to admit of any positive expression of its hardihood, further than that it is known to succeed well in some parts of the Province of Quebec. From the reports that have come to us from various sections, we believe that it will prove to be a very valuable variety over a large part of the country, but not quite as hardy as Red Astrachan or the Talman's Sweet. The tree is thrifty, upright habit, forming a tolerably rounded head, that requires considerable thinning out in order to obtain good-sized fruit. It bears young, abundantly, and every year.

The fruit is full medium size, nearly covered with crimson; flesh yellowish, fine grained, very tender, juicy, with a slightly vinous flavor; quality "very good." Ripens in December, and will keep until February.

It has many of the qualities of a good market apple—a healthy, early fruiting, prolific tree; fruit of good size, pleasing appearance, and very agreeable flavor. How well it will bear transportation to distant markets, and the rough handling too common in these days, we can not yet say.

NOVA SCOTIA APPLES.

We are indebted to Mr. R. W. Starr for the following descriptions of four varieties of Apples, which originated in Nova Scotia, and are much esteemed in that Province:

SUTTON'S EARLY was grown by Mr. Wm. Sutton, of Cornwallis, from seed of the Ribston Pippin. It has not yet been thoroughly tested, but it promises well. The fruit is large, conic, slightly ribbed; skin yellowish white, with faint russet markings around the **stem**; flesh white, juicy, **with a pleasant sub-acid flavour. Ripe from the** 20th to **the last of August. The tree is** thrifty, **with a spreading habit, and the** young shoots stout, dark **and downy.**

BISHOP'S BOURNE.—Another seedling of Sutton's from the Ribston Pippin. The tree is hardy, a quick grower, forms a spreading head, the young wood bright and tough. It bears abundant crops of fair fruit, which is much prized for stewing and baking, as it contains a great deal of saccharine, although classed as sub-acid. The fruit is of medium size, roundish conical, pale yellow in the shade, and obscurely splashed and striped in the sun; flesh is white, crisp, tender, juicy, mild sub-acid, slightly aromatic; season November **and December.**

MARQUIS OF LORNE.—A seedling from the Gravenstein, by Sutton. The tree is large, vigorous and spreading; young wood stout and dark; the leaves large, dense, dark green; the blossoms are large and deep rose-coloured; the fruit large to very large, oblate, sometimes conic; the skin smooth, yellowish white, thickly sprinkled with carmine **and splashed** with broken stripes of a darker shade of the same color; dots small and brown; stem short and small, inserted in a wide, deep, regular, russeted cavity; basin large, ridged and irregular; calyx large, open, with the segments reflexed; **flesh** white, breaking, somewhat **coarse** grained, juicy, pleasant, sprightly sub-acid; season November and December. A very promising variety.

Morton's Red.—This is supposed to be a native, having been found growing on the farm of the late Elkanah Morton, of Cornwallis. It is a moderately strong grower, with spreading, pendulous branches, a very good bearer and a good market apple. The fruit is of medium size, round, inclining to conic, and always fair; skin smooth, of a dull greyish white, nearly covered with light and dark red, through which the grey skin shows in faint striated markings; calyx inclined to large, closed; basin broad, shallow and regular; **stem medium, sometimes fleshy and** knobbed, inserted in a shallow even cavity; flesh white, tender, fine grained, juicy, pleasant sub-acid; season December and January, but will keep longer.

THE APRICOT.

This very handsome and delicious fruit can be grown in the open air only in the most favored parts of the Province of Ontario, and even there the fruit is very liable to be destroyed by late spring frosts, on account of the habit of the tree in putting forth its blossoms at the first approach of spring. The curculio also prey upon this fruit, and unless closely watched and kept in subjection, will not leave a single specimen to ripen. In other parts of the Dominion, this fruit can only be grown in the orchard-house.

It is propagated by budding on the Apricot, Plum or Peach. The Plum stock is much better than the Peach, especially for planting on heavy soils, the tree being healthier and the fruit of finer flavor.

The following varieties have been selected from some fifty names as most worthy of attention.

Black or Purple Apricot.—This variety is the most hardy of any with which we are acquainted, and it is mainly on that account that it is mentioned here. The tree is nearly as hardy as a plum, and **the** small purplish Apricots bear a strong resemblance to that fruit. The flavor is pleasant, though usually a little astringent, and in point of quality not to be compared to **the finer** sorts. Ripe in August.

BREDA.—This is a very productive and high flavored sort, fruit small, orange color, rich and juicy. Ripe beginning of August.

EARLY GOLDEN.—The fruit of this variety is small, color pale orange, juicy, sweet, and of good flavor. Tree vigorous and very productive. Ripe in July.

MOORPARK.—This old variety—for it has been in cultivation for about a hundred and fifty years—is one of the largest and best. The fruit is orange color, **with a red** cheek, sweet, rich, and juicy, with an exceedingly **luscious flavor.** Ripe in **August.**

RED MASCULINE.—**This is one** of the earliest sorts, and the tree among **the most** hardy, and productive. The fruit is small, bright yellow spotted with red, juicy and pleasant flavored, but **not rich.**

THE CHERRY.

This fruit is divided into two quite distinct classes, varying **not** only in the character of the fruit, but also in the hardihood of the tree. The class known as the Bigarreau and Heart Cherries yields larger and **sweeter fruit than** the other, which contains the Duke and Morello varieties; but the Dukes and Morellos are much hardier, withstanding a much greater degree of cold, and the fruit **is** far better for all culinary purposes.

The cherry makes a very pretty ornamental tree, and in the northern part of Germany the custom largely prevails of planting **it as a** road-side tree, so that the roads often pass, for many miles together, through an avenue of cherry trees. Such a custom **might** well be imitated in many parts of Canada, adding much to the beauty of the country and the comfort of the inhabitants.

The soil best suited to the cherry is a stony, gravelly, or

sandy loam, **deep and dry**. In a wet soil it will not flourish, but soon becomes **diseased and dies**. The Dukes and Morellos will grow in heavier soil than the Hearts and Bigarreaus, but it also **must be dry**. Indeed, **if the soil be** thoroughly drained to a good depth below the surface, especially if there be a porous subsoil through which the surplus moisture passes readily away, there the cherry will do well, even in strong clayey surface soil. Hill sides and even hill tops are better for the cherry than low bottoms or valleys.

The trees may be planted about eighteen feet **apart, indeed** the slower growing **Dukes and Morellos are far enough apart at** sixteen feet. They will require very little pruning, only an occasional removal of interlacing branches, and this should be done in July, when the wounds will heal quickly. They are propagated by budding; for although they can be grafted, yet in our climate this method is not as uniformly successful. The **best stocks are seedlings of** the varieties of cherry known as the **Mahaleb and the Mazzard, the** former being thought better adapted **than the Mazzard to a greater variety of soils.**

HEART AND BIGARREAU CHERRIES.

These thrive well in the warmer parts of Ontario, and along the borders of the great lakes, and **in** a few sheltered situations not immediately influenced by these large bodies of water. Some varieties do well also in the fruit districts **of Nova Scotia. In** the colder parts of Ontario, throughout the St. Lawrence and **Ottawa** Districts, and in all the other Provinces of the Dominion, with limited exceptions, the climate is too severe for their successful culture. Descriptions of a few of the **most desirable** sorts are **here given.**

BIGARREAU.—*Yellow Spanish.*—*White Bigarreau.*—On the whole, we give the **preference to this variety over** all the other light-colored cherries. **The fruit** is of large size, beautiful in appearance, and of excellent quality. The color **is a** pale yellow, handsomely marked with bright **red** dots, and marbled with red **on the** exposed side; the flesh is pale yellow, with a good deal of firmness, but juicy, sweet, rich, and of exceedingly agreeable flavor. It **ripens** about the first of July. The tree is a thrifty grower, and makes a large top with a handsome rounded outline. It is very productive, and is one of the varieties **recommended for** planting in Nova Scotia.

BLACK EAGLE.—As its name imports, this is a black cherry, **and** was introduced from England, where it was raised from a seed of the Bigarreau, described above, fertilized by the May-**duke.** It is very remarkable that the progeny of a yellow cherry fertilized by a red one, should be black, but such, nevertheless, is the received history of this variety. The tree is vigorous and of upright habit, usually bearing moderate crops, but sometimes the fruit is very abundant. The cherries are large, heart-shaped, color deep purplish black, continuing through the **flesh,** which is juicy, rich and high flavored. **Ripe in July.**

BLACK HAWK.—We have been **much pleased with this variety, and feel disposed to place** it in the front rank of the **Black Cherries.** It was raised by Dr. Kirtland, of Cleveland, Ohio. The tree has thus far proved to be healthy and vigorous, and abundantly productive. The fruit is large, very dark glossy black; the flesh dark purple, firm, juicy, sweet and rich. **It** ripens early in July, a little in advance of the Black Eagle.

BLACK TARTARIAN.—This variety is a very general favorite, and is probably more often ordered than any other one variety. The fruit is of the largest **size,** exceedingly showy, with a bright glossy skin **of the** darkest purple, heart-shaped in form, yet **so** regularly irregular in outline that it seems to have been hammered out at the blacksmith's forge. It is believed to have been intro-**duced into** England from Russia about the year 1796, whence **it has been** widely disseminated. The tree is a remarkably rapid and vigorous grower, erect in habit and very abundant bearer. The fruit **is** very large, **with a** thick purple flesh, almost firm, juicy, rich and excellent; stone quite small in proportion to the size of the fruit. Ripe about the first **of July.** Proves to be valuable in Nova Scotia.

COE'S TRANSPARENT.—This is an excellent variety of the tender fleshed, light colored sorts. The tree is healthy and vigorous, and a good bearer. The fruit is of medium size, round, **pale amber** color in the shade, and overspread with pale red in the sun with a peculiarly **mottled appearance**; the flesh is very tender, melting, juicy, with a **sweet** but very agreeable flavor; quality "best." It ripens about the last of June.

DOWNER'S LATE.—Was raised by Mr. Samuel Downer, near Boston, and is a valuable late variety, ripening about the first of August. The tree is vigorous, erect and exceedingly **prolific.** Fruit medium in size, bright red, borne in clusters; flesh tender, juicy, and sweet. Thrives well in Nova Scotia.

EARLY PURPLE GUIGNE.—The earliest good variety we have, ripening about the 15th of June. The tree is healthy, vigorous, somewhat irregular in habit of growth, a constant and abundant bearer. The fruit is a little below medium size, of a purple color when fully ripe, flesh tender and juicy, sweet and rich; quality "very good." Much esteemed in Nova Scotia.

ELTON.—There seems to be more of hardihood in this variety than is usual in this class of cherries, so that it will endure a greater degree of cold and **flourish** and bear fruit where **many of** its fellows perish. Those who desire to grow some **of the sweeter** cherries may succeed with this variety when the **other** kinds fail. **The fruit is** of large size, lengthened heart-shaped, yellow, with a **ruddy,** mottled cheek; flesh a little firm, juicy, rich, and of excellent flavor; quality "very good" to "best." It is ripe early in July.

GOVERNOR WOOD.—Ripening soon after the Early Purple Guigne, this **excellent cherry is the connecting link** between the earliest sorts **and the general** crop. It was raised by Professor Kirtland, of Cleveland, Ohio. The tree grows well and is very productive. The fruit is above **medium** size, very light yellow, with a red cheek handsomely marbled. The flesh is tender, sweet, juicy, and of an exceedingly pleasant flavor.

NAPOLEON BIGARREAU.—In point of beauty and attractive, showy appearance, there is none to excel this magnificent variety.

The fruit is of the very largest size; color, a beautiful amber yellow, handsomely spotted with deep red, and the glowing crimson cheek very finely marbled; the flesh is very firm, juicy and of excellent flavor. Ripens about the middle of July. The tree is an erect, vigorous grower, bearing good, regular crops. In our own experience with this variety, we have found it very liable to rot on the tree before it became perfectly ripe; in truth, all of this class of cherries seem to have this tendency in greater or less degree, and more if wet and warm weather prevail at the time of ripening than when the weather is cool and dry.

ROCKPORT BIGARREAU.—Another of Dr. Kirtland's cherries, of great beauty and excellence. The tree is remarkably healthy and vigorous, and forms a beautiful pyramidal head, and at the same time is an excellent cropper. The fruit is of large size, in color a beautiful bright red shading to pale amber; the flesh is nearly firm, sweet, juicy, of a rich and pleasant flavor. It ripens about the middle of June.

TRADESCANT'S BLACK HEART.—*Elkhorn.*—This is one of the first varieties introduced into Western Canada, and has there received a great many names. Of these the most common are Black Ox Heart, Ox Heart, and Black Heart. It is a vigorous, healthy tree, of erect habit, forming a tall pyramid, and an abundant bearer. The fruit is large, heart-shaped, having the same irregular surface as the Black Tartarian; color, a very deep purple, changing when fully ripe to a deep glossy black, flesh very firm and solid, purple, not very juicy, sweet and high flavored. Ripe late in July.

DUKES AND MORELLOS.

The varieties comprised under this head are more hardy than the Heart and Bigarreau cherries, consequently they endure severe cold much better, and may be successfully grown where the others fail. They are more acid also, some of the varieties abundantly so, and on that account are better adapted for cooking and canning than the sweeter sorts. We have selected half a dozen varieties which will be found to comprise all, and perhaps more than all, that it is desirable to plant.

BELLE DE CHOISY.—We have given this variety a place, because in point of flavor it is one of the best if not the best of this section; but it is such a very shy bearer in all our experience and observation, that we cannot advise any one to plant it. Yet when the fruit can be had there is no cherry more delicious; it is of medium size, bright red in the sun, pale amber in the shade; flesh very tender, melting, juicy, and of a most delicate and agreeable flavor. It ripens about the first of July.

BELLE MAGNIFIQUE.—The chief excellence of this variety is its lateness of ripening, it being in use about the middle of August. The fruit is of good size, bright red, with a juicy, tender flesh, of a sprightly, sub-acid flavor. It is desirable for cooking, and when allowed to remain on the tree until very ripe, is a pretty good dessert fruit. The tree is moderately vigorous in growth and an abundant bearer. We have found this variety to be exceedingly liable to the attacks of the curculio in our grounds, we think the most so of all the cherries.

KENTISH.—*Early Richmond.*—*Common Red.*—*Pie Cherry.*—*Montmorency.*—An old European variety introduced by the early settlers, and coming so nearly true from seed and yet sometimes varying so much that from all these shades of variation there has arisen considerable confusion. We notice that Mr. Downing, in his exhaustive work on the fruits and fruit trees of America, makes a second kind, which he calls the Late Kentish, but we have been unable to find any really permanent and distinguishing differences, so imperceptibly do these all glide into one another. Those that seem to ripen earliest will hang on the tree and continue as long as the latest, while in general appearance, size, color, flavor, productiveness and hardihood they seem to be substantially the same. Undoubtedly, taking all things into consideration, it is the most valuable of all the cherries that can be grown in the Dominion of Canada. In the first place, it is the most hardy variety, capable of enduring a very severe degree of cold, and of accommodating itself to any variety of soil, from the stiffest clay to the lightest sand. Then it is a very constant and exceedingly abundant cropper, coming early into bearing and continuing to extremest old age. When about half ripe, at which time the fruit is of a bright red, it may be used for pies, tarts and all cooking purposes, and when fully ripe, when it has become of a dark mahogany color, it is a very agreeable dessert fruit; and if there be any cherry that can be profitably planted for market, this is the cherry that will yield the most sure returns. The tree is a moderately vigorous grower, never becoming very large, and forming a rounded, spreading head. The fruit is of medium size, with a juicy, melting flesh, of a rich, sprightly, acid flavor, ripening from the middle of June to the end of July.

MAYDUKE.—Were this variety as hardy as the one last described it would stand at the head of the list, but although a very hardy sort, it is just a little less hardy than the Kentish. Owing to this want of hardihood the tree sometimes fails where the Kentish stands, and the crop of fruit is oftener injured or destroyed even where the tree survives. Yet every one should give this variety a trial where there is hope that any cherry will thrive, and if it succeeds he will ever after be gratified that he has made the trial. It is supposed that the Mayduke originated in France, whence it has been very widely diffused, and though it has been a long time in cultivation, none of the newer sorts have been found to be in all respects its equal. The tree is a vigorous, upright grower, and when young assumes a form much like that of a young Lombardy Poplar. It is a regular and abundant bearer. The fruit is of full medium size, borne in clusters, and when fully ripe a dark dull red. The flesh is tender, juicy, melting, and of excellent flavor. Ripe the latter part of June. Much esteemed by the fruit growers of Nova Scotia.

PLUMSTONE MORELLO.—This variety is very hardy, and of very slow growth; making, when worked on the Mahaleb Cherry stock, a nice pyramidal bush. Its dwarf habit has prevented this variety from being very generally planted, but its apparent hardihood makes it worthy of more extended trial. We have not found the tree to be as productive as the Mayduke, but it is usually mentioned as being a productive variety. The fruit is above medium size, dark red, with a tender and juicy flesh, of a sprightly, rich and pleasant flavor. It ripens early in August.

Reine Hortense.—An excellent variety, which will probably prove to be as hardy as the Mayduke. It ripens much later, and being much sweeter, it will be more generally preferred for the dessert. After a trial of fifteen years we have only one fault to find with it, and that is, that in some seasons too much of the fruit drops off soon after it has set. We have attributed this dropping of the fruit to chilly north-easterly storms occurring at that particular stage in the growth of the fruit. With this exception the tree is an abundant bearer, moderately vigorous in growth, perfectly healthy, and forming a handsome pyramid. The fruit is large, of a deep red color, somewhat mottled; the flesh tender and juicy, almost sweet, and of an exceedingly agreeable flavor. Ripe the latter part of July.

Starr's Prolific.—The worthy Secretary of the Fruit Growers' Association of Nova Scotia, to whom we are indebted for many favors, has kindly furnished us with the description of this variety, which is a native of Nova Scotia, and so much esteemed where it is known that we believe it to be worthy of wider dissemination.

It originated on the farm belonging to Mr. Starr's father, Starr's Point, from seed of the Waterloo.

The original tree is now about twenty-five years old, large, spreading and healthy, a constant and most prodigious bearer. The fruit is of medium size, roundish heart-shaped; color, bright red; flesh tender, **juicy, rich, brisk** sub-acid. Ripe about the first week of July.

THE NECTARINE.

This is only a Peach with a smooth skin, and the tree requires the same soil, cultivation, pruning, and manures as the Peach, and is propagated in the same manner, by budding on peach or plum stocks.

The fruit is more liable to the attacks of the curculio than the Peach, and on this account is even more difficult to secure than a crop of Peaches. The following varieties are the most worthy of attention by cultivators in Canada.

DOWNTON.—The fruit is of large size, greenish white, with a deep red cheek; the flesh also has a pale green cast, but is rich, melting and high flavored. Ripens the very last of August.

EARLY NEWINGTON.—A cling-stone variety, with large bright red fruit, very handsomely marbled and mottled with dark red, and covered with a thin bloom. The flesh is greenish white, except that next to the stone it changes to pale red; juicy, rich, and of excellent flavor. Ripe early in September.

ELRUGE.—Is esteemed one of the very best. Fruit is of medium size, yellowish green with a red cheek; flesh greenish white, very juicy, rich and high flavored. Ripe in the first half of September.

STANWICK.—For orchard house culture, under glass, this variety bears a high reputation. The fruit is of medium size, tender, juicy, and of superior quality.

VIOLET HATIVE.—*Early Violet.*—One of the most esteemed; handsome, and of delicious flavor. The fruit is of medium size, greenish yellow with a purple cheek, juicy and rich. Ripe latter part of August.

THE PEACH.

This delicious fruit can be grown in the open ground only in the warmer parts of the Province of Ontario, and then only in warm and dry gravelly or sandy soils, and in sheltered aspects not subject to late spring frosts. Trained against the wall, it does well in Nova Scotia, and other sections where the fruit buds are not killed by the winter's cold. In the earlier history of the country the Peach crop was more abundant and certain than it has been for the past twenty years. The clearing up of the country, with its consequent effect upon the humidity and electricity of the atmosphere, and the exposure of all things to the unbroken sweep of the winds, have wrought a change in the climate of the country not altogether favorable either to animal or vegetable life. When we, as agriculturists, better understand the influence of frequent belts of timber, composed of evergreen and deciduous trees, upon the life and health of ourselves, of our stock, of our crops and our orchards, they will then be esteemed as necessary and valued as highly as any part of the farm, and our crops of fruit will be less frequently injured or destroyed by sudden changes of temperature and predatory tribes of insects.

The soil must be warm, dry and porous, else the Peach will not thrive. In a stiff retentive clay the tree will not grow, nor in any cold, damp soil. The tops and sides of gentle slopes are usually more favorable than the bottoms of ravines and valleys. An abundance of lime in the soil is conducive to the health of the tree, and a regular dressing of wood ashes has always been found to be highly beneficial.

Peach trees may be planted twelve feet apart each way, and should be annually pruned back or *shortened in*. By this is usually meant the cutting off, every spring, of about one-third of the length of the previous summer's growth, and the thinning out of such twigs as may have become useless, or overcrowded. By this method of pruning, the trees will be kept in a neat, compact form, less exposed to injury from the winds, the branches less liable to be broken by any cause, and the tree more healthy and fruitful. If, however, instead of cutting away in spring one-third of the previous summer's growth, the growing shoots were checked by pinching the ends in summer, the wood would be better ripened, the tree kept more easily in shape, and the spring pruning reduced to a mere occasional thinning of superfluous shoots. We are fully persuaded that, in our Canadian climate, the more we control the form of our trees by summer pinching and the less of knife pruning we can get on with, not only of the Peach but of all our fruit trees, the more healthy and longer lived our trees will be.

Peach trees will not bear heavy manuring with stimulating manures; **they** make the trees grow too thriftily, **with soft, spongy wood.** The proper manures are wood ashes, lime, bone **dust, and perfectly decayed** barn-yard manure from some old heap or hot-**bed, the** latter to be used sparingly. The ground should be kept clean and never seeded down. They are propagated by budding on both Peach and Plum stocks.

A few of the best varieties, those that have been found best suited to this climate, are described below. If the peach growers of Western Ontario would turn their attention to the production of new varieties **from** seed, there is **no doubt a generation of** hardier sorts might be obtained, which **would be better adapted** to the country than most of those **now** in cultivation. Yet it must not be expected that the geographical **distribution of this tree can be greatly** enlarged **within the Dominion;** the warm soils **near the great lakes,** lying between lakes Erie and Ontario, **along** the **north shore of** Ontario and the south shore of lake Huron, where the air is tempered by those large bodies of water, will ever remain the most favorable to the production of the Apricot, Nectarine, and Peach.

The experiments already made by Mr. **Cowherd, of Newport,** Brant County, Ont., give promise of very favorable **results.**

CRAWFORD'S EARLY.—No variety of **peach is as popular** as this, and more trees are **planted of it than of** all the other sorts **put together. It is a truly splendid peach,** of large size, great **beauty of appearance, and** superior quality. The tree is healthy, vigorous and productive, and **the** fruit is large, yellow, with a very handsome red cheek; the flesh deep yellow, rich, sweet and high flavored. It ripens about the middle of September, and **is** much sought after in all our markets.

CRAWFORD'S LATE.—This variety is very much like the preceding in appearance and quality, but ripening about a fortnight **later.** It also is a splendid market variety, and greatly in demand for the purpose of canning, for which there is none better. **The fruit is** very large, yellow with a dark red cheek; flesh **yellow, juicy,** with **a rich vinous** flavor.

EARLY YORK.—The best early peach, ripening in the latter part of August. The Early Anne is ripe about a fortnight earlier, but it is not much larger than a nutmeg, and the tree such a miserable grower that we cannot recommend it. The Early York, however, is a vigorous, healthy tree, and bears abundantly. The fruit is of medium size, with a dark red cheek, flesh greenish white, very juicy, with a rich, sprightly flavor.

GEORGE THE FOURTH.—The healthy character of the tree and the high quality of the fruit of this variety have made it a great favorite. The fruit is large, white minutely dotted with red in the shade, the sunny side is dark red, often most beautifully mottled and marbled; the flesh is white, very juicy, and exceedingly rich and luscious. Ripe early in September.

HALE'S EARLY.—Comparatively a new variety, valuable on account of its productiveness and early ripening. It has been largely planted in some sections for market purposes, but its value as a market variety is somewhat doubtful. The fruit is of medium size, greenish white in the shade, but mostly covered with red; flesh white, juicy, sweet and of good flavor. Ripe a little before the Early York.

OLD MIXON FREESTONE.—An old standard variety that has borne the test of many years and is highly esteemed. The tree is healthy and vigorous, and bears good crops. The fruit is large, yellowish white marbled with red; flesh white, juicy, rich, with a very pleasant vinous flavor. Ripe middle of September.

RED CHEEK MELOCOTON.—Another very popular, well-known and long tried sort, which seems to thrive everywhere that the peach can be grown. It is the parent of the Early and Late Crawford, which have superseded it as market sorts. The fruit is large, yellow with a dark red cheek; flesh yellow, juicy, with a very agreeable rich, vinous flavor. Ripe about the middle of September.

TAYLOR.—Originated by James Taylor, Esq., of St. Catharines, an enthusiastic amateur fruit cultivator. The tree is vigorous, and seems to be more than usually hardy and healthy. The fruit is of large size, yellow with a red cheek; flesh yellow, juicy, with a fine aromatic flavor. Ripens just after the Early Crawford.

VAN BUREN'S GOLDEN DWARF.—We have not fruited this variety, but believe it to be well adapted to pot culture on account of its dwarf habit of growth. The fruit is said to be of medium size, of a golden yellow color with a red cheek; flesh yellow, firm, juicy and of good quality. It is a clingstone, a very undesirable character in the peach.

THE PEAR.

A strong clay loam, resting on a dry subsoil, is the very best soil for the pear tree. In such a soil it will be healthy and long-lived, and the fruit will be of the highest flavor. However, it will thrive in sandy and gravelly soils so long as they are dry; but in cold, wet soils the trees soon become diseased and worthless.

The climate in some parts of the Dominion is too severe for the successful culture of this fruit. In the Province of Ontario the Ottawa and St. Lawrence districts have been found too cold for most of the varieties in general cultivation, and in the Province of Quebec the pear can be successfully raised only in favored localities.

There is a disease, popularly known as the fire-blight, which attacks the pear tree, killing sometimes only the smaller shoots, sometimes entire branches, and not unfrequently the tree itself. Some varieties are very liable to this disease, as the Glout Morceau, and none are wholly exempt. The cause of it is yet unknown, nor has any certain remedy, or even preventive, been discovered. It usually makes its appearance in midsummer, blackening the bark and withering the leaves of the affected branches, giving them the appearance of having been scorched with fire. Prompt amputation of all the affected parts is believed to arrest the progress of the disease, and seems sometimes to save the tree. Those trees which are growing very luxuriantly in very rich alluvial soil, or that have been very highly manured with barnyard manure, seem to be the most subject to these attacks.

The best manures for the pear tree are wood ashes, lime and ground bones. These may be spread upon the surface of the ground, where they will become gradually incorporated with the soil. In our climate, great injury is often done by stimulating the pear trees to excessive growth. A short, well-ripened annual growth is all that should be desired.

This tree can be propagated both by grafting and budding. When worked upon pear seedlings, the trees naturally grow to a large size, and attain the height usual in pear trees. These are known as standard pear trees. It is difficult to transplant large standard pear trees with success, from the fact that the roots are poorly supplied with fibres, when grown in the manner in which they are raised in the nurseries in America. In England, where the importance of having an abundance of fibrous roots is understood and appreciated, nurserymen transplant their standard trees frequently, not only of the pear, but of the apple and other fruits, and also of ornamental trees, charging for such transplanted trees according to the number of times they have been transplanted. By each successive transplanting a larger number of fibrous roots are formed, so that after two or three removals, the roots, instead of looking like a two or three-pronged carrot, are a mass of fibres, resembling a fine, bushy head of hair. When planters in Canada are willing to pay the difference in the cost of growing such fibrous-rooted trees, they will find the nurserymen ready to supply them; but while the present practice prevails of buying always where they can be had cheapest, without regard to quality, nurserymen are forced to grow their trees with the least possible labor, and the trees are transplanted as seldom as possible.

Standard pear trees, as usually grown, do not require much pruning if they are attended to every year, and those branches removed which cross each other, or that are forming a distorted growth. Yet they are much better if trained as pyramids, branching near the **ground** and rising gradually in **a** symmetrical form. Grown in **this way** they are much better able to **endure the climate of** our colder sections, while they come **into bearing much sooner** than those with long trunks. **The method of** pruning to **form** such trees is the same **as** that which is fully described under the directions given for pruning dwarf pear trees. When grown in the pyramidal form **here** recommended, **the trees can** be planted nearer together, and thus they shelter each other **from the high winds.**

Dwarf Pear trees are **formed by budding upon low-growing** varieties **of Quince, which have the effect to lessen the size of the tree.** Some varieties of Pear **will not unite well with the** quince stock, **and** the only **way of obtaining dwarf trees of such varieties is** by budding the Quince **stock with** some **variety that** will **unite firmly with it,** such, for instance, as the Beurre d'Amalis, **and** then budding **the** refractory variety into that. This is called double working. Dwarf Pear trees attain to considerable **size** in favorable soils, but not to the height common in standard Pear trees, and usually come into bearing much **earlier, and in some** varieties the fruit is finer **and** higher flavored. These advantages, coupled with the fact that **the trees can** be planted closer together, and a greater number **of** varieties fruited on a smaller space, **constitute their chief recommendations.** The best distance **for Dwarf Pear trees is twelve feet apart** each way, while standard trees **require twenty feet.**

In planting Dwarf Pear trees, it is important that all **the** quince stock **should be set** below the surface of the ground. **If** the bud has been **inserted** high up on the stock, such planting would necessitate the placing of the lower portion **of the roots in** the cold subsoil, where they would **not only remain** inert, **but** become diseased, and cause **the tree to become** sickly **and** die. To prevent this, a few inches of the lower part **of** the quince root with the accompanying rootlets should be removed with a fine **saw,** so that when planted the whole of the quince stock shall be buried in the soil, and yet none so deeply down as to be below the stimulating effect of the warmth of the sun. Fortunately, the quince, when buried in warm soil, at once proceeds to throw out roots, so that in a few weeks new roots will be formed quite to the surface of the ground, fully supplying the place of all that have been removed.

The proper form of a dwarf pear tree, and the best form for a standard tree is the pyramidal. To produce this form it will be necessary to begin to prune the tree while it is quite young. Such is the desire on the part of purchasers to get large trees, that nurserymen get them up as fast as possible. Fig. 47 represents a dwarf pear tree at one year old from the bud, and the cross line, A, the place where nurserymen usually head it back in order that it may look as large as possible, whereas it should have been cut back at B. A tree that has been properly headed back when one year old, will, when its second season's growth is completed, have the appearance shown in Figure 48. The branches should now be shortened in such a way as to give a pyramidal shape to the tree, by cutting back the lower shoots to about eight inches from the body of the tree; those next above should be shortened about two inches more, and the next shortened yet a little more, until those nearest the leader are cut back to three or four buds from the base. The leader should be cut off at about half its length, so that another series of branches may be thrown out to continue the pyramid. At the end of the third season's

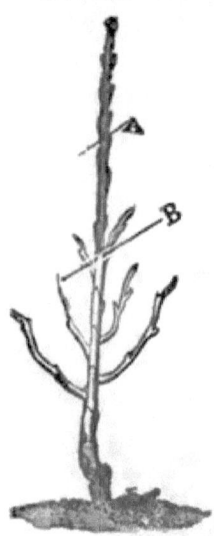

Fig. 47.

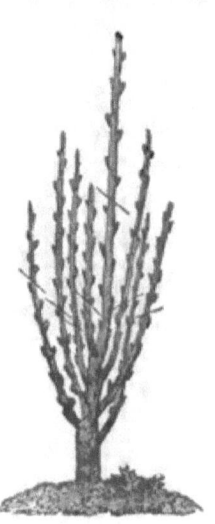

Fig. 48.

growth **the tree will** have the appearance shown in Fig. 49. **It should have** been stated that if the branches on the tree at the **end of** the second season's growth are too **numerous** to admit of all remaining, which will very probably be the case, enough of them **must** be cut entirely away **to give** plenty of room for the free **circulation of air and light,** upon which the full development of leaves and fruit so entirely depends. The like process of **cutting back the growth of the** previous summer must be again repeated, as indicated by the cross lines, keeping in mind that the **object for which you prune is to** bring the tree into a conical form. At the end of **the fourth** season the tree will **have the form shown in Fig. 50,** and the dotted line, A. B., **shows where the branches will** require to be shortened at the spring pruning. If summer **pinching of the** shoots is practised, very little **spring pruning will be required.** Summer pinching consists in nipping off **the point of the growing** shoot, usually with **the thumb and finger,** or it may **be** done with the knife. **The effect of this is,** of course, to

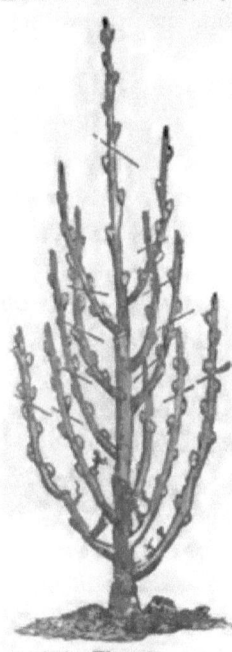

Fig. 49.

Fig. 50.

check the extension of the shoot, and also to send the sap to the buds below. If these buds do not break during the growing season, they will be considerably strengthened and increased in size, and either form fruit buds or send out strong shoots the next season. If the tree be growing rapidly, one or more of the buds near the end of the shoot will probably break and send out shoots the same season. Care must be taken not to perform the pinching so late in summer as to induce the formation of these shoots at a time when they can not ripen their growth before winter.

If it be desirable to check the growth of any branch that is absorbing too much of the strength of the tree and becoming too large in proportion to the others, it can be easily done by pinching the end in summer and stripping off a part of the leaves from that branch. If, on the contrary, you wish to induce a branch to grow more vigorously, shorten it back severely in the spring, and in summer pinch in the other branches and strip off some of their leaves, while you allow the shoots thrown out from the branch that was cut back to grow undisturbed.

In these suggestions mention has been made only of pruning in the spring, for the reason that experience has taught us that it is important that the wounds should heal over quickly. On this account the pear should not be pruned when the sap is not in active circulation, and should by no means be pruned in the fall. Besides this, it is very desirable to avoid the making of large wounds, as must be done in removing or cutting off large branches, and therefore pruning should be done while the tree is young, and systematically attended to every year. By doing this it will never become necessary to cut off large limbs, except in case of accidental injury.

Soil and exposure have a great influence on the quality of pears, an influence that has not yet been adequately accounted for or fully understood. This variation in quality may often be seen in the fruit of trees of the same variety, growing in soils apparently alike and but a mile or two apart. **As a rule, the** fruit from young trees is not **as fine** in quality as that from the same trees **at a more advanced age,** and that produced by trees growing in clayey soils with **a dry** bottom, not fertilized with highly stimulating manures, is **of better** quality than that borne by trees in a light sandy soil, or in a **damp soil, or** in a rich alluvial soil, or that are supplied too liberally with partially decomposed barn-yard manure.

Dwarf Pear trees are very apt to bear too much fruit, and it will therefore be necessary to examine them just after the fruit is set, and thin out **the pears.** No more fruit should be allowed to remain than the tree can bring to perfection of size and quality. The fruit on an over-loaded tree is sure to be small in size and poor in quality, while the tree is **often so severely over-tasked in** the effort to **grow and ripen its unequal burden,** that it becomes stunted, **sickly, and frequently perishes.** Just how much fruit **to leave and how much to take can only be learned by actual** practice. **The size, vigor and habits of the** tree, must be all duly **considered, and the** condition of the soil in which it is growing; the tendency in all cases is to leave too much fruit, and it is always advisable to go over the trees a second and a third time, removing those which give least promise of **coming to a full and well-developed maturity.**

The fruit of almost all varieties of **Pear is of much finer flavor if gathered a few days before it is fully ripe, and** allowed to **mature in the house. The best time for** taking the fruit from the trees is usually indicated by a slight change in the color of the pears, and by **the stalk** parting readily from the tree when the fruit is gently lifted. These remarks apply to the summer and early autumn varieties. After the fruit has been gathered, it should **be placed in** a box or keg and stored in a cool room, but not in the cellar, to ripen. If there be but a few specimens of any kind, these will ripen best if put into a paper bag, or wrapped securely in paper and placed together in a box. If spread out on shelves, or placed in drawers capable of holding a **much larger quantity, they lose much of** their flavor, and usually shrivel. But if kept in a body together, where there is sufficient quantity, or kept from too rapid evaporation by being wrapped in paper, their flavor and plumpness are fully preserved, and in due time the fruit will acquire its full color and perfect maturity, with more juiciness and richness of flavor than if allowed to ripen wholly on the tree. Many sorts, if allowed to remain too long on the tree, rot at the core, while others become dry, mealy and flavorless. By gathering and ripening them in the manner above described, these evils are lessened or wholly obviated, and fruit that would be otherwise worthless becomes not only good, but delicious.

Late autumn and winter Pears do not require such treatment, but on the contrary are allowed to remain on the trees as long as the season will admit. They should be gathered carefully without bruising, packed in barrels or boxes, and kept in a cool, dry cellar until they begin to show signs of ripening, when they should be taken to a room where the temperature is a little warmer, to complete their maturity.

Very few of the winter Pears which come to maturity after the holidays are worth growing in our climate. The best Pears are those that ripen not later than the middle of January; of those ripening after that time, none in our estimation are at all comparable in flavor to the Pomme Grise d'Or Apple.

The number of varieties of Pear now in cultivation is enormous, yet out of them all but a very few can be named that have proved themselves, after some years of trial, to be possessed of the qualifications which commend them to the attention of Canadian planters. Many varieties, which in Europe enjoy a high reputation, do not maintain their high qualities when transplanted to our soil and climate. Some varieties again are very fickle, exhibiting a high degree of excellence in one season, but almost tasteless the next. In selecting the varieties which are here described, the aim has been to mention only those which are really worthy of attention, and which combine in as great a degree as possible, hardihood and healthfulness of tree, with the highest quality of fruit.

The growing of Pears of the first quality for market, in such a way as to make it profitable, is attended with more difficulty than the profitable production of Apples, and will demand a higher order of horticultural talent. Yet such is the demand for finely grown Pears, that the early autumn varieties sell readily in our larger cities for from eight to fifteen dollars per barrel; while the later sorts, which come in after the great flood of autumn fruit has passed, command from twenty to thirty dollars per barrel. But these prices are obtained only for well grown fruit, fruit that can be uniformly grown only by a careful and judicious cultivator, whose trees are never suffered to weaken themselves with a superabundant crop, never over-fed with highly nitrogenous fertilizers, and never starved upon a parsimonious diet. No doubt the skilful cultivator of Pears for market will be amply remunerated, but let the impatient and unreflecting beware.

ANANAS D'ETE.—*Summer Pine Apple.*—This old pear from Holland is growing in favor with cultivators in Ontario on account of the healthy and vigorous character of the tree and the good quality of the fruit. In our climate it is by no means a summer pear, as its name would seem to indicate, but ripens the last of September, or more generally during the first ten days of October.

The fruit is above medium size, sometimes large, pear-shaped, color pale yellow; flesh is melting, fine-grained, buttery, sweet and high-flavored, quality "very good."

BARTLETT.—*Williams' Bonchretien.*—No pear has been more widely disseminated or is more universally esteemed throughout the Dominion than this variety, which is now about a century old. It originated in Berkshire, England, and was propagated by a Mr. Williams, of London, from which circumstance it received the name of Williams' Bonchretien. On its first introduction to America the name was lost, but a Mr. Bartlett, residing near Boston, disseminated it, and so it came to be known as the Bartlett Pear, by which latter name it is now better known all over this continent than by the original name by which it is known in England.

The tree is vigorous and upright, tolerably hardy, though not quite hardy enough to thrive well in the St. Lawrence and Ottawa districts of Ontario and other places of a like climate. In favorable climates it bears early and very abundantly. The fruit is of large size, yellow, with a slight blush on some specimens; flesh buttery, fine-grained, juicy, sweet, with a peculiar musky vinous flavor. Ripens about the middle of September. Well grown samples sell from seven to ten dollars per barrel in the city markets.

BEURRE BOSC.—Unfortunately this splendid variety is not sufficiently hardy to thrive well in those parts where the Heart and Bigarreau Cherries do not succeed. But in those places where it can be grown it has always maintained its reputation as a fruit of the "best" quality. The tree is a vigorous, somewhat irregular grower, producing its fruit not in clusters, as is usual with the pear, but singly, thus distributing the fruit very evenly over the tree, and giving to each specimen sufficient space to attain its full size without the necessity of thinning the fruit.

The fruit is large, tapering very gradually to the stalk, color yellowish cinnamon russet, sometimes with a ruddy glow on the exposed side; flesh very buttery, rich and delicious, quality "best." Ripe in October. This fruit always commands the highest market price.

BEURRE CLAIRGEAU.—Such are the vigor and healthy appearance of this tree, combined with early bearing and great productiveness, and such the beauty and attractiveness of the fruit, possessing also an excellent flavor, that it will doubtless prove to be a valuable and profitable variety. It is probably, on the whole, as hardy as the Bartlett, and nearly as productive.

The fruit is large, pear-shaped, color yellow shaded with crimson; flesh yellowish, juicy, buttery, with a pleasant vinous flavor; quality almost "very good." Ripe in November and December. Those who find the Bartlett to succeed well, may give this variety **a trial** with every expectation of success. **It** sells at present **in** New York city for twenty-five dollars per barrel.

BEURRE D'ANJOU.—In order more fully to test the value of **this variety for** Canadian planting, and to call public attention **to its** many valuable qualities, the Fruit Growers' Association of Ontario distributed a tree of it gratuitously **to** each of its members in the spring of 1871. The tree is very vigorous, healthy and productive; fruit large, obtusely pyriform; color greenish, with a brown cheek; flesh juicy, melting, with a pleasant, sprightly, vinous flavor; quality "very good." Ripe in November. The fruit sells in the Boston market for twenty-five to thirty-five dollars per **barrel.**

BEURRE DIEL.—This has been a **popular late autumn and** early **winter sort, and in warm, well-drained soils is usually very** good, **but in cold and damp soils is more** frequently very poor. In **our climate it seems to be very** variable in quality, judging **from** the samples that have been exhibited at meetings of fruit growers, and likely to be superseded in Canadian planting by the two last described sorts. The tree is very vigorous and a good bearer, and as hardy as the Bartlett. The fruit is large, yellow when ripe, often very considerably marbled with russet; **flesh** coarse grained, gritty at the core, but rich and **sugary in perfect** specimens. The quality of the fruit is usually better from trees **worked on the quince** stock, than from those on the pear. Ripe **late in November.**

BEURRE GIFFARD.—An excellent summer variety, ripening about **the** middle of August, of medium size, yellowish, with marbling of red on the exposed side; flesh melting, juicy, of a very pleasant vinous flavor, and richly perfumed; quality "very good." Like all early summer Pears, it does not last long, and is the better of being gathered early. The tree is healthy, but a slender grower, and fully as hardy as the Bartlett.

BEURRE SUPERFIN.—Those who have grown the old Brown Beurre and enjoyed its high vinous flavor, and have withal been disappointed to find it so variable and so subject to cracking, will be much gratified to find the flavor of their old favorite revived in this more recent and, so far as we are now able to judge, better and more reliable variety. The tree is very healthy and promises to take rank among the more hardy sorts, moderately vigorous in habit of growth, bearing tolerably well when it has arrived at maturity, but not beginning to bear while young. The fruit is medium in size, roundish pear-shaped, yellow, shaded with red on the sunny side; flesh buttery, melting, very juicy, with rich sub-acid flavor. Ripe in October.

BRANDYWINE.—With the exception that the fruit of this sort soon deteriorates after becoming ripe, we have been much pleased with this variety. The tree is sufficiently vigorous, upright in habit and an excellent bearer, and probably as hardy as most of our good varieties. The fruit is barely medium in size, yellowish green, with a ruddy brown cheek; flesh melting, sugary, juicy, with a very agreeable aromatic flavor; quality "very good." Ripe in the latter part of August.

BUFFUM.—This variety has been extensively tried in Canada, and the tree has been found to be tolerably hardy; but there is one very serious objection to it, and that is the very variable quality of the fruit. Sometimes it is very good, but oftener it is comparatively flavorless. In size it varies from medium to small; color russeted yellow, with a dark brownish red cheek; flesh buttery, not very juicy, sometimes dry, sweet and of pleasant flavor; quality "good," sometimes "very good.". Ripens in October. The tree is a strong, very upright grower, but there are other Pears much more desirable on the whole for our climate.

CLAPP'S FAVORITE.—In the hope of calling attention to this very promising Pear this description is given, and not because it has yet been proven to be valuable in our climate. It is claimed for it that it is a cross between the Bartlett and Flemish Beauty. The tree bears some resemblance to the latter in its upright spreading growth and dark reddish brown shoots, and if it should chance to prove as hardy it will certainly be a great acquisition. It is said also to be very productive, distributing its fruit evenly over the tree, and thus securing great uniformity in size.

The Pears are large, pale yellow, faintly marbled with red in the sun; **flesh** fine grained, sweet, juicy, buttery and rich; quality "very good." Ripe early in September or a little before the Bartlett.

DANA'S HOVEY.—This is also a new variety of great excellence, ranking next to the Seckel in flavor, and is probably the very highest flavored late December Pear in cultivation. It is small, resembling the Seckel in size and form, color pale yellow with considerable russet, flesh juicy, sugary, melting, with a rich aromatic flavor; quality "best." The tree is vigorous and retains its foliage late, **which is** usually an indication of hardihood and health. **This and the preceding variety are well worthy of the** careful attention **of our fruit raisers.**

DOCTOR REEDER.—A third new sort, which we feel persuaded **will prove to be hardy over** a very large part of the Dominion. The tree is vigorous, very healthy, and said to be a good bearer, the fruit is of medium size, yellowish russet; flesh fine grained, very sugary, buttery and highly perfumed. Ripe in November.

DOYENNE BOUSSOCK.—This tree is very vigorous, productive and healthy, and though not specially hardy, thrives well where the Bartlett succeeds. The fruit is above medium size, yellow, nearly covered **with nettings of** russet, with a brown-red cheek; **flesh** juicy, buttery, sweet, with a very agreeable aromatic flavor; **quality "very good."** Ripens early in October, and will probably prove valuable for market.

DOYENNE D'ETE.—This very small Pear, ripening about the first of August, is one of our most desirable, very early sorts. The tree is moderately vigorous, upright habit, and bears early and abundantly. Of its hardihood in our colder sections it is not possible to speak definitely as yet. The fruit is small, bright yellow, frequently handsomely shaded with red; flesh melting, juicy and sweet; quality "very good."

DOYENNE DU COMICE.—We have not yet seen the fruit of this variety, but entertain such high expectations concerning it that we are constrained to mention it here. It is described as a large Pear, of a greenish yellow color when gathered, becoming bright yellow when fully ripe, frequently shaded with crimson and fawn color in the sun; flesh melting, juicy, sweet, and rich; quality "very good" or "best." It is esteemed by those who are excellent judges as one of the best foreign Pears that has been introduced within the last twenty years. The tree is a fine grower and succeeds well on the quince. Ripe in November.

DUCHESSE D'ANGOULEME.—This fruit is beyond question of marvellous size, and some of the specimens that grace our autumn exhibitions are perfect leviathans, and usually the larger the fruit the better the quality. It is to be hoped that some benevolent minded individuals will continue to grow and exhibit these monstrous specimens just to keep us from forgetting to what size pears can be grown. But beyond this matter of exhibition the variety is not suited to the climate of this Dominion as a whole. Oftentimes, though blossoming abundantly, the trees do not set their fruit, and as a rule the summers are not long enough to give much flavor to that which may grow. In warmer latitudes it has been profitably grown for market, the large size and showy appearance giving it a ready sale at good prices.

EASTER BEURRE.—Those who wish to try a long-keeping winter pear cannot do better than to plant this variety, which will keep all winter and be just as good in the spring as it was in the fall. It is doubtless the best of its class, better, it is claimed, if grown on the quince than if grown on the pear stock. It is a fruit of large size, yellowish green with a brown cheek; flesh fine-grained, buttery, juicy, and as usually grown in this climate without much flavor. In very warm, dry, calcareous soils, and in favorable seasons, especially if in a sheltered position, it may be sometimes sweet and rich. The simple truth is that our climate is not suited to the production of late-keeping winter pears of high flavor, and when grown in a climate in which there is **sufficient** heat to impart a high flavor they cease to be late-keeping **pears**.

FLEMISH BEAUTY.—*Belle de Flanders.*—*Dundurn Castle.*—There is **no** pear that seems **to** be so entirely at home in this **Dominion as** this variety. Hardy, probably the most hardy of **all**, it will grow where any pear tree can endure the cold, and in every section it is spoken of with admiration. The tree is remarkably healthy in all soils and exposures, and bears abundant crops. The fruit is large, yellow, netted and marbled with russet, usually having a reddish brown cheek on the sunny side; flesh usually fine-grained, sometimes a little gritty at the core, juicy, melting, sweet and rich, with a **very pleasant and somewhat** aromatic flavor; quality "very good" **to** "**best.**" **Beyond** all question it is the most profitable **pear that can be widely** grown by us, and deserves a place in every collection. The only fault **it has is that** the fruit is so large and **heavy that it** is liable to be prematurely blown off by the high winds of autumn, and should, on that account, be planted in a place sheltered from the sweep of the winds which prevail at that season.

FONDANTE D'AUTOMNE.—*Belle Lucrative.*—This excellent variety can only be grown in perfection in those localities where the pear tree generally flourishes, the **tree** not being **suited to** severe climates, nor is the fruit full flavored if the tree be planted in cold damp soils, or where the summers are very moist and cool. But in all the better fruit-growing districts of Ontario and Nova Scotia it is grown to a high degree of perfection, save in exceptionally cold and **wet** seasons, when it is apt to fall below its full measure of excellence. The tree is a moderately vigorous grower, of erect habit, bearing early and abundantly. The fruit is of medium size; color a pale green or greenish yellow; flesh juicy, very sweet, melting and delicious; quality when in **perfection** "best." Ripe late in September. Some care needs to be taken in thinning out this variety, for it is very prone to overload, and an excessive crop injures the quality and flavor of **all** the fruit very considerably.

GOODALE.—Raised from seed by Mr. E. Goodale, of Maine. Enduring so well the severity of the winters there as to be esteemed "very hardy," and possessing also many good qualities, it is thought worthy of attention by Canadian growers, especially by those residing in those sections not altogether favorable to pear culture. The tree is a vigorous and thrifty grower, of upright habit, and said to be uniformly productive. We have never seen the fruit, but are assured by very competent judges that it is of large size, light yellow with a red cheek, with some markings of russet; flesh melting, sweet, juicy, a little gritty at the core, with a very pleasant musky perfume; quality "very good." It ripens in October.

HOWELL.—So far as this variety has been tried in Canada it seems to have given very good satisfaction. It is of recent introduction, and more time must elapse before its adaptability to our climate can be fully known. The tree is a free grower, of upright habit, and prone to run up without throwing out many branches, which defect may be remedied by timely summer pinching. It comes early into bearing and yields very large crops. The fruit is usually large, yellow with sometimes a reddish cheek; flesh juicy, melting, with a very agreeable vinous flavor; quality "very good." Ripens early in October.

JAMINETTE.—A very productive, early, winter Pear, of more than medium size; very juicy, sweet, and "good;" in favorable seasons, "very good." There is a healthy and hardy appearance to this tree which promises well for it in our climate; but it has not yet been very widely disseminated, and the hardihood of the tree in low temperatures has not yet been fully tested.

JOSEPHINE DE MALINES.—When the trees of this Pear have acquired some age, there is a very decided improvement in the flavor of the fruit, and it is then one of the most pleasantly flavored and agreeable of winter Pears. The fruit is of medium size, pale yellowish green; the flesh of a most delicate pink color, melting, juicy, sweet, with a very distinct, but delicate, quince flavor; quality "very good." It is in use during the month of

January. **The tree is** but a moderate grower, healthy and **productive, and while** young the fruit is very variable in **quality.** It is not probable that this variety will **be** worth **much in the colder parts of** the Dominion, more especially where the summers **are very** short or cool, for it requires considerable length of season **fully to** develop and flavor **the fruit.**

LAWRENCE.—This **variety is** worthy of trial wherever the Pear can be grown. The **tree is** of the more hardy class, very healthy, a moderate **grower, and** early and abundant cropper. The fruit is of medium **size,** color lemon yellow when **ripe,** with frequent traces of russet; the flesh is melting, juicy, **sweet, with** a very agreeable **aromatic** flavor; **quality almost " best." Ripe** in December.

LOUISE BONNE DE JERSEY.—**Such is the enormous productiveness of this Pear, and the uniform good** size and handsome appearance **of the fruit, that it has become** exceedingly popular. The tree **is healthy, a** very vigorous upright grower, and succeeds admirably when worked on the Quince stock. The fruit is better when grown on the Quince than on the Pear stock. It is of large size when well grown, but when the tree is overloaded, which is a very common occurrence, it is only of medium size. The color is a light or yellowish green on the shaded side, **dark brownish red** on the other; flesh **melting, very juicy, vinous, and in** the best specimens of **a rich pleasant flavor; quality rarely** above **"good."** Ripe late in September and **first of October.**

MANNING'S ELIZABETH.—**A small** August Pear of great excellence, **very sweet, sprightly, with** a fine aromatic flavor. The color **is bright yellow** with a very handsome bright red cheek; and **the** flesh is melting, juicy and delicious; quality "best." The tree is a moderate grower and very productive. It has not yet been sufficiently distributed throughout the Dominion to speak of its hardihood in our colder sections, but it can probably **be** grown without any difficulty where the Bartlett succeeds. **Ripe** in the latter end of August.

OSBAND'S SUMMER.—This variety has been very generally

grown by cultivators of the Pear, and has proved to be tolerably hardy as regards our climate, but quite susceptible to the disease known as fire blight. Indeed our own experience with it has been very discouraging, for as soon as the trees come into bearing they all go with this disease, and although we have made repeated trials, there is not now a bearing tree left.

The tree has an upright habit, is moderately vigorous, comes soon into bearing and yields abundantly. The fruit is small, clear yellow with a ruddy warm cheek, juicy, sugary, rich, with a pleasant perfume; quality "very good." Ripe about the middle of August.

SECKEL.—*Seckle.*—This is probably the highest flavored Pear in the world, and has become a standard of excellence by which the quality of other Pears is measured. The tree also is one of the most healthy, adapting itself to a very great variety of soils and climates, and remarkably exempt from diseases of every description, even escaping almost entirely the mysterious fire blight. It is also one of the more hardy sorts, capable of sustaining the rigor of a Canadian winter with almost the same endurance as the Flemish Beauty. It is also an abundant bearer, and although a slow grower, is erect in form, and makes a neat, compact head.

The fruit is small, of a yellowish cinnamon russet, with a ruddy brown cheek; flesh melting, very juicy, buttery, with an exceedingly rich spicy flavor, and very pleasant perfume; quality "best." Ripe in October.

It is an American variety, supposed to have originated on the farm of a Mr. Seckel, near the city of Philadelphia.

SHELDON.—After growing this variety for some time we are forced to the conclusion that it is of very variable quality, and that it will succeed well only on strong, well drained soils, abounding in lime. Possibly as the tree acquires age the fruit may be better and less variable, but in our experience the fire blight saves it from all the burdens of age. When well developed the fruit is above medium size, of a greenish yellow russet color, very juicy, with a rich vinous flavor; quality "very good;" but in our experience often very poor.

TYSON.—A medium sized Pear of great excellence and well worthy of trial. It is not probable that the tree is any more hardy than the Bartlett. It is an upright grower, thrifty and healthy, does not bear fruit very young, but bears large crops when it has reached maturity. The fruit is hardly of medium size, color deep yellow with a very handsome crimson cheek; flesh melting, juicy, very sweet, with a very agreeable aromatic flavor; quality almost "best." The fruit does not drop readily from the tree, but will often hang until it decays on the branches. It ripens early in September.

URBANISTE.—*Beurré Picquery.*—This variety has not been as generally planted as its merits deserve, and it is as yet impossible to speak confidently of its ability to endure a cold climate, yet such is the very healthy habit of the tree that we expect it will be found among the more hardy sorts. It does not come very early into bearing, but when it has reached its fruiting age yields large crops. The fruit is above medium size, of a pale yellow color; the flesh very melting, juicy, rich and buttery, and very pleasantly and delicately perfumed; quality "very good." It ripens in October and November.

VICAR OF WINKFIELD.—*Le Curé. Monsieur le Curé.*—We cannot advise the planting of this variety in our climate. After many years of trial and a not very limited opportunity of testing it as grown in various places, we are compelled to say that, in our judgment, it is an exceedingly poor Pear for one that has attained to so great celebrity. True, the tree is productive, and the fruit is uniformly fair and handsome, and that is about all that can usually be said in its favor. Once, and only once in our life, we tasted a Vicar that was really good, but happening another year to intimate to the gentleman who exhibited that specimen that it would be agreeable to see some more samples of like quality, he blandly replied that such specimens were produced only once in a decade. We therefore commend it to those whose patience can feed on quantity and wait for quality. It ripens in December and January.

WASHINGTON.—This pretty pear has given us such entire satisfaction that we feel sure lovers of good fruit will be gratified by having it brought to their attention. It can hardly be hoped that it will be extremely hardy, for it originated in the State of Delaware; but it will no doubt thrive well where most other sorts succeed.

The fruit is barely of medium size; the color a clear yellow, sprinkled nearly all over with small red dots, and which are more particularly abundant on the sunny side. The flesh is very juicy, sweet, melting, and of a very agreeable flavor; quality "very good." Ripe about the middle of September.

WHITE DOYENNE.—*Virgalieu.*—*St. Michael.*—*Butter Pear.* It is more than two hundred years since this variety came into cultivation, and it is worthy of the high estimation in which it has so long been held. It is a vigorous, upright grower, and ranks among our more hardy sorts, though not capable of enduring as severe cold as the Flemish Beauty. The fruit is full medium size, pale yellow when ripe, and sometimes has a bright red cheek on the side next the sun; the flesh is fine grained, buttery, with a high, rich, and delicious flavor; quality "best." Ripe in October, sometimes continuing into November. In Western New York the fruit has become so subject to spotting and cracking that the tree is much less cultivated than formerly. It may be that this difficulty will manifest itself among us; if so, there seems to be no alternative but to fall back upon other choice sorts of the same season, not subject to this affection.

WINTER NELIS.—A very healthy kind, and one of the more hardy class, which may be planted with confidence. The tree has a somewhat slender habit of growth, but it bears good crops. The fruit is of medium size, a good deal russeted, yellowish at maturity; flesh fine grained, buttery, juicy, sweet, with a pleasant aromatic flavor; quality "best." Ripe latter part of December, and always ripens well.

The following varieties originated in Nova Scotia, and are much esteemed by fruit growers acquainted with their merits. The descriptions have been kindly furnished by R. W. Starr, Esq. :

MARIA.—This fruit was first brought into notice by the late Hon. C. R. Prescott, and named by him in honor of his wife. It originated in the garden of the late —— Curran, Esq., of Windsor. Tree is hardy, small; young wood feeble, light colored. Fruit is medium in size, round, yellow, fine grained, buttery, rich; ripens ten to fourteen days earlier than the Bartlett; quality very good.

BURBIDGE.—One of the oldest native pears we have. The original tree is still standing on the farm of the late Col. Burbidge, near Port Williams, and though nearly a century old, is still vigorous. Tree large, upright; young wood stout and dark. Fruit small to medium, Bergamot shaped, skin greenish yellow, bronzed in the sun, sweet, gritty, but rich and high flavored; ripens a few days earlier than the Bartlett; tree is hardy and prolific.

LORD CORNWALLIS.—This was grown and named by the late Benjamin Woodworth, Esq., of Cornwallis. Tree medium sized, rather spreading; young wood greyish. Fruit large and handsome, pyriform, as brilliantly colored as Frederic of Wurtemburg, but, like it, rather variable; quality good; season October.

SUTTON'S GREAT BRITAIN.—A seedling from the Bartlett, by Wm. Sutton, of Cornwallis. The tree is vigorous and hardy; young wood very stout, short jointed, and dark. Fruit large to very large, pyriform, slightly bronzed or russeted in patches, and sometimes with a blush in the sun. Flesh is coarse grained, juicy, good. A good market fruit, ripening ten days after the Bartlett. The tree is a great bearer.

THE PLUM.

This fine fruit can be grown in much colder parts of the country than the Cherry, the tree being much hardier than any of the Heart and Bigarreau class. Wild Plums are found growing in all parts of the Dominion, and may by judicious cross-fertilization become the foundation of a very hardy and valuable race of Plums.

The Prunes of commerce are dried Plums, by no means as highly flavored as those which every Canadian housekeeper may provide by drying the Plums grown in our own fruit gardens.

The tree will grow in almost every soil, but it is most at home and yields its best and heaviest crops in heavy, clay loams. In sandy soils it is more subject to the curculio insect, for the reason that this insect when in the grub state can more readily penetrate into the ground to undergo its transformations into the beetle state. Common salt has been found to be an excellent fertilizer for this tree, promoting its health and luxuriance. Half a peck strewn, during the month of April, on the ground under each bearing tree will be enough. The black knot has been found to be a very troublesome disease, affecting the branches of the Plum tree, and if left alone in a few years causing the death of the tree. This disease is most prevalent upon trees growing in land that is imperfectly drained, and attacks the damson Plums in preference to all other varieties. Unfortunately, it is not confined to the damsons, but spreads first to the other purple sorts, and then, though in a less degree, to the yellow varieties. It is first seen as a soft swelling of the bark, which continues to increase in size until the outer cuticle of the bark is burst and the swelling assumes a rough, uneven surface. By degrees this becomes black and hard, rent with fissures, and quite dry. The cause of this disease is not yet known, and the best cure, besides growing the tree in a thoroughly drained soil, is persistent amputation and burning of these excrescences. Top-dressing the soil with wood **ashes**, and washing the bodies of the trees **with** a weak lye has been recommended as a remedy for the black knot, and will **no doubt** be found to be promotive of the health of the tree, even if **it do** not wholly prevent the growth of these unsightly excrescences. They **can, however, be** kept in complete subjection by planting **on** ground **where** no water stands in the subsoil, and by cutting off and burning the knots regularly as often as once a year. It **is** stated by F. R. Elliot, of Ohio, who is high authority in **fruit matters**, that if **the** tree **be** watered with a solution of copperas made by dissolving it at the rate of one ounce in two gallons of water the knots **will** disappear.

The Plum can be propagated both by **grafting and** budding. It is sometimes **worked on** the Peach **stock**, but such trees are worthless **in our climate.** The trees may be planted about sixteen feet apart, and headed low.

BAVAY'S GREEN GAGE.—*Reine Claude de Bavay.*—An excellent **late variety, ripening** in October, too late for some of the **colder sections, yet** ripening well in the favorable fruit districts of Nova Scotia and Ontario. The tree is a vigorous grower, and most abundantly productive. The fruit is of large size, greenish yellow, with splashes of deeper green; flesh yellow, sugary, rich and juicy; quality "best."

BRADSHAW.—*Blue Imperial.*—A very **large and showy fruit, of a** reddish purple **color, and** very pleasant flavor, though not of the highest **quality. The flesh is** a little coarse, yellow, juicy, adhering **a little to the stone;** quality "good." Ripe latter part **of August. The tree is** vigorous, of upright habit, and bears good crops.

COE'S GOLDEN DROP.—This is a very popular variety, but it does not ripen well in the northern parts of the country, except the season be warm and continue late. It is of large size, light yellow, with red dots on the sunny side; flesh **yellow,** firm, adheres to the stone, sweet, rich and delicious; ripe end of September. The tree is only a moderate grower, but quite productive.

DENNISTON'S SUPERB.—This originated near Albany, in the State of New York, and has considerable resemblance to the Green Gage, being of the "best" quality, but considerably larger than that old favorite sort. The tree is a much better grower than the Green Gage, and very productive. The fruit is round, medium size, pale yellowish green, not very juicy, but rich and of an excellent vinous flavor. Ripe the latter part of August.

DUANE'S PURPLE.—The tree is very vigorous and healthy, the fruit very large, reddish purple, covered with bloom, juicy, with a pleasant, not very sweet, but sprightly flavor; quality "good." Ripe about the middle of August.

GENERAL HAND.—The very large size and handsome appearance of this plum have caused it to be much sought after. The tree is vigorous, healthy and productive; the fruit of a deep golden yellow, not very juicy, but sweet and "good." It ripens in September.

GREEN GAGE.—*Reine Claude.*—In point of flavor this variety holds the first rank, and is more frequently asked for and less frequently planted than any other kind. Unfortunately, the tree is a most miserably slow grower, and makes a spreading, dwarfish tree; and nurserymen cultivate it very sparingly, or not at all, on account of its slow growing, spreading habit. The fruit is small, round, yellowish green; flesh pale green, juicy, and of a very sprightly, luscious flavor; quality "best." Ripe late in August.

IMPERIAL GAGE.—*Prince's Imperial Gage.*—This is a seedling from the Green gage, and is very nearly equal in flavor to its parent, and the tree is much more vigorous, growing freely and forming an erect, handsome tree, which is healthy and productive. The fruit is full medium size, pale green with a yellow tinge, and covered with an abundant white bloom. The flesh is juicy, rich, and of excellent flavor; quality "best." Ripe during the first half of September.

JEFFERSON.—Another first-class Plum, ranking in quality with the Green Gage, but very much larger and more showy.

The tree is but a moderate grower, though better in this respect than the Green Gage, and bears good and regular crops. The fruit is of large size, of a golden yellow color, with a purplish cheek; flesh orange color, very rich, juicy, and exceedingly high flavored. Ripe early in September.

LAWRENCE'S FAVORITE.—Also a seedling from the Green Gage and partaking very fully of the good qualities of the parent, while it is much larger in size, and the tree upright in habit and tolerably thrifty. The fruit is above medium size, in color a yellowish green; flesh greenish, juicy, very rich, with a remarkably pleasant vinous and delicious flavor; quality "best." Ripe about the end of August.

LOMBARD.—*Bleeker's Scarlet.*—*Beekman's Scarlet.*—This is an exceedingly productive sort, and the tree one of the most vigorous, healthy and hardy. The fruit is of medium size, red, with yellow flesh, which is juicy, sweet, with a very agreeable, pleasant flavor; quality "good." Ripe early in September.

McLAUGHLIN.—As this variety originated in Maine, and is an exceedingly healthy and hardy variety there, it will doubtless be found to be among the most desirable for our latitude. The fruit is large, yellow handsomely marbled with red, and covered with a light bloom; flesh yellow, juicy, sweet, and exceedingly luscious; quality "best." Ripe first of September.

POND'S SEEDLING.—*Fonthill.*—An English variety of great size and beauty. The tree is very vigorous and bears abundant crops. Fruit very large, bright red on a yellow ground; flesh yellow, juicy and sweet; quality "good." Ripe latter part of September.

PRINCE ENGLEBERT.—This promises to be a valuable variety, but has not yet been very generally disseminated. The tree is vigorous and exceedingly productive, the fruit large, deep purple covered with a blue bloom; flesh juicy, sweet and excellent; quality "very good." Ripe early in September.

PRINCE'S YELLOW GAGE.—This variety has been found to be very generally hardy and exceedingly productive, while the tree makes a vigorous, upright growth. Fruit of medium size, **deep yellow**, with an abundant bloom; flesh yellow, sweet and rich; quality "very good." Ripens early in August.

SHARP'S EMPEROR.—*Victoria.*—An exceedingly showy and popular variety. The tree is vigorous, and remarkable for its large, handsome foliage and great productiveness. The fruit is large, light purple in the sun, light yellow in the shade; flesh yellow, a little coarse grained, with a pleasant, somewhat vinous flavor; quality "good." Ripe the latter part of September.

SMITH'S ORLEANS.—Tree vigorous and productive; fruit large, frequently very large, reddish purple, juicy, rich and vinous; quality "very good." Has been very widely disseminated throughout Canada, and is a deservedly popular variety. Ripens about the first of September.

WASHINGTON.—This has been long known and very much esteemed by all growers of the Plum. It was first brought to notice by Mr. Bolmer, of New York City, in 1818, hence it is often known as Bolmer's Washington. The tree is vigorous, a good bearer, and forms a handsome rounded head, with conspicuous, large, glossy leaves. The fruit is very large, greenish yellow, very sweet and luscious; quality "very good." Ripe last of August.

YELLOW EGG.—This is another well-known and widely disseminated variety, very highly esteemed as a cooking plum. It is very large, yellow, somewhat coarse grained, sweet, with an agreeable mingling of acid. The tree is vigorous and productive.

THE QUINCE.

The successful cultivation of this fruit is confined within a small portion of the Dominion, extending but little beyond the limits of peach culture.

It thrives best in clayey loams that are well drained, though it can be grown upon any good, fertile soil, free from superfluous moisture. Being subject, in some degree, to a disease resembling, if not identical with, the fire-blight of the Pear, it should not be supplied with **fresh** and stimulating manures. Barnyard manure that has been composted with salt, at the rate of half **a bushel of salt to** every wagon-load of **manure**, and become thoroughly decomposed, makes an excellent fertilizer for the Quince, con**ducing** much to the health and fruitfulness of the tree, and size **and** flavor of the fruit.

The Quince may be planted ten feet apart each way. The pruning consists in thinning out the over-crowded branches, so as to give free circulation of air and light, and in cutting back the twigs that have borne fruit, to a good, strong bud, so as to produce new fruit spurs. It is best propagated by **layering in** this climate, though it can be grown from **cuttings** of the new growth taken off about a foot long and planted ten inches deep. The **month of September is the best time** for doing this, **and** where **there is danger of the** cuttings being thrown out by the **frost, they** should be covered with straw, leaves, or evergreen **branches on the** approach of winter.

ORANGE QUINCE.—This is the best variety for general cultivation. The fruit is large, with a smooth, rich golden yellow skin; ripening about the end of October. When well grown it commands a ready sale in all our city markets. It needs to be gathered and handled carefully; the least rough usage mars its beauty, and even slight bruises leave very unsightly discolorations.

PORTUGAL QUINCE.—This is such a shy bearer that it is only vexatious to plant it, though the fruit is excellent, being of milder flavor and more beautiful color when cooked than any other.

REA'S SEEDLING. — *Rea's Mammoth.* — This is somewhat larger than the Orange Quince, though after some years' trial it does not continue to be as much larger as it at first promised. In all other respects, color, form and cooking qualities, it does not vary materially from the Orange. It is thrifty, healthy, and tolerably productive.

ANGIER.—The fruit of this variety proves to be more valuable than had been supposed. It is used as a stock, on account of its thrifty growth, upon which to bud the Pear for the **purpose of making dwarf trees.** It is found to bear quite abundantly, **and** the fruit keeps longer than the Orange Quince, though **it is firmer fleshed and more acid.**

HARDY GRAPES.

Within a few years the cultivation **of hardy Grapes** has received a great deal of attention, and many good **varieties** have been added to the list, **some of them ripening much** earlier than the old Isabella and Catawba, **which once comprised our entire stock of varieties,** and **therefore better suited to our climate.** It is very probable that many more sorts will **be brought to the** attention of cultivators before another quarter of a century shall have passed; and it is to be expected that the judicious labors of the several Canadian hybridizers, who have made the vine a **prominent subject of** their operations, will be rewarded by the **production of some** new varieties which are eminently adapted to **our climate.**

One of **the first questions that occupies the** attention **of the** planter is **that of suitable soil.** From considerable observation and some experience in planting **the vine on various soils, we** conclude that it will thrive well **and bear abundantly** on sandy, gravelly, or clay soils, provided that **there be** no stagnant water **in the soil.** As a rule, also, the **vine** flourishes **best in soils** abounding in limestone, and where the surface is rolling, especially **on the** sides of hills and gentle slopes. Yet the **vine** will thrive **and bear abundantly on** a level **surface, and in any** soil that is thoroughly drained. As the cultivation of the **Grape** is extended and varieties are multiplied, it will doubtless be found that in certain localities the Grapes will acquire **peculiar** qualities and flavors, and that some varieties are better adapted to certain soils and localities than **others.** Already **we** see something of this; **but** we are not yet sufficiently advanced in vine-culture to be **able, save in** a very few instances, to point out these peculiarities.

Meanwhile we **may** plant our Grape vines on any soil that is suitable for **an apple** orchard with every expectation **of success.** In preparing **the** ground for planting, the first and most essential point is **to secure** complete and perfect drainage. This having **been secured,** it should be deeply and thoroughly tilled, as deeply **and thoroughly** as any land should be to yield a good crop of **Indian corn;** and when this has been done, it will be in a suitable condition for the reception of Grape vines. The deep trenching and very heavy manuring **often** advised is not only quite unnecessary, but positively injurious. The vine may seem to grow most vigorously and to bear fine fruit, but the tendency is to an unnatural growth, **of** a spongy texture, **less able** to resist the sudden changes and great extremes of temperature **incident to** our climate, resulting at last in disease and premature decay.

The **distances apart at which Grape vines should be planted** have **been variously stated by** different writers; but a more extended experience in the cultivation of our varieties in our soils **and** climate, has brought the most thoughtful cultivators to **the** conclusion that most of our vines should be planted not less than twelve feet apart each way. This is about the distance that present experience suggests as requisite for the most healthy development and most economical and profitable **culture of** the **Grape.** Parties interested in selling **a** large number of vines may continue to **recommend closer planting;** but experience is teaching us, and a sound **judgment, based** upon a knowledge of our climate **and of the habits of our** varieties of the vine, indicates that **this distance is the one** best adapted to our circumstances.

Of the **proper manner of** planting, it is hardly needed that anything should be added to what has been said on the subject of planting in general. The soil having been thoroughly pulverised by previous tillage, it remains only to make a shallow excavation of sufficient diameter to admit of the roots being all carefully spread out and extended their entire length, and then covered with fine soil to the depth **of** three or four inches, then gently pressed down with the foot. After the planting has been done in this manner, the surface should be covered, as far as the roots extend, with some sort of mulch, such as straw, leaves, or coarse litter. Planting may be done either in the fall or spring, at any time after the leaves fall in autumn, and before the buds burst in the spring, and when the soil is in a condition to be worked. The success of the operation depends more upon the care of the planter in the selection of suitable ground and its preparation, and in the planting of the vine, than on the season of the year when it is performed. When the vine is planted it should be cut back to two buds, and if the planting be done in the fall the mulching should be allowed to cover the vine during the winter, but removed just as the buds are swelling in spring, sufficiently to admit of their expanding without hindrance.

When the young vines begin to grow, all the shoots but one, usually all but the one nearest the ground, should be rubbed off. If the one nearest the ground seems to be feeble, or from any cause unsuitable, then the next shoot that is suitable should be retained, and all the others rubbed off. A small stake—a strip of lath will answer very well for a season or two—should be thrust into the ground at each plant, and the vine carefully tied to it as it grows during the summer. Beyond this, the only care required is to cultivate the ground lightly around the vines, not suffering any weeds to grow among them, and giving the roots every encouragement to grow and extend themselves, and allowing the canes to grow without any other restraint than merely tying them to the stake. This will complete the first season's growth.

It has been very generally recommended to prune the grape in the fall, but every year's experience confirms the opinion that in our climate it is on the whole much better to prune in the spring. In some places and seasons the weather will be such that pruning can be done in March, while in others it may be impossible to do it before April. But pruning the vine is not to be regulated by the day of the month. As soon as the weather has become **mild** enough to admit of the work being **comfortably done, it** will be the proper **time to** set about the pruning. The only objection that has been urged against pruning the grape **in the spring** is that the vines weep, or, **as some** say, bleed at **the cut, and** that this weeping is injurious. If pruned early, **as soon as** the weather will admit, this weeping will not **be** excessive, **and so** far from being injurious, is positively beneficial, serving to **check** the very rampant **wood** growth so common to most of our American varieties.

In the spring, then, of the second year the **cane** should be cut back to two **or** three eyes, and **as soon as the shoots** have fairly started, **two of the strongest should be selected, and** all the others rubbed off. **As the growing shoots** lengthen **they should be tied to the stake, and the** vines treated precisely **as in the preceding summer. During this summer preparations should be made for** permanently staking and trellising the vineyard. **This will involve** the necessity of deciding upon the method of training **to be pursued.** There are many methods practised, but **it is** not necessary that they should be all described. We shall content ourselves with two modes of training, either of which has been found to answer well in this climate, **and may be** known as the upright **and** the horizontal. **The upright trellis is** made in the usual form, by planting **posts along the row of** vines **and** stretching upon them three horizontal wires. The best wire is galvanized iron **wire, using number** ten size for the lowest one, and number **twelve for the** middle **and upper.** Each pound of **number ten will extend** twenty feet in length, and number twelve **will reach thirty-three feet.** Cedar, oak, or chestnut **will make good** posts, and the **two** posts at the ends of the trellis **will** require bracing to resist the strain of the wires. Some plant the end post very deep and in an oblique position, the top leaning from the row, so that the position of the post shall be a sufficient **brace.** Each vine having been pruned to form two canes, these **canes are** stretched horizontally along the lowest wire and securely **fastened there.** These **canes will** be the permanent arms of the vine, and will be allowed to extend until those of one vine nearly meet those of its neighbor, and then stopped. In the spring of the third year the buds on these now horizontal canes will start into growth, and those will be selected for training upon the trellis which are from eight to twelve inches apart, and all the rest carefully rubbed off. As the shoots grow they will be fastened in an upright position to the trellis. When they have made a growth of two feet in length, it is advisable to check them by pinching off the point of the shoot. This is done in order to check the upward flow of the sap, and cause the buds that are forming in the axils of the leaves to be more fully developed. The terminal bud, and sometimes more than one, will soon break, and continue their upward growth until they reach the top of the trellis, where they may be again pinched off, care being taken not to allow one cane to become longer than the others and so absorb to itself an undue amount of sap. If the vine be quite vigorous, some bunches of fruit will be developed this season at the base of these upright shoots, and one or two may be allowed to

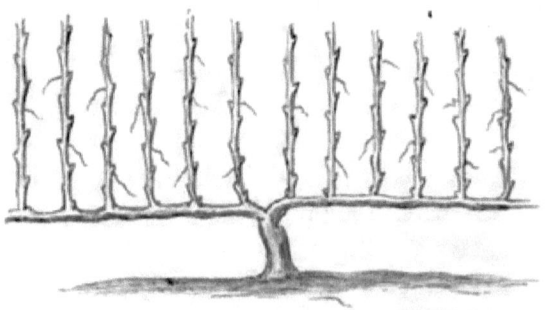

Fig. 44.

remain and ripen, regulating the quantity according to the strength of the vine, taking care not to allow too much fruit to remain while the vine is young, as that would prove a serious injury to the future health and fruitfulness of the vine. During the summer, the lateral or side shoots that may start from these upright canes are stopped or pinched back, to prevent them from extending too far. In the autumn of this year, after the leaves have fallen, the vine will have the appearance shown in Figure 44.

In the spring of the fourth year, each of these upright canes may be cut back to two eyes, and two canes be allowed to grow. These may now each bear two or three bunches of grapes, according to the strength of the vine, and be treated in all respects as the upright canes were during the last summer. In the autumn of the fourth year the vine will have the appearance shown in Figure 45.

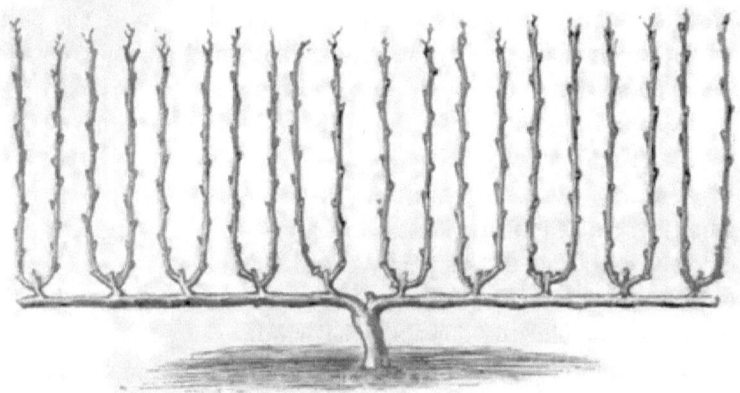

Fig. 45.

In the spring of the fifth and all subsequent years the upper of the two canes should be cut away entirely, and the lower cane shortened in to two eyes, which may be allowed to grow and form two canes as before, and each cane be allowed to bear three clusters of grapes. This completes the system, and the further pruning consists in annually cutting off the upper one of the two canes and shortening the lower cane to two eyes.

The HORIZONTAL MODE of training the vine, or, as it is sometimes called, the arbor system, consists in training the vine at first upright to the desired height, and then allowing it to run horizontally. There is no doubt this conforms more nearly to the natural habit of the vine, which grows perpendicularly for a time, and **until** it reaches a suitable support, when it stretches away in a horizontal direction, covering everything within its reach.

In preparing the trellis **for this system** of training, it is not **usual** to insert the posts in the ground **at all,** but merely to place **them** on the surface, with a flat stone under the foot. These **posts are usually made** seven feet in length, **placed at a** distance of **six** feet apart, and horizontal bars nailed upon **the top,** reaching **along the posts in two** directions, at right **angles to each other, and then braces are nailed from the posts to the horizontal bars. In this way a framework is formed upon the top of the posts,** which **keeps them in an upright position, and strips are nailed** across upon these horizontal bars so as to form a sufficient support for the vines. In this way the entire weight of the trellis, and of the vines growing upon it, rests upon the top of the posts, and being at an elevation of seven feet from the surface of the ground, **admits of cultivation underneath in every** direction, and dispenses **entirely with the use of wires. Besides,** there is no rotting off **of posts, no strain upon post or nail, no heaving out of place by the frost, nor blowing down by the wind.**

The vines are trained during the summer of the second year to the top of this trellis, by tying them to the temporary stakes planted near them; and when they reach the horizontal part, are **trained along the horizontal bars. If the vines are** healthy and **vigorous, they** will make considerable growth along the horizontal **bars during this summer, and they are** allowed to make all the **growth they will. It will be borne in** mind **that** up to the **present time the treatment of the vine has** been the same as that already described; **during the first year it was trained** as a single cane, in the spring of the second **year it was cut** back to two **eyes and two canes allowed to grow, and these** trained up to **and** on to the **horizontal trellis.**

In the spring of the third **year each of these** two canes is cut **back to about a foot below the horizontal** trellis, **and four canes** are led **up on to the trellis, two** from each cane. These four canes as they extend in length are fastened to the horizontal bars, and so separated as to give sufficient room to each. These growing **canes are** not stopped **at all or pinched back, nor are the laterals** that may grow pinched in, **for as the vine is now growing in a** horizontal position **there is no danger of any undue** determination of the sap to the extremities **of** the shoots, thereby robbing the lower buds of their due share of nourishment. Therefore in this horizontal method of training all summer pinching of the ends of **shoots** and of laterals is dispensed with, and all that is required **is to** keep down all sprouts **that** may come up from the roots, and to rub off the buds that start **out** along the main upright stem.

In the spring of the fourth, **and of all subsequent years, the vines will** be pruned by shortening in **the previous summer's growth to four, five, or** six buds according to **the strength of the vine and the amount of fruit it may be** safely allowed to bear; and as the vines increase in age and size the old wood can be cut **out** and replaced by new wood. The fruit will hang down from the trellis overhead, and be completely protected by the foliage growing above, while the leaves will be fully exposed to the full action of the light, the air and the **dews. At night** the heat radiated from the earth is not lost by being dissipated in the air, but is retained by the canopy of leaves overhead, **thereby** contributing to the perfection and **maturation of the fruit.**

We do not hesitate to **say that** for the more rampant growing **varieties, such as** the Clinton, Isabella, and others of like habit, **we are fully persuaded** that the horizontal trellis is much better than any other system of training the vine. These vines do not bear to be dwarfed **by** constant severe cutting and pinching. **The** results of this savage style of pruning have uniformly been, after a few years of struggling with the pruning knife, diseased vines, mildew and rot, resulting in loss of crop and frequently the death of the vines. It is only while the vines are young that they bear well; consequently it has been recommended to keep the vineyard always young by constant renewing of the vines, by layering the branches every few years, and raising new vines, and rooting out the old ones. But this is all wrong. The vine is naturally long-lived. In the Province of Ontario it has grown to measure four feet in circumference, and that system of culture must be bad that kills the vines off every eight or ten years.

The following varieties of grapes are worthy of attention; some of them have been already extensively tried and their reputation well established; others require more extended experiment before their exact worth will be fully ascertained.

ADIRONDAC.—This is one of the newer sorts, but has been fruited in the milder parts of Ontario for some years, and generally given good satisfaction. It ripens early, usually a few days before the Hartford Prolific, and will hang on the vine retaining its quality until the frosts cut the foliage. In size of bunch and berry it closely resembles the Isabella, and like it is black when ripe. The flesh is soft and breaking, with a sweet and agreeable flavor. The vine is not as vigorous a grower as the Isabella, and will probably bear closer planting.

AGAWAM—*Rogers' No. 15.*—In point of flavor we esteem this variety among the most desirable of Mr. Rogers' Hybrid Grapes. There is just enough of the native wild grape flavor remaining to give it a pleasant Muscat taste, while the flesh is tender and juicy. The bunch varies a good deal in size, which is a serious failing, but it bears large crops. The vine is very hardy and a rampant grower. Some complaint has been made of rotting of the fruit, and mildew of the vine, probably largely owing to the vicious system of pruning which has been practised— that of attempting to confine its vigorous habit within too small a space. The color of the berries is red.

ALVEY.—The berry of this variety is so small that it will never be popular as a table grape. The bunches are of good size, long, and well shouldered, and the berries, which are black when ripe, have a very pleasant, refreshing, vinous flavor. It is thought that it will prove to be valuable as a wine grape. It has not been sufficiently disseminated in the Dominion to test its hardihood.

AUTUCHON. — *Arnold's No. 5.* — This was raised by Mr. Charles Arnold, of Paris, Ontario, from seed of the Clinton, fertilized with the Golden Chasselas. The bunches are long, and sometimes shouldered, the berries hardly medium size, greenish yellow, resembling in flavor the White Chasselas. It is doubtful whether this variety is sufficiently hardy to endure the cold in the more severe parts of the country. It ripens about the same time as the Delaware.

BARRY—*Rogers' No. 43.*—The bunches of this variety are not very long, but broad and compact; berries large, round, and black, with a tender flesh, juicy and sweet; ripening about the same time as the Concord. It seems to be very hardy, and able to withstand severe cold.

BRANT—*Arnold's No. 8.*—Another of Mr. Arnold's seedlings, raised from seed of the Clinton, fertilized with the Black St. Peter's. The vine is a strong grower, healthy, and promises to be quite hardy. The bunch is of medium size, the berries small, black, free from pulp, very juicy, sweet, with a rich, aromatic flavor. It colors early, but improves in quality by being allowed to hang on the vines until frost. The wood ripens early.

CANADA—*Arnold's No. 16.*—Also from the Clinton, fertilized with Black St. Peter's. A very vigorous grower, and giving good promise of being hardy. The bunches are about the size of well grown Clintons, the berries somewhat larger, black, juicy, with a very agreeable, sprightly flavor, the best, in point of flavor, of all his seedlings. Ripe with the Concord.

CATAWBA.—This old and well-known variety cannot be grown in perfection save in a few favored localities. It requires a longer season, with a greater total of heat than our summers generally give us, to develop the full flavor and richness of this grape. Along the north shore of lake Erie it is oftener ripened than in any other part of Canada.

CLINTON.—One of our most hardy varieties, which has been very largely planted as a wine Grape. The vine is very vigorous, healthy and productive; the bunch of medium size, shouldered, **compact**; berries below medium size, black, **juicy**, with a brisk, somewhat acid, **vinous flavor**. The acidity is much ameliorated by allowing the **Grapes** to hang on the vine until after severe frosts. The Grapes **keep** well, and are very pleasant and refreshing in January and February. It is not much used as a table Grape on account of its acidity, **but is much** esteemed for cooking and canning.

CONCORD.—A very popular variety, **which** succeeds well in most of the Grape region of the Dominion. The vine is very healthy, moderately vigorous and exceedingly productive. Bunch of good size, compact and well shouldered; berries large, round and black, juicy and sweet, with considerable pulpiness. The skin is thin, and on that account the Grape needs to be handled with care in sending to market. It ripens fully ten days before the Isabella, and is more hardy.

CORNUCOPIA.—*Arnold's No. 2.*—Another product of Black St. Peter's upon the Clinton, raised by Mr. Arnold, of Paris, Ontario, and esteemed by him as one of the most healthy and productive varieties in cultivation. The bunch is large, shouldered and very compact; berries of medium size, black, juicy, without pulpiness, with a brisk, vinous flavor. Ripe with the Concord.

CREVELING.—*Laura Beverly.*—One of the most delightfully flavored early Grapes, ripening about the same time as the Hartford Prolific, but much superior in quality. There is no doubt but that it is identical with the Laura Beverly, which name it received from the Rev. Canon Dixon, of Port Dalhousie, who supposed for some time that his vine was an accidental seedling, and had not seen or even heard of the Creveling at the time he gave it the name of Laura Beverly. If Mr. Dixon's vine be a seedling, it is too exactly like the Creveling to warrant its cultivation as a distinct variety. They both have the bad habit of setting the berries imperfectly, so that the bunch is often not half filled. Could this defect be remedied, the variety would be worthy of all commendation. When well filled, the bunch is large, well shouldered, and tolerably compact; berries of medium size, black;

flesh tender, with scarcely any pulpiness, sweet, juicy, rich and fine flavored. The vine seems to be as hardy as the Concord, and moderately productive.

CROTON.—Not having fruited this variety, we can give only the testimony of others concerning it; but the fact that it ripens about the same time as the Hartford Prolific, makes it worthy of attention by Canadian cultivators, on account of its earliness. The vine is said to be hardy and vigorous; the bunches medium in size and shouldered; berries below medium, light greenish yellow, juicy, sweet and rich.

DELAWARE.—This is the best hardy grape, all things considered, that we have yet seen. It thrives best in sandy or gravelly loam, not so well in stiff clay. The vine is a good grower, not coarse, and requires a rich soil, that is thoroughly drained, to produce its finest samples of fruit. It is remarkably healthy, and sufficiently hardy to endure quite severe winters. When well cared for, it is exceedingly productive, and the bunches need thinning out lest it be too heavily burdened with fruit. Bunch is small, shouldered, compact; berries small, light red, and sweet, with a very pleasant, aromatic, vinous flavor. Ripe before the Concord, and very nearly as early as the Hartford Prolific. Is used both for the table and wine.

DIANA.—Possessed of many good qualities, it nevertheless ripens but little earlier than the Catawba, and therefore is not adapted to general cultivation in this Dominion. It thrives best on not very rich, clayey loam, well drained and warm, and abounding in limestone.

EUMELAN.—A hardy, productive and early ripening variety, but recently introduced; said to have a good sized bunch, with berry of medium size, bluish black, melting, sweet, with a sprightly, vinous flavor, and to ripen fully as early as the Hartford Prolific. The Fruit Growers' Association distributed a plant of this vine to each of its members in the spring of 1870, and in a few years its qualities and suitableness for the climate of Ontario will be well known.

HARTFORD PROLIFIC.—In general appearance of vine and of both bunch and berry this variety bears considerable resemblance to the Isabella, but ripens much earlier and is not as good in **flavor.** It is one of the earliest ripening sorts we have, and sells readily in the market at good prices. It has the defect of **dropping its berries from the bunch as soon as** ripe, yet this does not **take place every season. When ripe, however,** they should be **gathered and used,** as they do not improve in flavor by being allowed to hang on the vine, but on the contrary become musky, **and lose all** sprightliness. **The vine is about as hardy as** the Isabella, but not quite as vigorous in growth; the bunches large, shouldered, **tolerably compact;** berry large, round, black, moderately **juicy, sweet, with a good** deal of pulp.

IONA.—After some years of trial we are obliged to say that this Grape is neither hardier nor much, if any, earlier than the **Isabella.** Those who can grow and ripen the Isabella may hope **to succeed with this Grape,** but it will no doubt be better in **climates that** enjoy longer summers than those of Canada **generally.** The bunch is large, **loose, but shouldered; the berries are** full medium, red, juicy, sweet, with a pleasant vinous flavor.

ISRAELLA.—This ripens very soon after the **Hartford Prolific,** and on that account is well worthy of trial. Though sent out at the same time with the Iona and by the same cultivator, it was not as highly lauded, and has perhaps in consequence not been **very** generally tested in the colder parts of Canada. The vine is **vigorous, productive, and** probably will prove **to be** as hardy as **the Concord. The bunches are** above medium size, **shouldered** and **compact; berries large, black,** juicy, sweet, and without pulpiness.

ISABELLA.—One of the most vigorous, healthy and productive varieties in cultivation, and where it ripens well is one of the most profitable. Unfortunately it requires a longer summer than is to be found in most of the Dominion to ripen its fruit well, **and it** cannot endure exposure to great extremes of cold. It is **believed to be a native of South** Carolina. The bunches are large, loose, shouldered; berries blackish purple, juicy, sweet, with but little **pulp or** muskiness.

LINDLEY.—*Roger's No. 9.*—A very vigorous and productive sort, with a long compact bunch; berries medium in size, red, **juicy, sweet and** aromatic. Ripe just before the Concord.

LYDIA.—A white or greenish white variety that has been fruited in but a few places in Canada. The vine is not more **hardy** than the Isabella, and seems to be a shy bearer. Those who are anxious to obtain a Grape of this color might try this and the Martha. The bunch is short and compact; berries large, juicy, rich and sweet, with scarcely any pulp. Ripe at the same time as the Delaware.

MARTHA.—**Is said to be a seedling of the Concord. We** have not fruited it, but the few specimens we have seen did not equal the **Concord in quality.** Its admirers claim for it that the vine is as hardy, **healthy and productive, as the Concord.**

MERRIMACK.—*Rogers' No. 19.*—The vine has the same **character of** vigorous growth, combined with health and hardiness, that pertains to these seedlings. The bunch is short, but broad and compact; the berries large, round and black, juicy **and** sweet, with very little pulp; ripe about same **time as the** Concord.

OTHELLO.—*Arnold's No. 1.*—The largest, **both in** berry and bunch, and by far the most showy and attractive of all of Mr. Arnold's Seedlings. It was raised **from seed of** a wild grape of the Clinton **type, fertilized** with the Black Hamburgh. The vine is **a strong grower, and** very productive; **the** bunches are large, shouldered and compact; the berries large, black, with a firm, meaty **flesh, free** from all toughness, juicy, with a sprightly vinous flavor. **It** ripens about with the Concord. We think that in climates where the season is longer, it will be a sweeter and finer grape than it is here, and that it will not be likely to prove valuable in those sections where the Concord does not **ripen well.**

ONTARIO.—This is thought by many to be identical with the

Union Village, **but** our observations have not fully satisfied us that this is the **case**. It is an exceedingly coarse, vigorous growing variety, **not any** more hardy than the Isabella, with exceedingly **large, compact,** well shouldered bunches, and berries fully as **large as those of the** Black Hamburgh; black, juicy, with very little pulp, **and a** pleasant, mild, **vinous flavor.** It ripens **usually a little** before the Isabella.

REBECCA.—Is **not** suited to general **culture, thriving well only in a few favored** localities. It is a **white Grape, of** good quality, ripening **at the same** time as the Isabella. The vine is not vigorous, nor capable of enduring extremes of cold.

SALEM.—*Rogers' No.* 22.—**One of the best of the red-colored Grapes of Mr. Rogers'** Seedlings. A healthy and **vigorous vine,** bearing abundantly, having good sized, short, but compact **bunches, and** large, round, dark red berries, which are juicy, **sweet** and aromatic, **with very little** pulp; ripe about with **the** Concord. It is said **that this Grape** will keep well through the winter. We have seen samples exhibited the latter part of **January, in fine condition.**

WILDER—*Rogers' No.* 4—**The** best black grape raised by Mr. Rogers. **The vine is vigorous, healthy, and** productive. The bunches are sometimes large, shouldered, and compact; berries large, with very little pulp; **sweet, juicy, and** rich; ripe with the Concord.

MILDEW

Mildew is often spoken of as a disease of the vine; it appears on the **leaves,** sometimes extending to the growing shoots. This mildew is a parasitic plant, **and is not,** properly speaking, a disease, nor **even** the first cause **of disease,** but only comes in consequence of an enfeebled condition of the vine. These parasitic **plants** do not find in **the healthy vine** the conditions favourable to their development. It is when **the vine has** received some shock, has become in some degree **unhealthy,** that these parasites, ever ready **to** fasten on enfeebled and failing **vegetation,** finding conditions more or less favorable to their development, begin to appear. Having become once established, they prey **upon the vine,** make it yet more feeble, and hasten its destruction. There are some vines of so delicate and feeble a constitution that parasitic fungi find in them a congenial soil, and may **be** surely expected, sooner or later, to appear; but in vines of a robust constitution, like the Clinton, Concord, and many others, where we find these parasitic fungi in the form of mildew present, **we** may be sure that some cause is at work which has enfeebled **and** injured the health of the vine. Overbearing is a very common cause **of** sickly and enfeebled vines; injudicious pruning, especially **late** fall pruning, and severe **summer pruning are,** in this climate, **also a prolific source of injury to the vigor of the** vines. **It may be necessary, in order to** restore **the vines to** health, to destroy the fungi that are feeding upon them; but, unless the other enfeebling causes are removed also, and the vine wholly restored, these fungi will continue to appear year after year, in spite of all applications of sulphur or other substances destructive to them, and in the end the vine will perish.

Mildew should, therefore, be usually regarded as an indication of want of perfect health in the vine, and the **cause** of that failure of health be diligently sought for, and, if found, promptly removed. **Some of the** causes have been indicated, but there are **others,** and some of these it is not possible to remedy. The vines **of Europe thrive here** for a few years, but the extremes of temperature in our climate are too severe for their constitutional vigor; they become gradually enfeebled, mildew makes its appearance, destroys the foliage so that the wood cannot ripen, and the next winter they are irretrievably ruined. Flour of sulphur dusted upon the leaves is the best known agent for the **destruction of the mildew.**

CULTIVATION OF THE GRAPE UNDER GLASS.

The following hints are designed to aid those who are desirous of growing a few vines under glass, and who propose to be in this matter their own gardeners, and being therefore without the assistance of scientific cultivators, wish to avail themselves of plain, simple directions how to proceed. The writer, in preparing these suggestions, has availed himself of the very admirable little treatise by Mr. William Thomson, of Dalkeith Park, Scotland, making such changes as the difference in climate seemed to require.

SHAPE AND SIZE OF VINERY.

When the object sought in the erection of a **vinery is the production of** early Grapes, there is no form so suitable as a "**lean-to," with the roof** sloping full to the south-south-east. When it is desired to have late Grapes, say those ripening in August and September, the **span-roofed form is** best and most economical, and should **be placed with one end to the south and the other to the north, which will make the roof to slope to the east and west.** It is better that the house be of **sufficient size to be maintained** easily at a **uniform** temperature. If it be **very small, it is too** easily affected by the changes of weather going on without. Let it be, if practicable, say height of back wall **fifteen feet; width of house fifteen feet; height of front sashes two feet** six inches; **length forty feet, outside measurement.** A house of these dimensions has **a good length of rafter,** which enables the vines to **carry a large extent of foliage, and** become vigorous plants as compared with those **confined to a short rafter.** The **front sashes** should be **in sections, and hung upon hinges at the upper edge,** having a curved, notched iron **rod fastened on the inner** side of each section, so **that any one or all** of these sections can be opened to any desired extent, when **required for the** purpose of ventilation, or kept securely closed. The upper ventilators should be **three feet long by one foot wide, and** placed in the back wall eighteen inches **below the** plate. There should be a ventilator in each space between the rafters. The easiest arrangement for opening and **closing** them, is to swing them on a pivot, with **a** curved iron **rod** running from **the** edge of each ventilator **and** fastened securely **to** a larger rod, which **is run the whole** length **of** the house, and which is supported **on** brackets fastened in the wall and standing out about three **inches** from the **face** of the **wall.** This long rod is **very** readily and cheaply obtained by using inch gas pipe. At one end of this long rod, **and running at** right angles to it, is fastened a rod **or** bar to **act as a lever in** turning the long rod on **its axis.** From the **end of this** lever depends a handle, **which is** pierced at the **lower extremity** with numerous holes. **When** it is desired **to open the ventilators at** the **top of the house, they are** all openened simultaneously **and** to any desired **height, by means of this handle, which acting** upon the lever turns the long rod, and this turning of the rod pushes open the **ventilators. These are** kept open to any desired degree by slipping the lower end of the handle on to a peg fixed in the wall, which passes through any one of the several holes with which the lower end is perforated.

A good mode of building is to put up a frame, fill in between the studs with brick laid in mortar, making **a four inch wall,** and then plaster on the **brick. All** the interior of the house should be made as smooth as **possible, and the wood** work well **painted, so** that the house may be thorougly cleansed every year, and leave **no hiding place for insects.** The roof should be fixed, the astragals **reaching from the plate to the** ridge, and the glass bedded **in** putty, with **a lap of not** more than one-eighth down to one-sixteenth **of an inch.** If pieces of tin, four inches wide, be **first laid for the bottom** course, and then the glass laid **on,** lapping the eighth of an inch on the tin, it will be found **a saving** of glass in frosty weather. The rafters should be two by **six inches,** placed three feet ten inches apart, from centre to centre, **and** a vine trained under each rafter. Across the upper side of the rafters, and about midway of their length, should run a stringer of oak the whole length of the house, 3 x 1½ inches, upon which the astragals will rest, in notches cut in the upper side to receive them. At the bottom of these notches a small,

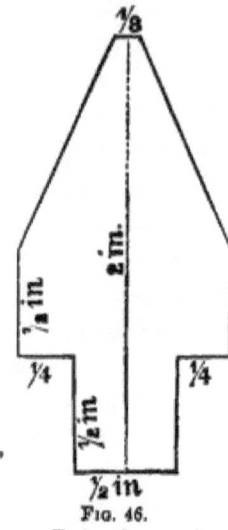

Fig. 46.

round three-eighths of an inch hole should be bored across the stringer, so that a drop of water running down the bottom of the astragal will not be stopped by the stringer, but may run on to the lower end. The astragals should be made of clear stuff 2 x 1 inch. The upper side should be rabbeted half an inch deep, with a seat of one-fourth of an inch to receive the glass, and the under side should be beveled off to a point of one-eighth of an inch in width, leaving only a depth of half an inch below the glass, which is fully one inch in thickness. The accompanying cut, Fig. 46, represents a section of an astragal.

Into the under side of the rafters should be screwed eyes or loops, with such length of rod that the wires, when drawn through them, shall be sixteen inches from the glass—the wires running the whole length of the house, at right angles to the rafters. These eyes should be fastened into the rafters every ten inches, thus bringing the wires not more than ten inches apart.

HEATING THE VINERY.

The best method of heating a vinery is by means of hot water, and in a house of the size above mentioned, in which it is intended to force early grapes, in order to heat it sufficiently there should be about one foot in length of four-inch pipe to every fourteen feet of cubic space, or say three hundred and twenty-five feet of pipe. As the heat is most needed at the front, it will be found a good arrangement to place five pipes along the front and ends, and two return pipes along the back—the pipes running under the walk which is carried around the house.

CULTIVATION OF THE GRAPE UNDER GLASS. 143

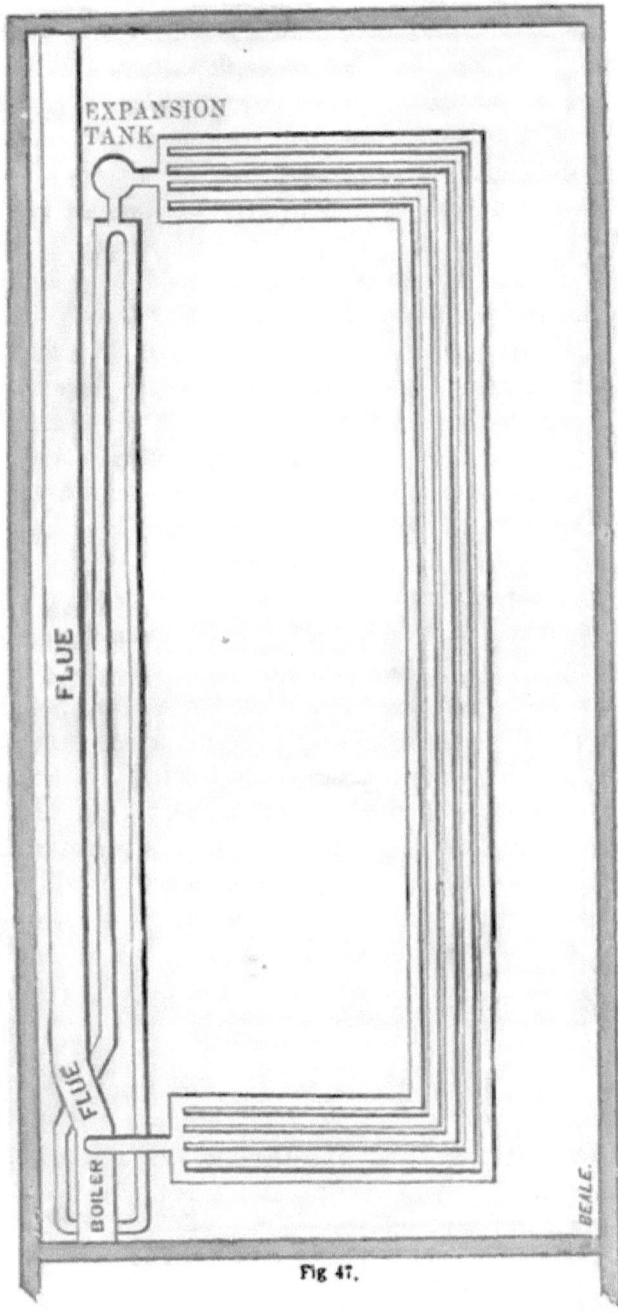

Fig 47.

Fig. 47 represents the ground plan of a vinery, showing the water-pipes and boiler. The hot water flows from the top of the boiler, runs through the pipes along the front and ends, and returns to the bottom of the boiler by the two pipes along the back of the vinery.

If a span-roofed house is preferred, the construction will be much the same as that already described. Of course there will be no back wall, but in place of it, another roofing of glass; and instead of the top ventilators being as in the "lean-to," there must be some arrangement made at the ridge of the roof. A convenient arrangement is to run the astragals to the ridge on the west side, and glaze that side tight to the top. On the east side, run the astragals only to within about eighteen inches of the top, and between every other rafter place a ventilator, three feet long and one foot wide, hinged on the upper edge, and rabbeted so as to lap over half an inch on the lower side and at the two ends, when closed. On the inside, near the lower edge, is fastened, with a staple, a small rod, with which the ventilator can be pushed open and kept at any desired elevation.

Or, instead of ventilators fastened on hinges, narrow sashes may be made to slide down and up between the rafters, which are opened and shut by a cord passing over pulleys. The only objection to this latter method is, that sometimes, in freezing weather, the sliding sash becomes frozen fast, so that it cannot be made to slide; though, with proper attention, it will very seldom be necessary to open the top ventilators in such weather.

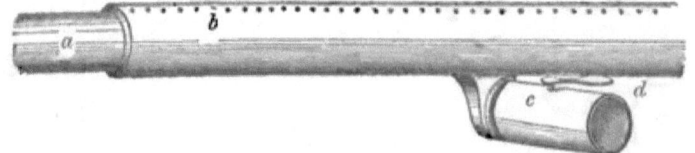

Fig. 48.

The above diagram illustrates the method of admitting fresh air into the vinery in cold weather, when it is impossible to open the side or front ventilators with safety.

a Represents the flow pipe running along the front of the vinery, and if there be several, the one nearest to the front wall; *b* is a tin or galvanized iron covering, made to enclose the hot water pipe, but having a diameter one inch more than the hot pipe it encloses, and brought down at the ends so as to fit tight at those points, thus enclosing a space of half an inch all round the flow pipe inside the sheath. This cavity is fed with fresh air from the exterior of the house by a pipe, *c*, five inches in diameter, which springs from the lower surface of the sheath, and passes through the front wall of the house to the external air. There is a valve, *d*, in the feed pipe to modify the supply of fresh air at pleasure. In the upper surface of the sheath is a double row of small holes, so that the moment the cold air comes into the hot chamber round the pipe, and gets hot, expanded and lighter, it makes its exit through these holes into the general atmosphere of the house. In this way a constant supply of fresh air can be obtained without causing a cold draught. This is more especially desired for houses used for early forcing, at which season the weather is nearly all the time so cold that it is unsafe to open the front ventilators.

It is always desirable to have some means of heating even a cold grapery, for it often happens that the warm days of early spring, which start the vines nicely, are followed by a period of chilly weather, accompanied by frosty nights, and unless the temperature of the house can be kept up the vines become severely chilled, and sometimes in a single night they will receive a shock from which they will not recover in a fortnight. For this purpose, however, a couple of pipes, running around the house, will be quite sufficient, and can be used at such times, either in the early spring, or when in bloom, or in the damp weather in the fall.

The best boiler, all things considered, for a small house, is the plain saddle boiler. It is quite unnecessary to enter upon a discussion here of the merits of the many boilers which have been invented, and all of which are advertised as "*improved*."

Those who wish to experiment in this direction, and spend considerable money in making these experiments, will find ample opportunity for doing so; the wise man will be satisfied "to let well enough alone."

The best method of heating all horticultural structures is by hot water. Common air always contains in suspension minute particles of animal and vegetable matter, besides being more or less filled with aqueous vapor. When this atmosphere is made to pass over highly heated metallic surfaces these particles of organic matter are decomposed by the heat, and resolved into their various elementary gases; and the suspended aqueous vapor is also decomposed, the oxygen thereof uniting with the hot iron surface, and the hydrogen mixing with the air. These changes make the atmosphere extremely deleterious to both animal and vegetable life. Metallic surfaces should never be heated above 212 degrees of Fahrenheit for all purposes of warming dwellings or horticultural buildings, and where the heating is done by hot water the most careless manager can never exceed this point. Heating by means of brick flues is not as objectionable as by hot air stoves or furnaces; yet in our extremely cold climate, rendering it sometimes necessary to heat the flues to a high temperature, the organic matter in the atmosphere becomes decomposed, and the expansion of bricks admits of an escape of gases from the fuel, through the fissures and joints.

Besides these reasons, a greater permanency of temperature is obtained by the use of hot water than is possible by any other method. Steam circulating in pipes will not maintain the same permanency of temperature. A tube filled with water at a temperature of 212° Fahrenheit contains 1694 times as much matter as one of the same size filled with steam. Hence it is that a given *bulk* of water, in falling from a temperature of 212° to 60°, will give out 228 times as much heat as the same bulk of steam reduced to the same temperature of 60°; or, in other words, a given bulk of steam will lose as much of its heat in one minute as the same bulk of water will lose in three hours and three quarters.

But this is not all the difference. The heat of the iron pipe must also be taken into consideration, which, if calculated at four inches in diameter and one-fourth of an inch in thickness, will, in the case of hot water, contain 4.68 times as much heat as the one filled with steam; so that in fact if the pipe, when filled with steam, cools down to 60° in one hour, it will require four hours and a half to cool the iron to the same temperature when filled with water. Nor yet is this all. As soon as the water in the boiler falls below 212°, all circulation of steam ceases; but in the case of water, the circulation is kept up until the water in the boiler falls to the same temperature as that in the pipes. Hence the temperature of the house is kept from falling below 60°, not only until all the water in the pipes, and the pipes themselves, have fallen to this point, but until all the water in the boiler, and the boiler itself, has reached the same temperature. From these observations it will be seen that a house heated with hot water will maintain its temperature six times as long as one heated by steam.

Again, in order to heat a building by steam, the pipes must be above the temperature of 212°, and as we advance above this point we soon reach such a degree of heat as we have already described as being prejudicial to that purity of atmosphere so essential to animal and vegetable life and health

BOILERS AND PIPES.

The efficiency of a boiler depends upon the quantity of surface exposed to the fire, and that should be in proportion to the amount of water contained in the boiler and pipes. A boiler which has a surface of seven square feet exposed to the fire will heat four hundred feet of four-inch pipe sufficiently for practical purposes. It is better that the boiler should have a capacity above the proportion of the pipes than below, for though the circulation will be slower, the temperature can be maintained at the desired point with a less consumption of fuel. The best material for these boilers is cast iron; they last longer than those made of malleable iron, because they are not as rapidly consumed by rust, and are usually less expensive in the first instance.

Experiments very carefully made by competent men have settled the fact that more heat will be given out by *four-inch* pipes, in proportion to the consumption of fuel, than by pipes of any other size. In laying down the pipes, they should never be fastened, but every facility should be given to them for motion lengthwise, by laying them on pieces of rod iron placed occasionally under them and upon the support upon which they rest. The linear expansion of cast iron is nearly equal to one inch and three-eighths in every hundred feet, when the temperature is raised from 32°. to 212°; and unless every freedom is given for the motion caused by this alternate expansion and contraction, the joints will very likely become loose and leaky.

In heating the vinery it is always desirable to economise as much heat as possible, hence it is well to run the smoke flue the entire length of the house, which may be done in a "lean-to" by running it along the back wall.

BORDERS FOR THE VINES.

If it be designed to force the vines for early fruit, it will be essential, in our climate, that they should be confined to an inside border. It is impossible to maintain anything like a corresponding degree of temperature between the root and the branches, if the roots are permitted to run in an outside border, and unless this is measurably maintained it is impossible to produce good grapes. But in cool graperies the borders may be open, and the vines allowed to ramble outside as well as inside.

In preparing the borders, if the subsoil be a retentive clay, and, as is usually the case, cold and wet, it is necessary to provide perfect drainage. To do this thoroughly, the whole of the soil of the size of the intended border, and to a depth of three feet, should be thrown out, and the bottom made to slope gradually to the front, with a fall of one inch to the foot, and along the front of the border, and just below the edge, a tile drain should be laid, with a like slope to carry off promptly all the water that runs to the edge of the border. The bottom of the border should then be covered with broken stone, or brick rubbish, or very coarse gravel, and this, if possible, covered with a layer that is a little finer, thus gradually increasing the fineness of the material until it approaches that of ordinary soil. This drainage should be nine inches deep, and be covered all over with an inverted sod.

The best soil with which to fill up the border is that taken from the surface of an *old* pasture, where the grass is fine and thick, paring off the sod to a depth of three inches—if abounding in calcareous matter, so much the better. Old grape growers say it should be composed of 65 per cent. of sand, 30 per cent. of clay, and 5 per cent. of chalk, with plenty of vegetable fibre, that is, roots of grass. But beware of decaying wood; every bit of this will be filled with spores of fungi, that will be certain to injure, and very probably destroy the vines. This sod and soil from the pasture should be stacked under cover for say six months, until the grass is dead and the whole mass dry; then broken up and mixed with lime rubbish, old plaster, if possible in the proportion of ten loads of loam to two of lime rubbish, one of charcoal, and two of fresh fermenting horse manure, and four hundred weight of coarse, broken bones. This should be thoroughly turned over several times, that it may be well intermingled, turning it, if possible, in frosty weather. If the soil be too strong in clay it may be improved by adding sand. If the soil be deficient in clay, increase the quantity of bones and horse droppings. Horn shavings are an excellent substitute for bones, or may be used with them. Calcined oyster shells are also useful, if they can be had. While preparing this compost for the vine border it should be kept dry.

The width of the border in the forcing house should be the entire width of the house, and the foundation laid up with stone or brick along the entire front, to the depth of the bottom of the border, so that the roots of the vines can have no opportunity of straying into the outer soil. In the span-roofed vinery the border should occupy not only the whole interior of the house, but a space on each side, equal, at least, to one-half the width of the house. It is advisable not to make the whole width of the border at the time the vines are planted, but in the forcing house make about eight feet in width along the front, or in the cool vinery make five or six feet inside and as much outside, along each side. This will afford sufficient room for the roots of the vines for the first year. The second year, add three feet to the inside border, or, if a cool vinery, add three feet inside and as much outside to each border, and at or about this rate every year until the whole width of the border is made up. If added as wanted, it will be sweeter and better than if it be all put down at once. The border in the vinery should be filled in so that the surface shall be from six inches to a foot above the surface of the soil outside. Allowance must be made for the settling of the soil, which will be about six inches.

The borders having been made, and everything ready for planting, the vines, which have been grown in pots, should have the soil well shaken out from the roots, the roots carefully disentangled, and any decayed portions cut off, then carefully and evenly spread out, and covered with the finely pulverized soil to the depth of four or five inches. The earth should be settled by watering moderately with tepid water, through a fine rose. When planted, the vines should be cut down to two buds. When these have got nicely started, rub off the weaker bud, and train the other under the rafter by tying it to the wires. During the first season, allow it to grow without any pruning or pinching whatever, carefully preserving every leaf it may form and every lateral that it may throw out. As the season advances, gradually give more air, so that by the middle of August the ventilators may be left open night and day. In this way a good healthy vine will be secured, with an abundance of roots, and with well ripened wood.

The second year's treatment begins with the cutting back of the canes in November, to within a foot of the bottom of the rafter. When this has been done, the inside of the vinery should be most thoroughly washed, and the vines painted with a paint composed of 2 oz. of soft soap, 2 oz. of flowers of sulphur, one gill of tobacco-water, and ½ oz. of nux vomica, mixed thoroughly in two quarts of water, to which enough dry clay, or slaked lime is added to bring the whole to a consistency of thick paint. This will destroy red spider and other insects that may be on them. The vines should then be laid down and covered with dry leaves, to protect them from frost. If it is desired to have ripe grapes about the first of July, fires should be started about the first of February, the vines uncovered, and, after the eyes are all evenly broken, tied to the wires.

As soon as the fires are started, the canes should be syringed with tepid water twice a day until the buds burst, and then all syringing of the vines should cease until they have fully expanded their first leaf. The temperature on starting should be between 40° and 45° at night, rising to 55° or 60° during the day. As soon as the buds are burst the heat may be increased at night to 45° or 50°, and so gradually increase the night heat a little, so that by the time the first leaves are wholly expanded the night temperature may be as high as 50°, running up in the day to 10° or 15° higher. The atmosphere should be kept sufficiently moist by placing metallic trays, containing water, on the pipes, and by sprinkling the border and paths, but never by syringing the pipes when they are hot. This year, the lateral shoots that start from the growing wood should be pinched at one leaf from the main cane, and those from last year's wood stopped at the fifth joint, and all the fruit taken off except one bunch, or, at most, two, if they are small. When the leading cane has reached two-thirds of the length of the rafter it may be stopped, and when it starts again, stopped once more, after it has made two more joints, repeating this process until growth ceases. The laterals must also be stopped every time they start, after making one joint more beyond the last stop. Air should be given more and more freely as the season advances, so that the wood may ripen well and naturally. After the leaves fall, the laterals should be cut off to the main cane, and the main vine cut back to six feet from the bottom of the rafter, all loose bark on the old wood removed, the cane washed with tepid water and a little soap, and painted with the mixture already mentioned. Wash all the walls of the vinery with hot lime whitewash, with a little sulphur stirred in it, and clean all the wood-work and glass thoroughly, especially all the nooks, corners and crannies, with plenty of soap and water. Lay down the vines, and cover well with leaves as before. Sometimes the mice get into the house, and finding the leaves an excellent place of concealment, take up their abode in them, and eat the bark of the vines. It is for the purpose of putting a stop to such mischief that the nux vomica is put into the paint. Perhaps a better way is to twist tightly some small straw ropes, and wind these securely around the whole of each vine, from the ground to the top, completely encasing each, and then laying them down along the front of the house. The mice will not gnaw through the straw rope.

In the third year the fires will be again started about the first of February, the covering removed from the vines, the vines well syringed twice a day with tepid water until the buds burst. As soon as it can be seen that two shoots are starting from one eye, rub off the weaker, and discontinue the syringing of the vine until the first leaf is fully expanded. The requisite moisture should be maintained by the trays of water on the pipes and sprinkling the floor.

As soon as the bunches can be discerned, the heat of the house, which has been maintained at from 45° to 50° by night, and from 10° to 15° higher by day, should be raised about 5° higher, and gradually increased, so that by the time the shoots have extended three inches in length, the heat will be raised to 55° or 60° at night, and from 65° to 75° by day. From this point there should be a daily increase of the temperature until the vines begin to bloom, when it should have reached a night temperature of 65°, and about 15° higher by day for

Black Hamburghs, and all the free-setting class. **In the case of Muscats, the heat should be 10° greater both night and day.** Lessen the amount of moisture while the vines are in bloom, and if the vines are occasionally jarred at this time, so as to fill the house with the pollen, the effect will be beneficial. In this way a good set of fruit will be secured, even on the Muscat vines. As soon as the fruit is set, **the heat should be** gradually allowed to decrease to 65° at night, **rising** to 75° or 80° by day with fire **heat, and up** to 85° or 90° with the sun. Also, as soon as the fruit is set, the house **should** be again supplied with moisture, and the vines well syringed daily.

There will doubtless be more fruit set than **the vines can be allowed to bear.** The best practice is to **take off all the** bunches on a shoot **but one, and** stop **the lateral on which it** grows **two leaves** or joints **beyond the** bunch, **and pinch in all sub-laterals,** (that is, laterals growing out of the lateral shoot), at the first joint, **and to re-pinch these as often** as they start again without **leaving any additional** joint. There will probably be still too **many bunches of** Grapes remaining, and these should be reduced to eight or ten bunches for each vine, always leaving the largest and best. The leading shoot from the main **cane** should not be allowed to bear any fruit.

The berries also will require **thinning out. In the case** of the free-setting varieties, this **should be done** as **early as** possible after the Grapes are set; in the **Muscats** it is better to wait **until it can be seen which of the berries** are properly set and taking **the lead. Care** must be taken **not in** any way to injure the remaining berries. There are Grape scissors made on purpose for this work, which will enable the operator with a little practice to thin out the berries readily and safely, and without injury to those that **remain.** Handle the fruit as little as possible. The object of this thinning is to give room to each berry to swell perfectly without being jammed, and yet so that, when ripe, the bunch shall be compact.

Air must be supplied in sufficient quantity to keep the foliage healthy and thick, and there will be no difficulty in doing this by means of the fresh air ventilator shown at fig. 48, which may be kept more or less open night and day, and in all weathers. Advantage may also be taken of the opportunity for diffusing ammonia through the house, by dissolving the sulphate or the carbonate of ammonia in the water trays on the pipes. This will have a tendency to thicken the leaves, and strengthen the whole plant. Yet this may be done to excess, and then, instead of a benefit, becomes a positive injury. A little guano, or pigeon's dung, or the dung of common barn-yard fowls, may be used instead of the salts of ammonia.

In watering the inside border, if the bottom drainage be what it should, give it always a thorough drenching, not a mere surface watering. Use soft, tepid water, soaking it thoroughly when the vines are started, and afterwards as occasion requires. Be careful not to tread on the border when newly watered. When the berries begin to color, increase the supply of air, night and day, and stop syringing the vines. Lessening the moisture will increase the flavor of the Grapes, but beware of the red spider, for with such power as the sun has in this climate, it is very easy to withhold moisture so much as to create a worse evil. When the Grapes are all cut, give the vines a thorough syringing with tepid water, and clean the foliage from all insects and dust. Keep the inside border dry enough to prevent the vines from starting into growth.

After the foliage is ripe and fallen, the laterals which have borne fruit must be cut back to one eye, those upon the growing cane cut back to the main vine, the main cane cut in to twelve feet in length, the vine washed and painted, the house most thoroughly cleansed, and the vines protected and laid down for winter.

When, in course of time, the spurs become too large and unsightly, a new cane may be grown by cutting down one of the vines every year and leading up a new shoot. If but one or two vines are cut back in each year, the whole vinery will be gradually renewed without materially lessening the supply of grapes.

DISEASES OF VINES.

Shanking.—This formidable disease **has been a fruitful theme of** conjecture, and many reasons have been assigned **for its cause,** and as many remedies propounded. It makes its appearance just as the grapes are changing from their acid to their saccharine state, arrests this transformation, the berry remaining acid, and becoming in a short time shrivelled. The little stem or *shank*, which attaches the berry to the bunch, decays, which is all the functional derangement apparent to the eye, hence the term *shanking*, applied to the disease.

It is probable that several causes may **combine in the production of this disease;** prominent among these are **over-cropping,** injury **to the foliage by** red spider, **or other** cause, **the roots** of **the vine having penetrated into a cold, wet** subsoil, or the **roots having made a late, succulent growth, by** reason of the **border being too rich** and damp, and perhaps too plentifully supplied with manure water. These causes may not all exist at any one time, but some one or more of them will be found to have just so far enfeebled the vine as to make its loss of vigor apparent in this way, when in nothing **else does it seem to manifest any** lack of healthy action. **The trouble** is thought by the ablest gardeners to **be owing to the want of well** ripened, fine and **woody roots at the time when winter sets in,** roots that are **ripened to their extremest points.** If instead of being thus ripened, **they are from any** cause coarse and soft, with a spongy texture, when winter sets in, all these spongy fibres will die and decay during the winter, back to the main stem roots, from which they issued. **When the vines start** to grow again the main roots throw out young fibrous rootlets to supply their place; but these are unable to supply the vine with sufficient nutriment to support both the requisite wood and fruit, hence the shanking of the fruit, while the other functions of the vine seem to be **performed in a** healthy manner. If it be certain that the shanking, when it appears, is not due to over-cropping, or injury to the foliage, nor to the roots having penetrated into the cold subsoil; and it should be remembered that these causes existing during the previous year, may be the occasion of imperfectly ripened roots, whose death during the past winter is now being felt in the shanking of the grapes; but that it is possible that it is owing to the border being too heavy, damp, and rich, the only remedy is to raise the roots, remove a portion of the border, and replace with compost in which there is a larger amount of lime rubbish, calcined oyster shells, and coarse bone, say double the quantity previously recommended, with only half the amount of dung. In this poorer and more porous border the roots will be more numerous, finer, and more woody, ripening well before autumn, and will survive the winter in a perfectly sound condition. It is easier to give one or two good waterings with liquid manure during the growing season, to supply the requisite nourishment, than to do without the healthy roots through which it is taken up into the circulation.

Rust on Grapes is believed to be caused by the application of sulphur to the hot pipes while the Grapes are yet young, and that this may be wholly avoided if sulphur be not used in this way until the Grapes have been set some time, and the skin become less tender and sensitive. The thick-skinned Grapes, such as the Muscats, are less liable to injury in this way. It is recommended by able Grape growers to paint the pipes with sulphur mixed with milk and water as soon as the red spider makes its appearance, which it will do in the hottest part of the house first, and repeat this painting once a week. It is considered the real specific for this great pest; yet, where the atmosphere of the house is kept at the proper moisture, and never allowed to get too dry, and the house properly cleansed every year, there is much less danger of its becoming troublesome. It will be seen, however, from what has been said on the subject of Rust, care must be used, lest in killing the red spider with sulphur, you injure the Grapes with Rust.

MILDEW of the vine has been a serious source of loss and disappointment. Strictly it is not a disease, but a parasitic, fungoid plant, which, under certain favoring conditions grows upon and derives its sustenance from the tissues of the vine. By its growth the further growth of the vine is arrested, and if sufficiently abundant the crop of fruit is lost, and the vine itself seriously and sometimes fatally injured. It is most likely to make its appearance in hot, dry weather, particularly if a draught of air be allowed through the house. By keeping the top ventilators open, and not suffering any draughts, the mildew may be wholly prevented. Little injury need be apprehended from it after the Grapes are once well colored.

There sometimes forms on the lower surface of the leaves a collection of little green warts. They are caused by a close, warm atmosphere, saturated with moisture, and can be prevented by maintaining a free circulation of air, moderately charged with moisture.

AIR-ROOTS on the vine are caused either by the atmosphere of the house being kept too moist, or because the border is too cold, or by both these causes acting together. When the natural roots are in a border that in texture, temperature and moisture is congenial to their growth, and the atmosphere of the vinery what it ought to be, there will be few air-roots.

As a rule, one pound of grapes to every two superficial feet of glass is a fair crop, yet a sound discretion must be exercised in the amount of crop, which should be proportioned to the vigor of the vines.

SELECTION OF VINES.

For a person who does not wish to force early grapes, but confines himself to a single cool grapery, the following selection will be found suitable, and at the same time give him a succession:

5 Black Hamburgh.
2 Muscat Hamburgh.
1 Royal Muscadine.

1 Chasselas Musque.
1 Buckland Sweet Water.
1 Golden Champion.

For early forcing, the following will be the most desirable and suitable sorts:

3 Black Hamburgh.
3 Muscat Hamburgh
2 Bowood Muscat.
1 Grizzly Frontignan.
1 White Frontignan.
1 Chasselas Musque.

FRUITING VINES IN POTS.

It is sometimes desirable to ripen a few grapes in pots. It can be done while the permanent vines are becoming established in their borders, preparatory to their first crop of fruit. They are often wanted for dinner table decoration,—and what can give the table a more charming appearance, in combination with flowers, than a vine laden with its tempting purple clusters! The following hints are intended to help those who are desirous of making the experiment.

It is of the first importance to obtain strong, healthy, well ripened, one year old vines, that have been well grown in eight-inch pots. These should be procured about the first of April. As soon as they are received, the ball of earth containing the roots should be well soaked with tepid water. They should then be potted in eleven-inch pots, first carefully loosening and spreading what root-fibres can be readily set free without breaking the ball to pieces, yet reducing the size of it by removing the loose soil at the top, and what may crumble off in liberating the ends of the roots. Some soil for potting them should have been provided similar to that used for the borders. The hole at the bottom of the pot should be covered with a potsherd, and the bottom filled, to the depth of at least two inches, with broken fragments of pots, or with small pieces of charcoal, or with half-inch ground bones. Over these should be spread a little moss to prevent the soil from being washed into the drainage. Upon the moss place about two inches of the coarser portion of the soil, and then proceed to plant the vine in the pot, pressing the soil in quite firmly around the roots and the ball in which they are contained. Fill the soil in the pot to about an inch from the brim. If the soil is not pressed down quite firmly in potting the vine, the water will soak through the loose, porous soil around the ball, without sufficiently wetting the ball and the roots it contains. Therefore pot firmly. Cut the vine back to three buds, and syringe with tepid water until they begin to break, and then suspend the syringing of them until the first leaf is fully expanded, and treat them in the same manner as the vines in the border. When the buds have started, select the strongest and rub off the others. It will be found a convenient arrangement to set the pots along the front of the vinery, as near the glass as possible, put a stick in the pot, and as the vine grows, tie it up until it reaches the wires, and then it can be trained to the wires in the same manner as the vines in the border. When the laterals start out, pinch them in beyond the first leaf, and repeat the pinching as often as a leaf is formed, leaving one new leaf at each pinching. When the main cane has attained a length of eight or nine feet, cut it back to six or seven feet. This will probably cause the laterals to start with more vigor, and they will require attention to keep them pinched in to their proper limits. When they have become brown at the base for a couple of inches, thus showing a ripening of the wood, they should be cut off down to the bud at their base.

During the growth of the vine, and up to the time of cutting off the laterals, the vines should be watered twice a week with manure water, commencing with a very weak solution at first, and gradually increasing the strength with the increased strength of the vine. But when the laterals are cut off, then cease the manure water altogether, and lessen also the amount of water given, gradually diminishing the waterings so as to ripen the wood thoroughly, yet not withholding water so as at any time to cause the leaves to flag. Copious waterings are very apt to cause the vine to start into a second growth, which must be avoided.

When the vine is full ripened, the pot should be plunged into the border in some spot where it will not interfere with the roots of the vines growing there, inserting the pot to a depth of six inches below the surface. The cane should be cut down and covered with some bits of old carpeting, or, if preferred, may be wound with straw.

In the spring, when the vines in the border are started, those in the pots should be taken out of the border and cut back to five feet in length, and the canes bent over and syringed, and treated in all respects as the other vines in the vinery. When the buds are all evenly broken, the cane should be tied to the stake in the pot, in an upright position, the shoots pinched in, leaving one leaf beyond the last bunch of fruit, and kept pinched in each time it starts. Water with manure-water twice a week, as was done last year, beginning with a weak preparation, and increasing in strength until the fruit is well colored. Only one bunch of grapes should be left on each shoot, and not more than five pounds on the vine.

The Black Hamburgh is the best variety for pot culture, and we advise amateurs to confine themselves to this alone until they have had some experience, and attained some skill in the management of pot vines, and then they may try their hand on such other sorts as they wish, with much greater probabilities of success.

THE BLACKBERRY.

But little attention has been paid to the cultivation of this fruit within the Dominion. The first variety that was sent out, known as the New Rochelle or Lawton, proved to be too tender to endure our climate, and the later introductions have not been very widely disseminated.

A deep, dry and rich soil is most favorable to the growth of this plant. **The canes** should be **planted** in rows eight **feet apart** and three feet **apart** in the row. **If the growing canes are pinched** back in **the month** of August, **they will** become **stocky, ripen their wood better,** and yield more and better fruit, than if left **to grow** unchecked. The old canes which have borne fruit **should be** cut out close **to the** ground as soon as **the** fruit is gathered, and if there be **a** superabundance of young shoots, they **should** be removed at the same **time.** A pair of shears with long handles, or a pruning **hook** with a long handle, **will be** found convenient implements for this **work.** All suckers **that come** up between the rows should be **cut up as weeds.**

The **cultivation consists** in keeping **the ground mellow and** free from weeds, and **in such an** annual **manuring with well-rotted barnyard manure as will be sufficient to keep** the ground **in a good state of fertility. Too much manure at** one time induces **a too luxuriant growth of** the cane, resulting in unripened wood that **is apt to suffer from the** frosts of winter. If the plants **have not** been properly pinched during the season of growth, **they** will require to be pruned back in spring to a height of about four feet, and the lateral branches to about sixteen inches.

The Blackberry is multiplied by transplanting the suckers, and by planting cuttings of the **roots.** When **the** variety is scarce, and it is desired to **multiply by as small divisions as possible, it will** be found advantageous **to prepare a** hotbed and plant **the root cuttings on a gentle bottom heat.**

The following varieties seem worthy of attention. Others **are** being **brought to notice,** but have not yet been sufficiently tested to speak **with** confidence of their merits. Could some one invent a Blackberry without thorns, yet as productive as those having thorns, and yielding fruit of as fine size and quality, he would deserve the lasting gratitude of every lover of this berry.

The Kittatinny.—This variety has the reputation of being **very hardy,** and so far as it has been tried seems to have given good satisfaction. The berries are large, slightly conical, and of a deep **shining** black, sweet, and with a rich, pleasant Blackberry flavor. The plant grows vigorously and bears abundantly, continuing to ripen its fruit for four or five weeks.

WILSON'S EARLY.—This variety ripens early, and perfects its entire crop in about two weeks. It seems to partake of the character of the Dewberry, the canes occasionally taking root at the tips. The fruit is very large, slightly pointed, deep black, and quite firm.

This variety was distributed by the Fruit Growers' Association of Ontario to all its members in the spring of 1871, so that its adaptedness to the climate of that Province will soon be thoroughly tested.

NEW ROCHELLE.—*Lawton.*—The climate is too severe for this variety anywhere beyond the Peach region. Within that limit it grows well, and bears very large crops. The berries are very large, deep black when fully ripe, and then it is soft, juicy, sweet, and of pleasant flavor, but if gathered too soon, when it first begins to get black, it is very sour and flavorless. Begins to ripen early in August and continues for five or six weeks.

THE STRAWBERRY.

Strawberry plants do not always produce perfect flowers. Some varieties produce flowers having only pistils and no stamens, these are called pistillate sorts; others produce flowers with both stamens and pistils, these are called hermaphrodite. In some of the hermaphrodite varieties the number of stamens is so few, or the development so imperfect, that there is not sufficient pollen to fertilize all the seed vessels. When from any cause there is no pollen to fall on the pistils, and thus to give vitality to the seed germ, then the receptacle or berry is not developed at all, and no strawberries are produced. When there is not enough pollen to give a grain to each pistil, then the seed germ at the base of that pistil is not vitalized, and the portion of the berry forming the receptacle of that particular seed does not grow to its proper size or attain its true character, and when any considerable number of them are not fertilized, the berry becomes deformed and mis-shapen. The Hovey's Seedling is an instance of a pistillate variety, one in which the stamens are wholly wanting; Russell's Prolific is an instance of one in which the stamens are defective, being too few or too imperfectly developed to thoroughly fertilize the fruit; while the Wilson produces a perfect flower with a sufficiency of well-developed stamens.

The following figure is a representation of a perfect flower, showing the stamens, with the anthers on their extremities, arranged in a circle around the receptacle or berry, which is studded all over with slender hair-like pistils. Varieties which produce such flowers have an abundance of pollen, much more than enough to supply every pistil with the requisite fertilizing agent. Hence such varieties always have perfectly formed fruit, and if the plant produces an abundance of flowers there will be an abundance of fruit.

Fig. 49.

Fig. 50 represents a pistillate flower. It will be at once seen that there are no stamens, and consequently no anthers, arranged around the berry, though there are plenty of pistils bristling over its surface. Unless these pistils receive pollen from some other strawberry flower, there can be no vitalizing of the seed germ, and, in consequence, no swelling and growth of the receptacle, or, in other words, no berries. If, then, the garden be planted only with Hovey's Seedling, or any other merely pistillate sort, there

Fig. 50.

will be no fruit; but if there be planted near them some of the Wilson, or any other sort having an abundance of stamens, there will be fruit on the pistillate as well as the staminate sort, provided both are in bloom at the same time, so that the pollen may fertilize them. Hence it will be seen that in planting strawberries attention must be given to the character of the flowers, else there may be a fine growth of plants, and an abundance of blossoms, but no fruit.

The SOIL for strawberry plants should be deep, well pulverized and rich. A deep strong loam is the soil best suited to all varieties; but any soil that is well drained, well pulverized to a depth of sixteen inches, and well enriched, will make a good strawberry bed. There are some varieties that yield their finest fruit, and in greatest quantity, in a clay soil. Of this class are Triomphe de Gand and Jucunda, but they can be made to yield very fine fruit on sandy soil that is highly supplied with fertilizers. It has been said that it is possible to injure the strawberry crop by too high manuring, the plants growing vigorously, but running to vine and not to fruit. Such is not our experience. We have applied well decomposed manure in great quantities to all the leading varieties, and have found the fruit to be increased in proportion to the increased growth of the plant. Much has been written concerning special fertilizers for the strawberry, and great stress laid upon the use of tan-bark and other substances, but the best special manure we have found has been that from the barn-yard. It should be remembered that thorough cultivation and high manuring are the secrets of success in the cultivation of the strawberry, and that a much larger return will be obtained from one quarter of an acre that has been thoroughly prepared by deep subsoil plowing, cross plowing, thorough pulverization and abundant manuring, than from a whole acre that is skimmed over and half manured. We are fully persuaded that our strawberry growers generally err in planting too much land, and that they would find their profits much increased if they would lessen their acreage and double the cultivation and enriching of that which remains.

We have found the early spring to be the best TIME for setting strawberry plants. When but a small bed is to be planted, and the plants are near at hand, they may be set at any time by taking suitable pains, and selecting suitable weather ; but when any large quantity is to be planted, there is danger that there will be a great many failures in fall **planting,** unless the weather is unusually favorable in September. If set later than September, there is great danger that the plants will not become sufficiently rooted before **winter sets in** to enable them to pass that trying season safely. In those parts of the country where the snow does not lie on the ground all winter, and consequently **can** not to be relied **upon as** a protection to the plants, **it is very** desirable that they should be lightly covered **with** branches of evergreens, **leaves, or straw. This protects the crowns of the** plants, in **which the fruit buds are enveloped, from the frequent** alternate freezing **and** thawing to which they might be otherwise **subjected, and** which often kills the fruit buds before spring.

The best PLANTS for setting out are strong, well-rooted runners. Theorists would have us believe that the first plant that forms on each runner is better and more productive than the subsequent plants on the same runner ; but this **is mere theory,** without foundation in fact. Provided the plants be well **rooted, the** last one on the runner is as good and **as** productive as the first, under the same treatment. **In field culture it is** found con**venient to set the plants** in rows, three feet apart, **so** that they **may be** tilled **with a horse and cultivator, and** the plants one foot apart in **the row. These should be** carefully tilled with cultivator and **hoe during** the first season, and until the berries are beginning **to swell in the second.** After the fruit **has been** gathered, the ground should be mellowed up, the weeds destroyed, and the plantation tilled until the fruit begins again to swell in **the** third season. This crop of fruit should be the last, and after **it** is gathered the plantation should be ploughed up and devoted **to some** other crops for a few years before strawberries are again **planted**

A good method of PREPARING the ground for a strawberry plantation is to seed it down with clover. During the winter give the clover a good heavy top dressing of ashes. When the clover comes into bloom the next summer, plough it all under, using a chain, if necessary, in order to cover it. In the fall cross plough, following the plough with the subsoiler. In the spring put on all the manure from the barnyard that can be had, plough it under by crossing the last furrows, and again follow with the subsoiler. Now sow with carrots or mangolds, and keep them clean. In the fall, if the soil be clayey, plough again, and leave the ground rough during the winter. In the spring, put on all the old, fine, thoroughly decomposed manure, that has been provided, together with any fine ground bones there are to spare, and harrow it in with a two-horse cultivator, run as deep as possible. Finish by pulverizing well with the harrow, and then set the strawberry plants. Ground that has been prepared in this way is much easier kept clean, and will produce healthier plants and larger berries, and more of them, than any slip-shod style of cultivation.

In garden cultivation, the ground may be laid off in beds, and the plants set in rows two feet apart, and one foot apart in the row. After taking two crops of fruit, it will be found a saving of labor to spade the plants under, and rely upon another bed, which was set out in April previous, in preference to keeping the old bed clean.

A good supply of MOISTURE during the time that the fruit is swelling and ripening, is a very essential thing in successful strawberry culture. In many parts of the country we are liable to have dry weather during a great part of June, just when the strawberry needs a great deal of moisture. In order to lessen the evils of this dry spell, recourse should be had to mulching, and as it can not yet be quite certainly foretold what the weather is to be, the mulch should be put on about the first of June. The most convenient and best mulch that can be applied is short grass, cut from the lawn or meadow. This will scatter no seeds, will keep the fruit from the dirt, and will, in many seasons, double the value of the crop.

Strawberry plants are very easily raised from seed. **The fruit should be gathered when it is fully ripe, and crushed with dry sand enough to** separate the seeds from each other, **and then sown,** sand and all, on the surface of a bed, prepared by thorough pulverizing and abundant manuring with old compost. If kept shaded from the direct rays of the sun, and kept moist by gentle waterings, with a fine rose, every day, the seed will germinate and the plants appear **in** about six weeks. After these have made four or five leaves they may be pricked out into another bed, where **they will** have room to grow. It is well to protect them with **a covering of a** few **leaves during the** winter. **The** first **year of fruiting they are very likely to make great promises, which they never afterwards keep, so that** too much reliance **must not be placed on the appearance of the first fruiting.**

The Alpine varieties should always be propagated from seed, **for the reason that** the berries are always much finer from young seedlings than from old plants, or from the runners of those Alpines that throw out runners. Some of the Alpines are what are termed *bush* plants; they never produce runners, and must be multiplied either by division of the **old plant or by seed.** Some **of** the Alpines **are monthly fruiters, and, in cool,** moist **seasons** especially, **if growing in a generous** soil, they will bear fruit continuously, **from June to November.** The Mexican everbearing, **which was introduced to** public notice with a great flourish of trumpets, as being something quite extraordinary, is an **instance of** a monthly Alpine variety.

Varieties of Strawberries.

The name of these is legion, and it would be a very profitless waste of time to endeavour to describe a hundredth part. **Very few** varieties succeed well over a large territory in all soils **and** climates; many are extremely fastidious, and never do well **beyond the spot that** gave them birth. Therefore it is wise to buy new varieties sparingly, and rely for the supply upon well-known and long-tested sorts. The following descriptions will be confined mainly to those sorts which are now prominently before the public, and will give as concisely as possible the prominent characters of each.

AGRICULTURIST.—On sandy soils it is almost worthless, requiring altogether too much coaxing and petting to get a fair crop of fruit. On some clay loams, with high culture, it gives a good crop of large, conical berries with long necks, of light crimson color, sweet and rich. Pistillate.

AUSTIN.—*Shaker.*—A large berry, soft, white flesh, very acid, and having very little flavor.

BOSTON PINE.—*Bartlett.*—Is tolerably productive in some rich and deep soils, if grown in hills and the runners kept off. It has the merit of being of excellent flavour, and of ripening early. The berries are above medium size, light crimson, sweet and rich. Hermaphrodite.

CHARLES DOWNING.—This variety is attracting considerable attention, and has the reputation of being very productive, with very large deep scarlet berries, which are sweet, juicy and rich. Hermaphrodite. We have not fully tested its merits.

COLFAX.—Not worth growing. Berries small, soft, and sour. Very productive.

DOCTOR NICAISE.—With high culture, the berries are often immense; but they are too few to make it a very desirable variety. The berries are usually of a cock's-comb shape, scarlet, juicy, sweet, but not high flavored. Hermaphrodite.

GOLDEN QUEEN.—An old variety with a new name. It is Trollope's Victoria. It was first brought to our notice by an itinerant pedlar, who had a basket of the fruit, and was soliciting orders for it as something new.

GREEN PROLIFIC.—A very large and a very sour berry, without flavor, but the plant is very vigorous and productive.

HOVEY'S SEEDLING.—This has been a very popular sort, and did a great deal to awaken attention to the cultivation of the strawberry. The **plants** are hardy and vigorous, yielding moderate crops of large and finely flavored fruit. It is a pistillate sort, hence it **can not** be **fruited** without planting some pollen-bearing sorts **near by.**

JUCUNDA.—In some localities this variety succeeds very well, while in many other places it **is almost a total failure.** It prefers a strong soil, and succeeds **best** grown **in hills, with** the runners **cut off.** The berries are large, light scarlet **in color,** with moderately firm flesh, and not very high flavor. Hermaphrodite.

LA CONSTANTE.—This is another of those fastidious sorts, that, in a few localities, bears good crops of fruit, but that on the whole seems to suffer from our hot summers, **and to prove very often** quite unsatisfactory. It is a large, **bright** crimson berry, with a firm flesh, of a rich and delicious **quality. Hermaphrodite.**

LADIES' PINE.—**This originated with** W. H. Read, **of** Port Dalhousie, **Ont., and is one of the most** delicious of strawberries. Unfortunately **it is too** unproductive to retain a place in our gardens. Pistillate.

LENNIG'S WHITE.—*White Pine apple.*—*Albion White.*—Another very finely-flavoured strawberry, but a very **moderate** cropper. The best white variety in cultivation. **The berry is** large, white slightly tinged with **pink, soft, juicy,** sweet and **rich, with a** very decided **pine-apple flavor. Hermaphrodite.**

NAPOLEON III.—**This variety appears to be both** vigorous **and productive, yet it has not been** sufficiently long in cultivation **here to speak very** decidedly of its qualities in these respects. **The berry is large,** light scarlet, tolerably firm, juicy and rich. **Hermaphrodite.**

NICANOR.—A **very** productive variety, with a good deal **of uniformity in the size** of the fruit, but hardly large enough to **please** The berries are only of medium size when there is a **full** crop; bright scarlet in color, tolerably firm, rich and of pleasant flavour. Hermaphrodite.

PEAK'S EMPEROR.—We **can only** say of this that the berries are large, dark crimson, firm, with a pleasant, sub-acid flavor. Its qualities of vigor and of fruitfulness have not been tested in this country.

PRESIDENT WILDER.—There are two varieties bearing this name,—the one originated in Europe, and but very little known in America; the other raised by the Hon. Marshall P. Wilder, President of the American Pomological Society. The latter variety has been very widely disseminated, and we may soon hope to see how well it will adapt itself to all soils and localities. In the grounds of the originator it is very productive, and the berries are large, bright crimson scarlet, sweet and rich.

RUSSELL'S PROLIFIC.—For all practical purposes this variety should be treated as pistillate, though there are usually a few stamens more or less perfect. We have noticed that it thrives best, and the berries are of better flavor, in sandy soils, and that if plentifully supplied with pollen there is an enormous crop of fruit, which is large, light crimson, soft, and pleasantly flavored.

TRIOMPHE DE GAND.—So widely has this variety been disseminated that it is now well known, and has proved itself to be better adapted to a great variety of localities than is usual with European sorts. It is vigorous and hardy, yielding its largest crops and finest berries in clayey soils, with high culture in hills and with the runners cut off. Though the flowers are hermaphrodite, there is frequently an insufficiency of pollen to fertilize all the seed germs, hence the fruit is sometimes misshapen, and the apex of the berry hard. The berries are large, light crimson, firm, bearing carriage well, glossy, pleasant flavored but not rich.

TROLLOPE'S VICTORIA.—*Golden Queen.*—*Trembly's Union.*—A large, handsome and excellent English variety, which has been a good deal disseminated under one name or the other. The plants are vigorous and healthy, but only medium in productiveness. The berries are very large, light crimson, juicy, rich, and with a peculiarly pleasant and almost aromatic flavour. Hermaphrodite.

WILSON.—The most widely distributed and most generally grown, especially for market, of all the varieties. The plants are very hardy, vigorous and exceedingly productive in all soils, localities and climates; there is no other sort that has been found to adapt itself to all situations so well as this one. The berries are large, dark crimson when fully ripe, moderately firm, with a sprightly acid flavor. Hermaphrodite After producing one or two full crops the plants begin to fail, and on this account new beds should be planted frequently.

THE RASPBERRY.

The varieties of the Raspberry in cultivation among us are derived either from the European or from the Red or Black Raspberries of America. Those that derive their origin from the European or from the Red American, multiply by suckers which come up from the roots, while those that spring from the Black Raspberry are increased from the tips of the canes, which, bending over until they reach the ground, take root at the extremities.

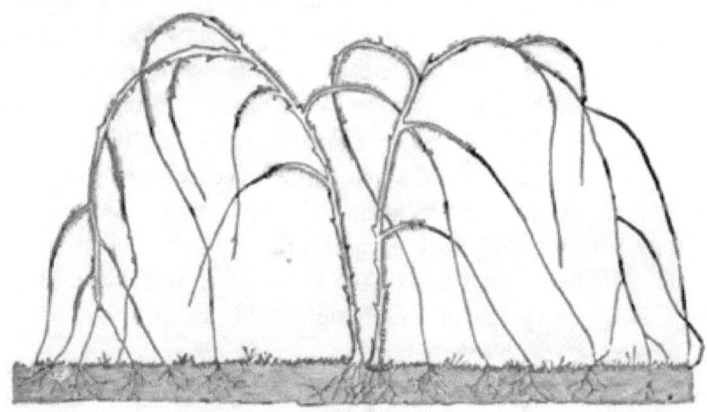

Fig. 51.

Fig. 51 represents a plant of the Black variety, with the tips of the branches taking root in the soil.

In the autumn, the suckers may be taken up from the parent

plant with a spade, and those that take root at the tips of the new canes, may be removed by cutting *the rooted tips* off from the parent cane, and lifting *them* from the soil. These may be then planted out where they are intended to remain, and covered with coarse manure to the depth of five or six inches. Treated in this way they will make stronger plants during the next season, than when set out in the spring. If the transplanting is done in the spring, the plants should be mulched to the same depth, as a protection to the roots against the heat of summer.

The Raspberry produces the best and finest fruit in a deep, moist, and very rich soil, and whenever these conditions can be secured, no difficulty will be experienced on account of the character of the soil. But it will be at once seen that such requirements can not be met in land that is badly drained, or where a hard, unbroken subsoil is allowed to lie near to the surface. There are places where the ground is naturally underdrained, the soil of good depth and great fertility, but these are highly favored spots, and most cultivators will find it necessary to prepare the ground by deep ploughing, the application of manures, and perhaps by underdraining. If water stands in the soil at a depth of eighteen to twenty inches from the surface, it must first be removed by underdrains, for nothing is more injurious to the Raspberry than stagnant water at the root. This may seem strange to some, after having already said that it delights in a moist soil, but plants make a great difference between moist and wet. A thoroughly underdrained clayey loam is the very best soil naturally for the most economical cultivation of this fruit. The plough should be run as deep as possible, and if the plough can be followed by the subsoiler, right behind it in the bottom of the furrow, so much the better.

The plants should be set in rows six feet apart, and two feet apart in the row. Six feet may seem to be a great distance between the rows, but if the plants have proper culture it will soon be found not to be too much for convenient use of the cultivator. In a small garden, where the horse and cultivator cannot be used, the rows may be set four feet apart. **If** set at two feet apart in the row, the plants will soon form a continuous hedge, and any suckers appearing between the **rows, unless** wanted for a new plantation, **should be** treated as weeds and thoroughly cut up.

The plants should be prepared for setting **out** by cutting **back the cane** or top to within three or four inches of the root. **A growth** of leaves or shoots is not wanted from this cane; such growth only serves to exhaust **the** plant; but what is wanted is a good strong growth of new shoots from the root. These will survive the winter and produce fruit the next summer, while all the growth from the top or old cane will only die when autumn comes; and **if this top** should bear fruit, **as** it very likely **will,** the effect is **to exhaust** the root and enfeeble, if not wholly ruin, the young **root sprout that forms the** cane for next year. If no sprout comes up **from the roots, and survives the summer, though** the top **you plant may bear leaves,** and shoots and fruit, in the **autumn it will die, and** the whole plant with it.

The Raspberry is a sort of biennial plant; the canes that **come up** from the root this season will bear fruit next summer **and die** in the autumn, and if from any cause no new canes come up during the summer to supply their place, there will **be nothing** to continue the plant another year, and it wholly fails. **For this** reason **it is** best to cut away the **top when planting,** leaving only enough to **show its position after it has been set out.**

The **cultivation during the first season** after planting will consist in keeping the **soil well stirred on** the surface and free from weeds. Those who **wish to** economize ground and labor may plant bush beans between the rows, without injury to the Raspberry plants. In the autumn or very early in the spring, but better **in the** autumn, the plants should be liberally supplied with barnyard manure spread on the surface over the roots. This should be allowed to remain there, becoming gradually in**corporated** with the soil by the tilling, and renewed as often as **it becomes** wasted, so that the roots may be kept cool and moist **in summer,** and protected from the extremes of the winter's frost.

During the first season's growth after planting, the young canes that come up from the root should be pinched off at the tip, with the thumb and finger, as soon as they reach the height of fourteen to eighteen inches, and any side shoots they may throw out should be pinched in when they are a foot long.

In the second summer more and stronger canes will come up from the root. These may be allowed to grow until they are twenty-four to thirty inches in length, when they should be pinched-in, and the side branches that may be thrown out should be stopped when they are from eighteen to twenty inches long. It will usually be found that the main canes will require to be pinched-in some time in June, and the side branches early in August; yet the cultivator will remember that this pruning is to be done, not according to the almanac, but when the canes have reached the requisite length, be the month or day what it may. If the plants are thoroughly pruned in this way, they will be stocky and strong, capable of standing upright, and keeping their crop of fruit well above the ground, out of the dirt. During the second season, the canes that grew the first summer will yield a nice crop of fruit, as much as the plant ought to produce. As soon as the fruit has been gathered, the canes that produced it should be cut off at the ground and removed. They are of no further use; as the autumn comes on they will die, and by removing them as soon as the fruit is gathered, more room, light and air are given to the young canes that have come up during the season, and that are to bear the fruit next year. And of these young canes, if any of them should be weak and slender, it is always advisable to cut them away also at this time, leaving only those that are vigorous and capable of supporting the crop of fruit.

In the autumn a further supply of manure should be furnished, and it may be here said, once for all, that this manuring should be performed every fall, and that he who does it with a liberal hand will be liberally rewarded in the quantity and quality of the fruit. Besides enriching the soil, the surface just over the roots and where the cultivator does not reach in passing between the rows, should be covered to the depth of four to five inches with coarse barnyard litter, such as straw, or corn stalks, or refuse hay. If these cannot be had in sufficient quantity, recourse may be had to rotten chips or rotten tan-bark, sawdust or shavings, with which some ashes have been mixed. This mulching serves a very important purpose in preserving the plants in a healthy and vigorous state, and securing a large crop of large fruit.

In some parts of the Dominion, where the snow does not remain on the ground constantly during the winter, it becomes necessary to protect some of the more tender varieties. This is most conveniently and cheaply done by bending the canes carefully over, making the bend as near the ground as possible, and throwing a little soil on the tops. When the plants are ready to start in the spring they are gently lifted, the soil shaken off, and the canes fastened in an upright position by tying to a stake or trellis. When the ground is covered with snow to a depth of two or three feet all the winter, no such protection is necessary; and we have noticed that those plants, whose roots are well protected by a liberal mulching, are seldom injured by the winter, though there was often no snow at all on the ground. With proper attention to the pruning of the plants while they are growing, and keeping the soil well enriched and the roots protected with a good mulch both winter and summer, there will be much less complaint of injury to the canes by the winter, and a fine crop of large and handsome fruit will well repay all the labor bestowed.

The following varieties have been selected from a very long list, as being the most worthy of attention in this climate.

BRINCKLE'S ORANGE.—*Orange.*—This is the highest flavored, large-sized, light colored raspberry in cultivation, and well deserves a place in every garden throughout the Dominion. It is not perfectly hardy in those parts where the snow does not cover the ground all winter, but after growing it for at least a dozen years, it has proved so nearly hardy, and such an abundant bearer, that we place it in the front rank. Indeed, when it has been grown in rich, deep soil, and well mulched, it has not failed at any time to yield a fine crop of fruit. The berries are of large size, light orange color, juicy, sweet, and rich. The canes are strong, exceedingly productive, and continue in bearing in moist seasons for about six weeks.

Belle de Fontenay.—*Belle d'Orleans.*—The best of the autumn-bearing varieties of the Antwerp class. It has the fault of sending up a great quantity of suckers, which require to be kept down with the hoe like so many weeds. If the canes are cut to the ground every spring, the fall crop will be much better than if the canes are allowed to remain and bear a summer crop. In the more northern parts of the country, it will be necessary to cut down the canes in spring, in order to get the autumn crop sufficiently forward to ripen the fruit; and indeed it is doubtful whether it will even then ripen in those parts where the summers are very short and cool.

The berries are large, dark crimson in color, juicy, with a very pleasant, sprightly flavor; the canes are stout, and moderately productive.

Clarke.—A variety but recently brought to notice, and thriving better than most of this class on a light sandy soil. It has been claimed for this variety, that it is perfecty hardy, but we have not found it to be more hardy than the Franconia, nor as hardy as the Philadelphia.

The berries are of large size, of a bright crimson color, juicy, sweet, and of excellent flavor. It continues to ripen for a long time, and is an abundant cropper.

Davidson's Thornless.—*Thornless Black Cap.*—This variety of the Black Cap has the great merit of being destitute of thorns, save a very small one on the leaf stalk. Those who have had experience of the many and sore scratches, to say nothing of torn garments, that one is sure to get in gathering the fruit of the American Black Cap, will be able to appreciate the comfort of picking berries where there are no thorns to lacerate the hands and tear the clothes.

The berries are about the size of the average Black Cap, ripen early, are black, sweet, and well flavored. The plants are vigorous, very productive, and perfectly hardy.

FASTOLLF.—An old English variety, of fine appearance and excellent flavor, too soft to endure transportation to a distant market, but very valuable for home use. The canes are strong, with stiff spines, and bear abundant crops of large, purplish crimson berries, sweet, rich, and high flavored.

PHILADELPHIA.—This variety is also almost free from spines, and one of the most hardy and prolific in cultivation. It does not take root from the tips of the young canes like Purple Cane, to which it seems to be nearly related, and throws up suckers quite sparingly. For these reasons, it has been found to be a valuable variety to cultivate for a near market, and is particularly well adapted to sandy soils.

The berries are of full medium size, globular in form, dark red, not rich, but of a pleasant sub-acid flavor. The canes are stout, erect, and branching; the leaves thick and tough, and do not suffer in times of drought, and the crop is exceedingly abundant.

FRANCONIA.—This is a very valuable variety, being nearly hardy, and very productive. The berries are large, dark purplish red, sufficiently firm to carry well to market, and of a rich, sprightly and agreeable flavor. It has been in cultivation for a long time, and stands next to the Philadelphia in hardihood and productiveness, while it excels that variety in size and flavor of the fruit, and firmness of berry.

FRENCH.—*Vice-President French.*—Originated by Dr. Brinckle, and named by him after one of the Vice-Presidents of the Massachusetts Horticultural Society. It is a valuable variety, ripening a little later than most other kinds.

The fruit is of full medium size, of a deep crimson color, tolerably firm fleshed, sweet and of excellent flavor. The canes are strong, erect, and very productive.

GOLDEN THORNLESS.—This is a variety of the Black Cap

family, rooting at the tips of the young canes, but the berries are of a deep dull orange. It is the most productive and the berries are the largest of any of the Yellow American Raspberries. The canes are very nearly thornless, moderately vigorous, perfectly hardy, and enormously productive. The berries are about the size of the Mammoth Cluster, very firm, juicy, and pleasant, but not high flavored. We have never seen any of the American Yellow Raspberries that were equal in flavor to the Black Caps, but this variety is the most desirable and valuable of any of the Yellows, and makes a very pleasing addition to one's list of sorts.

HORNET.—A European variety, not as hardy as would be desirable, though thriving well where the winter snows are deep. The berry is very large, showy, deep crimson, juicy, and of fine flavor.

IMPERIAL.—We have found this variety more hardy and more productive than Hornet, and the fruit nearly equal to it in size, of a bright red color, tolerably firm, juicy, and of excellent flavor.

KNEVET'S GIANT.—An old English variety that deserves more attention than it has received. It is a very strong grower, nearly as hardy as the Franconia, quite hardy when there are deep snows through the winter, and exceedingly productive. The berries are of the very largest size, of a deep red color, quite firm, juicy, and of excellent flavor. We fully believe that in the vicinity of Ottawa and Montreal it might be profitably grown for market, and would certainly be one of the most attractive berries that could be introduced.

LUM'S EVERBEARING—*Autumn Black Cap.*—A very productive fall-bearing variety of the Black Cap. The berries are about the usual size of the fruit in this class, and perhaaps a little more juicy. In most of our country it will be found necessary to cut down all the canes in the spring even with the ground, and not seek to obtain the double crop, for unless this is done, the autumn crop will not ripen before the frosts set in.

If the canes are cut down in **the spring the** young shoots are forced on more rapidly, and will begin to ripen their fruit about the first of September. We advise those who live in those parts of the **country where** they find it difficult to raise apples, and where **pears are** almost an impossibility, **to** give this and the **Belle** de Fontenay a **trial, treating them as here** recommended, and see if in this way **they are not able to secure a crop of** autumn raspberries that will in **some measure compensate for the loss** of other fruits.

MAMMOTH CLUSTER.—The **largest and best of** the varieties of the Black Cap **family. The** canes **are very strong,** branching, perfectly **hardy, and** enormously **productive.** The berries are large, **black, with a** handsome **bloom, juicy, sweet,** and fine flavored. It ripens later than Davidson's Thornless, in this **way** continuing **the season of this** class of **fruit.**

NAOMI.—We give **this variety a place here** merely to **say** that, after having grown **it for** several years, we fail to **see** sufficient **difference between it and the** Franconia to make **any distinction. It is no** more hardy, nor any more productive, **nor different in size** or flavor of fruit.

PURPLE CANE.—This native variety is hardy, very **productive,** and ripens its fruit early and all at once. The **canes are strong and tall, perfectly hardy, and root at the tips. The berries are of medium size, of a purplish maroon color, too soft** to bear **carrying to a** distant market, but **good for home use, sweet, juicy, and** rich.

THE CURRANT.

It is quite common to find the Currant **bushes in some neglected part** of the **garden,** nearly hidden by the grass and weeds, and yet bearing considerable crops of fruit. But though the great vitality of the plant will enable it to endure such treatment, it **will** repay a more generous treatment in both size and quality **of fruit.** While thriving well in almost every soil, it will produce the best results in a well-drained clayey loam, which is deep and rich; and if liberally supplied with **manure of any** description, the crop of fruit will be immense.

The Currant is easily propagated by cuttings or by layers. If the cuttings are taken off in August, made about six inches long, and planted with the top bud just even with the surface of the ground, and then covered when winter sets in with a mulch of coarse litter six inches deep to prevent them from being thrown up by the frost, they will make stronger plants the next season than when planted in spring. The mulch should be taken off in the spring, so as not to interfere with the growth of the cuttings.

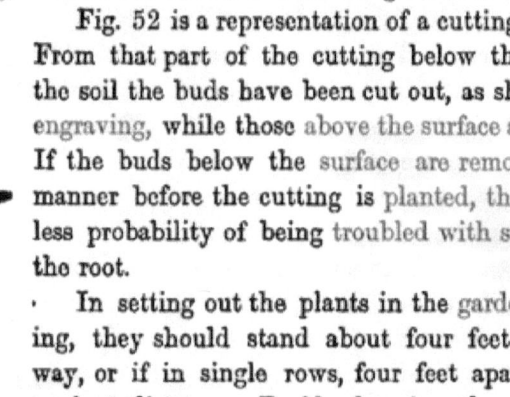

Fig. 52 is a representation of a cutting as planted. From that part of the cutting below the surface of the soil the buds have been cut out, as shown in the engraving, while those above the surface are retained. If the buds below the surface are removed in this manner before the cutting is planted, there is much less probability of being troubled with suckers from the root.

In setting out the plants in the garden for fruiting, they should stand about four feet apart each way, or if in single rows, four feet apart is a convenient distance. Besides keeping the ground rich and clean between the bushes, it will be found that a heavy mulch, such as is recommended for the Raspberry, will be of great advantage, especially in very hot and dry seasons. A little pruning will also be serviceable, enough to keep the head open, and occasionally thin out the old wood, so as to keep the top in a healthy and vigorous condition.

Fig. 52.

The following varieties are those most worthy of attention:

BLACK NAPLES.—This is the best of all the Black Currants; the fruit is large and fine, and the clusters are both larger and more numerous than in any other black sort.

CHAMPAGNE.—A very handsome pale pink variety, esteemed on account of its peculiar color more than for any special quality of the fruit.

CHERRY.—The largest Red Currant, very **showy, and sells well in market. Is** hardly as productive in our climate **as the** Red Dutch, and decidedly more acid. Bunches quite short.

GLOIRE DE SABLONS.—A very prettily striped variety, red and **white, but** small in size, and valuable chiefly for its ornamental **appearance.**

LA VERSAILLAISE.—So **very closely** resembling the Cherry Currant in size, color **and flavor,** that having the one we have no occasion for the other.

RED DUTCH.—This **old,** well known and long tried sort is yet a very valuable variety, of good size, fine color, rich acid flavor, long clusters and exceedingly productive.

VICTORIA.—A valuable, late ripening **sort.** The fruit is **of a** bright red **color, as** large as the Red **Dutch. The** bunches **are** very long, **and hang** a fortnight **longer than other sorts. It** is an abundant **bearer, and greatly lengthens the** Currant season.

WHITE GRAPE.—**The best White** Currant; berries very large, **not so acid as the red** varieties, and **of** good flavor. An exceedingly productive and valuable sort.

THE GOOSEBERRY.

In the climate of Great Britain, the **Gooseberry is** grown in great perfection, but with **us, it is only in** comparatively a few favored localities **that any good measure** of success crowns our **efforts.** It is usual for cultivators **to** say, that the *mildew* is so bad that it destroys **the crop, and** even ruins the plants. For all practical purposes, this statement is sufficiently exact, though the real **difficulty lies,** not in the mildew, but in such a condition **of** the epidermis **or** outer skin of the leaves and fruit of the Gooseberry, as to provide a suitable bed for the growth of the minute fungoid plants which constitute mildew. This condition is doubtless produced by a state of atmosphere incidental to the climate of this country, the effects of which we do not know how **fully to counteract.**

In those parts of the Maritime Provinces where the **sea fogs** prevail, the European varieties of the Gooseberry succeed, but farther inland, beyond their influence, the same difficulties are experienced.

The foreign, or European varieties of Gooseberry, suffer more from this peculiar condition of our atmosphere than some of our native sorts, and doubtless the cultivation of the English varieties will always be attended with great difficulty. It is almost useless to undertake their cultivation in a sandy soil. In a deep and very rich clay loam, they may thrive, but they will require careful culture, thorough pruning, abundant manuring, and in most places to be thoroughly mulched with hay or straw, or some coarse material, and well watered. An occasional sprinkling of salt on the mulch, in moderate quantity, has been found to be serviceable in helping to maintain a suitable humidity.

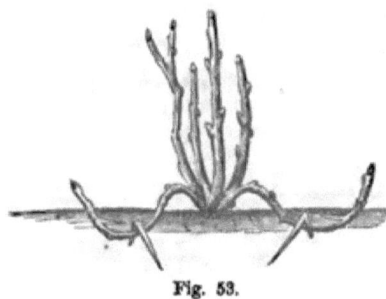

Fig. 53.

The propagation of the Gooseberry is both by cuttings and by layering. Usually cuttings will succeed well. New varieties are obtained from seed. Seedlings of European varieties have not proved to be suited to our climate, but there is every reason to believe that seedlings from some of our native sorts may yet be obtained of good size and flavor, and which will be adapted to the climate, and free from mildew.

The process of layering is shown at fig. 53. It consists in bending down a branch, on one side of which a tongue has been cut with a sharp knife, and fastening the cut part below the surface of the soil, by means of a hooked peg.

The varieties of foreign Gooseberries are too numerous to be given here, and every year gives us additions to the list. They are all fine berries where they can be grown, and all subject to mildew, in most places and seasons.

There are some American varieties which have been found to be usually exempt from mildew. They are not as large and showy as the English sorts, but we must content ourselves with these until better are produced. We consider the two described below to be the best.

DOWNING.—Was raised by Mr. Chas. Downing, of Newburgh, N. Y., and has proved to be the best of the American sorts thus far. The berry is of medium size, of a light green color, and very good flavor. The plant grows upright, with shining, deep-green leaves, and is very productive.

HOUGHTON.—The fruit is not as large as the Downing, is of a pale red color, sweet and good. The plant grows well, but the branches are slender, with a somewhat drooping habit, and exceedingly productive.

THE CRANBERRY.

We desire to call attention to the cultivation of this fruit, believing that there are many acres now lying wholly neglected, covered with rushes, coarse grasses, stunted bushes, and possibly intermingled with vines of the Cranberry, which are well adapted to its successful growth, and which, by the application of a little labor and capital, might be made to yield a handsome revenue. At present this fruit brings high prices in all the cities of this continent, selling readily at from eight to ten dollars per barrel; and should it ever happen that the supply becomes equal to the demand in America, the fruit can be put up in barrels, and shipped with perfect safety across the Atlantic.

Cranberry plantations have been found to yield an average crop of one hundred bushels to the acre, taking one year with another, though it is no uncommon thing to gather two hundred and three hundred bushels to the acre. It is one of our hardiest fruit-bearing vines, growing wild in many of our marshes; it is very prolific, requires but little care after being once fully established, and will remain without renewal on the same ground, and continue to bear abundantly for an indefinite length of time. The fruit is much esteemed and in good demand, and when properly handled, will keep fresh a twelvemonth and bear transportation without injury.

In selecting a location for a Cranberry plantation, it is highly important to avoid those places where the water must be stagnant,—such soil is sodden and cold, and the roots will rot in it. If it cannot be so drained that the water will be at least one foot below the surface of the soil, it is unfit for Cranberry culture. Yet we have no confidence in an upland plantation. The Cranberry is a semi-aquatic plant, and requires a constant supply of water, therefore, it is necessary to select a place which can be abundantly supplied. It is also very desirable in our climate that it should be well sheltered from cold, raw winds, and if it have a southern exposure so much the better. If it be possible to secure a piece of ground that can be overflowed at pleasure, having in reserve a sufficient body of water higher up for this purpose, it will be of great advantage. This may often be secured by erecting two dams, one above the Cranberry beds and the other below. By means of the upper dam a body of water may be kept always at hand, which can be let on to the Cranberry plants at pleasure; and by means of the lower dam, with properly arranged gates, the water can be kept on the beds at any desired level. In this way the plants can be protected from late spring frosts that would kill the blossoms, or from very early autumn frosts that would injure the fruit before it is fully ripe. During winter the water should be kept so deep that it will not be frozen through to the ground, and this may protect the plants from too great a degree of cold. During the summer the water should be drawn off to about one foot below the surface of the beds, so that the roots may find moisture all summer, and yet the soil above not be filled with stagnant water. Again, the water should not be too cold. Some locations that are supplied with water from springs in the adjacent bank are unsuitable, because the water is very cold. This may sometimes be remedied by cutting a ditch along the border, and draining off the **cold, icy** spring water, or gathering it into a reservoir, where it **will be** warmed by the sun and air before it reaches the plantation.

The **soil** must not be too rich. The vines may grow in good alluvial soils, and seem very flourishing, but they will not bear **fruit.** Clay and marl are wholly unsuitable, and heavy soils in general are not adapted to the growth of this plant. Air, water, and pure sand form its food, and where these can be had in suitable combination it will thrive best. Cranberry cultivators say that the best soil is *beach sand.* This is the soil of the celebrated Cape **Cod** Cranberry plantations, either naturally or supplied artificially. **The sand** is light **and porous, admitting** air and **moisture freely to** the roots of the vines, while weeds and **grasses, which would** choke them, **can not grow in it. Where** beach sand can not be had, **any clean sand—the** more **free from all mixture of** vegetable matter the better—may be used. **Some** have found pure gravel—the cleanest is the best— **to be a** good substitute for sand. Next to beach sand is *peat,* and this is almost always present in wet grounds. The peat requires some preparation before it is fitted for Cranberry culture. The top turf requires to be taken off to a depth sufficient **to** remove all roots of grass and weeds, and the bared surface **left** exposed to the action of the frost **and weather for** one year. **This** treatment **will make it light and porous,** preventing that **caking and cracking which is sure** death to the Cranberry. **Where the soil is not** naturally either a sand or peat, and the location **seems otherwise** well suited to the cultivation of the Cranberry, it may be possible **to** supply pure sand or gravel. After taking **the** turf off from the beds to a depth that will remove all the roots of grass and weeds, the bared surface may **be** covered with sand to the depth of four or five inches, or **with** gravel to about half that depth.

Overflowing the beds can be very easily effected, if the arrangements in the way of dams already suggested have been provided. **About the** end of **October is the** proper time to let on sufficient water to overflow the plantation to such a depth that the water will not be frozen through to the ground during the winter. The water should be allowed to remain until such time in the spring, usually in May, as the weather becomes mild and vegetation commences, when it should be drawn off just to the tops of the vines. This will give the plants the benefit of the increased warmth of the weather, yet at the same time protect them from frosts. The water can be allowed to remain at this point until the season has become so far advanced that the danger from frosts is past, and then it should be drawn off entirely. The necessity for this arises from the extreme sensitiveness of the blossoms, and the same is true of the unripe fruit, to frosts. If it be possible to have a reservoir of water retained by a dam above the beds, with which to flood the plantation at will, the water may be drawn off earlier in the spring, and a longer season be thereby secured than would be safe without such an arrangement; for if a frosty night threatened after the water had been drawn off, the plants could be again covered with water from the reservoir, and thus kept safe from the frost. Again, in autumn the unripe fruit could be protected from premature frosts, and sometimes the entire crop preserved, by letting on the water whenever danger of frost was apprehended at night, and drawing it off in the morning. In this way also the plants may be protected from the ravages of insects. It is liable to attacks from two kinds of worms; one of these destroys the vines, the other the fruit. By submerging the vines for a few days, as soon as these begin to appear, they will be drowned out and the plantation preserved.

Planting the Cranberry can be best done in the latter part of May or the beginning of June. The roots are placed in the soil, the vine spread out and covered so as to leave only the tips of the branches out. Set in this way each branch will form a plant. The closer they can be set the sooner they will cover the ground. The Cranberry will also grow from cuttings. Some planters run the vines through a straw-cutter set to cut them in lengths of about two inches, and sow these pieces broadcast over the ground. These are then well harrowed in, when they soon root, spring up, and speedily cover the ground. Others plant in drills, but the method pursued is of little consequence if the ground has been so thoroughly prepared before planting that there will be but few weeds to contend against. If the ground is likely to be full of weeds and grasses, it will be necessary to plant the vines in such a way that they may be thoroughly weeded out, for the Cranberry is not able during the first years to choke them, but on the other hand is in great danger of being choked by them.

The cultivation is confined chiefly to the three years immediately after planting, and consists in keeping all grass and weeds from getting a foothold. The best method of doing this is not by hoeing, but by pulling the grass and weeds up with the hand, loosening the ground if necessary with a digging fork, so that the roots of the weeds may be drawn out entire. After the third summer, the vines should have so fully covered the ground as to choke out all grass and weeds and require but little attention.

In selecting plants to set, care must be taken to procure fruitful plants, for there are plants which are very fine-looking and vigorous, but which yield little or no fruit. In gathering plants from our marshes, some attention must be paid to this matter, by noting during the previous autumn those which are fruitful, or labor and time will be both lost and great disappointment follow.

The varieties of the Cranberry seem to be quite numerous, differing chiefly in size and shape of berry. There seem to be three tolerably well defined sorts, known as the Cherry, the Bugle and the Bell Cranberries, which are readily recognized by the form of the fruit, but beyond this difference in form there seems to be nothing to distinguish one from the other. As long ago as in 1856 a letter was published from Professor F. Shepherd, of Western Reserve College, Ohio, in which he mentions a variety of Cranberry which he saw growing on the upland in great quantities in various parts of British America, particularly on the Neepigon coast of Lake Superior. Should any reader of these pages know of any locality where such a variety of Cranberry is now growing, he will confer a great favor by communicating the information to the author.

Fig. 54.

Fig. 54 is a representation of a branch of the Cranberry vine and fruit, of the Cherry variety.

HUCKLEBERRY OR WHORTLEBERRY.

This neglected fruit deserves more attention than it has yet received. In many respects it possesses better natural qualities than either the Currant or Gooseberry. The northern species are all perfectly hardy, and many of them very productive, and wholly free from the thorns that make the Blackberry, Raspberry, and Gooseberry, such uncomfortable things to handle. The berries are firm, and will bear carriage to market much better than Strawberries or Blackberries. Thousands of bushels are gathered from the woods, and sell readily in market. Why should not careful cultivation and selection result in the same improvement of this fruit that has been obtained by the cultivation of the others? Beyond doubt, it would; and as the woods and marshes will not always afford a supply of these berries, we desire to call attention to the Huckleberry as a promising subject for horticul-

HUCKLEBERRY OR WHORTLEBERRY.

tural experiment. Seed may be secured by crushing the berries and mixing them with some fine sand. This may be sown in a bed of finely pulverized soil, covering with very fine mould, to the depth of not more than a quarter of an inch. The bed should be kept moist, screened from the direct rays of the sun, and when the seedlings are a year old, they will require to be transplanted to where they will have room to grow and bear fruit. From these, selections could be made of the finest and most desirable, which could be propagated by layering, or grafting, or budding, upon those which were of inferior quality.

Fig. 55.

Fig. 55 represents a branch of the Huckleberry laden with fruit.

THE KITCHEN GARDEN.

The Kitchen Garden deserves more attention from our farmers than it has generally received. The products of a good garden are worth all that they cost, for the single purpose of supplying the farmer's table with that variety of food which the best development of body and mind require. It is no uncommon thing to find the table of a well-to-do farmer very scantily supplied with vegetables. Beyond that great staple, the potato, there is seldom any vegetable on the table, year in and year out. Sometimes a little variety is obtained by cooking a few of the field peas when green, or a few ears of corn, which the good wife gathers, robbing the farm stock of their coarse fare, that she may give a little variety to her table. The delicious wrinkled garden peas, not only more palatable but more nutritious, are wholly unknown, and so of all the comfortable and wholesome variety of culinary products of the well-managed garden. This is a great mistake. Man does not live by bread alone, even in a mere physical view of that statement. A considerable variety of food best develops the physical part of our being. There is also a subtle correspondence between the texture of our bodies and that of the food we consume. The consumption of the coarsest products only, will tend to make coarse men. A well-stocked and well-kept garden is a sure concomitant of a more intelligent and more refined yeomanry.

Besides this, the influence of the garden and of the pleasant fruits and vegetables it yields, upon the minds and hearts of the children of the farm, is fruitful of good. Too little is done to make home attractive. It should be the most lovely spot on earth to all its inmates. "Be it ever so homely, there is no place like home," but we should not travestie this heaven-im-

planted sentiment of our nature by making no place so **homely as home.** Rather will the wise father seek to **foster this love of home, by** gathering about the farm-stead **that** which shall make it pleasant **to the** eye and dear to the heart, that shall minister **enjoyment** to mind and body, and link the thought of it in the **memories** of his children with every **comfort and** every joy. Who can wonder that the children of some of our cheerless farm houses have no pleasant thoughts of home, and leave it as soon as they are fledged? No wonder they seek their enjoyments elsewhere, perhaps in places where they learn the ways **of** vice. No wonder that so many sons of farmers leave the farm, so bleak and cheerless, and un-home-like, disgusted with its labors and **all** they have known of the farmer's life. **There is no reason why** the farmers of Canada **should not enjoy every real comfort, dwell** in the **most pleasant of homes, beautiful in all their surround-**ings, **have their tables** supplied with all the most delicious fruits **and vegetables of** our climate, and their door-yards an Eden of delightful bowers, bright with blossoms laden with sweet perfume.

But there is another view to be taken of this subject **by those** farmers residing upon the suburbs of our thriving **towns and** villages. A well-conducted garden is a paying thing. The time **and** labor bestowed on the garden may be made to yield a handsome revenue. Vegetables **and** small fruits **may** be grown in excess of the wants of the farm house, and the surplus will always find a sale in the town market, if of good quality, and usually at decidedly remunerative rates. In this, as in all departments of industry, skill in producing fine products will have its sure **reward. The careless** and unthinking cultivator **will, in** the end, be driven from the field by the man who uses his brains and makes himself informed upon the best modes of culture, and **studies** the requirements of his soil and of the plants he cultivates. **In these** pages will be found some hints that will help the Canadian farmer to an acquaintance with the requisites essential to success in the cultivation of the garden, and such descriptions of the several vegetables and of the culture required by each, and of the several varieties at present most esteemed in Canada, that he can, with a little practice, become a successful grower of garden products.

The soil which is *best* suited for the production of vegetables is what is termed a rich loam, fully a foot in depth, with a sandy or gravelly subsoil, through which the surplus water readily filters. This is the character to be most desired, and the nearer it approaches to this the better it will be. A poor, light, thin soil, and a heavy, tenacious clay soil, are alike to be avoided. Sometimes a soil may be greatly improved by deep ploughing, so as to bring up the subsoil and mingle it with the soil, but it is oftener the case that the subsoil is sterile, and requires to be gradually worked up and brought into contact with the ameliorating influences of the atmosphere. Hence, in selecting a place for the garden, if there be none on the farm of the desired depth of soil, that should be preferred where the subsoil can be most readily brought into a fertile condition. If the subsoil be so tenacious or so compact that the water finds its way through it slowly, it will be necessary to under-drain the garden. And just here it is probable that many readers will stop, and say if that be necessary, they must just give up the idea of a garden altogether, for they cannot afford to under-drain. Were nine-tenths of our farmers to set themselves to work systematically to under-drain their farms, taking one field a year until the whole farm was under-drained, they would get back their entire outlay in five years by the increased production of their farms. But men are slow to believe this great truth. Yet what is true of the farm is doubly true of the garden. Peter Henderson, himself a most successful gardener, gives an account of a man who had a ten years' leasehold of eight acres. For three years he cultivated the land as a market garden, barely making both ends meet. At this time he was persuaded by Mr. Henderson to under-drain this land, of which he held only a lease having now but seven years to run. At the expiration of his lease he bought the eight acres, paying therefor twelve thousand dollars, and all this sum he had saved from the sale of the products of his garden since he had under-drained the land. He found that it paid him well to under-drain; and though, from the peculiar nature of the circumstances in which he was placed, he obtained a much larger return from his eight acres in a few years than our farmers may expect to get, yet the fact that under-draining will pay the cultivator handsomely still remains.

If, then, the subsoil be retentive, do not be deterred from under-draining enough ground to furnish a comfortable garden. If the products are all consumed in the family, the under-draining will pay in the greater ease of cultivation, and the greater satisfaction of producing that which is satisfactory in quantity and quality. If it be desirable to cultivate also for market, the increased returns will soon balance all the expenditure. There is nothing lost in putting the ground into that condition which is the most favorable to vegetable growth. Hence, in preparing the ground for a garden, it should be thoroughly ploughed and cross-ploughed, and the subsoil well broken up by the subsoil-plough following in the bottom of the furrow at each ploughing. When the ground has been thus thoroughly and deeply broken up, it should be well harrowed, and, if full of lumps, well rolled, until every clod is crushed and the soil made fine and mellow.

An abundance of manure should be applied to the garden and thoroughly incorporated with the soil. This every farmer should have in abundance in his cattle-yard, and use with an unsparing hand. If he can conveniently increase the quantity by obtaining the refuse hops from some neighboring brewery, or horn scrapings from a comb manufactory, or the refuse of a pork-packing establishment, he will find them to prove very beneficial. Indeed, the garden is very much benefited by an occasional change of manures. It seems as though, by the constant use of any one manure, the plants failed to derive the proper nutriment from the soil, but, by changing from one to another, the fertility is better kept up. We have found an occasional use of ashes, leached or unleached, to be of great benefit; and the farmer who does not find it convenient to obtain any other than barn-yard manure, may effect a change by ploughing under a crop of clover every five or six years. This, of course, will necessitate an occasional change in the garden spot. But in whatever way it is done, this variation in the character of the manure applied will be found of essential benefit. Finely-ground bones is probably the best commercial manure within the reach of our farmers. This can be had at about twenty-five dollars per ton, and will pay well if applied once in four years as a rotation manure. With soil thoroughly under-drained, well and deeply pulverized, and abundantly supplied with manures, the foundation is laid for successful gardening.

ASPARAGUS.

This is a valuable early vegetable, perfectly hardy, and perennial; consequently, a bed of it will last for twenty years. The ground is prepared by deep ploughing and subsoiling, or by trenching with a spade, at the same time incorporating with the soil an abundance of manure. The Asparagus delights in a rich alluvial soil, in which sand predominates. It is usual to obtain plants of two years' growth for forming a bed. These can be had of any nurseryman or market gardener. When it is not convenient to procure the plants, seed may be purchased of the seedsmen, and sown, either in the fall or spring, in drills a foot apart. The seed should not be sown very thick, and after the plants appear they should be thinned out, if necessary, so as to stand about four inches apart in the row. If these have been well cared for they will be quite large enough to take up when one year old and transplant into the permanent bed. Some sow the seed on the intended bed, and never transplant at all. In that case the rows should be about eighteen inches apart, and the plants nine inches apart in the row. If plants are set out it will be found convenient to stretch a line, and with the spade cut a trench about six inches deep. In this trench the plants are set, spreading the roots out carefully, and the crown covered about two inches deep with earth. The best time for setting the plants is in the spring, after the ground has become settled, usually from the middle of April to the middle of May. As soon as weeds begin to make their appearance, which they will usually do before the Asparagus buds appear, it will be found a very expeditious, and at the same time convenient method of destroying them, to give the beds a light raking with the steel rake. This raking may be repeated, if required, until the Asparagus buds show themselves at the surface.

The after cultivation consists chiefly in keeping the ground free from weeds, and the surface loose and friable. In those parts of the Dominion where the snow does not lie on the ground to a sufficient depth to keep the ground from being deeply frozen, it will be found advantageous to cover the bed with coarse manure, to the depth of four or five inches. As soon as the stalks are dead in the fall, they should be cut down at the surface of the ground and the top dressing of coarse manure put on. Although the plant is sufficiently hardy to endure the frosts of winter, experience has shown us that the plants which are thus protected start earlier in the spring, and, as it is always desirable to get fresh vegetables from the garden as early as possible, this light winter protection becomes very desirable. As soon as the weather becomes settled in spring the coarser parts should be raked off, leaving only the fine manure. Salt is a special manure of great benefit to this plant in those parts of the country lying remote from the sea shore; though it is said that, in the vicinity of the sea, its use is not attended with any benefit. It should be applied in the spring to the surface of the ground, strewn upon it at the rate of three pounds to the square yard. Being naturally a marine plant the salt supplies that which is wanting, in our inland districts, to the health and vigor of the plant, while it destroys many weeds and worms in the soil which are prejudicial. When the bed is not covered with barnyard litter in the fall, a top dressing of a couple of inches of well rotted manure should be spread over the bed, just as the plants begin to start in the spring.

CUTTING the buds for the table may be begun the third spring. It is the practice of many to cut the buds two or three inches below the surface, and, in most works, this is the direction given. But why we should take so much pains to secure a long, white, woody stalk, which no cooking will make tender, and no person can eat, is more than we can understand. It is the practice of the writer to cut the buds, when three to five inches long, just above the surface of the ground, thus securing for the table all the green portion, and leaving the white part in the soil. In this way there is no danger of injuring the buds yet below the surface, and the work is much more expeditiously performed. This cutting should not be continued too long. When the beds are young the buds may be cut a couple or three times over, but when the beds have become established the cutting may be kept up for three or four weeks. As soon, however, as the plants begin to show any signs of weakness the cutting should be discontinued for that season.

The buds are cooked by boiling them in water for twenty or thirty minutes, until they become soft. Some toasted bread is then laid out upon a dish, the cooked asparagus spread upon the toast, and melted butter poured over the whole. In this manner the buds are kept entire and brought to the table. Others cut the sprouts or buds into small pieces about half an inch long, and cook and serve the same as green peas. Others prefer to treat them simply as greens, and use them with vinegar.

VARIETIES of Asparagus are mentioned by writers, and of late much has been said about Conover's Colossal Asparagus. We have no confidence in the existence of any such varieties, much less do we believe they can be perpetuated by sowing the seed. A possessor of this Colossal, confident of its superiority in size over all others, recently exhibited some of his best **samples at the Massachusetts Horticultural Society's Exhibition, and was badly beaten by** larger and **heavier specimens** of the common **Asparagus, which** made no **pretensions whatever to** being *colossal*. **High** cultivation, plenty **of manures judiciously** applied, **with a deep** alluvial soil, will **make all the** difference **we have** yet seen, **without** trying to make **people believe** that **it is a** different **variety.**

BEANS.

It is usual to **separate beans into two classes, the one** comprising all those **varieties** which **have a dwarf or bushy habit of** growth, **the other** embracing those **which have a climbing habit,** and **require a pole or** other **support. The first class is called** Dwarf, **or Bush Beans; the other, Pole, or Running Beans.** They are **all very sensitive to frost, and on** that account **should not** be **planted until the weather is** warm enough to plant Indian Corn.

BUSH BEANS do **not** necessarily require a rich soil, indeed they will grow in poor soil, but they yield much better in land that has been well enriched. Nor are they very particular as to the character of the soil, **so** long as it is warm and **dry.** Wet **soils,** and shaded situations, are very **unfavorable to their culture. They are** usually planted **in hills,** which **may be such a** distance **apart as is most convenient to the cultivator. If the** ground is **to be tilled with the aid of a horse, the hills will** require to be **set in rows three feet apart, and the hills two feet** apart in the **row. If intended to cultivate wholly** by hand, the hills may be eighteen **inches apart each way. As** the young plants are subject **to the depredations of** cut-worms, it is well to plant eight beans **in each** hill ; **but if five** grow, it will be sufficient. Sometimes they are sown in drills three inches deep, and eighteen inches apart, and the beans dropped about two inches apart in **the drills.** The following varieties are the most desirable.

EARLY VALENTINE.—This bean is not excelled by any in the **tender succulence of its** pods when green. They are of moderate size, thick and fleshy, and continue in use for a long time. As a shelled bean, it is not desirable. It is very productive, and comes into use in about seven weeks from the time of planting. The ripe bean is of a salmon color, marbled with purplish rose. The flowers are white.

EARLY MOHAWK.—This variety is one of the most hardy sorts, enduring cold winds and chilly weather, and even light frosts, much better than any other kind. On this account, it is a valuable variety to plant in those places which are subject to late frosts and chilly winds. It comes into use about a week later than the Early Valentine, is very productive, the pods are tender and good, and if they are gathered as fast as they become fit for use, a good supply will be kept up for some time. It is not desirable as a shelled bean. The bean is drab-colored, variegated with purple, and the flowers are a pale lilac.

REFUGEE, or *Thousand to One*.—Not an early bean, coming into use in about eight weeks from the time of planting. It is extremely prolific, and the pods are quite thick and fleshy, and of fine flavor. It is much esteemed as a snap-bean, but not much used when shelled. The flowers are purple, and the beans light drab color, spotted with purple.

NEWINGTON WONDER.—Much esteemed for private use, on account of the particularly tender and crisp character of the pods. It is exceedingly productive, comes into use after the early varieties are over, and continues for a considerable length of time. The beans are small, light brown, and not used as shelled beans. They require the whole season to ripen perfectly.

WHITE MARROWFAT.—This is the well-known white bean so largely cultivated for market. It is an excellent variety when used as a shell bean, either green or ripe; indeed we esteem it as the best of all the bush beans for this purpose. It is not a very early variety, requiring to be planted about the tenth of June, in order perfectly to ripen its crop. It is quite productive, yielding from twenty to thirty bushels per acre, and usually selling at about one dollar per bushel.

Wax or Butter Bean.—A variety of recent introduction, but very popular in our markets as a snap or string bean. It is a very productive variety, with thick, fleshy, yellow pods, and which continue in use a long time. The beans, when ripe, are black, and not desirable for shelled beans. To our own taste the pods lack sweetness and richness of flavor.

Pole Beans, or, as they are sometimes called, Running Beans, require some support, and on that account are not as generally planted as the dwarf varieties, which do not require to be furnished with poles around which they may twine. Besides, they are usually not as hardy, suffering severely from the slightest frost, and require a light but rich soil. Yet there are some varieties that are exceedingly desirable, and those who grow Indian Corn may avail themselves of the facility which the corn furnishes of providing poles for the beans. The Cranberry varieties can be grown by planting a few beans in the corn-hill at the time of the second hoeing, and as they grow they will twine around the corn-stalks for support. In this way the farmer can raise enough to supply his own table without any serious inconvenience. On account of the tender nature of this class of beans, it is of no use to plant them until the warm weather has fully set in, and the soil become warm and dry.

Red Cranberry.—An old and favorite sort, one of the most hardy and productive of its class, and more generally cultivated than any other pole bean. It will ripen its crop in about three months from the time of planting. It is frequently used as a string bean, the pods being tender and succulent, and retaining this character for a long time, but its chief value is as a shelled bean, used before it has become ripe. The beans are of a deep purple color.

White Cranberry.—Some prefer this variety to the preceding on account of the color, and as a shelled bean, both green and ripe, it is of great excellence. It does not come to maturity as quickly as the other sort, and on that account cannot be ripened in all seasons in some parts of the country. It usually requires a season of fifteen weeks from the time of planting to bring it to maturity.

CASE KNIFE.—This is an exceedingly prolific variety, requiring about the same length of season as the White Cranberry, and like it of a clear white color, and of excellent quality as a shelled bean, both green and ripe.

CONCORD.—On account of its early maturity, as well as its general good qualities, this variety is deserving of attention in our Canadian climate. Planted after the commencement of warm weather, it will begin to ripen in about ten weeks. It is a healthy and productive sort, of excellent quality as a shelled bean both in the green and ripe state, but is not valuable as a string bean.

LIMA BEAN.—This variety is universally esteemed to be the best of all this class, but unfortunately our climate is too short for its maturity. Often the frost comes just as the beans are becoming large enough for use, and as it is also one of the most tender of all the pole beans, the labor of a whole summer perishes just at the point of fruition. Yet there are some parts of our Dominion, particularly the more favored sections of Ontario bordering on the lakes, where this bean can be successfully grown; also, by taking a little pains to start them about the tenth of May, under a sash, and then transplanting them into the open ground after the weather has become quite warm and settled, the season of growth may be so lengthened that beans may be had large enough for the table, even though they may not ripen. We have been most successful in planting them upon pieces of inverted sod, cut about two inches square, and placed either under a sash, or in some warm, sunny corner, on the south side of a building or of a high board fence. When the weather has become fully settled into summer, the beans are removed, with the bit of sod in which they are growing, to the permanent ground, without in the least being checked in their growth. This ground should be in a warm and well sheltered part of the garden, and where the soil is warm, dry, and rich.

The pods are always tough, and can never be used as **a** string bean, but **the** full-grown **beans, while yet green, are** the most delicate and delicious of all beans. When ripe they are of a dull greenish white, flat and broad kidney-shaped.

Beans, of all kinds, cannot be relied upon to germinate when **they are** more than two **years old.**

BEETS.

This valuable vegetable forms a very important crop with our market gardeners, ranking second only **to the cabbage. In some** of its varieties it is a most valuable farm crop, while **the finer** sorts are both pleasing to the eye and **pleasant to the palate when** placed on the dinner table.

The most favorable soil is one that is light, deep, and dry, though well enriched. When grown in heavy soil, particularly **that which is damp and cold,** it is apt to be coarse, and of poor **flavor.** In a poor soil it becomes tough and full of fibre. The **use** of coarse manures makes the roots forked and ill-shapen. If the ground be well dressed with fine, well rotted manures, the roots will be smooth and solid.

The ground having been prepared **by thorough** pulverizing, the seed may be sown in drills, an inch and **a** half deep, and about eighteen **inches apart, dropping the** seed every two inches. For early summer **use they should be** sown as soon as the ground has become settled, but for autumn and winter use, about the middle of May. When the young plants are about three inches high, they should be thinned out, by pulling up the weakest, so as to stand from four to five inches apart. The young beets that are thus pulled out make excellent greens, cooked tops and all, and dressed with vinegar. By taking out a part each day, the table may be supplied with them for a week or two.

The subsequent cultivation consists in keeping them free from weeds, and the surface of the ground loose and mellow. When the surface of the ground is frequently stirred, the plants will grow better, because of the mellow condition of the soil, and in time of drought will suffer far less than if the earth is left undisturbed and allowed to become hard. The reason of this is, that when the surface is mellow evaporation does not take place as rapidly as when it is hard, and the moisture in the soil, instead of going off into the air, is retained to supply the roots of the plants. Besides this, the frequent stirring admits air into the soil, and the air furnishes food to the roots as well as the water, so that whether there be weeds to destroy or not, these stirrings of the surface are beneficial to the growth of all plants.

Beets are not only valuable for summer use, but they may be preserved through the winter, and used whenever desired. Those that are intended for winter use should be gathered before the frosts become severe, for if they get severely frozen before they are taken up the exposed part will decay. In taking them out of the ground, care should be had not to injure or bruise the roots, and in taking off the leaves not to cut the crown of the beet. After removing them from the ground, they may be left exposed to the air long enough to dry, and then removed to a cool cellar, and packed in fresh earth or sand, alternate layers of roots and earth, so that they shall be well covered. If carefully gathered, and stored in this way in a cool cellar, they will keep quite sweet and good until June. It is, however, a very common error to keep them in a warm cellar, and in such a place they lose much of their freshness and flavour. It is better that the cellar should be so cool that the thermometer shall stand at freezing point, or a very little above, than to keep them warmer.

In growing beets for table use, it is not desirable to see how large they can be made, for the large, overgrown specimens are coarse and lacking in flavor, but the rather to grow them smooth, firm and fine grained. The test of a good beet is in the close, compact character of the flesh, with fineness of grain, free from fibre, and perfect smoothness of exterior. Therefore, in selecting roots from which to raise seed, those should be chosen which are well formed, free from forks or branches, smooth, of medium size of the variety, and having the color indicating a pure strain. These should be planted out during the latter part of April or beginning of May, according to the character of the season, where they will not be near any beets of another variety that are going to seed. The seed will usually ripen in August, may be gathered when dry and preserved for future use. Beet seed possesses great vitality, and, if it has been kept dry, will grow, though it may be five or six years old. If the seed be soaked in warm water for a few hours just before planting, it will germinate quicker and more certainly.

The following varieties will be found to be the best for table use:—

EARLY BASSANO.—Fig. 56 shows the form of this variety of beet. This variety is shaped much like a white turnip, with a slender tap-root. The exposed part of the root is brown; beneath the surface of the ground it is a clear rosy red. The flesh is nearly white, with circles or veins of bright pink, not very close-grained, but tender, sweet and pleasant. It is a very early sort, introduced from Italy, and much valued on account of its coming so soon into use. Many esteem it so highly that they make a second sowing late in June for winter use. The roots from the early sowing would not be suitable for the table in winter, becoming too tough and fibrous.

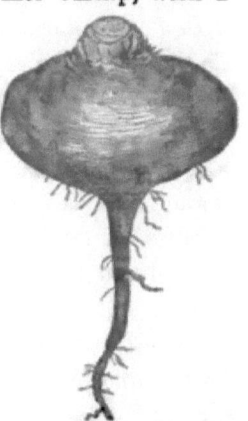

Fig. 56.

EARLY BLOOD TURNIP.—Succeeds well everywhere, and is much esteemed on account of its healthy character and uniform excellence, and is more universally planted than any other sort. It is shaped much like a smooth, well-formed, globe turnip, being about four and a half inches deep by four inches in diameter. It is very smooth and handsome, with a deep blood-red flesh, often with veins of lighter red, very tender and sweet.

It is but little later than the Bassano, and keeps well for winter use.

Long Smooth Blood.—One of the best, especially for fall and winter use. It is long, round and free from rootlets, of fine quality, and of a deep blood-red color. In flavour and tenderness of flesh it is superior to the common long blood beet.

Carter's St. Osyth.—This is a comparatively new sort, much esteemed in England, and, so far as it has been tested here, maintains its English reputation. It is a long beet, very sweet, rich, fine grained and crisp, and will doubtless become a general favorite.

BROCCOLI.

We give this name a place here, merely to say that the distinction between Broccoli and Cauliflower seems to us to be without a difference. It is said to be more hardy than the Cauliflower, and on that account can be left out all winter in places where the winters are mild, but as we never have such winters in Canada, this difference has no practical existence here. It is also claimed by some that it is more sure to head than the Cauliflower, but this opinion has obtained merely because the Broccoli is planted for fall use, and having the benefit of cool and moist weather, heads well, and so will Cauliflower when treated in the same manner.

The cultivation and treatment are in all respects the same as for Cauliflower, and will be found under that head. The following are the leading varieties:

Purple Cape.—The heads of this variety are, as the name indicates, of a purplish color, which are of good size, close and compact. Cooking destroys the purple, so that on the table it has a whitish green color. It is an excellent variety, and heads well.

White Cape.—Is said to be not quite so hardy as the Purple, but in all other respects differs nothing from it, only in color, being of a creamy white.

WALCHEREN.—Another white variety, producing very large and firm heads. It is as large and fine as most Cauliflowers, and is said by those who can see the difference between Broccoli and Cauliflower to endure both heat and cold, and dry weather also, better than a Cauliflower.

BRUSSELS SPROUTS.

Fig. 57 shows the form in which it grows. This singular variety of the Cabbage family is little cultivated in our climate. Our summers seem to be too hot for it, and it very frequently becomes badly infested with green fly or aphis. It looks like a tall-growing variety of Cabbage, with a tuft of leaves and sometimes a well formed head on the top, and a large number of small Cabbage heads growing out of the sides of the stalk in the axils of the leaves. When the summer is cool and moist, these little heads are very tender and sweet, resembling a Cauliflower in flavor, but in hot, dry summers they are apt to be strong and sometimes bitter.

Fig. 57.

There can really be no object in cultivating it, except for the oddity of the thing, a well-grown Cauliflower being fully equal to an entire plant of Brussels Sprouts in quantity and quality, and much more likely to yield an adequate return for the labor bestowed. Those who wish to give it a trial should cultivate it in all respects as they would a Cabbage, and cook and serve as if it were Cauliflower.

CABBAGE.

The soil best suited to the growth of the Cabbage is a deep and very rich loam. The plants flourish best in a cool, moist season, and are impatient of long-continued droughts and extreme hot weather. Hence in this climate our best heads are generally obtained from late-grown plants, which grow rapidly and form compact, tender heads as the autumn weather comes on. Frequent stirring of the soil is exceedingly beneficial to the Cabbage, and an abundant supply of well rotted manure essential to the attainment of the best results. Ashes and lime are excellent manures for the Cabbage, and best of all finely-ground bones, at the rate of a ton to the acre, sown broadcast on the ploughed ground and harrowed in. It is said by experienced market gardeners that the liberal use of ground bones or a liberal application of lime to the soil will prevent the attacks of the maggot in the root, which insects are often very injurious to the young Cabbage plants.

To obtain early Cabbage, the seed is sown in September, about the fifteenth of the month, and the young plants set out in a cold frame just before winter, about the first of November, and protected from the extreme cold, by placing double sashes over them. Another method, and the one most commonly practised among our farmers, is to start a hot-bed in March, and in this sow the Cabbage seed. For late Cabbage, the seed is usually sown about the first of May, in a prepared bed or cold frame. In all these cases the Cabbage plants are subsequently transplanted to the open ground, which has been previously prepared to receive them, choosing a damp, cloudy day, just after a shower, for the transplanting.

Cabbage may be preserved for winter use in a cool cellar or root house, where the thermometer is kept just above the freezing point. The best manner of doing this is to pull up those having good, solid heads when they are dry, strip off a few of the outer leaves, and plant them out as it were in some fresh earth, **in the** cellar, setting **the** Cabbages as close together as they **will stand**, and burying **the roots** in the soil. Secured in this way, they can be conveniently procured at any time **in** the winter; and where there is not sufficient room to store away the entire winter's **supply, a** few can be placed **in the** cellar, and advantage taken **of** occasional mild weather **during the** winter, to replenish the **store** from the pit outside.

The usual method **of storing** Cabbages in a pit, and one that is found to answer every purpose, is to dig a trench about one spade length in depth, in the bottom of this trench **place a couple** of rails, and upon these rails place the Cabbage, **head down, having** first plucked off a few **of the very loose outer leaves, and bringing** the remaining **leaves close around the head. The** trench is usually made wide enough **to hold three heads of cabbage.** They are packed **in closely, then covered with earth, until about half** the length **of the stalks is covered,** and then a few inches of straw laid upon the earth; and this covered again with soil until the stalks are completely hidden, forming the covering into a sharp ridge. Care must be taken that the water which may find its way into the trench shall be able to run freely away. Stored in this way, Cabbage will keep perfectly until spring.

Cabbage seed will germinate freely when four years old, if it **has** been well preserved. **To keep seeds sound** they must be kept dry.

The following varieties, though by no means all that are in cultivation, **are among the** best, and will be found to be every way satisfactory.

EARLY YORK.—A well-known early variety, much esteemed everywhere, and easily distinguished by its peculiar habit, **and the** deep pea-green color of the leaves. It forms small, solid **heads,** roundish oval in form, which **are tender and** of good **flavor.** As they are never large, the plants may be set eighteen **inches apart** each way.

EARLY WAKEFIELD.—The variety raised in America under

this name, is a favorite with the market gardeners around New York City, on account of its rare combination of earliness and size, being much larger than the Early York, and very sure to produce a good crop; in other words, to head well. The form of the head is pyramidal, rounded at the top, and the head is also quite solid. On account of its greater size, it sells better in market than the Early York. There seems to be a difference between the American and English varieties of this name, the American being better and earlier; hence it is necessary to be particular to procure American-grown seed.

LITTLE PIXIE.—Is a very diminutive but early sort, of dwarf habit, the whole plant being not larger than some good cabbage lettuce. The flavor is delicate and the heads solid. It seems to be more of a fancy sort than one of general utility.

WINNINGSTADT.—We esteem this one of the most valuable of all the Cabbages. It heads freely, bears drought and heat remarkably well, and keeps well through the winter. Though often mentioned as a summer variety, and answering that purpose as a second early sort remarkably well, when the seed is sown early, yet it is as a fall and winter cabbage that it is most valuable. The heads are of a conical form, very compact and solid, and the stalk short. It is a profitable market variety, always meeting with a ready sale.

PREMIUM FLAT DUTCH.—This is also a very popular sort, forming large, round, and solid heads, which are broad and flat on the top, stalk short. It is a very large-growing variety, and keeps well, remaining fresh and crisp until late in the spring; at the same time quite tender, sweet, and good.

DRUMHEAD SAVOY.—All the Savoys may be readily distinguished from the other Cabbages by the peculiar wrinkled appearance of the leaves, and the looser, less compact structure of the heads. They are extremely hardy, bearing well a considerable degree of frosty weather, which, indeed, so far from injuring them, seems to improve their quality and flavor. This variety is shaped much like the common Drumhead Cabbages, hence its name. The heads are large, round, a little flattened at the top, and quite compact. This is the best of the large Savoys, heads well, is tender and of fine flavor, and retains its freshness and flavor late into the spring. The seed should be sown early in this climate, as it needs the whole season to perfect itself.

GREEN GLOBE SAVOY.—For domestic use this variety stands, in the estimation of the writer, without a rival. In fineness of texture, sweetness and delicacy of flavor, it is unsurpassed; yet such is the passion for size among buyers in our markets, that delicacy and excellence of quality are quite overlooked, and a hundred heads of Flat Dutch will be sold for one of this sort. It is very hardy, heads freely, is smaller than the Drumhead Savoy, and has the leaves very finely wrinkled. It attains its highest excellence late in the season, after the advent of frosty weather, and retains its freshness late in the spring. Those who can enjoy fine quality in a Cabbage will plant this sort for their own table, and the coarser varieties for market. Figure 58 is an engraving of this variety.

Fig. 58.

RED DUTCH.—This variety is used for pickling. It retains its crispness and freshness when pickled better than the white kinds, which soon become tough and wilted, and besides this its bright color gives it a very pleasing appearance.

CARROTS.

The soil best suited to the cultivation of this vegetable is a deep, rich, sandy loam; wet and cold soils are very unfavorable. It is not necessary that the soil should be very highly enriched with manures, but it is very important that it should be most thoroughly pulverized to a good depth. Some of the writer's best crops of Carrots have been obtained by turning over a good clover sod late in August, on ground that had been previously well subsoiled, harrowing lengthwise of the furrow, and in the spring mellowed up thoroughly with a two-horse cultivator. The seed should be got in as soon as the ground is warm, and sown with a liberal hand. It pays better to thin out the young plants afterward, than to be so sparing of seed as to have large blanks in the rows. The young plants are so feeble, that when they stand singly they are often unable to force their way through the crust that frequently forms over the surface of the soil, but when sown thick, their united efforts seem to be able to break the crust that was too strong for a single plant. It is a great mistake to sow Carrots on ground that is full of seeds of weeds. If it be possible to till the ground with some hoed crop, such as early potatoes or early cabbages, the season before, and after the crop is taken off plough and harrow, and when the weeds start harrow again with a heavy harrow, and in this way turn up as many of the weed seeds as possible to the surface, and after they start to grow kill them with the harrow or two-horse cultivator, much labor of weeding the next season after the ground is sown to Carrots will be spared.

The seed should be sown in drills about one inch deep and twelve to fourteen inches apart. Just as soon as the rows of young Carrots can be seen, they should be gone over with the hoe and carefully cleaned out. If once the weeds are allowed to get the start of the young Carrots and choke them, an irreparable injury will have been done them, and the labor of weeding more than doubled. In their earlier life Carrots are feeble plants, and easily stunted and injured by an overgrowth of weeds. When they have become fairly established they should be thinned out to about four inches apart, and the ground kept clean, and stirred frequently during all the growing season.

In the autumn the roots should be taken up and secured before the frosts are hard enough to injure them, that is, before the frost is hard enough to freeze the ground. Those that are intended for the table should be placed in alternate layers of fresh earth, and stored in a cool cellar. Those intended for the barn may be laid in ridges and covered with earth and straw so as to exclude the frost. Care should be used not to bring too large a quantity of Carrots together. In large heaps they will not keep so well as in smaller—at least, such has been the writer's experience. Those in the large heaps decay, as if they had fermented.

Every farmer should raise enough Carrots to supply his milch cows liberally. The animals thrive well on them, and the quantity and quality of the milk are improved. The finer varieties are a very desirable addition to the dinner table, and are exceedingly nutritious and wholesome. Used in soups, or boiled and dressed with cream, they are very palatable.

Carrot seed cannot be relied upon that is more than two years old. It is usually stated that two pounds of carrot seed are sufficient for an acre, but we have found it much more economical to use at the rate of five pounds to the acre.

EARLY HORN.—This is the variety to cultivate for the table. Fig. 59 is a correct representation of its peculiar form. It is short, terminating abruptly, with a very slender tap-root; the flesh is of a deep orange-yellow color, crisp and very fine grained, and of the richest and most delicate flavor. It does not require, when grown for table use, to be thinned out in the row to more than two inches apart, and may be used as soon as it is half grown. Some use this variety not only for the table but for their stock; and, where the soil is naturally thin, and underlaid by a sterile or tenacious subsoil, this is a more profitable variety to grow for all purposes than the long-growing kinds. It matures earlier than the other sorts, and on that account can be grown where the summers are very short. Those who have thought the Carrot too strong flavored for a table vegetable, will be much pleased with this.

Fig. 59.

EARLY FRANCE.—A small, almost globular-rooted sort, very early, and **well** adapted for forcing—in truth, hardly desirable for cultivation in **any other way than** under glass. It is of a **mild and delicate flavor, and near large** cities, where high prices **can be obtained for the** earliest vegetables, **may be** grown with profit.

LONG ORANGE.—This is the well-known **and** long-cultivated yellow-fleshed variety, **which** is by no **means** unworthy of a **place in the garden, and** makes an excellent **farm crop on suitable soils.** The flesh is tolerably close-grained, **tender and** sweet. **If used for the table the roots should be pulled when** young, **for they are better and milder flavored when half-grown** than at maturity. As a field crop it will yield from **six to eight** hundred **bushels to** the acre, and is probably the most nutritious **sort grown for stock feeding.**

ALTRINGHAM.—**A** deeper colored variety than the **Long Orange, with a crisp flesh, which is** mild and pleasant flavored. **Those who grow Carrots for market find this to** be a very saleable **kind, probably on account of its bright, lively** color, as much as its good qualities.

WHITE BELGIAN.—Grown **only as a field crop for** stock feeding, too coarse **and lacking in flavor for** a table variety. It yields large acreage returns, **and sells for as much** per ton as the Long Orange; but **we very much** doubt whether the average crop from **an** acre will yield as much nutriment as an **acre of** Long Orange. For milch cows the Long Orange **is the preferable variety, imparting to the** butter a richness **of flavor and color that cannot be obtained from** the White **Belgian.**

CAULIFLOWER.

The soil best suited to **the cultivation of the** Cauliflower is **a deep** rich loam. This should **be well** pulverized, and abundantly supplied with manures **that have** been well rotted. **Lime,** ashes and ground bones are **very** valuable fertilizers for **this** vegetable, and though the main supply should be drawn from the farm-yard, **yet** the occasional use of these **will be found** exceedingly beneficial, and especially on land that has been long tilled. Common salt is said to be valuable as a fertilizer for the Cauliflower, but we have never **tested its worth.**

If **early** Cauliflowers are desired, the seed should be sown in **a hot-bed** in March or **very early in** April, according to the **season.** As the plant is almost hardy, **care** should be taken not **to keep** the young plants too close, but raise the sash and admit **air in** moderate weather, gradually increasing the quantity of air until **the** plants **are so** well hardened as to need covering only **in extreme weather.** If they have been judiciously **treated** they **will endure** safely ten degrees of frost, **and may be set out** in the **open ground** as soon as **the soil is sufficiently settled** to be worked. **The secret of obtaining** good early Cauliflowers lies **in getting them well forward before hot** and **dry weather** sets **in.** **During the cooler and usually showery weather of** April **and May, such** growth will be secured as to ensure a well-formed head or flower. But if they are not set out until nearly all danger of frost is passed—which, in this country, is usually from the first to the fifteenth of June—they will very surely be overtaken by hot weather, and possibly dry as well as **hot,** and then the flowers will be small, tough, **and** strong-**flavored.** The only remedy **we** have seen suggested for this **state of things, is to** mulch the ground heavily with strawy **manure, and sprinkle that** with salt. This will tend to keep the soil **cool and moist, and** mitigate **the** effects of the heat and drought. **But the better way is to get** the plants early into the ground, **and then they are sure to** form good heads, unless **the weather in May be** unusually **dry.**

For late **Cauliflower, the seed may be** sown in May or June, **in the open** air, in a **prepared bed, on the north side of** some **building or** tight board fence, where they will be least exposed **to the** depredations of that little black beetle, familiarly known **as** jumping Jack. If he should make his appearance, a liberal **dusting** of **soot,** or plaster, **or** ashes, will be found of benefit.

As soon as the plants are large enough, they may be set out in the open garden, choosing a dull day, after a rain, if possible. These will come into head during the cool and usually moister weather of the latter part of September, and of the month of October. If any have not formed heads when the severe freezing weather begins to come on, they may be taken up and planted as close together as they will stand, after removing a few of the loose outer and lower leaves, in some fresh earth in a cool cellar or root house, and they will there be very sure to form flowers of delicate tenderness, from the time they are put into the cellar until Christmas, or possibly later. Indeed, we esteem it very desirable to have fifty or more plants that have not headed, to stow away in the root house at the beginning of winter, that a longer term of this most delicious vegetable may be enjoyed. Cauliflower seed that is four years old may be safely relied upon, only provided that it has been kept dry.

The Cauliflower should be used while the head is compact and looks white like a curd, and indeed in this state it is often spoken of as the "curd." If it be allowed to remain, the surface, which is nearly smooth in this state, gradually becomes uneven, and finally branches out, and runs up into flower stalks. It is cooked by boiling it in water in which enough salt has been dissolved to give the water a decided saline taste. This seasons the vegetable much better than it can be seasoned in any other way. After it has been boiled long enough to become tender, which is usually from twenty to thirty minutes, it is taken up into a dish and melted butter poured over it, when it is ready for the table.

If any of our readers have not been in the habit of using the Cauliflower, we feel confident that one season's trial of it will make it ever after a necessary of life.

There is not much occasion to multiply varieties, and probably the best for our climate are the two following :

Early Erfurt.—This variety is especially valuable for early sowing. It heads well, is a dwarf, compact grower, and the heads are of good size, with a close white curd.

WALCHEREN.—Remarkable for its hardihood, being **able to** endure the cold and the heat and the drought much better than other varieties. The heads are large, compact, even, with a fine white curd. The leaves of this sort are broader and less pointed than those of other sorts.

STADTHOLDER.—Is **much esteemed by the** London market **gardeners.** Head large, **compact, and fine.**

LE NORMAND.—Has proved a valuable variety, usually heading well, despite considerable heat and drouth. The heads are large, often very large, firm, white, and compact.

CELERY.

This delightful salad is seldom grown **by our farmers, for the** reason, probably, **that the method of growing it, which is laid down in most books on gardening,** involves a great amount of **labor, and to** a large degree such as can be performed only by hand; but this labor, it has been found, can be nearly all dispensed with, and the growing of celery has been very much simplified, so that we may hope that its cultivation will not be long confined to the gardens of gentlemen in towns and of market gardeners. Besides being a most agreeable addition to the farmer's own table, he may, if living near a suitable market, **make the growing of it a source of profit.**

To grow Celery well, a small piece of ground should be made very rich by **working into it** a liberal supply of short, well-rotted, barnyard manure, and thoroughly pulverized and raked off quite smooth and clean. This is for the seed bed, and need only be large enough to **grow** as many plants as it may be thought desirable to have. It should be in some warm, sunny spot, and the soil light and dry. After the bed has been prepared, rows may **be marked** out across it about six inches apart, and the seed **sown in** the marks thinly and then covered by patting with the **back of** the spade. This should be done as soon in the spring **as the** ground has become a little warmed and in good working order.

The seed does not germinate very quickly, and therefore, as soon as the rows can be seen it will be necessary to run the hoe between them and clean the bed of all weeds. This should not be done, however, when the plants are wet with dew or rain, as this has a tendency to cause them to rust; and this suggestion should be borne in mind throughout the entire season in all the operations connected with this vegetable. After the plants have become fairly distinguishable, they should be thinned out sufficiently to give those that remain free access to light and air, which will leave them about half an inch apart.

When the plants have filled up the space now allowed them, and seem to be crowding each other, we have found it to be of decided benefit to select some cool but dry day, and prick them out into another bed, which has been previously prepared in the same way as the seed-bed. We first give the young Celery plants a thorough watering with a watering-pot having a fine rose, soaking the ground well, and then, as soon as the leaves have become dry, carefully pull them out of the seed-bed and plant them in the new bed, in rows eight inches apart, and four inches apart in the row. If the transplanting is done just before sundown, and the earth firmly pressed about the roots, and as soon as the work is completed the bed nicely watered from a fine rose, the plants will need no protection from the sun, unless the following day should be unusually hot. The object of watering the seed-bed before pulling up the plants is to enable the operator to draw them easily from the soil and without breaking the root fibres, and the bed into which they are planted is watered as soon as the work is done in order the more completely to settle the earth about the plants, and this transplanting is done just before sundown so as to avoid the heat of the sun, which might cause the plants to wilt, and is apt to make the ground bake if allowed to fall upon it just after it has been watered. This operation of transplanting small plants is what is termed " pricking out."

Some persons trim off a part of the foliage of young plants, Celery and other plants, when they transplant them or " prick them out," but it is a very mistaken practice. It originated, doubtless, in the idea that inasmuch as a large part of the roots were either cut or broken off in taking up the plant, it was therefore necessary to restore the balance between the top and the root by taking off a part of the top also. If the directions given in the preceding paragraph are followed, and the ground in which the young plants are growing thoroughly soaked, and the plants carefully pulled, not dug, the roots will draw out of the soil without being much, if any, broken. If by chance any should be materially deprived of their roots, such had better be thrown away. It is cheaper to set out only good plants, and never spend labor on a poor thing shorn of half its roots and top. Another very important matter in transplanting is to firm the earth well about the roots. More plants die in the process of transplanting, from neglect to press the earth gently, but firmly, about the roots, than from any other cause.

By transplanting the Celery into a new bed, where the plants can have more room, we secure nice stocky plants, with an abundance of root. Such plants will produce fine, solid heads or bunches, while those that have been drawn up will always be weak and spindling, and yield but a wretched crop. After transplanting, they will need to be kept clean and the soil stirred occasionally, so that they make a strong healthy growth, always remembering not to work among them when the leaves are wet. Early in July it will be time to prepare the ground for planting out the Celery. A piece that has been cleared of a crop of early cabbage, or peas, or beans, if it was heavily manured in the spring, will be just the place for Celery, requiring only to be ploughed and well harrowed, so as to pulverize it thoroughly. Upon this the Celery may be planted in rows, three or four feet apart, and six inches apart in the row. These plants should be taken up carefully, allowing as much earth as possible to adhere to the roots, and set out without disturbing the ball, at the same time pressing the soil firmly about the root. The directions already given in regard to transplanting from the seed-bed may be advantageously followed here, except that the plants can not now be pulled out of the soil, but must be gently lifted out with a transplanting trowel. In a couple of days they will have thrown out new roots, and if they have not been allowed to get wilted, will begin to grow vigorously. Nothing more is requisite than to keep the ground free of weeds, until after the middle of August, being careful, in hoeing, to draw the earth more towards than from them, yet not to hill them up, nor by any means to let any of the soil get into the heart of the plants.

Towards the end of August, when the Celery has made some eight or ten stalks, forming a good shield around the heart so as to protect that part from the soil, the earth should be drawn up to the plants as high as to the first leaves. It is well to hold the stalks together in a bunch with one hand, while with the other the earth is drawn around the plant, always being careful that the soil is not drawn up so high as to get into the heart. When the heart stalks have grown up to the height of the outside leaves, then the earth should be banked up against the plant to very near the top. This is all the earthing up the plants will need. Much of the labor of this may be done by running a light plough with a steady horse between the rows, throwing the earth towards, not on to the plants, and finishing with hoe and spade. When the heart has again grown up above the outer leaves, the Celery will be fit for use.

By this method of growing Celery a much better article is obtained and with much less labor than by the old mode of digging out trenches in which to plant it, and then earthing it up gradually every few days. The best Celery is that which is the most crisp, tender and sweet, and that can be best obtained by securing a quick growth. By earthing up after the weather has begun to get cool, at which time the plant grows most rapidly, and doing it at two instead of a dozen operations, a quick growth of the heart or centre stalks is secured.

It is prepared for use by removing the outer stalks, washing off all the adhering soil in clean water, cutting away the corky bark of the root, **and** dividing the root into pieces, leaving the stalk adhering to each portion of the **root**. These are placed in an upright position, **in a** glass about **one-third full** of **water, and set** on the table. **The** water will **prevent it from** wilting, **and preserve the** stalks fresh and crisp.

It can be stored for winter **use in a cool root-cellar, by taking** it up in a dry day and planting the roots in fresh earth **in the** cellar, much in the same way **as** recommended for Cauliflower. The cellar must not be kept **too** warm ; as near 30° Fahrenheit, as possible, or just above freezing, is warm enough. In such a cellar we have kept it in excellent condition, and find it **more** convenient than keeping it in the ground. But those who have no such cellar can keep it in trenches made in **a dry spot where** no water will settle **in them. The trench should be dug as narrow** as **possible and as deep as the length of the Celery. In this** trench **the Celery is placed in an upright** position, packed close so as **to fill it entirely, with the** green tops just on a level with **the top** of the trench. In order to have it keep well it must be **covered** gradually with straw, as the weather becomes colder, until by the holidays it is covered from a foot to eighteen inches deep with straw. If, however, this be all put on at once **in the** fall, the Celery will spoil. Covered gradually **as the** weather becomes colder, commencing the covering **as soon as the** ground **has frozen to the** depth of **a couple of** inches, the Celery will keep well, and can be easily **got at any day in** the winter. If snow falls in the meantime to such a depth that the frost cannot reach the ground, that will of itself be a sufficient covering, if it can be relied upon to remain ; if not, a covering of straw should be laid upon the snow, which will help to keep it from melting. But the straw used should be clean, not that which has been used as bedding for the farm stock. From such straw there might leach down upon the Celery a dirty water that would **impart to** it a decided barnyard flavor.

The best variety of Celery is the Sandringham Dwarf White. It has a fine nutty flavor, is crisp, tender and solid. There are other good varieties, some of them having red tinted stalks, but this is the best, and no one who has once grown it will ever want any other for his own table.

CRESS OR PEPPER GRASS.

This is an early spring salad, used either by itself or mixed with Lettuce. It has a warm, pungent taste, hence its name of Pepper Grass. It grows readily in any garden soil, and may be sown just as soon as the garden can be worked. The young leaves are always the best, which should be cut before it begins to run to seed, and as it grows rapidly, if it is desirable to have it long in use, seed should be sown two or three times, with an interval of ten days or a fortnight between the sowings. The surface of the bed should be raked smooth and fine, and the seed sown thickly in shallow drills and slightly covered. The seed will grow when five years old.

CURLED CRESS is the variety most generally grown, on account of its handsome appearance, which makes it very suitable for garnishing dishes, as well as for use as a salad.

WATER CRESS differs materially from the Cress or Pepper Grass of our gardens, being a hardy perennial plant, growing along the margins of streams and ponds, but is much like it in the peculiar pungent taste of the leaves, and is used, particularly in the spring of the year, as a very agreeable salad. When once sown along a running stream or pond, it will rapidly increase and spread, and those who have such a place on their farms, can easily supply themselves with this very agreeable and healthful spring salad, at the mere cost of gathering it when wanted. And if residing near a market, especially that of a large city, they will find it a very profitable crop to raise. A basketful will sell for fifty cents, and as an ordinary waggon will carry some two hundred such baskets, in a city where there is a sale for such a quantity, a hundred dollars can be taken for a single load.

Gentlemen who are desirous of growing Water Cress for their

table, and yet **have** not a convenient stream of water, may adopt the following method, which is said to answer the purpose **well**, though we have never given it a trial. It is simply to prepare a hot-bed, as early in March as possible, and plant it with the Water **Cress.** In this, if kept pretty close, it is said to grow very luxuriantly, and can be cut as **it is wanted.** It will soon grow up again after being cut, and requires only to be watered freely twice a week, to give an abundant supply. When the sun becomes hot, it will be necessary to whitewash the glass to prevent the plants from scalding. If plants can not conveniently be had, no doubt they can be raised in the bed from seed, only requiring longer time to get established.

CUCUMBERS.—The soil best suited **to the growth of the Cucumber, is a light, friable loam, thoroughly drained and in good heart.** Those **who grow this vegetable in** quantity for market, find a well-rotted **sod to be an excellent manure for them,** turning it **under in the end of** August, and ploughing again in spring, and giving a third ploughing just before planting. If the object be to get cucumbers for pickling, there is no occasion to plant before the first of July, and by planting late, the vines make such rapid growth as soon to get out of the way of striped bugs **and other** insect pests. The hills may be placed at four feet apart each way, and a dozen **seeds sown in each, and if** too many should survive the attacks of their numerous foes, **they may** be thinned out to four or five plants in each hill.

It is a good plan to put a shovelful or two of thoroughly rotted manure in each hill, and work it up with the soil before planting. **In this** way the manure is economized and applied more directly where it is wanted, than by spreading it broad-cast over the whole ground.

When Cucumbers are wanted for the **table** or market in the beginning of summer, it is necessary to have recourse to frames, **in order to** get the plants well started in good season, and to get them so large before they are exposed in the open ground, that they will escape the ravages of the striped bug. The best way of raising them, is in a cold frame on pieces of inverted sod, **in the same manner as recommended** for the Lima Bean. This should **be done** about the middle of May, **the** sod cut into pieces about **four inches** square, and three or four seeds planted on each piece. **Care must be taken not** to allow the **plants to** get drawn up, but **by giving plenty of air keep them stocky and hardy.** When **they have three or four rough** leaves, they can be transplanted by **lifting up the bit of sod and** setting it in the hill where it is intended **they shall grow.** It is best to do this transplanting just before **sundown, so that the plants may have the** night in which to **recover from the disturbance, but if the removal be carefully made they will not feel the change. If water be given at the time of transplanting, let** it be a thorough soaking, sprinkled on **through a fine rose,** that will sink down below the roots.

When the cucumbers are large enough to cut, the vines should **be examined every day,** and all that are large enough, and all **that are misshapen, imperfect or worthless,** taken off; for if any **are allowed to remain on the vine to ripen, the** crop will be **materially lessened, the energies of the vine** seeming to be directed to the ripening of those that are **left on, instead of** the setting of more fruit. If it be desired to save seed **from any, a few** of the best formed may be left on a vine that is quite removed from those of any other sort, and allowed to ripen. They intermingle so readily **that** it is difficult to get pure seed when more than one variety is **raised in** the same garden. Careful gardeners keep a vine **in a frame where it can be well** secured from the pollen of any other **sort, until the desired** number of fruit has set, fertilizing the pistillate **flowers by hand. The** seed has great vitality, retaining the power of germination for **eight or ten years.**

The following sorts will **be found** the most profitable.

EARLY FRAME.—An old and well-tried variety, much esteemed **on** account of its vigorous **and productive** character, and the **tender quality and agreeable flavor of the fruit.** It is used both **for the table** and for pickles.

WHITE SPINE.—A great favorite with market gardeners

because of the great productiveness and healthy habit **of the vine,** and the handsome appearance and excellent quality of the fruit. Besides, it does not change to yellow on approaching maturity, and retains its freshness of appearance for **a long time.**

LONG GREEN TURKEY.—Is an excellent productive sort, the fruit sometimes measuring sixteen inches in **length, firm,** crisp, having few seeds, and of good flavor.

There is no end of varieties grown in frames, some of them nearly a yard in length, **but** probably the best of **them is** SION HOUSE IMPROVED.

CORN.

As **every tiller of the soil knows how to grow Corn, it** will not **be expected that we should give very minute** directions on this head. **Yet we have noticed** that comparatively few of **our farmers grow** those varieties of corn that are best adapted for **table use** when green, but content themselves with some ears **taken** from their field varieties, while it is yet in the milk. Although these are often very good, we think there are garden varieties which are much sweeter, more tender, **and, what is well** worth considering, lasting much longer in that soft state **in** which they can be used for the table, than any **of our field sorts.** It is **to these we desire to** direct attention, believing that those who may be induced to **try them** will **thank** us in their hearts for bringing them to **their notice.**

The cultivation of these varieties of Corn differs in no way from the ordinary treatment. They flourish best in a warm, dry, loamy soil, that has been well enriched and thoroughly tilled. The seed should not be planted until settled warm weather, the young plants being very sensitive to frost. It may be planted in hills in the usual way, or in drills four feet apart, and about eight inches apart in the drill.

EARLY EIGHT-ROWED SWEET.—Aftery trying a good many varieties, we give this the decided preference over all others, as the best variety for table use. It is a good cropper, continues in use for some time, and is of a very rich, sweet, and pleasant flavor. By planting as soon as the weather will admit, which varies in different parts of the country from the 20th of May to the 10th of June, and again planting three weeks later, a supply of most delicious Green Corn can be had until frosts cut it up in the fall.

STOWELL'S EVERGREEN.—Has the merit of being a late variety, and remaining soft all the season, but it does not compare in quality, in our estimation, with the Early Eight-Rowed.

WHITE PARCHING.—This is the very best Pop-Corn, and every child should be made glad with a store of this for the winter evenings. It is an eight-rowed Corn, ears about six inches long; kernels small, flinty, and of a semi-transparent white. When parched it is snowy white, very tender, brittle, and sweet. Always select the slender, small-sized ears that are well filled with only small white kernels, for seed corn, and keep it pure, as any mixture will impair its quality as a Pop-Corn. It is best when grown in dry, sandy or gravelly soil, and when the summers are warm and short.

ENDIVE.

This salad plant is not much used in this country, Celery and Lettuce taking the place. It thrives in any good garden soil, and may be sown in drills about a foot apart. The seed should be sown thinly and covered but slightly, and after the plants are well up, they should be thinned out to about ten inches apart in the rows. As this salad is usually wanted for winter and early spring, the seed may be sown about the middle of July. In order to prepare it for use it is necessary to blanch the leaves. This is done by drawing the outer leaves together over the centre, and tying them fast with a string, or a mat may be thrown over the plants. In order to keep them through the winter, it is necessary to transplant them on the approach of severe weather into some fresh earth in the cellar. The plants should be taken up with a ball of earth about the roots, and after planting in the cellar, it is well to moisten the earth with a little water.

GREEN CURLED.—This is the best sort, hardy, tender, and crisp.

EGG PLANT.

Fig. 60 is an engraving of an Egg Plant with fruit. This is a very tender vegetable, requiring a long season, and can be raised in our climate only at considerable pains-taking. It can not be made with us a crop of much profit, and will be grown in

Fig. 60.

small quantities by market-gardeners near our large cities, and by those who have such a partiality for it that they are willing to take the requisite trouble. It requires a longer season to perfect its fruit than the Tomato, and the young plants are yet more sensitive to chilly winds and spring frosts. The seed should be sown in a hotbed in March, or in a flower-pot or box of earth, and started in the kitchen window, in the same manner as Tomato plants are started, and treated much in the same way, except that even more care must be used to keep them from being chilled, especially when they are transplanted into the open ground, for if they get badly chilled they seem to get over it very slowly. For this reason it is necessary to wait until the season is well advanced, and all danger of frost is past.

LONG PURPLE.—This is probably the most hardy sort, maturing its fruit the soonest, and the most desirable for our climate.

The fruit is usually cooked by cutting it into slices about half an inch in thickness, parboiling these in a little water, and frying in butter, seasoning with salt and pepper. Sometimes they are broiled, like a beefsteak or mutton chop, on the gridiron, or fried in a batter.

GARLIC.

This vegetable thrives best in a rich, light soil, made fine and friable. The sets are planted in rows a foot apart, and about four inches apart in the row, some time in the latter part of April or beginning of May. They need no special cultivation, other than to keep the soil loose and free from weeds. When ripe the tops wither, and the crop is harvested in the same manner as onions. It is used to flavor soups and stews, having an intense onion flavor.

HORSE-RADISH.

In very rich, deep, and mellow garden soil this root will grow rapidly, and can be cultivated at a good profit. It is worth upwards of one hundrd dollars per ton, and in such soil will easily yield three tons to the acre. Besides, it can be planted with some early crop, such as early cabbages, and made to occupy the ground after the first crop is taken off. Market gardeners preserve all the small branching roots, breaking them off from the main root in preparing that for market, and cut them up into pieces about six inches long, and varying from one-half to one-fourth of an inch in thickness. These are packed away in moist sand in a cool root-cellar, until wanted for planting in the spring. Early Cabbages or early Cauliflower are planted in rows two feet apart, and eighteen inches apart in the row. Between the rows of Cabbage a row of these Horse-radish cuttings are planted by making a hole with a stick deep enough to set the Horse-radish with the top about two inches below the surface. By planting it so deep it will be longer in making its appearance above ground, and so not interfere with the cultivation of the Cabbage. By the time the Cabbage is taken off the Horse-radish will be nicely started, with plenty of time to make fine roots before winter; and as it will now grow rapidly, will only require to be once well hoed over after the stumps of the Cabbage are cleared off.

The plant is perfectly hardy, and makes its growth mainly during the cooler autumnal weather. It should be dug just before the ground freezes, the small roots broken off and stowed away for cutting up, when there is leisure for it, and the main roots cleaned by removing the green tops and washing in water. It is now ready for sale, and is bought by weight in the large cities, where it is grated and put up in glass jars. The consumption seems to have more than kept pace with the supply, as the price has considerably increased within the past ten years.

For home use a few roots will suffice, which may be packed in earth, and kept in a cool cellar, where they can be obtained at any time. Grated and moistened well with good vinegar, it is used with meats, and is both an agreeable and wholesome condiment. The young roots, grown as described, are the best; when allowed to get old, they become tough and stringy.

KOHL-RABI.

Fig. 61 is an engraving of this plant. This is a sort of above-ground turnip, not very generally used, and possessing no special qualities that we can discover which render it particularly desir-

Fig. 61.

able. If **sown too** early it becomes strong in flavor and **woody**, but if sown about the middle of June, in rows eighteen inches apart, **and thinned** out so as **to stand** about eight inches apart **in the rows, they will** form after the midsummer heat has begun **to wane,** and be more likely to be tender, especially should the **season be showery.** The bulb is the **part which is** used, which is boiled, and treated in the same manner **as the** turnip.

The **WHITE and PURPLE** are the sorts grown for table use, and are more likely to be tender and palatable **when about** three inches in diameter, than if allowed to become larger.

LEEK.

A very hardy plant, **and of easy** cultivation, **flourishing in** any mellow soil that is abundantly supplied with manure, **and capable of** enduring twenty degrees of frost without injury. **The seed, which must not be** more than two years old, should **be sown in a well-prepared seed bed, in** drills about eight inches apart, as early in April as convenient, **and the** bed kept **clean and friable.** In July, ground that has been occupied by early **Peas may be ploughed and harrowed, and the plants set** out in **rows a foot apart and six inches apart in the row, planting** them **rather deeply in the soil.** Or the seed **may be sown where the plants are** to remain, if preferred, by making little trenches some **six inches in** depth, and sowing the seed in the bottom of these **trenches, covering it not** more than half an inch deep, and as the **plants grow,** gradually filling up the trenches with soil, which **serves to blanch the** bulbs, and make them of a milder flavor.

The **bulb is the part** used, sometimes in soups and stews, and sometimes **boiled alone and** served with melted butter. **They** are fit for **use in October, and** can be preserved in earth **in the** cellar for winter.

LONDON FLAG.—This is the sort most commonly grown, and **is about** an inch and **a quarter in diameter.**

MUSSELBURG.—Does not differ materially from the preceding, though perhaps is usually a little larger.

LETTUCE.

An important vegetable with the market gardener, and one that is very acceptable in spring to **every lover** of salads. Those **who** desire to supply it as early as possible, will sow seed of some of the hardiest sorts, such as the Brown Dutch, or Hardy Green Winter, about the middle of September, in a warm exposure and in rich soil. In about a month later the plants will be ready for the frames, into which they must be transplanted, and as the weather becomes severe, protected with a sash, or in favorable positions, with dry leaves. The plants **are sufficienty hardy to** endure a cold of twenty degrees below **the freezing point, and** consequently only require a slight protection. **We believe that** in our **climate, the north side of a building or high board fence is much** better than the south side, or any side where the sun **can shine directly upon the sash.** A uniform cold temperature, provided the cold be not greater than that mentioned above, is less likely to prove injurious to the plants than one that is frequently changing under the action of the sun's rays. A frame three feet by six will hold six hundred plants. As soon as the ground can be worked in the spring, these plants should be set out between the rows of early Cabbage that have been wintered **over in the** same **manner, thus** economizing the **ground, because the** Lettuce will **be all** fit for cutting and used before the ground will be occupied by the Cabbage. Those who do not wish to take this trouble to secure fine early Lettuce may sow the seed in a hot-bed, or in a cold frame, or in the open air, according to the time when they wish to use it, or the conveniences they may have for growing it. If in the open air, a warm, sunny and well-sheltered spot is to be chosen, where it is possible, and the soil made rich with well-**decayed** manure, and worked up loose and fine. We have **noticed** that although the Cabbage Lettuces will often head well, if allowed sufficient room in the seed bed, they usually head more **uniformly if** transplanted, and are in less haste to run up to seed. The secret of making Lettuce brittle and tender lies in securing a rapid growth, which can be best done in a rich, warm soil, well supplied with moisture, but the water, however, must not be allowed to stagnate in the soil. Lettuce will head best before the hot weather of summer comes on, and consequently such plants as are not expected to head until mid-summer, will make finer heads if planted where they will be shielded from the sun during a part of the day.

ALL THE YEAR ROUND.—This variety of Cabbage Lettuce remains a long time without running up to seed, the heads are small but close, and the plants hardy, enduring both heat and cold well.

BROWN DUTCH.—The heads are of medium size, not very solid, but they are tender and of good quality. The plants are very hardy, and on that account well suited for wintering over, and form heads freely. It does not endure heat well, and can not be so well relied upon for summer use as some other sorts.

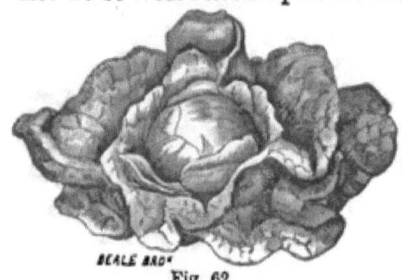

Fig. 62.

DRUMHEAD OR MALTA.—Fig. 62 is a representation of this variety. The heads are large and compact, tender, well-flavored, and nicely blanched in the centre. It remains in head for some time without running to seed.

TENNIS BALL.—This is one of the best sorts for forcing under glass. The head is small, very compact, slow in running to seed, and blanches finely. The plant endures cold remarkably well, and grows best in cool weather, but is not suited to our hot summers.

NONPAREIL.—One of our best summer varieties, enduring the heat, forming fine, compact heads, which are well blanched, tender, and of good flavor, and slow in running to seed.

PARIS WHITE COS.—The Cos varieties of Lettuce do not form such cabbage-like heads as the preceding sorts. The heads are more conical, not solid, and do not usually blanch well **without being tied up,** though this variety is somewhat of an **exception to this remark, the** heads blanching tolerably well without tying. It is an excellent and very popular variety, being **very** brittle **and well flavored,** and makes **an excellent summer Lettuce.**

Lettuce seed will grow when it is three years old.

MELONS.

Our seasons are short for the production of fine Melons, and even with the aid of hot-beds in which to start the seeds, we do not always succeed **in ripening off the crop before frost.** Nor have we found it to be of any advantage **to give the plants a very early start so as to lengthen the season of growth,** for, in truth, **they will not grow in the open ground until the warm weather has fairly set in, and the nights are no longer chilly, not to say frosty.** Besides, they seem to be so **sensitive to a** sudden **chill,** that plants started early under glass have need to be har**dened** off with great care, for the cold seems to so shock their constitution that they do not recover from it for a long time, so much so, that plants raised from seed sown much later are often much the larger and healthier by the first of August. We have succeeded best by planting the seeds on pieces of inverted sod, cut about two inches square, which have been placed for a few days before **planting in a cold frame, and the sash** kept tight, so as to warm the sod thoroughly with **the sun heat.** As soon as the plants make their appearance give air as freely as possible, that they may not be drawn, but kept stocky and hardy. **Such seed** planting need not be done before the first of May, and **the** plants should not be set out in the open air before the ground has become quite warm, and the nights no longer cold.

A light, friable, and warm soil, with as sunny an exposure as **possible,** and, if it can be, sheltered from west and north-west **winds, is** the best place for Melons. It need not be very rich, **only enough** thoroughly rotted manure worked into the spot where the plants are set to give them a good start. During the dry weather of summer, it will be of advantage to give them a good **watering with** weak manure water twice a week. The Melon **Bugs, too,** will need watching, and the very best remedy **we have ever found for these is a good hard** pinch between the thumb and finger.

When the **weather has become warm enough, the** plants **should** be carefully lifted, with the piece **of sod on** which they **are growing,** and set **out three or four in a place,** and these places about four feet apart each way. If the transplanting has been well done the **Melons will not feel the removal,** and will need only the usual **care of occasional stirring of the soil, to keep** it loose and free from weeds. We have succeeded also **very** well, in favorable seasons, by planting the seed in the hill where the Melons are to grow, and thus avoid the labor and care **of** growing in a frame and transplanting. It needs to be done as **early as the season will** admit, which will be as soon as the **ground is warm enough to** enable the seed to germinate, and not **to rot. When sown in the open air the** plants are more liable **to be lost by** a late frost, for there is no convenience for protecting them after they **are above ground, and then the** only remedy is to plant again.

It is extremely difficult to speak of the varieties of the several classes of Melons, usually known among us as Musk **Melons and Water Melons,** on account of the great tendency to deterioration **by cross fertilization.** The pollen from one variety **is carried to the flowers of** another, and new varieties are in this way constantly springing up, and such is the facility with which this intermingling **of** sorts takes place, that it is almost impossible to keep a variety pure **if any other be** raised in the garden. The only way to get pure seed is to grow the Melon in a frame, and, by means of the sash, keep it well secured from **any** chance of mixture until the young Melons are set.

GREEN CITRON.—A medium-sized **Melon, with a thickly-netted green skin; the flesh** green, thick, very juicy, and of a sweet and **excellent** flavor. It is of good constitution, **and** bears abundantly, and is one of the best sorts.

NUTMEG.—Medium-sized, **roundish oval, with a pale green** skin, which is very thickly **netted; the flesh is green, very sweet,** rich, and very highly **perfumed.**

BAILEY'S ECLIPSE.—This is much esteemed in England, and **should** be equally fine here. It is said to be a round, handsome Melon, weighing from three to four pounds, beautifully netted, with a pale green, rich, luscious, and melting flesh.

THE GROVE HYBRID.—Another English **variety, which is** said to be truly splendid, ribbed and slightly netted, weighing from four to six pounds, the flesh pale green, **rich and luscious.**

LARGE YELLOW CANTALOUPE.—A large yellow-fleshed sort, an abundant cropper, **and probably as good as any of the red or yellow-fleshed Melons, none of which are as sweet and high-flavored as the green-fleshed Melons.**

BLACK SPANISH WATER MELON.—This is a large variety, having a deep red-colored flesh, and of very fine sugary flavor. It is very productive, has a healthy constitution, and is one of the best for our climate, as it matures its fruit early.

ICE CREAM.—When pure the flesh is a yellowish-white, with white seeds, which render it quite distinct from most other Water Melons. **It is a prolific variety, ripening early,** sweet **and fine flavored, and well suited** for our short summers.

These varieties are probably the best for general cultivation **in our climate, but, after all,** there will be seasons every now and then in which even these will not ripen well, or until so late a period in the season that their flavor is impaired. Melon seeds will preserve their vitality for eight or ten years; and old gardeners say that seed which is four or five years old will produce vines which set their fruit better than those raised from fresh seed.

ONION.

The best soil for Onions is a deep, rich, loamy, mellow soil, on a dry bottom. A sandy loam that is strong enough to raise good crops of Corn and Potatoes will make an excellent ground for Onions. In selecting a place for growing this vegetable, it is well to choose one that has been previously well tilled with hoed crops and kept clean—such as has raised a fine crop of Beets or Carrots. The Onion is an exception to the general rule of rotation in crops, and not only can be grown successfully upon the same ground for many years in succession, but the bulbs are better and finer, after four or six years of cultivation with this crop, than during the first year. It is also necessary that the ground be highly manured and well prepared.

The preparation consists in ploughing the ground deep, harrowing thoroughly, breaking up all the lumps, if any, and making it as fine and light as possible. It should be manured with fine, thoroughly rotted barn-yard manure, at the rate of twenty-five tons to the acre, and, besides this, all the cleanings of the pig-stye, poultry-house, and earth-closet that can be spared, should be worked in with the harrow. Pure ground bones, at the rate of a couple of tons to the acre, may be used every two or three years with most decided benefit. If at any time it is decided to grow enormous specimens, that will take prizes at our agricultural shows, there is nothing like a barrel or two of Onions, well rotted, wherewith to dress the bed in which it is designed to grow them.

The surface of the ground should be finished off as nearly level as it can be done, and cleaned entirely of stones, sticks and rubbish. If it is intended to grow Onions on a large scale, it will be advisable to use a machine made expressly for sowing the seed, and which sows two rows at once, making the drills and sowing at the same time. If only a small garden-bed is required, the drills should be drawn about a foot or fifteen inches apart, **and the seed sown thinly**, so that they may **be about one inch apart in the** drill. **The** drills should be very shallow, mere scratches into which to drop **the seed, and the covering is best** done with a light **roller, run over the ground lengthwise of** the drills.

Onion seed will germinate when **two years old,** but it is not **as** likely to produce as vigorous **plants as fresh seed** raised the previous summer. It is **very easy to** test its vitality by placing **a** few seeds upon some **damp** cotton or a bit of wet **moss in a** warm room; **if it be fresh,** it will sprout in **three or four days.** Four pounds **of fresh** seed will **be enough to sow an** acre with the sowing machine; and when **sown in the garden** by hand, an ounce should be enough **for four hundred feet of** drill. The seed **should** be sown just as **early as** it is possible **to** get the **ground in good** condition; the **earliest** sown yield the heaviest crop.

As **soon as the** plants can be seen, the ground should be hoed **carefully** between the rows, and the weeds thoroughly **cleaned out.** The hoeing should be shallow, taking care not to draw the earth up around the plants, but to keep the ground **level** and clean. As soon as the Onions are **an** inch **or** two high, they should be thinned out to two inches apart in the row. At this distance apart they may **be allowed** to grow for a time, **and the young** onions used **for the table or sold** in the market, **by gradually** thinning **out to four** inches apart, until they begin **to be too much crowded.** In field culture, or where there is **no market for these** very young onions, the plants may be thinned **out to four inches apart** as soon as they are well established.

Timely and **thorough** cultivation is of great importance to the success of this crop, as it is, indeed, the secret of all profit**able culture.** If the weeds once get the start they will materially **injure** the growth of the plants, if not entirely ruin the crop; **hence, do** not let the weeds start at all, but hoe before they **become visible.** Thus, much **time** and labor will be saved, and the crop cultivated at far less expense than if the weeds once get a foot-hold.

In wet seasons onions sometimes grow thick-necked. To remedy this, growers are in the habit of gently bending down the tops, late in July, with the hoe handle, which checks their growth and makes them form better bulbs.

In August, or early in September, the onions will be ripe, which is indicated by the dying off of the tops. They may now be pulled or raked out, and left spread out to dry in the sun for two or three weeks, by which time they are ready for market or storing for winter use. In keeping them over winter, it is safest to place them where they will be free from frost, yet it is also necessary that they be kept cool and dry, with plenty of ventilation. They do not keep well in ordinary cellars; these are usually too close and damp, and too warm. The writer makes a practice of keeping them in a cold chamber, the floor of which is covered to the depth of a foot or more with perfectly dry soil. Upon this the Onions are laid six to eight inches deep, and some of this dry soil thrown over them, covering them to the depth of about six inches. This soil has remained in this chamber for many years, and is therefore perfectly dry, and although the frost penetrates the chamber, yet the dry earth seems to be a sufficient protection to the onions. It has never been renewed or changed, the same earth being used year after year. After being placed in this chamber, and covered with the dry earth, the Onions are never disturbed until they are wanted in the spring, when they always come out quite fresh and sound.

Market gardeners, who find it to their advantage to supply the market with early Onions of good size in the green state, grow them from "sets." These sets are raised from seed the year previous, wintered over, and planted out as early as possible in the spring. To obtain the sets, which are very small onions, a poor piece of ground is selected; this is ploughed and harrowed, and thoroughly pulverized in the manner already described, but no manure is applied. After getting the ground as fine and smooth as possible, the **seed** is sown in drills about nine inches apart, **and** sown very thick, **so** that the Onions shall grow as small as possible; there is no danger of their being too **small;** the smallest will make as fine Onions next year as the largest, while if they are more than half an **inch** in diameter there is danger that they will not increase **in size but** run to seed. As soon as these little Onions get ripe, **usually in** August, they are pulled up, spread out and dried, and **stored** away where they will keep cool and dry, and be protected from severe frost, the same as any other Onion.

Early in the spring, as soon as the ground can **be nicely** worked, the beds for planting these sets are got ready by thorough pulverizing and heavy manuring with **all the well-rotted barn-yard** manure and bone dust that can be spared. Seventy-five tons **of** fine barn-yard **manure to the acre is not found** to be any too **liberal** a dressing, **which should not be buried deep,** but worked into **the** surface of **the soil. The sets are planted in** this bed in rows nine inches **apart and three inches apart** in the row, by pressing each **firmly into the soil** just deep enough to be covered. After the **bed is** planted, the roller should be drawn over it, so as to press the soil firmly around the bulbs. As soon as the Onions show themselves above ground enough to distinguish the **rows, the hoe** should be run between them, and the ground between the onions broken up with the fingers. This will destroy the young weeds, and give the plants a good start, so that with a couple more such hoeings they will be large enough for market early in June, and the ground cleared **of them in** time for a crop of Cauliflower **or** late Cabbage. **In the vicinity** of large cities this is found to be a profitable **mode of cultivation.**

In raising onions from seed, **it** is important to procure American-grown seed. For some reason European seed, whether from Great Britain or the continent, often fails **to** form good, solid **bulbs.** Some varieties are not grown from seed, such as the Tree **or Top Onion** and the Potato Onion, but by planting the bulbs. **The following** varieties are selected as being the most worthy of attention in our climate.

WEATHERSFIELD **LARGE** RED.—The skin of this variety is a

deep purplish red, neck of medium thickness, the flesh of a purplish white, tolerably fine grained, and with a strong flavor. It is very productive, grows to a large size, and is much valued on account of its excellent keeping qualities, which make it a suitable sort for shipping to distant markets.

YELLOW ONION.—This also is a valuable and popular market sort. Much confusion has arisen by reason of its having been called "Silver Skin" by New England growers, thus confounding it with a medium sized variety having a silvery white skin, grown for pickling, but which is a poor keeper. The true Yellow Onion is above medium size, skin yellowish-brown, deepening in color by age or long exposure to the sun; the flesh white, fine grained and mild flavored. It yields large crops, the bulbs being of uniform good size, with very small necks, and keeping well.

DANVERS YELLOW.—A sort of sub-variety of the old Yellow Onion, more globular in form, having a yellowish-brown skin, that becomes greenish-brown if long exposed to the sun; the flesh is white and mild flavored. It also is an excellent cropper, but has not the reputation of being as good a keeper as the old Yellow.

SILVER-SKIN.—This is the sort that is so much used for pickling, and, when full grown, is a very handsome, medium-sized bulb. To grow them for pickling, the seed should be sown thick, on not very rich soil, so that the bulbs may be small. The outer skin is silvery-white, hence the name; the neck small, the flesh white, sweet, very mild flavored, and fine grained. It produces good crops of uniform-sized bulbs, and is a very agreeable variety for home use, but unfortunately it is a very poor keeper in our climate.

POTATO ONION.—Very desirable for home use on account of its very mild, sugary, and excellent flavor. In the estimation of the writer it is the most agreeable of all the Onions. The bulbs are of medium size, sometimes large, with a coppery-yellow skin. It does not produce seed, but multiplies under ground, hence the name potato-onion. To obtain large-sized bulbs for the table, the small bulbs from the previous year are planted very early in the spring, as early as possible, in soil prepared and well manured in the manner already described. These are set in rows a foot apart and five inches apart in the row, and by the middle of summer will have increased to fine-sized bulbs, after the manner of onion sets. To increase the quantity of bulbs, the large bulbs are planted in the same way and at the same time; these will subdivide, forming usually one, and frequently two, large bulbs, and a numb of smaller bulbs. They do not keep as easily as the Weathersfield Red and Large Yellow, but, buried in dry soil in the manner already mentioned, we have found no difficulty in keeping them through the winter.

Fig. 63.

Top or Tree Onion.—This sort derives its name from the singular manner in which it multiplies, producing on the top of the stalk, instead of flowers and seeds, small Onions. These little Onions are kept over winter, and treated in all respects the same as onion sets, planting them in the spring and using them in the green state during summer. To obtain the little Onions, some of the large bulbs must be allowed to ripen, and be kept over winter; in the spring they should be planted in rows about fifteen inches apart, and ten inches apart in the row. These will throw up a stalk in the summer, upon the top of which the little bulbs will be formed. Some market gardeners use this variety instead of growing Onion "sets," in the manner de-

Fig. 64.

scribed above. We have not been favorably impressed with the quality of this variety for the table, and have found it not to keep well through the winter.

PARSNIP.

In selecting ground for the growing of Parsnips, it is very desirable to obtain land that last year was very highly manured, and thoroughly and deeply worked. It delights in a deep, rich, well pulverized soil, of a sandy or light loamy texture, and forms smoother and better roots when the enriching has been done the year previous, and the manure in this way thoroughly incorporated with the soil. If the manure be applied the same season, it should be such as has become most thoroughly decomposed. Coarse manures cause the roots to branch and fork, and become very rough and uneven, and sometimes it has seemed as though the flavor was affected also.

The seed may be sown as early in the season as the ground can be prepared, which preparation is the same as for carrots or beets. The sowing should be done as evenly as possible, yet thickly, in drills about sixteen inches apart. The seed will germinate more quickly if it be soaked in warm water for a few hours before planting. None but seed of the previous summer's growth should be used, as it can not be depended upon after it is a year old. After the plants are well started, they should be thinned out to about six inches apart in the row. They should be hoed and kept clean in the same manner as carrots.

As frosts do not injure the Parsnip, the roots can be left in the ground all winter, and by spreading a few leaves or evergreen boughs over a part of the bed before the ground freezes, the frost may be prevented from penetrating to such a depth as to hinder digging, and the roots taken up as wanted. In many parts of the country the snow falls, before the ground is frozen, to such a depth as to give all the protection needed. The roots retain their flavor better when left in the ground. Yet, sometimes it is necessary to store a limited quantity in the cellar for winter use. In taking the roots out of the ground, care should be used not to **cut or break** them, for those that are whole retain their **freshness** and flavor much better **than those that are** broken or **cut with** the spade. By digging **a trench** close beside the row **as** deep as the roots extend, **they can** be easily taken out without injury. After digging they should be allowed to dry a few hours in the open air, the leaves all removed, and then packed in fresh earth in the cellar or root house. This is a favorite vegetable with most persons. Boiled and served with butter, or sliced, dipped in batter and then fried, it is most delicious for table use. The farmer will also find it a very valuable root for **his farm** stock, more nutritious than Turnips or **White Carrots, and one** that they **will eat with great relish.**

The **varieties of the Parsnip do not seem to be as marked as** in most **other vegetables.** Soil and season seem to make more difference **with** it than variety.

The Long Hollow Crown is thought to grow more smooth **and** regular, and to be of a finer and sweeter flavor than the common Dutch or Guernsey.

The Student was obtained from the Wild Parsnip, through successive sowings by Prof. Buckman, of the Royal Agricultural College at Cirencester. We **have grown what we obtained** for this variety, which has been recommended as being peculiarly sweet, mild and pleasant, but failed **to find in it** any qualities which **make it superior to the Hollow Crown.**

POTATO.

It is not necessary **to give** Canadians any instructions in growing potatoes. Every farmer's boy knows that the best soil for this most common and important vegetable is a light loam, that is in good tilth and well drained, though potatoes can be **raised** on heavier soils, especially if they are dry. He also knows **that** the very best manure is a good clover sod turned under with all the top that might grow between haying and the end of August—the more the better. If this be cross-ploughed in the spring and well harrowed, it will make a splendid piece of ground for potatoes, much better than can be obtained by manuring a piece that has been under the plough for a long time.

It has long been a vexed question whether it is better to plant potatoes whole or in pieces, large tubers or small, and which produce the best crop. The question is not fully settled yet, but perhaps the experiments of those who have raised fine crops of potatoes without planting the potato at all, may help to throw some light on this subject. When the celebrated Bresee's Potatoes were first introduced, we mean the Early Rose, Bresee's Prolific, &c., such was the anxiety to get them, that good-sized tubers were sold at fifty dollars each, and when they became more plenty, at a dollar per pound. In order to supply this demand as speedily as possible, a hot-bed was prepared in the early spring, and a potato cut in two, lengthwise, and laid with the cut side down upon the soil and the sash kept closed. As soon as the sprouts were long enough, say a couple of inches, they were cut off, leaving a part adhering to the potato, and planted out in the hot-bed. The portion of the sprout remaining attached to the potato after a while sent out new shoots, which were in turn cut off in the same way and planted out. Those that were planted out in the hot-bed soon struck root and grew, and when they became long enough the tops of these were cut off, or as a gardener would say "headed back," and planted out. In this way, by multiplying cuttings and enlarging the hot-bed room as needed, a great many thousand rooted cuttings were obtained, and these, when the weather became suitable, were planted out in the open ground, and in due process of time grew and produced tubers, which were as large and fine as those produced from whole or cut Potatoes.

From this we learn that potatoes may be raised from cuttings of the sprouts alone, without planting any part of the potato, and that in all probability it is of most importance to plant healthy, perfectly-ripened tubers in suitable soil, and these are usually those of medium size of the variety.

After the Potatoes appear above ground, they require to be kept clean with hoe and cultivator, and the custom is to draw the earth gradually to the plant, until quite a hill or ridge is made. Some, however, advise deeper planting, about eight inches, and level cultivation, claiming that in this way a larger proportion of large potatoes is obtained, and that if the tops are cut down by late spring frosts, the part of the stalk below the surface will send up new shoots, and save the crop, only it will be later in ripening.

Some gardeners are very desirous of securing a few very early potatoes, and to accomplish this end have recourse to forcing. This is done by making a good bottom of manure, about two feet deep; upon this is spread good rich soil to the depth of eighteen inches; then the potatoes are placed upon the earth, and four inches more in depth spread over them. This will leave the top of the ground inside of the frame from six to eight inches below the sash. As soon as the tops appear above the surface, they will need the usual attention of airing by day and covering at night, until the weather has become settled, and danger from cold storms is over.

New varieties are raised by sowing the seed contained in the potato balls, which grow on the tops. We have seen very fine-sized tubers raised from seed sown in the spring, though it is more common to gather only small tubers the first year. From these tubers a crop of Potatoes will be had in the autumn of the second year, and from this crop an opinion may be formed of the productiveness, size and quality of the new seedling sorts.

There are a great many varieties in cultivation, but it is quite foreign to our purpose to enter into a description of any more than those which are more especially regarded as garden varieties.

ASH-LEAVED KIDNEY. — A small, smooth-skinned, white-fleshed sort, one of the earliest, and long grown by gardeners as a forcing variety, but of no account except for its earliness.

EARLY HANDSWORTH.—This has the reputation of being a very early sort, with dwarf-growing tops, and also most productive and fine-flavored. The tubers are round, white, and of medium size. It will probably prove a good variety for forcing.

EARLY GOODRICH.—An early and prolific variety, but which in our grounds is of decidedly inferior quality. It is a white potato, oblong in form, tapering somewhat towards one end. In other places the quality may be better, as soil has much to do with the quality of all varieties.

EARLY ROSE.—With us this has proved to be the best of all the early sorts, of good size, very prolific, cooking dry and floury, and of fine flavor.

WHITE PEACH BLOW.—An excellent late variety, color white, with pink blotches about the eye; dry, mealy, and of good flavor. It is usually healthy and very productive.

With the Early Handsworth, Early Rose and White Peach, Blow, a continuous supply of choice potatoes may be had the whole year through; yet there are other sorts already announced in seedsmen's lists, and others yet to come, some of which will in time supplant the varieties of to-day, for the potatoes of thirty years ago are not those now most esteemed. This change is a law of nature, and "passing away" is written upon all her works. All sorts sustain their nutritious qualities best if cooked with the skins on. When boiled, they are placed over the fire in cold water sufficient to cover them, and, as the water boils, a little more cold water is added to check the boiling, so that the potato may be cooked through without bursting. As soon as they are soft, the water is poured off, and the kettle allowed to stand over the fire long enough to allow the moisture to evaporate. This is said to be the very best method of boiling potatoes.

PEAS.

Judging from the quality of the Peas one finds on the tables of our hotels, particularly in rural towns and villages, but few of our people know what Green Peas really are. It would seem as though, as a people, we are content to supply our tables with the field Peas which we grow for our swine, and put up with these dry, flavorless things, when we might just as well have those that are sweet, rich, and delicious. We hope that our readers, who so far honor us as to look into these pages, will give some of the varieties of table Peas which we shall mention a trial, and if they have never used any other than the field Peas for their table, we feel assured they will thank us for calling their attention to these far preferable varieties.

The best soil for Peas is one that is light and rich, partaking more of the sandy character than of the clayey. Yet they may be grown on any soil that is well worked to a good depth, and well drained below. It is not desirable to manure ground for Peas the same season they are planted; the fresh manure causes the Pea to produce vine more abundantly than Peas. For this reason it is better to select a piece of ground that was well manured the previous year, and sow the Peas as soon as possible after the frost is out of the ground. They may be sown in rows, the space between the rows varying according to the growth of vine of the variety sown, leaving nearly as many feet between the rows as is the ordinary height of the vine. This is necessary, to give room for the vines where they are not supported by brush or stakes, and that is now quite an unnecessary labor, since the introduction of short-growing sorts of the flavor and sweetness of the best Marrowfats. It is well to sow them in drills about four inches deep; sown at this depth they suffer less from dry weather, to which we are frequently subject. The shorter growing sorts will be sown thickly, the taller should be sown thinner, decreasing the quantity of seed as the height to which the vine grows increases. As soon as they appear above ground they will require to have the soil stirred with hoe or cultivator, and the weeds kept in subjection. This should be kept up until they take possession of the ground, which they will soon do. It is a good practice to soak the seed in a little tepid water for four or five hours before sowing; this helps forward their germination, and enables them to appear sooner above ground. Peas are not to be depended upon to grow after they are two years old. By sowing a few every fortnight until the first of June, they may be had in succession for a long time. To enjoy Green Peas in perfection, they should be gathered when about three-fourths of their full size, and cooked the same day they are taken from the vines. It is often compulsory on those who live in the cities to use Peas that have been picked, perhaps, for two or three days, and, as they measure better when full grown, often when they are too large; but those who can gather them from their own garden ought to have them when at their best, and cooked when fresh gathered.

There are many really good varieties, but we mention only a few which seem best adapted to our wants.

McLean's Little Gem.—A green wrinkled marrow, combining the excellence of the late wrinkled Peas with early maturity. The habit is dwarf, not usually more than a foot in height, and very prolific. The Peas have the delicious sweetness and flavor of the tall-growing wrinkled sorts.

McLean's Advancer.—A dwarf blue wrinkled marrow, also of excellent flavor. The vines grow about two feet high, and are abundant croppers. They may be sown in rows eighteen inches apart, and require no brush or stakes.

With these two varieties alone one may enjoy the most delicious Green Peas for a long time. If desired to have some late Green Peas, the Little Gem will yield a crop if sown about the middle of August.

Daniel O'Rourke.—This is a favorite early sort, especially among market gardeners. It should be sown in rows about two and a half feet apart, on account of its length of vine. It is of hardy constitution, and very prolific.

CHAMPION OF ENGLAND.—One of the tall-growing sorts, usually about five feet high, but long known as one of the finest quality. Its great length of vine is a serious inconvenience, and it is doomed to be crowded out by some of the shorter-growing, and therefore, more manageable varieties.

LAXTON'S ALPHA.—A new sort that we have not grown, but is highly commended by others, as the earliest blue wrinkled marrow, being earlier than McLean's Little Gem, and wonderfully productive. It is said to be a cross between Laxton's Prolific and McLean's Advancer. It grows about three feet high.

McLEAN'S WONDERFUL.—Another new wrinkled marrow, growing about three feet high, of robust habit, very prolific, and said to be of excellent flavor.

We name these new sorts, believing they will prove to be valuable varieties with us, not growing so tall as to require supports, and possessing the richness and delicacy of flavor so much desired.

PEPPERS

Being naturally tropical plants, it is necessary to start the plants in a hot-bed, or in the house, in order to give them a longer season than they could have when sown in the open ground. The seed is sown thinly, and about half an inch deep, in the month of April, and the plants cared for in the same manner as Tomato plants. When the weather has become settled, and frosts no longer feared, the plants should be set out in the open ground, choosing a light, warm soil, with a sunny aspect, and planting them in rows eighteen inches apart, and twelve inches between the plants in the row.

In some places they are grown extensively for pickle manufacturers, and sold to them by weight. When grown for this purpose, they are usually planted in rows about two feet apart, and the plants fifteen inches apart in the row. The thick-fleshed varieties are preferred for this use, and these usually yield about three tons to the acre.

The principal use of Peppers in this country is for pickling or for flavoring other pickles. They are used in the green state, an opening being made in the side of the pod, the seeds taken out, and the pods soaked in salt and water for twenty-four hours, changing the water after they have lain in it for twelve hours. They are then drained, put into jars, and covered with cold boiled vinegar. The jars are tightly closed, and after remaining in this condition for three or four weeks, the Peppers will be ready for use.

The ripe pods may be dried in a moderately heated oven, then pulverized, and sifted through a fine sieve, first taking out the seeds, and then tightly corked in glass bottles. This will make as pleasant a Pepper as the Cayenne of commerce, without the admixture of red lead with which it is often adulterated.

BELL PEPPER.—The pods of this variety are very large, and when ripe, of a glossy, bright coral-red. It is early, thick-fleshed, less acrid than most of the other sorts, and much used as a pickle.

LONG RED PEPPER.—The form of the pods is long and conical, when ripe of a brilliant red, thin fleshed, and exceedingly acrid. It is an excellent variety from which to make a domestic Cayenne pepper.

SQUASH PEPPER.—In form something like a Tomato, with a smooth glossy skin, brilliant coral-red when ripe, with a thick skin, less acrid than the Long Red, but hotter than the Bell.

SWEET SPANISH.—One of the largest and also one of the earliest, color brilliant scarlet, and the flesh of a mild pleasant flavor. Makes excellent pickles.

RADISHES.

The soil for these should be a light sandy loam, dry and warm, especially for very early crops; later in the season it should be also deep, that it may be moist. Those who desire to enjoy Radishes as early as possible, can grow them in a hot-bed having a **very** gentle bottom heat, giving them plenty of air in fine weather, and watering **with** tepid water. **The seed may also be sown** in some sunny spot in the open ground, sheltered **if** possible from the **colder winds, as soon as the** weather becomes balmy in spring. **The excellence** of this **vegetable** consists in its being crisp, tender and mild; and these requisites can only be secured **by** a quick growth. When the hot weather of summer sets in, the Radish **is** apt to be too pungent to be agreeable, and is better flavored at this time if grown as much in the **shade** as possible.

The seed is sometimes sown broadcast, **but** more commonly in drills about half an inch deep and six inches apart. After the plants are up they should be thinned, so as to stand about an **inch apart. The** seed will keep **its vitality** well for three years, but after **that time is not to be relied upon.** It **is a very** common **practice to sow Radishes among Beets, or Onions, or** Cabbage, as **the crop is taken off before they can interfere** with these **later** vegetables, and in this way ground is economized. Early Radishes command a quick sale in our town and city markets. The chief labor connected with their cultivation **is** that of cleaning and bunching them **for sale, which, by the** way, is no small item.

There are a great many varieties, but **the** following are quite sufficient and the most desirable:—

French Breakfast.—An excellent variety for forcing in hot-beds, **olive-shaped,** scarlet with white tip, very tender, **pleasant flavored and handsome.**

Rose Olive-Shaped.—This is a very fine early variety, oval in form, skin deep **rose** color, flesh tender and excellent.

Long Scarlet Short Top.—A favorite market sort, suitable **for** open garden culture, color deep pink, flesh **white, crisp** and **mild** flavored; usually about six inches in length when in its best condition for the table.

Chinese Rose Winter.—The best winter Radish. The root is cylindrical in form, terminating abruptly in a slender tap-root, and of a bright rose color. The flesh is firm, breaking, and generally of a pleasant mild flavor, much less pungent than the Black Spanish, and far more pleasing in appearance.

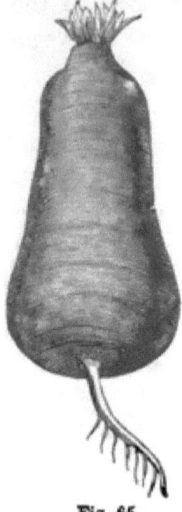

Fig. 65.

The seed of this, and of all winter Radishes, should be sown about the first of August, in light, friable, yet rich soil, and the plants thinned out to about six inches apart in the row. They may be used during the month of October as wanted, but when cold weather approaches they should be taken up and stored in fresh soil in a cool cellar or root-house, where they can be had for use at any time during the winter. We have kept this variety packed in this manner in the root-house in fine condition until April. If the weather in September is hot and dry for any length of time, the winter radishes will usually be more pungent than if the weather be showery.

RHUBARB.

The Rhubarb, or Pie Plant, as it is very commonly called, grows well in any rich soil free from stagnant water, and responds most bountifully to generous culture. Indeed it seems to be scarcely possible to get the ground too rich, and regular annual top dressings of manure are needed to bring out strong and broad leaf-stalks. It is for these leaf-stalks that it is cultivated, and these are used in various ways, chiefly in the making of pies and tarts, or, when stewed, as a sauce. They are best when young, early in the spring, and are prepared by peeling off the outside skin, cutting them up in slices, and stewing in a saucepan with plenty of sugar and very little water.

It is propagated by divisions of the root, which are planted in soil that has been prepared by deep ploughing and abundant manuring. In the spring of each year a heavy coat of manure should be spread on the surface of the ground around the plants. When new varieties are wanted they may be obtained by sowing seed. Some of the plants will be good, which may be selected and planted out, and the remainder thrown away. It will require three years to raise plants from seed that will give stalks fit for use, while those from divisions of the roots, leaving an eye or bud upon each piece, will yield stalks fit for use in one year.

It is a perfectly hardy plant, but will start earlier in spring if covered in the fall with a little coarse litter to keep out the intense frost; and as a great part of the comfort, and to those who cultivate for market, the profit, of growing the Rhubarb, is to have the stalks for use as early as possible, a little labor bestowed in the fall in protecting it from severe frosts is amply repaid. Where the snow falls before the ground freezes and remains all winter, keeping the frost out entirely, or nearly so, such fall covering will not be needed. A plantation once formed and properly cared for will last for fifteen years.

The best varieties are the following:

MYATT'S LINNÆUS.—Is early, very productive, has a fine spicy flavor and is moderately acid.

MYATT'S VICTORIA.—Of large size, and is the variety chiefly depended upon by market gardeners for the main crop. Not so early as Linnæus, but larger and yielding a much greater weight per acre.

SALSIFY or OYSTER PLANT.

The Vegetable Oyster is a perfectly hardy plant, enduring our winters without protection as perfectly as the Parsnip. When cooked, the flavor much resembles that of the Oyster, and it is very much relished by nearly every one. It is coming rapidly into more general use, and in some places largely cultivated for market, finding a ready sale.

A light mellow soil, such as that in which Carrots are grown, suits it best, and it should be pulverized and enriched in precisely the same manner as for Carrots. The seed should be sown early in spring, in drills about fourteen inches apart and about an inch deep, and, when the plants are fairly started, should be thinned out to about five inches apart in the row. It is not safe to trust to seed that is more than two years old.

The cultivation is the same as that of Beets or Carrots, keeping the ground well stirred and free from weeds. In October the roots will have grown to their full size, and may be used as desired for table or market. When severe weather approaches, a few may be covered with leaves or straw, to keep out the frost, so that they can be obtained for use during the winter, or they may be taken up and packed in fresh earth in a cool root-cellar. The remainder may be allowed to remain unprotected until spring, when they can be taken up as soon as the frost is out, and used or sent to market.

They are prepared for the table by slightly scraping the roots then they are cut in thin slices, and boiled in a very little water, seasoned with salt, until tender. When thus cooked, cream is poured in, with a little cod-fish picked fine, and the whole allowed to boil up, when it is ready to be dished for the table. The cod-fish, if used very moderately, greatly increases the oyster-like flavor, for which this vegetable is so much esteemed. Some boil the roots entire until quite tender, then grate fine, make into balls, then dip in batter made of white of eggs beaten up with a little flour, roll in grated cracker or bread crumbs, and fry in a pan until brown.

SQUASH.

This common and useful vegetable may be grown in any soil that is well drained and rich. The seed should not be sown until warm weather has fairly set in, and the danger of frost passed, for the seeds will rot if the ground be cold, and a slight frost kills the young plants. When the soil is in good tilth, we have grown them as we do Pumpkins, among the Corn, but the better way is to grow them by themselves, mixing a couple of shovelsful of well-rotted manure with the soil in each hill. For the bush varieties the hills may be three feet apart each way, but the running kinds will require not less than six.

It is well to prepare the hill by stirring and loosening the soil to the depth of about eight inches, raising it a couple of inches above the general surface of the ground, and making it some eighteen inches broad. In this hill plant a dozen seeds, for though three or four plants will be sufficient, there are so many enemies to devour the young plants, that what with cut-worms, squash bugs, striped bugs, and all sorts of bugs, the cultivator will possibly not have more than three or four vigorous plants left. Should more than that number escape, it is a very easy matter to pull out the surplus. The cultivation will consist in keeping the ground free from weeds and occasionally stirring the soil in the hill around the plants. The more rapidly they can be made to grow during the first week or two of their life, the sooner will they be out of danger from their insect foes. The seeds retain their germinating powers for a long time, and may be expected to grow even when six or eight years old.

The Squash is prepared for the table by simply boiling it in water until quite soft, it is then mashed, the water strained out by pressing in a colander, and then it is seasoned with pepper, salt and butter, or cream, to suit the taste. There is an endless list of varieties, and these are multiplying continually. It is in fact difficult to keep any variety pure, if more than one be grown in the garden, so easily do they mix and cross with each other. We have been best suited with those named below.

SUMMER CROOK-NECK.—This is the best flavored of all the summer Squashes, though none of them are equal in delicacy and sweetness to the later sorts. It is a bush variety, the fruit crook-necked, color yellow, skin thin, covered with warty excrescences, and fit for use only while the skin is tender and easily broken with the nail. As it ripens, the rind becomes hard, and the flesh watery and coarse.

YELLOW BUSH SCALLOPED.—A very early sort, and on that account and its productiveness largely grown for market. It is not as sweet and rich as the Summer Crook-Neck, and like it must be used before the rind becomes hard.

AUTUMNAL MARROW.—An excellent autumn Squash, frequently known by the name of Boston Marrow. It is about nine inches in length by seven in diameter, somewhat oval in shape, with large, fleshy stem, skin thin, orange-yellow when fully ripe, the flesh salmon-yellow, dry, fine-grained, rich, sweet and excellent. If carefully gathered without bruising, and stored in a cool, dry, airy place, free from frost, they will keep all through the winter. In a damp cellar they are sure to rot. This is a running sort, and requires to be planted in hills six or eight feet apart. There is a bush variety much resembling this in appearance, smaller in size, requiring a shorter season in which to mature, keeping well in winter, though not as fine flavored, which may be substituted for this in those parts of the Dominion where the season is found to be too short for the running sort.

Fig. 66.

CANADA CROOK-NECK.—We esteem this to be the best of all the crook-neck Squashes. It is small when grown unmixed with other sorts, weighing not more than about five pounds. The color is light yellow, flesh orange yellow, fine-grained, sweet, dry and of excellent flavor. We have found no trouble in keeping this variety through the winter, provided only that it be not kept in a damp place, but dry and free from frost. It is a very prolific variety, matures well in our climate, and is deserving of cultivation anywhere.

HUBBARD.—Without question the very best winter Squash,

and, when it can be obtained pure, will not fail to give satisfaction to the most fastidious. The Squash is somewhat oval in shape, about ten inches long and seven broad, and weighs about eight pounds. The shell is very hard, color greenish olive or bluish green, in this somewhat variable; the flesh is a rich orange-yellow, very fine-grained, dry, sweet and delicious. We have no trouble in keeping it through the winter in a dry, frost-proof cellar. It requires plenty of room, say about eight feet apart each way between the hills, and as it needs the whole season in the most favorable parts of Ontario, it will no doubt be well to give it a warm soil and warm aspect in the colder parts of the Dominion.

Fig. 67.

YOKOHAMA.—This is said to mature earlier than the Hubbard, and to be nearly as good. We have not grown it, but if it be found difficult to mature the Hubbard in any of our colder sections, it would be well to give this a trial, as it has the reputation of being fine fleshed, sweet and excellent.

SEA-KALE.

Our climate is so severe during winter, that it is not as favorable to the cultivation of this vegetable as the more open climate of England, where it is cultivated in every gentleman's garden, and also largely grown for market. We do not advise our farmers to attempt its culture; it does not repay the labor and care requisite for its production as a market vegetable, and we mention it here for the guidance of those who are willing to be at the necessary labor and expense, for the sake of having it on their tables for a short time in spring. We cannot have it all through the winter, as in England, unless we cultivate it under glass, and it is only in spring, after the weather has begun to moderate, that we can hope to get up heat enough to start it into growth.

A bed of Sea-Kale is started either by procuring the plants from some gardener, or by raising them from seed. Some sow the seed where the plants are intended to remain, but the better way is to prepare a small bed in which the seed is to be sown, and grow the plants for a year in this bed. The seed cannot be relied upon after it is two years old. The bed should be prepared by making the soil fine and rich, and the seed sown thinly in drills about an inch deep and a foot apart. The plants should be thinned out to about an inch apart as soon as they appear, and when they are well established, thinned again to three inches apart. During the summer the ground should be frequently stirred and kept free from weeds. In autumn the plants should be covered with five or six inches of earth and some coarse litter.

The next spring, as soon as the ground can be worked, a piece of deep, rich, sandy soil should be selected, ploughed and subsoiled to the depth of fifteen inches. Upon this the plants should be set out in rows three feet apart, and two feet apart in the row. In planting, the crowns should be set not less than two inches below the surface. During the summer the ground must be kept clean by frequent hoeings, and if dry weather sets in, the plants will need watering. The plants must not be allowed to run up to seed, but the seed stalks kept cut down as often as they appear. At the approach of winter, the ground should be covered to such a depth with coarse manure, or leaves or straw, as will keep out the frost. Salt is a good fertilizer for this vegetable, strewn over the ground in the spring in moderate quantity.

After the weather becomes mild, usually towards the end of March, the covering should be removed from as many plants as it is desired to force into early growth, and a twelve-inch flower-pot inverted over each plant; or, instead of pots, we have sometimes seen boxes used. Over these pots or boxes fermenting manure should be heaped to such a depth as to generate a heat of between fifty and sixty degrees, which will usually require about two feet in depth of manure. It is usually recommended to mix leaves and fresh stable manure in equal quantities, but it is not always possible to get the dry leaves, and not at all necessary. Care must be taken in placing the pots or boxes over the plants, that all holes are closely stopped, and the rims sunk in the soil, so as to prevent the entrance of any rank vapors from the fermenting manure. In from four to six weeks, the plants will probably have grown up inside the boxes or pots some six or eight inches in length, when the shoots may be cut for use. After cutting away the sprouts fit for use, the crowns may be covered with fresh soil to the depth of three or four inches, the pots replaced, and the manure, etc., replaced as before. In this way another cutting may be had from the same plants. When done cutting, the greater part of the manure should be taken off, and the remainder worked into the bed as a dressing.

The plants which are not forced in this way should be covered early in the spring with ten or twelve inches of sand or other light soil. The sprouts growing up through this will be blanched, though it is thought that the flavor is not quite equal to that of the plants which have been forced.

It is prepared for the table by boiling for about twenty minutes, in water that has been seasoned with salt, when it is taken up, laid upon toasted bread, and drawn butter poured over it. It is used as a substitute for Asparagus or Cauliflower, and those who are fond of either of these will enjoy a good dish of Sea Kale.

SPINACH.

Any good garden soil, that has been well enriched, will grow Spinach. It should be well pulverized with plough and harrow, or spade and rake, just as early in the spring as possible, and liberally dressed with well rotted manure. The seed should be sown as soon as the ground can be got ready, in shallow drills, about half an inch deep and nine inches apart. Sowing should be repeated at intervals of a fortnight, in order to keep up a succession for use. The seed retains its vitality for several years, and may be safely used when three years old.

It does not require any special cultivation, other than stirring the soil and keeping the weeds down, and the crop is usually fit for use in five or six weeks. The young plants should be thinned out so that they will stand about nine inches apart, and the later thinnings may be used as greens. Unless the individual plants have plenty of room they will run up at once to seed.

The earliest crops are obtained by sowing seed in September, in rich soil well prepared, thinning out the plants to six or nine inches apart, and, on the approach of winter, covering them thinly with straw, so that they may have a slight protection. This covering will not be needed where the snow falls before the ground is frozen and remains until spring. In the spring the covering is removed, and the plants thinned out as they increase in size, until the whole crop is used or marketed, which will usually be early in May, quite in time to use the ground for some other crop, such as Cabbage, Cauliflower, &c. When well grown, the leaves of Winter Spinach will measure two feet in circumference.

The leaves are the part that is used. These are rinsed in clean water, and boiled in the least possible amount of water, which has been seasoned with salt. They will be cooked in about fifteen or twenty minutes, when they should be placed in a colander, the water drained carefully off, and then seasoned with butter and pepper. Some, however, prefer it dressed with vinegar and hard-boiled egg.

ROUND-LEAVED. — This is the favorite sort with market-gardeners, and their main dependence both for spring and fall sowing. The leaves are large and fleshy, and rounded in form. It is very hardy, suffering but little from the severity of winter. In dry and warm weather it is very apt to run to seed.

LARGE PRICKLY.—Is an excellent variety for fall sowing, being very hardy, yet requiring a light covering of straw where snow cannot be depended upon. The leaves are large and thick, and of excellent quality.

FLANDERS.—This variety is highly spoken of by those who have raised it, many giving it the preference over the Large Prickly. It is believed to be fully as hardy, and, consequently, equally adapted for wintering over, while the leaves are larger, thicker, and more succulent. It grows quite bushy, and, therefore, needs to be thinned out to about nine inches apart.

NEW ZEALAND.—This is botanically quite a different plant from the common Spinach, though for all practical purposes and uses it ranks with it. It needs the same soil and cultivation, except that being a larger plant, it requires more space for its development. Well grown plants measure five and six feet in diameter. Many sow in a seed-bed or in a frame, and afterwards transplant to three feet apart each way. In deep and rich soil it grows with great luxuriance, especially in hot weather. The leaves can be gathered and used as they grow, and if not kept too closely cropped, each plant will continue to yield its leaves all summer long. It is very easily grown and very productive, but will not withstand frost.

TOMATO.

Not very many years ago, the Tomato was occasionally seen in village gardens, under the name of Love Apple, cultivated on account of its beauty of appearance, as an ornament merely, but now that it has found its way to our tables, it is grown by every one who makes any pretensions to keeping a garden, and hundreds of acres in the vicinity of the large towns and cities of America are devoted to its culture. Every farmer residing convenient to market, finds it profitable to grow a proportion of Tomato, and the yield and price rarely fail to be such as to give a fair return for the labor. The earliest ripe Tomatoes brought to market command the best prices, and hence there is a great desire to get them early. We doubt, however, if on the whole it pays our farmers to provide the necessary hot-beds and sash required to grow a crop of very early Tomatoes, because such are the facilities for transportation in these days of steam, that the more Southern grower supplies the earliest Tomatoes in spite of all we can do, and by the time we can possibly get ours ripe, the price is so materially affected by the supply from more sunny latitudes, that the pay is not an adequate return for the investment.

Those, however, who are very anxious to get Tomatoes as early as possible, should provide themselves with a hot-bed about the middle of March, varying somewhat as to date according to the locality and the season, placed in some spot well sheltered from the prevailing cold winds. In this the seed should be sown in drills about three inches apart, not too thickly, and the sash kept close until the plants appear. As soon as they begin to show the second leaf they should have plenty of air whenever the weather will permit, taking care at the same time that they do not get chilled. In about three weeks it will be necessary to have some more hot-beds ready into which to transplant the Tomato plants, setting them about four or five inches apart each way. A sash will hold about fifty plants when thus transplanted, consequently two sashes will be required for every hundred; and as an acre holds some five thousand plants, fifty sashes will be needed to grow enough for an acre. After they have been transplanted, the same care will be required as before, giving water when needed, and sufficient air to make the plants strong and healthy. We think the better way for us to proceed is to wait until later in the season, say about the tenth of April, before sowing, and then during the first week of May they might be transplanted into a bed of ground made very rich, well exposed to the sun, and well sheltered from winds, and so arranged, that, at night and in very chilly weather they can be covered with boards. The best way would be to make a frame on the sides, as if for sash, and lay the boards across the sides of the frame. As the plants begin to crowd **each** other again, they can be again separated **by** taking up every alternate plant, **and** setting these out in **an** adjoining **bed. In this** way the plants **can be** allowed **all the** space they **require,** will grow **strong and stocky, and be in fine** condition for planting in the open ground when danger of frost is **over, and** will be more likely to be healthy and valuable, grown by the inexperienced in this **way, than if** they attempted to use sashes. In this manner something may be lost in the matter of earliness in the ripening of a few Tomatoes, but a **great deal** is saved in the matter of hot-beds and sashes. **Tomato seed will** retain its vitality for five years.

Those who desire to raise only a few **plants for home use, can** start them in the house by sowing the **seed in a** box filled with good rich soil, **and keep it in a warm kitchen** window. **The** kitchen is the **best room in the house** for plants, because the air is filled **with moisture from the water** that is kept almost constantly on the stove, in the various operations of cooking and **washing that are carried on there.** When the plants are fairly started, if they stand too thick, enough may be pulled out to give the remainder sufficient room; and if these are needed, they may be planted in another box of earth, kept shaded and well watered for a few days, when they will have taken fresh **root,** and may be set in the light. As often as the weather will permit, the boxes should be **set outside the** window, where they will get the sun and air, and **be** sheltered from chilly winds, not forgetting to **take them in if** the weather should suddenly change **to a colder temperature, and** always at night. In this way strong, stocky, and healthy plants can be grown, which may be set out, and sheltered with boards for a time, until the weather **becomes warm enough** to put them in the open garden.

We have known an enthusiastic Tomato grower save his crop from an untimely June frost by placing small heaps of shavings **around his** Tomato plantation on the north, east and west sides, and when the thermometer indicated the approach of frost, he would light his **piles of shavings** and rubbish on the windward side, and the wind would blow the warm smoke over the plot of ground and thus save the plants from the frost. In his locality there was no danger of frost when the wind was in the south, hence he placed no heaps of combustibles on that side. In this manner he has saved his crop of Tomatoes not once, nor twice, but several times, and as he usually plants an acre or more, and markets the crop, it is quite a material item with him.

For early Tomatoes, it is desirable to select a light, dry and warm soil; if not rich enough to give the vines a good start, a little well-rotted manure should be worked into the soil where each plant is set, and in such soil three feet apart is a good distance to plant them. For the main crop, they may be set in heavier soil, that is well drained and rich, at four feet apart each way. When those plants which are intended for the early crop have set their first clusters of fruit, it will hasten the swelling and ripening of the fruit to cut off the vine a little beyond the clusters, and as often as it starts again into growth to pinch out all the young shoots, not allowing the plant to make any more growth or set any more fruit. In hoeing, the earth should not be drawn up to the plants but from them, and the roots made to feel as much of the sun's heat as possible.

There is no doubt that something can be gained in the way of early maturity, by annually selecting for seed, the first well formed Tomatoes that ripen and sowing only such seed. Every year, some new sort is advertized which is to be from ten to thirty days earlier than any other, but it never turns out to be any earlier than those that have been in cultivation for years. We advise every Tomato grower to save his own seed from his earliest good specimens, and let the "greenhorns" buy the wonderful novelties.

When there is no lack of space, the simplest mode of cultivation is to keep the ground free from weeds, and allow the Tomato vines to spread over the ground. In small gardens they may be tied to stakes or a trellis, or kept up by a hoop placed around the plant and supported by stakes at any desired height from the ground. In small gardens they have a very handsome and **neat** appearance when **trained in** some one of these methods, besides, a larger crop **may be** secured in this way from a **small piece of** ground.

The Tomato is used in a great variety of ways. Peeled and **sliced,** it is eaten without **cooking,** dressed with vinegar and **pepper, or** sugar and vinegar, **or sugar and cream,** or seasoned only **with** salt, or with mustard **and vinegar,** according to the fancy **of each.** It is cooked by stewing, by frying, by boiling, by baking, stuffed with finely chopped meat and bread crumbs, and roasted—in short, in every conceivable **way that** ingenuity **can** devise.

Varieties have become greatly multiplied, **but beyond the** gratification **of curiosity, there is no need of growing more than** two or three.

EARLY SMOOTH RED.—**This is the earliest variety of them** all, medium **in size,** round, smooth, and of good quality. Those who are seeking for an early sort will find this to ripen a little in advance of all the rest, and by carefully saving the seed of the first to ripen, will in a few years succeed in ripening it in their grounds before any of the new extra early sorts.

GENERAL GRANT.—The best of all for the main crop. **The** fruit is large, smooth, flattened, solid, and **of excellent** quality. **If the** seed of this variety be saved only from smooth and well-formed fruits ripening **first,** it will be found to ripen close upon the heels of **the Early Smooth Red, and** to yield a fine crop of truly splendid **Tomatoes.**

With these two varieties the cultivator might well be content, for there are none in **all** the list yet grown to excel them.

FEJEE.—A large, solid, and pleasant flavored variety, of a nearly pink color, but late.

RED CHERRY.—Small, round, produced in clusters, used for pickling, too small for anything else. There is also a yellow variety.

RED PLUM.—Nearly plum-shaped, small, scarlet, very uniform

in size, productive, also used for pickling. There is likewise a yellow variety.

STRAWBERRY.—This is a different species, having a peculiar flavor, thought by some to resemble that of the Strawberry. Used for preserves, with the addition of lemon-juice, or stewed and served like Cranberries.

TURNIP.

To nearly every Canadian tiller of the soil this is a well-known vegetable as a field crop, and its cultivation well understood. Of the cultivation of the Turnip as a garden vegetable it is only necessary to say, that for the production of early Turnips, where that is desired for market or table purposes, it is highly important to select a light soil, sandy or gravelly, and enrich it abundantly with manure. In all other respects the cultivation will be the same, only on a smaller scale, perhaps, than the ordinary farm crop. We have thought that the late Turnips were better and sweeter than those usually brought to the table during the heat and drought of midsummer. The seed should be sown in drills about eighteen inches apart, and the plants afterwards thinned out to about six inches apart in the row. The seed will retain its vitality for a number of years, and can be safely relied upon even when four years old.

For winter use it is necessary to put the Turnips into pits, and cover with straw and earth sufficiently to exclude the frost, taking care not to put too many in one heap, as they will not keep so well in large bulk as in bodies of only three or four barrels in one heap. Where the soil is perfectly dry, even in wet seasons, or can be made so by drains, trenches may be dug in the ground to such a depth as can conveniently be done without admitting water into the trench, and about three feet wide, and the Turnips placed in these trenches, and covered with straw and earth. Where a trench cannot be dug without danger of water, they may be packed in ridges on the surface, and covered, only the covering will require to be put on thicker, to exclude the frost, than when they can be put below the surface.

The following varieties are the most desirable for garden culture.

Nimble Dick.—The earliest Turnip, white and flat, of good quality, and much prized by those who grow Turnips for market.

Golden Ball.—A yellow-fleshed variety, globular and smooth, sweet and of good flavor.

Purple-Top Strap-Leaved.—A flat, smooth Turnip, with a slender tap-root, firm fleshed, sweet and mild flavored. An excellent variety, and yields good crops.

Yellow Malta.—A small, early, yellow-fleshed variety, of fine grain and good flavor, probably the best yellow Turnip for summer use.

Sweet German.—The best table variety with which we are acquainted for late fall and winter use. The seed should be sown from the first to the tenth of July in good, deep, rich soil, and the Turnips will be large enough for the table in October, and much sweeter than if sown earlier. It resembles the Swedish Turnips in form, but is white fleshed, fine grained, solid, sweet and of superior flavor. It will keep in fine condition until June, retaining its fresh, crisp character and sweet flavor. It is not always quite as smooth in form as a Turnip raiser would desire, but it more than makes up in sweetness and quality what it lacks in beauty of form.

HOT-BEDS.

Perhaps the first thing to be provided, in preparing a hot-bed, would be the frame, which is a sort of box without a bottom, nine feet long, six feet wide, two feet deep at the back and eighteen inches in front, level at the bottom but sloping gradually from the back to the front at the top. This, if made out of pine plank two inches thick, and dove-tailed together, will be substantial and lasting. The sides should be enough higher than the front and back to keep the sash in place, projecting upwards about the thickness of the sash. Such a frame will hold three sashes.

The most convenient size of sash is six feet by three, the sash bars being all six feet long without any cross bars, and the glass laid with a lap of an eighth of an inch, the lowest light lapping about a quarter of an inch on the frame of the sash, and the upper light inserted, at the top, in a groove in the upper sash frame. In order that this may be done, it will be seen that it is necessary that the rabbet of the sash-bar or astragal shall be made to lie flush with the upper surface of the lower sash frame. Glazed in this manner, the rain falling on the sash runs off with nothing to hinder its descent. The sash-bars should be made stronger than those of ordinary window sash, and in the form shown for green-house astragals at page 142.

These having been provided, it is necessary then to procure the material for producing the heat. This should be a quantity of fresh horse-dung, to which may be added, if convenient, leaves equal in bulk to one-half of the manure, or instead of leaves, the straw used in bedding. These should be well mixed and thrown compactly together into a heap to ferment. After the fermentation has become lively, the heap should be turned over, shaken out and re-formed, and left for three or four days until fermentation sets in again.

If the ground be of that porous character that water will not settle into a pit two feet deep, such a pit may be dug out, of the width and length requisite to receive the frames, and the manure now placed in the pit. But if the ground be of such a character that water would settle into pits dug in it, the bed must be formed wholly on the surface. In placing the manure now, it should be put into the pit or built up in the form of the frames gradually, packing it as solid as possible, and beating it well down with the back of the fork, so that it may be alike firm and solid in all parts. When this is completed, the surface should be level, and the manure about two and a half feet deep throughout the entire bed. If built on the surface of the ground it should be made a foot wider than the frame, so that it may project six inches in front and rear when the frame is set in its place.

The frames are now to be placed upon the top of the manure, and the sashes laid on and kept close until the fermentation again sets in. At first this will be violent, and the thermometer will rise to about a hundred degrees if plunged in the manure, but in about three days the heat will subside. When this takes place, and the thermometer plunged in the manure has gone down to ninety, the soil should be put in the frames and spread out evenly to the depth of six or eight inches.

This soil is prepared during the fall by mixing together some well rotted sods, which have been thrown together early in the summer for this purpose, and one-third its bulk of old, rotted manure. Rotted refuse hops from the brewery make an excellent manure for this purpose.

The situation of the hot-bed should be well sheltered from the westerly and northerly winds, and have a full southern exposure. Such a shelter can be made, when necessary, by planting a double row of evergreens on the north, east, and west sides of the ground set apart for the frames. In most parts of our country the westerly are the prevailing winds, and it is of more importance to have the shelter on the north and west sides than on the east. Until the evergreens become large enough, a high board fence may be erected, but in a few years the trees will make a most effectual shelter. The Norway Spruce and the White Spruce are excellent trees for such a purpose.

Beginners are very apt to keep their frames too close and the heat too great. If the result be not the entire burning up of the seeds or plants, it is very sure to be the production of long-drawn, spindling, sickly plants, too tender to be ever of any value. The remedy for this is to lift the sashes, and let in air. This may be very nicely regulated, from the merest crack to any width. When the weather and strength of the plants will admit, the sashes may be drawn off entirely.

COLD FRAMES.

These are the same frames and sash as have been already described, placed upon a bed of soil, but without any manure or heating material beneath. All the heat, in this case, is obtained from the sun, which, being confined and the air excluded, soon warms the soil to a considerable degree. They are very useful in protecting nearly hardy plants during the winter and early spring, and in giving them a gentle warmth above that of the outside atmosphere.

TOOLS.

Of ploughs and harrows, and cultivators, spades and shovels, it is not necessary to speak, but there are a few garden implements that are not as generally employed as their utility deserves.

THE STEEL RAKE is the best instrument for destroying very young weeds in a wholesale way. It can be had of many sizes, varying from eight to twenty inches in width. Two or three days after planting, the ground should be raked over with the steel rake; this loosens the surface, and destroys untold numbers of sprouting weeds. In about a week after, the raking should be repeated, and as the weeds will then be just starting again, another crop of them will be destroyed. It is quicker done than to go over the ground with the hoe, and more effectual.

THE SCUFFLE HOE is the best form of hoe for working between narrow rows when the plants are small. They can be had of varying widths, and should be about three inches narrower than the space between the rows.

THE DIGGING FORK is a better instrument than the spade for loosening up and turning over the soil. It enters the ground more easily, and the soil is pulverized better by striking it with the back of the fork, when turned over, than can be done with the spade.

THE PRONGED HOE is better than the common blade hoe, for more work can be done in a day with it, and better done and with greater ease, than with the old blade hoe. Of course, it should be used before the weeds get a start, as it is much easier and cheaper to kill weeds just as they are breaking through the surface of the ground, to say nothing of the feeding of the weeds and the maturing of weed seeds for another crop.

THE FLOWER GARDEN.

The desire to make one's home attractive and pleasant is prominent in the mind of every right-thinking person, not merely for his own enjoyment, but more for the sake of his children. Home should be the most attractive place our children can find, and all the charms that we can throw around it will be as so many links to bind them to the spot that is to them both a sanctuary and a shelter. Besides this, the surroundings of home have a formative power upon the character of those who dwell there, and a stranger may tell much of the mind and heart of the inmates by looking at the door-yard.

To encourage and help those who are striving to twine some flowers in the strands of daily toil, who are wishing to set those plants which, though not ministering food to the eater, shall cheer with their winsome beauty the dwellers at home, smile out a welcome to the entering guest, or greet with a cheery pleasantness the passer-by; to help such have these pages, devoted to the Flower Garden, been penned.

Our Canadian climate may not be the most favorable for lavish display of floral beauty, yet there are many beautiful things that will endure our climate, and, if it be necessary to bestow more thought and care upon the culture and protection of the trees, shrubs, and plants which we desire to have about our dwellings than is requisite in more sunny climes, this very care only heightens our enjoyment, and deepens our love for the things we thus cherish. Take courage, then; the Canadian's motto is "to make a path where he cannot find one," and if the floral treasures of the tropics do not grow naturally in our northern land, we will set about our homes those things which harmonize better with the natural features of our country, and compel

many of the plants of the tropics to blend their beauty and fragrance, during our brief warm summers, with the **hardier** beauties of **our sterner** climate.

We possess a wealth of beauty in **our Evergreens, and much of comfort, too,** for they **can** be **so planted** about the farmstead as to shelter the buildings from the keen frost-laden blasts **of** winter, making the spot within their shielding influence **several** degrees warmer, and a great many degrees more comfortable, than out where the wind sweeps on with unbroken power. We have a goodly number of these which are native to the soil, and those who wish to increase the variety may add to our **own** White Spruce, Hemlock Spruce, Balsam Fir, White Pine, &c., the Scotch **and** Austrian Pines, the Norway Spruce, and the rarer, **but equally hardy, Nordman's** Fir and Eastern Spruce.

We **have deciduous trees, too, of great** loveliness, and these **may be so interspersed with the Evergreens** as to heighten each **the beauty of the** other. A most graceful tree is our drooping Elm, and with it, all the Maples,—the Red, the Sugar, and the **Silver** Maple,—with the Birches and the Oaks, flourish throughout the Dominion. To these may be added the Mountain Ash, both of Europe and America; and Maples, and Oaks, **and** Birches and Elms of other climes, as may best please the taste of the planter. And if he have a little knowledge of their several tints of foliage, and particularly of their autumn **hues,** and of their natural forms and habits of growth, he can so plant them that through all the changing year they shall minister to the homestead both grace and beauty.

But it is hardly within the scope of this humble treatise to dwell upon the subject of the planting and management of trees around our dwelling-places, and the formation of lawns and parks. The time, we trust, is near at hand when the desire for home embellishment in the planting of trees shall attain such a position among us, that Canadians will require and receive, from abler hands, a work that shall treat specially of the planting of ornamental trees, and give such hints concerning their arrangement and disposition in groups or avenues, or single specimens, and such descriptions of their several characters, peculiarities, and beauties, and adaptation to soils and climate, as shall give a new impetus to the planting and culture of trees, for their own sake, throughout our entire Canada.

Turning to our humble but grateful task, we propose first to enumerate some of those flowering shrubs which have been found to thrive well in the greater part of Canada, and which contribute so much, at their several periods of blooming, to make the door-yard and garden lovely and gay; and, at the same time, give such suggestions concerning the soil and cultivation best adapted to each as shall be of service to those who care for what they plant, and take delight in their perfect development.

HARDY FLOWERING SHRUBS.

THE BERBERRY.—*Berberis.*—There is not a shrub more hardy than this, adapting itself also to every variety of soil. It is found in Northern Europe, Asia, and America, inhabiting the valleys of the more northern portions, but climbing the hill-sides of the warmer latitudes. Its flowers are yellow, produced in long, pendent racemes, and usually in great profusion. The fruit is of a most brilliant crimson, often remaining on the bush all winter. When laden with its yellow blossoms or with its coral-like berries, it is an object of much beauty. It should be planted at a little distance from the dwelling, for although its fragrance is pleasant when borne in on the air, when too near it is so strong as to be sometimes disagreeable. It will thrive in every description of soil, but seems to fruit more abundantly in that which is dry and poor. There is a variety with purple leaves and purplish fruit, which is even more ornamental than the common. It is known as the *Purple-leaved Berberry.* This variety is propagated by layers, while the common is grown from seed, sown in the fall in drills, and covered about an inch deep. The Berberry does not require trimming, assuming naturally a graceful form, growing yearly more dense by shoots thrown up **from the crown, but never** sending up suckers from the **roots.** The bark and root are used for dyeing linen and leather, imparting **to** them a **bright** yellow color. The fruit is very acid. It is sometimes **pickled,** but used more **as an** ornament **than a** pickle. **Boiled** with sugar, it makes **a pleasant** jelly, and of a most beautiful color.

CAROLINA ALLSPICE.—*Calycanthus.*—This shrub will hardly thrive, we fear, in the colder parts of the Dominion, except where the snow falls to such a depth as to cover it entirely during the severity of winter. In such places, and in the vicinity of the great lakes and other large bodies of water, it will live and thrive, making a moderate **annual** growth. At Halifax it is grown, **but only** in sheltered **situations.** It is very desirable for its **peculiarly formed chocolate-colored flowers,** which **have a very delightful fragrance of ripe fruits,** a mingling of the odor of Pine **Apples and Melons. In our** climate it is quite a **low shrub,** rarely attaining a greater **height** than three or four feet, growing best in strong, loamy soil. It is propagated by layers, **but** chiefly from the nuts, which mature abundantly in warmer climates.

CANADIAN JUDAS TREE.—*Cercis Canadensis.*—To some, this **pretty, low** growing tree, is known as **the *Red-Bud*, from** the appearance of the branches, which, early in the spring, are profusely covered **with clusters of** pretty pea-shaped blossoms, of a ruddy pink color. The leaves are very pretty also, being very regularly heart-shaped, and of **a rich** green. The blossoms appear before the leaves are expanded, and thus give to the tree a very pleasing appearance. It grows slowly, seeming to prefer a rich loam, and a somewhat sheltered situation. In favorable localities it attains **a** height of twenty feet, but with us it may be set down as rarely **exceeding** twelve or fifteen feet. We know it to be quite hardy in the greater part of Western Ontario, and believe that it will make a handsome shrub in most parts of the Dominion. It has not been planted as generally as its beauty deserves, hence there has not been the same opportunity to learn of its hardihood. We have added the name "Canadian," which is its specific botanical name, to distinguish it from the European Judas Tree, which is not as hardy nor as handsome. The name "Judas" Tree, seems to have originated from the supposition that it was the tree whereon Judas hanged himself.

DOGWOOD.—*Cornus Florida.*—Like the Judas Tree, this is strictly a tree of low growth, attaining ordinarily a height of from twelve to twenty feet, and has been almost as much neglected by planters because, like it, this beautiful little tree may be found growing naturally in some parts of the Dominion. But they are both well deserving of a prominent place in the attention of all Canadians who wish to adorn their rural homes. In spring, the Dogwood is very conspicuous when covered with its flowers, which are surrounded with large floral leaves, nearly white, and beautifully shaded with rosy purple. These petal-like leaves are no part of the true flowers, but infold them as an involucre. There are usually a dozen small flowers thus surrounded, in one head, by these floral leaves, and as they are borne on the extremities of the branches, cover the little tree with a seeming mass of bloom. The flowers usually open in the month of May, and continue for some time. These are succeeded by berries, which become of a most glowing scarlet color as the autumn draws near, standing out above the foliage. And as autumn advances, the foliage itself changes to a most gorgeous purple, becoming more deeply tinged as the days pass by, until the upper surface of the leaves is suffused with a rich crimson and the under side becomes a glaucous purple. There is not among all our hardy, large shrubs, anything more charming, both in spring and fall, than this native tree. We have no doubt but that it will be found to be as hardy as the Sugar Maple, delighting most in a moist and shady situation, becoming dwarfed when planted in very dry soils, or exposed places.

DOUBLE-FLOWERING ALMOND.—*Amygdalus.*—Those who live where the Peach tree will flourish and blossom, can enjoy the beauty of this charming tree, but in the colder parts of the country it suffers too much from the severity of the winter. **It grows to the ordinary size of** the Peach tree, and has the same naturally **straggling habit of** growth, which requires to be **corrected by a little** heading in. The flowers are very double, looking like little rosettes, of that peculiar pink shading best described as a peach-blossom color. These expand before the leaves have made much growth, and are borne in great profusion, literally covering the tree with little roses. It thrives best in warm, dry and light soils, not doing well in clay, and refusing to live if it be wet and cold. It is propagated by budding on either Peach or Plum stocks.

DWRAF DOUBLE-FLOWERING ALMOND.—This charming little shrub, scarcely exceeding two feet **in height, is of the same** tender **character as its larger relation,** not being able to endure extreme **frosts, and thriving best in** light soils that are warm and **dry. Where the snow** falls early, and deep enough to cover it **during the** severe winter weather, we believe it might be safely **wintered** out of doors. Yet even in our coldest latitudes the beauty of this little shrub might be enjoyed by growing it in a small tub, which could be plunged in the soil during the growing season, and removed in autumn to a dry cellar or any other shelter, where the thermometer did not fall to zero, taking care to prevent the roots from becoming quite dry. Or if taken up carefully in the fall, with **a** ball of earth **about the** roots, wrapped in a mat **and placed under shelter** and **covered** deeply with leaves, it could be replanted in spring, and would flower abundantly. The blossoms **are very double, of** the same lovely peach-blossom color, and cover the **shrub in one** mass of bloom. We like it best when **budded on the** Plum stock, on account of its propensity to throw up suckers from its own roots, which soon cause it to have **a very** untidy and neglected appearance. When budded on **Plum or** Peach it can be kept with a short, clean stem, which is **a most decided** improvement.

Dwarf Double-White-Flowering Almond.—A lovely shrub, in all respects like the foregoing, requiring the same soil, climate and treatment, but having pure white double flowers. It is also much improved by being worked upon a Plum or **Peach** stock.

DEUTZIA.—This genus of plants derives its name from *John Deutz*, a resident of Amsterdam and distinguished patron of botany, in whose honor it was so called by **Thunberg**. It comprises several very handsome shrubs.

DEUTZIA.—*Double Crenate-Leaved.*—A variety of recent introduction, one of the most charming of them all. It is quite hardy in the western part of Ontario, and in warm, dry soils, as distinguished from those that are wet and consequently cold, will probably prove hardy throughout the Dominion. It is a vigorous growing shrub, blooming most profusely, the flowers expanding in July when most other shrubs are out of bloom. The flowers are very double ; white, tinted with rose color on the outer surface of the petals, and hanging like little bells from the branches. We do not know a more beautiful and desirable shrub than this, and hope that it will yet be found in every collection, however small, in the Dominion.

Rough-Leaved.—A very desirable variety, growing to the height of six or eight feet, and most profusely covered in June with white, sweet scented flowers. It is very hardy, and in well drained soils will thrive well in all parts of the country. It succeeds well in the vicinity of Halifax, Nova Scotia.

Slender-Branched.—A dwarf-growing shrub, of very graceful habit, and exceedingly pretty when loaded with its elegant pure-white flowers. It also is very hardy, and will no doubt winter safely in any part of the Dominion, for in the coldest latitudes it will be securely covered with snow. If taken up in autumn and potted, it may be flowered most beautifully in March in a cool green-house. To flower it well, it must not be forced rapidly, but kept in the coolest part of the house, and allowed to come forward slowly.

DOUBLE FLOWERING BRAMBLES.—*Rubus.*—There are two varieties, the one white and the other rose-colored. They will grow wherever the Blackberry thrives, and are very ornamental when covered with their pretty double flowers. **They are easily** propagated **from** cuttings of the roots.

FILBERT, PURPLE-LEAVED.—*Corylus.*—This is a most conspicuous shrub, particularly if planted so that its large dark purple leaves are contrasted with the lighter green foliage of adjacent plants. Its beauty lies entirely in the color of the leaves, and as this continues to be a dark purple nearly all the summer, it is a constant object of attraction and enjoyment. It has not yet been much planted in Canada, but from what we have seen of it, we believe it will prove to be hardy, and to thrive in all soils.

HAWTHORNS.—*Cratægus.*—These are among the most beautiful and interesting small-growing **trees** which we have, and give to the grounds in early **summer a most** ornamental appearance, diffusing at the same time an agreeable fragrance. They **thrive** well in the vicinity of all our large bodies of water, at Halifax, in Nova Scotia, as well as along the shores of Lake Huron. They prefer a rich, limestone soil, though they will grow in any soil that is not filled with stagnant water. In the colder sections they should be planted in positions that are sheltered from the prevailing winter winds. Propagated by budding on the common Hawthorn of the English hedges. There **are** many varieties, but the following **are** the most attractive and desirable.

HAWTHORN.—*Double-White.*—Is very pretty when covered with its small, **double, white** flowers, and contrasts finely with the colored **varieties.**

Double Rose-Colored.—The flowers are large and very showy, of a deep rose color, shaded with crimson, and produced in great profusion.

Single Scarlet.—When in full bloom it is exceedingly **showy,** but the flowers do not last long under a hot sun.

New *Double Scarlet.*—We have not yet seen this variety **in** bloom, but it is described in England as the most desirable of all, on account of the perfectly double character of the flowers, and their great depth of color, which is there a bright carmine red.

HONEYSUCKLES.—*Lonicera.*—These are very hardy shrubs, growing in the open air about Stockholm, in Sweden, and St. Petersburgh, in Russia, and may be safely planted anywhere in Canada. They adapt themselves to almost every soil, and endure any exposure. They may be grown from seed, which should be sown in the autumn, or from cuttings.

Pink-Flowering.—A very showy variety, producing bright red flowers, which are delicately veined with white.

Red Tartarian.—The flowers of this variety are of a very bright pink, and appear about the end of May.

White Tartarian.—Differs from the preceding only in the color of the flowers, which are white.

LILACS.—*Syringa.*—These are well-known hardy shrubs, which grow well everywhere, in every soil, and all exposures. They have become so generally diffused that they are hardly held now in the estimation which they really deserve. Yet their beauty has been celebrated in verse, for it is of the Lilac the poet is speaking:

> "Various in array, now white,
> Now sanguine, and her beauteous head now set
> With purple spikes pyramidal."

There are a few varieties that are worthy of special attention. Among these we place the

Persian Purple.—It is one of the most graceful and pleasing shrubs in any collection. The leaves are small, and the spikes of flowers so large and heavy that they bend the spray, and hang like nodding plumes. The catalogues advertise a *White* variety, but though we have bought it several times, in hopes to secure so desirable a shrub, we have never yet seen it; the flowers have all been a sort of faded purple.

Chionanthus Leaved.—It is very distinct in both foliage and flower, and blooms quite late. The flowers are purple.

Virginalis.—The flowers are pure white, borne in large full spikes, and exceedingly pretty.

Prunus Triloba.—We esteem this a great acquisition to our list of hardy **shrubs,** and well **worthy of** a place in the **most** select collection. It has not yet been planted sufficiently long, **nor in places** sufficiently various, **to** enable us to say that it will **endure the** winter in our colder sections; but we believe that in **those** places, at least, where it is covered all winter with snow, **it** will thrive perfectly. **The** flowers are nearly double, of a clear pink color, large size, and borne in great profusion. It is cultivated by budding on the plum stock.

Purple Fringe.—*Rhus cotinus.*—Known under different names, as Venetian Sumach, Smoke Tree, Love-in-a-mist, this shrub has found its way into most collections. In the neighborhood of our great lakes it endures the winters perfectly, but **at** Halifax, and in similar localities, it requires a somewhat sheltered position. **The shrub** has a very irregular habit of growth, and **any attempt** to prune it into regularity only seems to increase the deformity or render it conspicuous. Left to itself, branching to the ground, its irregular growth is concealed by the foliage, and when covered with its peculiar feathery fringe, it is most interesting and ornamental. When these floral panicles first appear they are of a light green, which at length changes to a reddish brown, that, after a time, deepens into a purplish shade. At this time it often looks like a cloud of smoke issuing from the ground, or early in the morning, when covered with dew, like a rising mist. These floral panicles continue a long time, and make the shrub well worthy of the general esteem in which it is held.

Rose-Acacia.—*Robinia hispida.*—Also sometimes called the *Moss Locust,* **is** an exceedingly handsome shrub. Its habit of growth is spreading and irregular, and the branches are covered thickly with stiff hairs, hence the name of Moss Locust; but the flowers are produced in great profusion, hanging in dense racemes, and are of a most beautiful rose color. It begins to flower when not more than eighteen inches high, and grows slowly to a height of from three to five feet, in very favorable localities attaining to ten feet. The flowers appear in July, are pea-shaped, and borne in clusters like the common Locust, but have no perfume. We believe it will thrive anywhere in Canada, the snow protecting it on account of its dwarfness, in those parts where the winters are severe. It has the fault of throwing up suckers from the roots, in which way it propagates itself, but its beauty fully compensates for all its faults.

ROSE OF SHARON, or ALTHEA.—*Hibiscus Syriacus.*—These shrubs bloom so late in the season, in August and September, when no other shrubs are in flower, that they are very desirable. They are not particular in their choice of soil, though they seem to thrive best in a deep loam. Sometimes the twigs suffer during the winter, but when sheltered by neighboring evergreens or covered beneath the snow, they pass safely. But in bleak situations, especially where exposed to the sweep of wintry winds, they will perish. There are numerous varieties, differing only in their flowers. Some are single, and of various shades of blue, purple, or red, or are white, or white with violet centre; others are double, and of similar colors. In form the flowers resemble those of the Hollyhock. There is also a variety having the foliage marked with light yellow, known as the Variegated-leaved Althea; its flowers are double, and of a purple color.

JAPAN QUINCE.—*Cydonia Japonica.*—This shrub is one of great beauty, and much more hardy than the Quince we grow for fruit. So far as we are informed, it thrives well in all parts of the Dominion, though we can speak positively of it only in Nova Scotia, and in the vicinity of the lakes and River St. Lawrence. It is simply splendid when covered with its large, showy blossoms, and the scarlet varieties look truly like a burning bush. It is in blossom early in spring, before the leaves are fully formed, and when used as a garden hedge, presents a most charming appearance. And even after the flowers are gone, the neat, glossy green leaves have a very pleasing effect. The fruit is not fit for use. It can be propagated from the seed, and in this way new varieties are introduced, differing in the coloring of the flowers from the parent. Any particular variety may be propagated by **root** cuttings. The following varieties are quite distinct, and **worthy** of attention.

Scarlet.—**The** flowers are produced in great profusion, and **are of a bright** scarlet-crimson color, giving the shrub a very **brilliant** appearance.

Double-Flowering.—A **variety of the** preceding, producing, **flowers** that are semi-double.

Blush.—Very pleasing when grown with the Scarlet, from the contrast of color; the flowers of this being a delicate pink or salmon color, shading to white.

Umbelicata.—Produces brilliant rosy-red flowers, and large, showy fruit. **Of a more** vigorous habit, forming a large shrub.

SPIREAS.—**This is a** most **useful** genus of plants for the Canadian cultivator, many of the species having been introduced from Siberia, and therefore **able to endure the** cold of our **most** rigorous **winters,** and all of them natives of cool regions. Many of the varieties are plants of great beauty, and by a judicious selection of sorts, may be made to bloom over a period of three **months.** They are of easy culture, delighting in a moist, rich soil, becoming stunted in that which is very dry or poor. They are **propagated** by cuttings, by layering, and by seed. **We have not** space **for the** description of all the varieties that have been introduced, and make a selection of those which will be most useful and pleasing **in our climate.**

Double-Flowering Plum-Leaved.—This variety we place at the head of the list for **its beauty and hardiness.** We believe it will thrive anywhere **in** Canada, and that it will be a constant pleasure to its possessor. In May it is covered with pure white double flowers, wreathing the slender branches throughout almost the entire length, each one looking like a miniature white rose. **After the** flowers are gone, the leaves through the summer are a **bright, glossy** green, changing, as autumn approaches, to yellow **and orange,** and red, and scarlet. Such is the variety of coloring, **so** harmoniously blended are the tints, that one will look at it again and again, and wish it might thus remain for ever. It does not produce seed, but is propagated from green-wood cuttings and layers.

Lance-Leaved or Revesii.—Could we assure our readers that this elegantly graceful shrub was as hardy as the Plum-leaved, they would as surely plant it, for though differing from it entirely in habit of growth, form and color of foliage, it is in nothing behind it, save hardihood, and in some respects is more attractive. The Plum-leaved is quite erect in form, this most gracefully pendulous; and the leaves are not oval, but narrow, pointed, and deeply serrate, changing late in autumn to a purple hue, but not as gaily painted. But there is a brilliancy in the snowy whiteness of its flowers, and a charming grace in its lovely, airy form, that is not to be surpassed. And though we have seen it suffer in the open winters of these lake regions, doubtless, in the regions of all winter snow it would be perfectly hardy. There is a double-flowered variety of the Lance-leaved, differing in nothing from this, save that the flowers are double. They are not so tender that any need hesitate to give them a trial; if in the region of open winters with but little snow, give them the shelter of some friendly evergreen that will stand between them and the rough wintry wind that most commonly prevails, and it will not be often that they will suffer. To decide which of these two varieties of the Lance-leaved is the prettier, will be no easy task; many, perhaps most, will prefer the double; but there is a peculiar, charming brilliancy in the flowers of the single variety that the double does not possess. They blossom a few days earlier than the Plum-leaved, and like it, are usually propagated by layering and from cuttings of unripe wood.

Eximia.—This is a very fine variety, producing its flowers in spikes. They are of a bright rose color, and appear in July.

Billardi.—Another rose-colored variety, which keeps in bloom throughout July and August.

White Beam-Tree Leaved.—A very pretty white flowering sort, introduced from the north-west. It has a very dense, bushy habit, and blooms in July, the flowers entirely covering the plant.

Callosa.—There are two, the white flowering and the rose-colored. The flowers are produced in broad panicles, and continue nearly all summer.

SIBERIAN PEA-TREE.—*Caragana*,—A very pretty and hardy shrub, producing an abundance of yellow pea-shaped flowers in spring. It thrives in any soil that is not wet, and makes a good substitute in our severer latitudes for the Laburnum. It is propagated by seeds, which it yields abundantly.

SILVER BELL.—*Halesia.*—The four-winged fruited Halesia is quite hardy, and will grow in any soil or exposure, but thrives best in a rather poor, sandy soil. It presents a very pleasing appearance when loaded with the pretty, white, bell-shaped flowers, which appear in June. They are propagated by seed.

SYRINGA or MOCK ORANGE.—*Philadelphus.*—There are several varieties of this shrub, all of which are of easy culture, and thrive in any good garden soil. They are quite hardy, and are propagated by cuttings, or layers. They come into bloom in July.

The *Garland* is the best known, producing a great profusion of white, sweet-scented flowers, whence the name of Mock Orange. It is of this the poet is speaking:—

"The sweet Syringa, yielding but in scent
To the rich Orange, or the woodbine wild."

The *Hoary-Leaved* is a very beautiful variety, having large white flowers and downy leaves.

The *Large-Flowered* is not as fragrant as the *Garland*, but the flowers are larger and more showy.

SNOWBALL or GUELDER ROSE.—*Viburnum.*—This is a well known and favorite shrub, quite hardy, and accomodating itself to a great variety of soils and situations. It is of very easy culture and can be propagated by cuttings or layers. It flowers in June, and is a very showy object when covered with its rounded panicles of white blossoms. There is a variety known by the name of *Macrocephalum*, which is comparatively rare, and produces much larger heads of bloom than the older sort, and therefore thought to be more beautiful. It is certainly well worthy of a place in our collections. *Plicatum* is the name of another new variety which is said to bear large clusters of snow-white flowers in great profusion, and to be really a fine shrub.

TAMARIX.—We hope these very beautiful shrubs will prove to be hardy in a large part of the Dominion. As yet, they have not been sufficiently known and cultivated among us to decide the question of their hardiness, but they will, no doubt, thrive in the greater part of western Ontario, and in the vicinity of large bodies of water. Their leaves are very delicate and heath-like, and when covered with their spikes of pink flowers, they present a charmingly graceful appearance. There are several varieties, but the *African*, blooming in spring, and the *German*, blooming in August, are the best with which we are acquainted.

WEIGELAS.—These beautiful shrubs do well in Nova Scotia, and generally throughout Canada, and well deserve the high estimation in which they are held. They grow well in any good garden soil, are easily propagated from cuttings or layers, and remain a long time in bloom.

Rose-Colored.—This was introduced by Mr. Fortune, from China, and created a great sensation on its first appearance. It is one of the best, if not the best, of all the varieties. The flowers are rose-colored, and are produced in the axils of the leaves throughout nearly the entire length of the branches. They begin to expand as the leaves appear, but continue on the shrub until after the leaves are fully grown.

Amabilis.—Much esteemed on account of its flowering in the end of summer. The blossoms are not quite as large as Rosea, but are much the same in color, the leaves are larger, and the habit of the plant is more drooping.

Hortensis Nivea.—The flowers of this variety are pure white, and very abundant. In habit, it is somewhat more vigorous and upright, and larger in the leaf.

There are many more varieties, but these are the most distinct. A variegated-leaved variety of the Rose-colored Weigela is well worthy of attention, from the pretty yellowish-white border of the leaves and dwarf habit of the plant.

WHITE-FRINGE.—*Chionanthus Virginica.*—One of the most desirable flowering shrubs in cultivation, on account of its beautiful racemes of delicate white flowers, which have the appearance of a paper fringe. It thrives well in Nova Scotia, and will probably adapt itself to the climate of Canada generally, but it has not yet been sufficiently widely planted to ascertain just how much cold it will endure. It succeeds best in a light loam, and may be propagated by grafting it on the Ash.

There are many other shrubs which might be grown in some parts of the country, with varying success, but although some of them are very handsome, they suffer so often from the effects of our climate that their cultivation is not satisfactory. Among these we name the *Laburnum,* an exceedingly beautiful tall-growing shrub or small tree, especially when covered with its long, hanging racemes of yellow flowers, from which it has received the name of Golden Chain. The *Japan Globe Flower* is so often killed back that its beauty is quite lost, and the *Flowering Currants* very frequently have the blossom buds destroyed, and the same is true of the *Forsythia.* Probably in those places where the snow falls deep enough to cover them, they would escape all injury. From those described a selection may be made that will suit the locality of each cultivator, and the most worthy of his attention.

HARDY CLIMBING SHRUBS.

These are often very desirable to cover a wall or fence, or to train about the pillars of a verandah, or upon a lattice or screen. There are but few that seem to be well adapted to our climate, and of these the following will be found to be the most satisfactory.

VIRGINIA CREEPER.—*Ampelopsis hederacea.*—This is perfectly hardy everywhere, and being a rapid grower will soon cover the desired space. The flowers are insignificant, but the foliage is handsome, being of a bright, shining green in summer, and in autumn changing to a variety of rich shades of scarlet, and crimson, and purple. It will grow in any soil and any aspect, requiring no culture, and clinging firmly to the wall or other support by the rootlets thrown out at every joint.

Ampelopsis Veitchii is a miniature variety, with smaller foliage and finer stalk, but like it clinging firmly, growing rapidly and densely, and changing in autumn to crimson and purple.

TRUMPET-FLOWER.—*Bignonia Radicans.*—Like the Ampelopsis, this throws out rootlets at the joints and clings firmly to wall or board, and soon covers its support. It is a very showy climber when in bloom, producing large trumpet-shaped flowers, which are of an orange-scarlet color, appearing in August and continuing for some time. It is hardy in a large part of the country, though we judge that it would not endure the cold of our severer sections. It thrives best in a loamy soil, not too wet.

BRITHWORT or DUTCHMAN'S PIPE.—*Aristolochia sipho.*—A most interesting climbing plant; the leaves are very large, often ten or twelve inches across, of a dark green color, and the flowers, which are produced in July, are yellowish-brown, resembling in form a meerschaum pipe. It does not seem to have been much planted in Canada, but we have no doubt it will prove to be generally hardy. It grows in any fair garden soil, and raises itself by twining around its support, hence it should be trained about a pillar or on a lattice and not against a bare wall.

CLEMATIS or VIRGIN'S BOWER.—There are several varieties of these elegant slender-branched shrubs. They are suitable for training upon trellis work, but can not cling to the face of a wall. The most of the more showy varieties require some winter protection. Where there is snow all winter it will be quite enough to lay them on the ground, and allow the snow to cover them, but where the snow does not lie all winter, it will be necessary to throw some **litter over** them before the ground freezes. **Instead** of training the large-flowering species upon a trellis, they **may be** allowed to spread over the ground, merely confining them to the bed it **is designed** they should cover, and **in this** method they **make most** beautiful bedding plants. The flowers are often three **to four** inches in diameter, **usually** white, or purple, **or** blue, of various shades and tints, exceedingly brilliant and showy.

American White.—A **native** variety, sometimes found on the banks of our streams, supporting itself by twining its petioles **or** leaf-stalks, around the branches of shrubs or low trees. It blossoms in August. The flowers are white, succeeded by seed vessels having long feathery appendages which are very handsome. It will grow some twenty or more feet in a season, but the greater part dies back **in winter, leaving a foot or two near the ground** from which **the new growth starts out** the next season.

Sweet-scented European.—The flowers are small, white, and **very sweet-scented.** There is a light purple variety that is sweet-scented, **called** *Odorata.* They both flower in August and **September.**

Viticella.—Flowers reddish purple, produced in great abundance from June to September. There is a double-flowered Viticella, which is much admired; another called V. *Venosa,* in which the purple petals are veined **with crimson;** and yet another called **V.** *Purpurea,* having a red band **in the** centre of each petal.

Lanuginosa.—Has very **large** pale blue flowers, and there is a sub-variety, *Candida,* which has large, handsome white flowers, that is thought to **be the best** white.

Honeysuckles.—*Lonicera.*—These favorite climbers are too **well** known to require description. Seed sown in the autumn, after they are ripe, will come up the next season, but if allowed to become dry they seldom grow until the second year.

Scarlet Trumpet.—Quite hardy, yielding trumpet-shaped **flowers, of a** rich scarlet on the outside and orange within, not **perfumed.**

Yellow Trumpet.—Differs from the foregoing only in the color of the flowers, which are light yellow throughout.

Monthly Fragrant.—A very sweet-scented variety, blooming all summer, flowers white, changing to straw color.

Halleana.—Pure white flowers, which in time change to yellow, very sweet scented, and produced in great profusion from June to November.

Japan Golden-veined.—The leaves are very prettily veined with yellow, flowers perfumed, habit of growth slender and delicate.

WISTARIA, OR GLYCINE.—These most beautiful climbing shrubs will no doubt require protection in winter in those parts of the Dominion where the Peach tree does not flourish. In Nova Scotia they require to be grown in very sheltered situations; and where the climate is too severe for them to remain on the trellis all winter, they can be taken down, thrown on the ground, and if the snow cannot be depended upon to protect them, covered with leaves or straw. They require a well-drained soil that is moderately rich; in soils too damp, or if over-fed, the flower-buds are more likely to be injured by the winter. The flowers appear in spring just before the leaves, in racemes of about ten inches in length, hanging like bunches of grapes, in hundreds of clusters. While young it does not blossom abundantly, but as soon as it has become well established, it will bloom with increasing fulness from year to year. Where it does not require winter protection it can be made to assume the form of a tree, by training it to a stake of the desired height, and not allowing it to find any further support. After a time the stem will become stout enough to be self-supporting, when the stake may be removed. The plant finding nothing further to climb upon, will eventually give up trying, and make a pretty round-headed shrub. In August they usually blossom a second time, but not near as profusely as in the spring.

Chinese.—Grows very rapidly, and will cover a very large space; produces large hanging clusters of pale blue flowers.

Chinese, White.—Resembling the preceding in habit of growth, but producing white flowers.

Magnifica.—The flowers are pale lilac, the plant vigorous and of a hardy character, foliage like the American.

American or *Frutescens.*—Flowers pale blue, clusters not so long as the foregoing sorts, and habit of growth not so vigorous. There is also a white variety, called *Frutescens Alba.*

Ivy.—*Hedera.*—There seems to be some difficulty in making this beautiful evergreen climber thrive in our climate, more probably because of our hot suns than because of the frost, for we have noticed that it will grow on the north side of a building, especially if sheltered from the sweep of winds. It will cling by its own rootlets to the face of a wall without any help of man, and soon cover it with a mantle of green. Those who have a wall, the north side of which they wish to cover, will probably succeed in doing it with this plant, but it is of no use to try to grow it where it is exposed to the sun.

But there is a use to which the Ivy may be put in any part of Canada with complete success, and that is *indoor decoration.* No matter how dark the room, how great the dust, how various the temperature, so long as the roots are not frozen, whether lighted with gas or coal-oil, the Ivy will grow. Placed in a pot or box on the floor, it may be trained to festoon a window, or ornament a door-way, to run as a border or cornice of green around the room, or in any form or fashion fancy may decide. Of course, if the dust is occasionally sponged from the leaves in tepid water, and the fresh air allowed to visit it now and then, it will well repay the attention bestowed.

There are many varieties of the Ivy, all of which have their own peculiar beauty. The leaves of some are blotched with gold, as the *Aurea Marmorata ;* some have the edges of the leaves margined with white, as the *Marginata Argentea ;* some have lobed leaves, as *Lobata ;* some palmate leaves, as *Palmata,* and the variety called *Tricolor* has its leaves marked with green, white and rose-color.

HARDY HERBACEOUS FLOWERS.

We group under this head some of the most interesting and desirable of our hardy plants, whose foliage may nearly or quite disappear upon the advent of winter, but whose roots remain unharmed in the soil, and send up in spring new shoots, stalks, and leaves, bearing flowers, and often maturing seed before the return of winter. All the care these require is to keep them free from grass and weeds, giving them an occasional top-dressing of well-rotted manure, and when they seem to have become overgrown or tired of their position, giving them a shift to a new spot, and, if need be, dividing the root. They should be transplanted in spring, if possible. Among these will be found some of our most showy flowers, some of them exquisitely fragrant, and old favorites that no one can do without.

Achillea.—*The Milfoil or Yarrow.*—The varieties of this plant are mostly very hardy, of easy culture in any garden soil, and those named worthy of a place in the garden, especially on account of the length of time they continue in bloom. Propagated mostly by dividing the roots.

Millefolia Rosea.—Produces rosy-lilac flowers, grows a little over a foot in height, and blooms from June to August.

Millefolia Rubra.—Deep red flowers, which continue all summer. Plant grows about fifteen inches high.

Ptarmica Pleno.—Is double white, flowers in July, and attains a height of about eighteen inches.

Microphylla.—Produces white flowers in July, and is quite attractive on account of its neat, pretty foliage.

Aconitum.—*The Monkshood or Wolfsbane.*—Very pretty tall-growing plants, blossoming freely in spikes, varying from eighteen inches to three feet in height; singularly formed, resembling the cowl or hood of a monk, and are mostly of some shade of blue. They are all violent poisons if eaten, and must not be allowed to find their way into the salads or greens. They are grown from seed and by divisions of the root.

Californicum.—A very robust variety, attaining a height of from two to three feet, and blooming in September. The flowers are pale blue, veined with purple.

Japonica.—The flowers are deep blue. It grows about eighteen inches high, and blossoms in August.

Napellus.—Flowers in June, which are a light azure, tipped with yellow. Grows eighteen inches.

Oriental.—About eighteen inches in height, flowers light cream-colored, tipped with yellow, appearing in July.

Versicolor.—Flowers blue and white, appearing in July and August, stalks eighteen inches.

AQUILEGIA.—*The Columbine.*—This is an old and favorite flower, flourishing in any garden, perfectly hardy, and multiplied into an indefinite number of varieties, bearing single and double flowers of every shade of blue, purple, black, rose-color, red, reddish-brown, striped and variegated. They blossom in June and July, require no special culture, and are propagated from seed and by dividing the roots.

CAMPANULA.—*The Bell-flower.*—There are a number of pretty flowers that belong to this group, some of them perennials, and others lasting only for two years. The Canterbury Bells belong to the biennials, being raised from seed sown in the spring, transplanted in August or September to the place where they are to remain, and flowering the following summer. As the plants die after ripening the seed, a continuous supply of these flowering-plants can be had only by sowing seed every year.

Some of the Campanulas are of very slender, graceful habit, such as the C. Rotundifolia, often known as the Harebell. It is of this pretty, delicate plant that Sir Walter Scott is speaking, when he describes the step of the fair Lady of the Lake as being so light that

> "E'en the slight Harebell raised its head
> Elastic from her airy tread."

Others again are more robust, growing from four to five feet high, and often used, especially by our Anglican forefathers, to decorate their halls and stairways, and as summer screens in the fireplace.

Carpatica.—These are of dwarf habit, growing only some six inches high; there are two varieties, one with white flowers, the other is tinted with azure.

Coronata.—Is a very pretty semi-double, profuse bloomer, with pure white flowers, in July and August, growing to the height of eighteen inches.

Grandiflora.—There are two varieties, both growing about eighteen inches high and flowering in July, the one pale blue and the other a semi-double white.

MEDIUM or CANTERBURY BELLS.—These are biennials, and are all very showy, the colors red, white and blue, and both single and double. Seed should be sown every year.

Persicifolia.—The flowers of this are large and showy, the plants perfectly hardy perennials, growing about three feet high, and blossoming in June and July. There are both double and single varieties of blue flowers and of white.

Pyramidalis.—Very showy, forming a pyramid five feet high, and covered with a profusion of large blue flowers for two months. The flowers continue better if the plant be partially shaded from the sun. The seed is usually sown in the autumn, soon after being gathered. These come up in the spring, are kept clean and free from weeds during the summer, and in October transplanted to the bed where they are to remain. They require a light protection of leaves during the winter in our climate where unprotected by snow, but should not be dressed at any time with manure. They usually bloom the second year, though sometimes not until the third.

Rotundifolia.—Is a native of this continent, probably to be met with in Canada as well as in New England, grows about a foot high, of slender habit, and produces drooping, fine blue flowers in July. It is the Harebell, both of England and America.

Trachelium.—Grows about three feet high, preferring a loamy soil, has large heart-shaped foliage, and produces double blue flowers in July and August. May be propagated by sowing the seed or dividing the roots.

CONVALLARIA.—*Majalis.—The Lily of the Valley.*—The delicate beauty and grace of this modest flower, combined with an exquisite sweetness of perfume, have made it an universal favorite, welcomed alike in lordly hall, or peasant's hut. From its crown of broad and bright green leaves rises a single stalk bearing a number of pretty bell-shaped flowers, the edges neatly turned back. It is perfectly hardy, thrives well in any thoroughly drained soil, preferring a shady spot, and spreading rapidly enough by its delicate creeping roots. There are two varieties, one with pure white flowers, the other, with rose-tinted blossoms.

DELPHINIUM.—*The Larkspur.*—The herbaceous varieties are very desirable showy plants, some of them very tall, running up to five and six feet in height, and producing a fine effect when planted among shrubbery; others, more dwarf in their habit, growing about two feet high, and requiring a place in the border. They flourish in any good garden soil and are perfectly hardy. Choice and perfectly double varieties are multiplied by dividing the roots; by sowing the seed of those that produce seed a variety of shades of color will be produced, some very closely resembling the parent, and possibly one or two in a hundred better than it.

Formosum.—A tall-growing variety, blooming very freely throughout July and August. The flowers are large, deep azure, with white centre, and veined with a reddish purple. There are many seedlings from this, varying in shade of color.

Grandiflorum.—Very showy, growing from two to three feet high, and comprising many hues of blue, and purple, and white. In bloom all summer, and perfectly hardy,

These are named as samples of the tall and the short-growing sections; beyond this there is only an endless confusion and commingling of varieties once thought to be distinct, but now so completely lost in each other by cross-fertilization, that they have no very distinctive characters. All are beautiful, and new **seedlings are being constantly produced,** crowding out the **old** favorites, to be in turn supplanted by those that come after.

DICTAMNUS.—*The Fraxinella.*—This singular plant has an odor something like that of lemon-peel, especially noticeable if the leaves or stalk be gently rubbed. In warm midsummer weather, when the plant is in bloom, the odor is strongest, and it is said that **an inflammable** vapor is **exhaled** from its resinous secretions in sufficient quantity to admit of being set on fire, though we have never tried the experiment. There are two varieties, a red and a white flowered, both blooming in June and July, and growing to the height of about two feet. In Nova Scotia it requires to be planted in favorable situations, and to be protected in winter. In Western Ontario it seems to be sufficiently hardy in well-drained soil, but very impatient of wet. It is raised from seed, which should be sown in the autumn as soon as ripe.

DIANTHUS.—*The Pink.*—An universal favorite that needs no description, finding a place in every garden, and consisting of many varieties. These varieties are such as to be worthy, in many cases, of individual mention, and requiring often various treatment.

Garden Pink.—This is **sufficiently hardy to** endure our **winters,** suffering **only if** allowed **to become** large, when the **shoots form such a mat that they** damp off or rot from excess of **moisture.** It requires a good, rich garden soil, that is thoroughly **well drained.** We have found that by layering the shoots after the plants **have done flowering,** and thus keeping up a supply of young plants, there is no difficulty in preserving them in the climate of that part of Western Ontario **within the influence of the lakes,** but if this **be neglected, they are almost sure** to go in **winter with** the damp. Florists have laid down certain rules, by which the quality of the flowers **is decided;** those having large and **broad petals,** with finely **fringed edges,** the ground color being **white or rose, with a** dark velvety eye, and a delicate lacing of the same color as the eye around the entire margin or the petal, stand in the **front rank**. The method of propagating by layering is described **under the** head of *Carnation;* new varieties are raised from **seed**.

China Pinks.—These last only **two years**, being biennial. They are dwarf in their habit of growth, quite **hardy**, producing **most** beautiful flowers, both the first and second year, but more strongly the second season. The flowers are richly marked with dark shades of crimson, with edgings of rose, pink, or white, in endless variety of pattern, but have no perfume. Seed should **be** saved from the double varieties, in order to secure a large proportion of double flowers. The HEDEWIGII and **HEDEWIGII-LACINIATUS** and DIADEMATUS are very large **flowering varieties of** the China Pink.

Carnations.—These are the most beautiful of the tribe, and at **the same time** deliciously scented. In the open ground they suffer from **the severity of** our winters, and sometimes from the **heat and** drought of summer; but when well grown, they can be scarcely excelled, vying even with the rose in beauty of appearance and sweetness of perfume. They are divided by florists into *Flakes*, those having two colors only, with large stripes quite through the petals; *Bizarres*, which are variegated with not less than three colors, irregularly striped and **spotted**; and *Picotees*, which have a clear white or yellow ground, laced or edged with scarlet, rose, or purple.

We layer Carnations when the flowers begin to fail, taking off all the lower leaves of the young shoots with a sharp penknife, and cut **a** tongue, passing the knife upwards half through the joint, then fasten the shoot to the ground with a hooked peg, bending carefully at the cut but not breaking, and cover **about** two inches deep with pure sand. By watering occasionally, if needed, to keep the soil moist, the layers will root in from four to six weeks, and may then be separated from the parent plant, and either potted or set out in open border. By covering lightly with evergreen branches, they will pass the winter safely in open border, or if potted should be plunged in a frame, and covered in same manner. Leaves would be a good covering, but they make a harbor for mice, and mice are very fond of Pinks.

They require a good, deep and well enriched soil. If potted, the soil used should be well-rotted sods, mixed with well-rotted old manure, in about equal proportions. If not sufficiently porous to allow the water to pass readily through, it should be lightened by adding sand sufficient to make it porous. Those wintered in pots may be planted out in the open ground as soon as the weather has become settled in spring.

The Winter-flowering or *Tree Carnation* is a very pleasing addition to this tribe of plants, enabling us to enjoy their beauty and fragrance nearly all the year. In summer these require to be kept in a cool and airy place, so that they may become stocky and vigorous for winter blooming. In autumn they should be removed to the green-house or window, and allowed plenty of air, not forcing them forward rapidly, but permitting them to come into bloom without any crowding.

DIANTHUS BARBATUS.—*The Sweet William.*—There are now some beautiful strains of this much-admired flower. The Auricula-flowered is one of the most showy and handsomely marked. It is easily raised from seed, and choice varieties may be perpetuated by layering or dividing the roots. It will flourish in any good, well-drained garden soil, but in some parts of the country, where there is but little snow, will require winter protection.

DIGITALIS.—*The Foxglove.*—These are beautiful ornamental plants. The large thimble-shaped flowers are produced in dense spikes, three and four feet high, of various colors, purple, red, rose, and white, very neatly marked with minute dots within the bell. Some of the varieties are perennial, but those usually grown in our gardens are biennial, requiring to be raised from seed every year, in order to keep a succession of flowering plants. A new strain, known as the Gloxinia-flowered, is much admired, the flowers bearing a marked resemblance to those of the Gloxinia. They are all poisonous plants if taken into the system; and an intoxicating drink is sometimes made by steeping the leaves and stems in water, making a Fox-glove tea. They thrive in any garden soil, and **may** be made perennial by dividing the roots, after they have done flowering, in the fall. **They appear** to best advantage when planted among shrubbery. In the neighborhood of **Halifax,** Nova Scotia, they **require** favorable situations, and to be protected in winter; and the same will hold true of all sections where the winters are severe, and the ground not covered continually with snow.

DICENTRA.—*The Bleeding Heart.*—This is one of the most beautiful and most hardy of all our herbaceous plants, one of the few that does not flourish well unless it has a season of frost, and will thrive throughout the Dominion. The plant has a very neat and graceful habit, its leaves are a light transparent green, and the heart-shaped **flowers, arranged in bending** sprays, are of a bright rosy pink, **with pearly white corollas, set** in frosted silver. The flowers are produced in great profusion, and continue during the month of May. It grows in any well-drained garden soil and is well worthy a place in every Canadian garden. There is a pure white-flowered variety of recent introduction, which is much admired and believed to be perfectly hardy.

FUNKIA.—*The Day-Lily.*—These are also perfectly hardy, of very easy culture, growing in any garden, and very ornamental. Each flower lasts only for a single **day, but** the plant continues in bloom for some **time. They are all** propagated by divisions of the roots in spring.

The White Day-Lily.—Has large, tube-shaped, very fragrant, white flowers, **produced** in succession upon stems about two feet **high.** In flower **in July.**

The Blue Day-Lily.—Produces light blue flowers in the same **manner,** but they are not fragrant nor **as** large as the white. **Blooms a little** earlier than the white.

The Variegated Day-Lily.—Is **a** blue-flowered variety with handsomely variegated leaves ; **very attractive.**

HELLEBORUS NIGER.—*The Christmas Rose.*—This interesting plant derives its **name of Christmas** Rose from its habit of blooming in **England** at Christmas time. It is a most **hardy evergreen-leaved** plant, flowering **here** about the first of December, and continuing to throw up its **flower** stems, if the weather **be not too severe, all** through the winter. Where covered with **snow** sufficiently to **protect** it from **extreme** frosts, its pretty **flowers may be found under** the snow. The flowers are single, **of a blush white color,** tinged with green, **and** resemble a small **single rose. It is propagated by** dividing the roots in spring.

IRIS.—*The Fleur-de-lis.*—There are **many** varieties of **Iris, the most of them being hardy and some exceedingly** beautiful. As the **different varieties require somewhat different treatment,** the culture adapted to each **is given** below, with a description **of some of the most** interesting and desirable sorts.

Germanica.—**This is the one so** commonly seen in all **our gardens, perfectly hardy in all parts** of Canada, and flourishing in every soil and with the most negligent treatment. The flowers **are large, dark purple and light blue, appearing in June.**

Susiana.—**One of the most beautiful, tuberous rooted** varieties. **The flowers are very large and showy, the colors being a variety of** shades of **brownish purple, very prettily mottled and** spotted, **which** appear in June. **It is important that the** roots should be **taken up as soon as the leaves begin to die down, which is about the first of August, and** kept dry in **some cool** place until **October, when they should be again planted. In** places **where the winters are open they are the better for a** slight protection of **litter. If the roots are allowed** to remain in the ground **they** commence **to grow in the fall, and this young growth being killed by** the **frosts, the plant in consequence dies.**

Persica.—**This beautiful variety is very sweet-scented, and comes into** flower very early **in spring. Its** colors **are blue, yellow,** purple, **and** white. **It is one of** the most **charming things** possible for window culture, **and may be** grown in **sandy soil in pots, or in moss, or in** water. **It is bulbous-rooted, growing best in a sandy soil,** and requiring plenty of moisture, but not stagnant water. It is perfectly hardy where snow covers the ground all **winter,** but in other places should receive a slight **protection.**

Xiphium.—This is also a bulbous-rooted variety, known **as** the Spanish Iris, and described in catalogues under the name of Iris Hispanica. It is very hardy, and the flowers are very **pretty,** displaying nearly every shade of light and dark blue, brown, purple, yellow, and white, and withal **very** sweetly scented. It will thrive well in any good garden soil.

Xiphioides.—This has obtained the name of English Iris, and is called Iris Anglica in most catalogues. It is bulbous-rooted, of more robust habit than **the Spanish, and** produces flowers as various in color, **and as handsome. It also is perfectly** hardy, and **will do well in any friable garden soil.**

All of **these bulbous-rooted sorts** should be planted **in** the fall, about **three inches deep, and allowed** to remain for three years, **when they will require to be** taken up and the bulbs **separated.** They are best suited in a rich loamy soil, that is thoroughly drained.

Some new sorts have been introduced from Japan and the Mountains of the Caucasus, which are said to **be** very distinct in habit and color, and very beautiful, but **we have not** seen **them.** *Kampferi* is an example **of the Japanese Iris,** said to produce flowers six inches in diameter; while *Violacea* comes from the Caucasus, **and produces flowers of** a rich, deep violet-purple. These **will probably prove to be** hardy, and add to the number of a family **already rich** in most beautiful flowers, well adapted to our climate, and of easy culture.

Laťhyrus.—*The Ever-blooming Pea.*—A perennial blooming Pea, which thrives well in our climate, producing its flowers in **long** succession. It will thrive in any good friable soil, and makes a pretty plant for an arbor, trellis, or screen, attaching itself to any support by means of tendrils. There are three varieties, *Latifolius,* which produces pink flowers; and *Latifolius alba,* having white flowers; and *Grandiflorus,* which has very large rose-colored flowers. They are easily raised from seed, beginning to flower the second year, but increasing in profuseness of bloom until they are four or five years old.

LYCHNIS.—*L. Chalcedonica.*—A native of Russia. The flowers are borne in trusses, and are either white or brilliant scarlet, and both single and double. The single are easily raised from seed, the double can only be propagated by dividing the roots early in spring, or by cuttings. The single varieties seem to be perfectly hardy in our climate, but the double require a slight protection where the winters are open. The double varieties are truly splendid, especially the scarlet-flowered, and continue in bloom from June until autumn.

L. Fulgens.—Is a hardy species from Siberia, its flowers are scarlet, about an inch in diameter, very showy, but single. There are double white and double scarlet varieties of this species, which, like the double varieties of Chalcedonica, require to have some protection during our open winters,—as we have learned to our cost,—and which are not easily to be obtained.

L. Flos-cuculi.—This is the Ragged Robin of English flower-gardens, a deservedly popular flower, of easy cultivation, growing in any loamy, well-drained soil. The flowers are very double, and of a deep pink color. There is also a double white variety. They are easily propagated by divisions of the root. These suffer more when the winters are open than when the ground is covered with snow.

L. Senno.—A new species from Japan. There are white and red varieties of this also, and it will probably prove to be hardy in our climate.

PŒONIA.—*The Peony.*—The herbacious Peonias are among the most hardy and most showy of our border flowers. They will adapt themselves to almost any soil, though they prefer a rich, deep loam. Once planted they should remain in the same border for a number of years, receiving in early spring a top-dressing of well-rotted manure, to encourage their growth, and improve the size and beauty of their blooms. They are multiplied by dividing the **root**, taking care to have a bud upon each piece. A piece of root without a bud will remain many years in **the soil** seemingly **alive, but** we have never known one to throw up **a shoot.** They thrive best if the **roots are divided** in September and planted out in the border, **but they are** tenacious of life, and can be transplanted **in the spring or fall,** though when transplanted at these **times they will not** usually blossom well the next year. There are many varieties of herbaceous Peonias, **and** more names in our nurserymen's catalogues than distinct varieties, the distinction being in many cases without any important difference. Having flowered or seen in flower some hundred different names, we select from them the **following as being the** most distinct **and** worthy of **cultivation, and they are truly a** most superb collection of **most showy flowers.** Those who have seen only **the old crimson** *P. Officinalis,* have usually **formed the opinion that the scent of the flowers is** unpleasant, but the **perfume of these is sweet, in many instances** resembling that of **the Rose.**

Festiva Maxima.—This is a favorite variety, **on** account of the size, purity, and beauty of its flowers. They are very large and full, of the purest white, with occasional streaks of carmine, which serve to relieve the sameness **and heighten the** snowy whiteness of the flower.

Queen Caroline.—A worthy companion to the preceding, perfect in **form, very large and double, in color** a rich deep rose, truly a perfect **beauty.**

Whitleji.—Is a white flower with light cream-colored centre, very large and double, changing to pure white when open **for** a time.

Humei.—A large, showy, very double flower, of a **purplish-**rose color, continuing in bloom later than most of the other sorts.

Delachii.—Is a very dark purplish crimson, much resembling **Potsii, but** more double, and on that account to be preferred.

Queen Victoria.—A very large, showy flower; the outer **petals are of a** clear rose color, the inner petals nearly white, **slightly tinted with pink.**

Centripetala.—The flower is peculiarly formed, the petals of the outside row are large, and of a fine rosy-pink color, those of the next row are narrow and fringed, while the centre-petals are full-sized and broad.

Victoria Tricolor.—The outside petals are light rose, mottled with pink, the centre petals yellowish-white, with occasional markings of red. The flower is large and full.

The *Tree Pæonias* are very beautiful, but they all require protection during our severe winters. Possibly they may be sufficiently protected by the snow where it falls deep enough to cover them, and remains through the winter, but in all other places they should be planted in favorable positions, where they will be sheltered from the sweep of chilly winds, and protected with straw or branches of evergreens tied over them during the winter. There are many varieties of these also. Alba Variegata, Gumpperii, Parmenteri, Reine Elizabeth, and Robert Fortune, are among the best and most distinct.

THE PHLOX.—There is an almost endless list of the varieties of Phlox, all of them beautiful, yet not all equal in beauty. All are perfectly hardy, enduring our most severe winters without even the slightest protection, and may be grown in any garden where the soil is rich and friable, but flourishing in perfection where the soil is very deep, moist, rich, and loamy. The Phlox is somewhat impatient of drought, and holds its colors better and its bloom longer if planted so as to be somewhat shaded from the fierceness of the sun, yet not under the drip of trees. It is easily propagated by division of the roots, which may be divided when the plant has done flowering or early in spring. New varieties are raised from seed.

The varieties in cultivation have been divided into Early Flowering and Late Flowering. New and improved names are being constantly produced by the florists, so that the favorites of to-day, 1872, will probably be discarded in a few years to make way for those of more recent introduction. Meanwhile those who plant the following names will be sure to have most beautiful flowers, **the** most desirable and most distinct of **those** now in cultivation.

EARLY FLOWERING.—*Suffructicosa.*—*Her Majesty.*—This is **the most** perfect white variety that has hitherto been produced. The flowers are pure white, of the finest form, very fragrant, and **borne on a** fine compact spike. The plant is of a dwarf habit, **yet** vigorous and healthy.

John Cumming.—A very fine flower, perfect in form, of a deep rose color, with a distinct dark crimson eye.

Mrs. Graham Sterling.—The flowers are very fragrant, and of the finest form, color pure white with a dark crimson eye.

Othello.—This forms a grand spike of finely developed, very dark crimson flowers, delicately shaded.

William McAuley.—This also makes a most beautiful **spike** for exhibition; **the** flowers are very large, perfectly formed, of a **beautiful light rose,** handsomely shaded.

The Deacon.—A deep rosy purple flower, with a light crimson **eye,** of large size and of the finest form and quality.

LATE FLOWERING.—*Decussata.*—*Madam C. De Bresson.*—One of the most beautiful, attractive and showy flowers in the whole range of varieties. The flowers are large, white, with a full bright carmine centre, which makes a most pleasing contrast.

Duke of Sutherland.—Makes a magnificent exhibition spike; the flowers are of fine form, dark rosy crimson with a very dark eye.

Madam Delamare.—The flowers have a novel appearance, being of a bright rosy salmon color with a fine black centre.

Monsieur Delamare.—Is exceedingly attractive on account of the dazzling red color of the flowers, handsomely set off by a black centre.

Madam Verschaffelt.—The spikes are large and very showy, **covered with** a great profusion of flowers of a bright lively salmon **color.**

Venus.—The flowers are silvery white, with a bright, violet-**purple eye, very pretty.**

There is a very dwarf, spring blooming Phlox, called by botanists *Phlox Subulata,* and known by the common name of *Moss Pink.* It never grows more than a few inches in height, and produces varieties with flowers of pink, purple, and white, and some that are eyed. A bed of these is very pretty in May, easily grown, requiring only to be divided and planted in a new bed once in two or three years.

SPIREA.—*The Meadow Sweet.*—These are all perfectly hardy plants, enduring our most severe and changeable winters without injury. They thrive best in a loamy soil, deep, rich, and well drained. In such situations they grow finely and flower most abundantly. There are several very pretty and desirable species which are well worthy of a place in the most choice flower garden. They are all of easy culture and increased by divisions of the roots.

Filipendula.—The double flowered variety is very pretty. The flowers are white, very double, resembling the beautiful *Spirea Prunifolia,* which is described among the shrubs. It grows about eighteen inches high and blossoms in June and July.

Japonica.—This is now advertised, sometimes as *Hoteia Japonica,* sometimes as *Astilbe Japonica.* But by whatever name it may be called, it is one of the most graceful and beautiful little things with which one can ornament a garden. The foliage alone is very pretty, but when this is crowned with its neat spikes of white feather-like flowers, it is charming. If taken up in the autumn, carefully potted and set away in the cellar until February, then brought into a warm room, it will blossom beautifully and make a most elegant window plant.

There is a variety the foliage of which is handsomely variegated with bright yellow, especially in the early part of the season, but in nothing else differing from the preceding.

Ulmaria.—The double-flowered variety of this species is by far the most desirable. The flowers are produced in large corymbs, of a snowy whiteness. The species is a native of

Great Britain, abounding in rich, moist meadows, and scenting the air with its **perfume**.

Lobata.—The flowers of this species are a deep pink, arranged **in corymbs, and** borne upon **a tall flower stalk. They are very pretty, and** contrast finely **with the** white flowering species. This is a native of the prairies of America, and is sometimes **called the** "Queen of the **Prairie."**

Palmata.—A new **species** introduced quite recently from Japan, believed to be hardy also, but has not yet been sufficiently tested in our climate to settle this **point.** We have not yet seen the flowers, but they are said to be of a beautiful crimson purple, and borne in broad corymbs. The bright red stems and palmately lobed leaves give it a **distinct appearance from the** older sorts, and we hope our plants will favor us with a sight **of** the flowers during the **coming season.**

TRICYRTIS.—This new herbaceous flowering plant is perfectly **hardy in our** climate. The stalk and foliage are killed by the **frosts,** but the roots pass the winter safely, and throw up their **shoots** the next season. The flowers, however, are produced too late to make it much of an addition to the garden, for they scarce make their appearance in our climate before the autumn frosts cut the plants so severely as to spoil all their beauty. But if carefully potted in September, before the frosts appear, it will make one of the most beautiful of late fall or early winter-blooming plants for the window or green-house that we possess.

The flowers have **a very** marked resemblance to some of the Air-plants or Orchids. They are of a pearly white, beautifully dotted with clear **purple,** and have a sweet perfume, much like that of the Heliotrope.

VIOLA.—*The Violet.*—There are many species **of this "wee modest** flower" scattered with lavish profusion through every land and every clime. There are many to be found growing wild **in favorable** places in all parts of the Dominion, but although they are not wanting in beauty, they have none of them the **sweet perfume of** the European violets. Hence we seldom see the American violets cultivated in gardens, save in the children's garden; their appreciative love for the friends of their woodland rambles leading them to transplant them to their own flower beds.

The English Violet.—Both single and double, is one of the first of our spring flowers, the blossoms often hidden by snow when winter lingers in the lap of spring. The flowers are most delightfully fragrant, a small bed filling the garden with perfume, and a flower or two scenting the whole room. Nor is there anything pungent or cloying in the odor; we can never get it in too great abundance. Its balmy sweetness seems wafted in gentle undulations, just breaking with sufficient force upon the senses to fill them with delight.

This species delights in a deep, rich, moist soil, sheltered, if possible, from bleak winds, but more especially sheltered from the hot scorching suns of summer. In a dry and sandy soil it will not flourish. Sometimes, when the winter is open, they suffer much from the sudden changes of weather, many plants perishing; but when they have once become well established, some survive or new ones are produced from seed, so that they are not wholly lost. When there is a covering of snow through the winter, be it ever so slight, they come out in fine condition.

We cannot understand how any old-countryman can afford to be without this lovely reminder of home, and are sure that no Canadian who has once enjoyed its sweetness and beauty will willingly be without it.

There are varieties known as the *Giant, Czar, King, Queen,* somewhat larger than the English, but not more sweet, and some not as abundant bloomers.

The *Neapolitan* is not sufficiently hardy for our climate.

The *Cornuta* has light mauve flowers, which are fragrant. It has been lately used for bedding purposes in England, but here it would not bloom in summer, though hardy enough to bear the winters.

VIOLA TRICOLOR.—*The Pansy.*—This beautiful and universal favorite needs neither description nor praise; it is **known to the young and old**, and is cherished alike by both; to the latter especially dear for its many long-time associations, as well as its **intrinsic beauty.** In the cooler and moister climate of Great Britain, **with** winters less rigorous than ours, it flourishes in per**fection.** Here the hot, dry summers parch it, and the hard winter frosts pinch it, but with a little care on the part of the cultivator, it can be grown here in great beauty, unfolding its lovely flowers **in** abundant profusion through the spring and autumn months. In the colder parts of the country, where the snow will protect it all winter, it should be grown in great perfection.

By selecting a spot on the north side of **buildings or of a high** fence, where the **soil is, or can be made, deep, light, rich and** moist—selecting for fertilizer that from the cow stable, and applying it liberally—the **Pansy** can be well grown in any part of the land. When hard freezing weather approaches, a **light covering of brush will** collect, in most places, enough snow to give the **plants all** the protection they need, or if not, a few branches of evergreens will be quite sufficient. Protection from the sun, both in winter and summer, is of more importance in our climate than protection from frost. This is secured by making the Pansy **bed** on the north side of some object that will afford this shade, while it does not subject the plants to drip, nor rob them of their nourishment. They are propagated by cuttings when it is desired to preserve some particular variety, but when that is not essential, by sowing **the seed.**

Pansies have been divided by florists into Selfs, Yellow-grounds, White-grounds, **and** Fancy. The *Selfs* are mostly of **one** color, and may be dark, or white, or yellow; *Yellow-grounds* are those in which the ground-color is yellow, belted with some shade of purple; *White-grounds* are belted in the same manner **upon a** light cream or pure white ground; *Fancy* Pansies are of **many colors,** blotched, laced, marbled, veined, pencilled, and **shaded in every** conceivable fashion. In Scotland they are all grown in great perfection, and new, choice varieties sell at five **shillings sterling each.**

Here, we have hardly attained to the same nicety of discrimination with regard to Pansies as obtains in the Old World. Without troubling ourselves with minute distinctions, the flowers are admired for their beauty; yet even the child in Pansy-lore will prefer those that are most circular in outline, and whose colors are pure and distinct.

YUCCA.—*Adam's Needle.*—We desire to call attention to the Yucca, a most beautiful and interesting plant, yet very seldom to be met with in our gardens. The peculiar foliage is so strikingly in contrast with that of all other plants that for this alone it is always desirable, yet in addition to this, its appearance when in in bloom is exquisitely charming, especially when seen by moonlight. The variety known as *Filamentosa*, so called from the threads that hang from the edges of the leaves, is the only one that we know to be sufficiently hardy to endure our climate. Very probably some of the other species, such as *Y. Gloriosa*, would winter safely beneath the snows of more northern localities, when it would perish in the open winters of the lake regions. We most sincerely hope that every one who has a garden will, at least, plant the *Filamentosa* and enjoy its rare beauty.

To enjoy this plant to the best advantage a bed should be prepared, of light rich soil, that will hold at least half-a-dozen plants at about two feet apart each way. The first season they will not be likely to bloom, but they will bloom the second, and increase in size, and in a few years completely fill the bed. They should be allowed to remain in the same bed without being disturbed, for as they increase in size and strength they will flower more and more abundantly.

It is propagated by dividing the roots, and very readily from seed. The seedlings differ considerably, and we hope some lover of flowers will take this plant in hand, and, by sowing seed, raise some new and desirable hardy varieties.

The flowers are borne on tall branching flower stems, from four to six feet high, which are nearly covered with large, bell-shaped, creamy-white blossoms. Mr. E. S. Rand, living near

Boston, Massachusetts, mentions a bed of ten Yuccas planted four years, which produced fifteen flower stems, none of them less than six feet high, **and** upon which the flowers were numbered by thousands. The flowers appear in July **and continue** for a **long time.**

BULBOUS-ROOTED FLOWERS.

Under this head are grouped a class of flowers of great beauty, easy of culture, and **many** of which are most admirably adapted for window culture and winter blooming. Some of these are most easily grown in those parts of Canada where the snow falls soonest and remains the longest, requiring **no other protection** than that mantle which **nature provides for her children of the soil, and** under **which she so lovingly wraps them from the frost.** In those places **where the ground is** often bare during a large part of the cold season, and the frosts penetrate to considerable depth, the tender care of the cultivator must supply the needed covering, and some coarse litter be spread over them of sufficient depth to prevent the frost from penetrating far into the soil below.

This class of plants is seldom troubled with insects and is measurably exempt from diseases, and by a proper selection and treatment may be had in bloom, in some or other of its members, all the year round. Many of these add to the charms of beauty the most delightful perfume, and whether blooming in a bed under the window or upon the flower-stand in the room, will fill the house with their pleasant odors.

A want of knowledge of the habits and true methods of culture of these flowers has, we are persuaded, been the hindrance hitherto to their general **introduction** into our flower gardens. **We have** often known our nurserymen and florists to receive orders in the spring for bulbs that should be planted in the fall, and which, if taken up and transported to the purchaser in spring, **will be** very sure to perish. It is hoped that the hints here given will be so clear and practical that all doubt and misapprehension will be **removed, and that** those who take pleasure in their gardens and windows, will **be** enabled to grow them **with** entire success.

Another reason why every possessor of the smallest village lot **may** enjoy the pleasure which these flowers will afford, is **that they require but** little space and **can be** had at very little **cost.** It is true that those who must have the latest novelty can **have it** only at **considerable** expense, but **those** who are willing **to have pretty flowers** without inquiring whether they are of the latest introduction, and **can** enjoy the beauty or fragrance of an unnamed tulip or hyacinth **just as keenly as though** it bore the title of some noble Countess or Royal Prince **or Imperial** Majesty, may buy them of our dealers at very moderate **prices.**

The most of these bulbs are grown in Holland, where **soil,** climate and cheap labor conspire to render their production much less expensive than it would **be here.** For this reason our florists annually import them from that country, and have them on hand, ready for their customers, in time for planting at the **proper season.**

Those who wish to have a bed of these bulbs under the window should choose, if possible, a window that looks toward the south. The most of them are natives of **warm** climates, and delight in all the sunlight and sun-heat we can give them. They also prefer a rich and moist sandy loam, yet one that is **readily** drained, free from all stagnant water in the soil. If the **soil be** not naturally of this character, the labor necessary **to make it so will** be most amply repaid. If the subsoil **be naturally** porous, all that will be needed will be to work into the surface sufficient sand **and** thoroughly rotted manure to make it rich and light to the depth of eighteen inches. But if the subsoil be a retentive clay, it is very desirable that it should be removed from under the intended bed to the depth of a foot at least, and an under-drain made from the bottom **to** the most convenient outlet, so as to carry **off all** the water that would settle into the place from which the clay is removed. The place occupied by the clay sub-soil should be filled up with broken stone or coarse gravel, putting the coarser portion at the bottom and the finest at the top. The surface soil should be kept separate from **the subsoil** when digging out the **bed, the subsoil** taken away, and the surface soil mixed with sand and old rotted manure, and decayed leaves, if they can **be had, until it is quite** light, loses nearly all its adhesive or sticky character, if it had any, and then spread over the drainage until the bed is filled again. It is not desirable to raise the bed more than an inch or two above the natural surface of **the** ground after it is settled, but when first filled in it should be raised about four inches, to admit of the settling of the newly-disturbed earth.

Those who are willing to take the **trouble to** prepare a **soil** by gathering a few **wheelbarrow loads of** sod from an old pasture, every summer, **and stacking them in some** out-of-the-way **corner** in alternate layers of sod and cow-manure, will secure just the best dressing for these and all other flower beds that they can **have.** Of course its value will be enhanced if they can add to it ground bones, horn scrapings or horn piths. This heap, after lying for two or three months, should be cut down with the spade and thoroughly worked over and commingled. If **this** can be done two or three times, at intervals of a month or so, during the year, so much the better, and when it is a year or more old it will be in just the right condition for use. The proper time for applying it to **the** bulb bed will be in the autumn, when it may be spread on the surface to the depth of an inch or two. **This will** also be just the soil to use for pots if it is desired to grow any of the bulbs in the window, adding to it enough sand to make it light and free from adhesiveness, if it be not already there.

Further directions for the successful cultivation of the several varieties will be given in the paragraph devoted to each, where the peculiar treatment that may be best suited to that particular species will be fully described.

If a bed be planted by setting little clusters of Snow-drops and spring Crocus here and there, but leaving sufficient room between in which to plant Hyacinths and early and late Tulips, interspersed with English Iris, a few Meadow, Japan and Tiger Lilies, with some clumps of Colchicum or autumn-flowering Crocus, it will be an object of beauty and interest nearly all the summer, and will not require to be disturbed for three or four years. From the time that the Tiger Lilies are done blooming until the autumn Crocus appear there will be a lack of flowers, which might be supplied by sowing some Portulaca seed on the bed in the latter part of May, which will cover the surface without injury to the bulbs, and blossom abundantly in August, continuing until frosts destroy the plants.

THE HYACINTH.—This grows best in light, but rich, sandy soil. The best manure is old cow-dung that has been thrown into a heap and thoroughly rotted, and consequently entirely free from any straw or litter. If it can be mixed with an equal bulk of dry leaves when placed in the heap, and occasionally worked over during the season, so that the leaves shall be thoroughly blended with the manure, its quality will be much improved. Soot makes a very good dressing for the Hyacinth bed, if used in moderate quantity, and powdered charcoal seems to give a greater intensity to the color.

There is now hardly any conceivable color which is not to be found in the Hyacinth blooms. Many exercise their skill and taste in planting them in such a manner that the color of each shall increase the effect of that next to it. Those who have the opportunity of selecting the bulbs for themselves should take those which are solid and heavy, and have the surface covered with a thin clean skin. Avoid those that seem hollow at the top, and do not esteem them according to the size, for that varies much with the variety, some being always large. Those that are large, but light and scaly, and those that are double-crowned, are not desirable. The single-crowned, hard, smooth, and usually medium-sized bulbs, give the best bloom. The single varieties are the best for growing in the house, while in the open bed the double will give the prettiest flowers, taken singly, and the single the most flowers and finest spikes.

October is the best time for planting, though it can be done at any time before the ground freezes. The bulbs should be set four inches deep and about six inches apart. The planting should be done when the ground is dry enough to be in a fine, friable condition, and in dry weather. As soon as the ground begins to freeze, and where snow cannot be relied upon for a covering, the surface of the bed should receive a light covering of leaves or strawy litter, held down by a few sticks so as not to be blown off, and thick enough to prevent the frost from penetrating into the bed.

When grown in pots, those bulbs which have no offsets or sprouts near the base, which are perfectly sound, and are the heaviest in proportion to their size, should be selected. These should be planted in six-inch pots, one in each pot. If it is desired to have a succession of bloom, it is well to pot as many as it is desired should bloom at one time, and then make another potting about three weeks later. The method of potting is this: place a bit of broken crock or a pebble over the hole in the bottom of the pot, then fill in an inch deep of broken pieces of crock, or small bits of charcoal, or coarse gravel, or coarse ground bones, so as to secure perfect drainage, then fill up to within two inches of the top with the soil from the compost already recommended, composed of rotted sods, cow-dung, and pure sand, packing it firmly and nearly solid into the pot; then place the bulb on this soil, and fill in around it with more of the same, ramming it in firmly with a blunt stick. When finished, the top of the bulb should just appear above the soil, and the earth be within about half an inch of the rim. Give it a good watering now, thoroughly soaking the whole of the earth in the pot. When done potting, let them be taken to a dark, cool, cellar, free from frost, the soil kept moist, until the pot is filled with roots, which can be ascertained by placing the left hand over the top of the pot, inverting it, and then hitting the rim smartly against the edge of bench, or table, or cellar-bin, so as to knock the ball of earth loose from the pot, when the pot can be gently lifted with the right hand enough to see whether the white roots have run through the soil. When they have filled the earth with roots, then they are ready to be removed to the room in which they are to bloom; there they should be placed in the window, where they will have abundance of light, and can be maintained at a temperature not colder than fifty at night, or more than seventy-five by day.

They will now soon begin to show leaves and push forth the flower stalk, and will require to be watered oftener, enough to keep the soil moist, not wet, but when the flowers are beginning to open, the watering may be increased, and the ground kept well saturated. After they have become expanded, the flowers will last longer if the temperature of the air can be kept at about sixty during the day, but this is not an easy matter in the sitting-room, where one likes to have the flowers, that their beauty and fragrance may be constantly enjoyed.

After the plants have done blooming, the watering must be gradually diminshed until the leaves become yellow, when it should cease, and the pots be laid on their sides on a shelf in the cellar, there to remain until wanted for planting in October. It is not desirable to flower a Hyacinth bulb in a pot more than once, the next year the pot-flowered bulbs should be planted in the open border, and a new stock secured for potting.

Hyacinths may be grown in pots of moss or pure sand, first putting the drainage into the bottom of the pot as already directed, and using moss or pure sand instead of soil for planting the bulb. Or, they may be grown in water, either in glasses, known as Hyacinth glasses, which can be obtained of the florist, of various patterns, or, instead of a glass, in a Turnip or Carrot hollowed out so as to hold the bulb and sufficient water below it. By hollowing out the root in such a way as to leave a part of the crown in a circle around the Hyacinth, the leaves will grow up out of the root and conceal the bulb, producing a pleasing effect.

BULBOUS-ROOTED **FLOWERS.** 315

The glass or hollowed root should be filled with water just so that the bottom of the bulb may touch the water. Rain-water is the best for this purpose, and for watering those growing in pots, and should be luke-warm when used. After the bulbs have been set in this manner, on water, they should be kept in a dark place until the glass is nearly filled with roots, when they should be brought to the light. It will save the necessity of changing the water if a bit or two of charcoal is placed in it, but if this be not done, the water should be renewed about once a week, using tepid water. Bulbs flowered in water will not bloom the next year, and are usually thrown away when done flowering. If it is desired to preserve them they should be planted in earth as soon as the flowers fade, and if well cared for they will bloom again the second year.

It is utterly useless to give our readers a list of names of choice Hyacinths, for in a few years they would drop out of the florist's catalogues to make way for new comers. The named varieties are sold at higher prices than the unnamed, but these can be purchased in different colors kept distinct, and either single or double. Nor is it of any practical benefit to describe the methods used for increasing or propagating them, it being much more economical to buy them already grown.

AMARYLLIS.—These bulbs require very different treatment from the Hyacinths, and can not be relied upon for out-door culture in our climate, but for the green-house or window many of them are very desirable. They do not require that the soil should be made very rich with manures, but flourish best in good sandy loam, or old rotted turf that has been made quite light with sand, and is somewhat rough and lumpy. The bottom of the pot should be filled with a couple of inches of drainage, over which is placed a little moss to prevent the soil from washing into and choking it up. This is the more important because these bulbs will not require re-potting for several years, indeed flourish much better if allowed to remain without being re-potted, provided the soil be kept sweet and the drainage perfect. When potted, the top of the bulb should be level with the rim of the pot, and the soil half an inch below the rim, so as to admit of easy watering. When first planted it should be watered copiously.

After being potted they should be placed in a temperature of about fifty degrees, and not be watered again until the leaves begin to grow. When these begin to start the pots may be brought into a room where the temperature is about seventy degrees, gradually increasing the watering as the leaves and flower-scape increase in size. The best time for starting the bulbs into growth is in January, and the heat while the plant is blooming should be hardly as great as after it is done blooming and while it is perfecting its leaf growth. After that is perfected, which will usually be in July, the watering should be gradually diminished, so that they may be at rest about the first of October. While at rest they should be kept in a temperature never lower than fifty degrees, and if possible, not much above sixty degrees.

While at rest they should never be watered again until they begin to grow. When they are ready they will start, and watering before this time only tends to injure the roots and produce decay. As a rule they will begin to grow in January, and attain their full growth in July. Just after they have attained their full growth, which may be known by the leaves ceasing to elongate, is the best time to re-pot the bulbs, if it be necessary; but re-potting should be avoided as long as the soil remains sweet. After re-potting they will require to be kept in the shade for a few days, until again established, giving just water enough to prevent the leaves from flagging. Indeed, after the growth is over, this is all the water that any of them will require. But in treating these bulbs we should not be guided by the almanac, but by the indications of the bulbs themselves. Sometimes they will have completed their growth by May, and show a disposition to rest; such a disposition should be humored, and water withheld until the plant shows that it requires it again, by starting once more into growth. Sometimes they will take a midsummer rest and bloom again **in autumn, and make a** second growth **after** the second bloom, **and during this period of growth they will** require careful **watering.**

Seedlings can be grown by **sowing the seed in** June, keeping **the soil** moderately moist **until the** young plants appear, **then increase the** waterings **as their** growth demands, and keep **them** growing as long **as they** are willing. By keeping the ground a little damp while they are at rest, **they may be** kept in foliage for a couple of years, when they should be treated as old bulbs. The third year many of them will show bloom.

The following varieties will be found to be **the most manageable** and desirable **for green-house or window culture.**

Belladonna.—The **Belladonna Lily, as it** is often **called,** requires only **that care should be taken to** grow the foliage **well** after the **bloom is over, and if this** be attended to, it will be found **to be of easy culture,** under the treatment above described. **The pot may** be plunged in the open border about the middle of June, and allowed to flower there, but it must be removed to the window or green-house to perfect its leaf-growth before the appearance of frost. The flowers are produced in spikes, and are **of a** lovely rose color.

Formosissimus.—This is the variety so **well known under** the name of Jacobean Lily. In some parts **of the** country it may be grown in **the open border,** when the **season** is long enough to admit of its **being** put out in May, but it will do best to grow it in a pot, and **treat it as a** window or green-house plant, in the manner already **described.** Its flowers are a brilliant scarlet, and appear before the leaves.

Purpurea (Vallota).—This retains its leaves all the year **round, and** should not be dried off like the others, but receive **less water in** winter or when **taking its rest.** Its natural habitat **is in wet** grounds; hence it requires to be abundantly supplied **with** water during the growing season. It has very brilliant scarlet flowers, which are produced in great abundance.

Johnsoni.—Is **a very** handsome hybrid variety, requiring the same treatment as *Belladonna,* and produces scarlet flowers with a white stripe.

Vittatum.—Exceedingly pretty. The flowers are white, with a red stripe. Should be treated in the ordinary manner.

CROCUS.—The pretty spring-flowering Crocus, succeeding the Snow-drop in their period of bloom, are very easily grown, requiring only to be planted in a light, but rich, moist soil, and left to grow as they please, giving them an annual top-dressing of very old and most thoroughly decomposed manure. They should be planted in the fall, about three inches deep, and an inch apart each way, and allowed to remain in the same bed for a number of years. Such a bed will improve in beauty for some time, and will only require to be replanted when the bulbs begin to grow out of the ground—for the young bulb is annually produced upon the top of the old, and in process of time approaches the surface.

The Crocus beds require the same treatment as directed for Hyacinths, and indeed, it is desirable to plant them together in the same bed, so that after the Crocus are done blooming the Hyacinths may take their place. They may be also grown in pots in the house, or in water or sand. They should be allowed to make their root growth in a cool place, and when the flower-buds appear, have plenty of light and air, and not too much heat.

The Autumn-flowering Crocus are botanically different plants from the other, and are called Colchicum. These are perfectly hardy, and as easy of culture as the spring Crocus. They throw up their flower stalk and blossom late in autumn, but the leaves and seed appear next spring.

The Spring Crocus are yellow, blue, purple, white, and striped; the Autumn are purple and white.

DAHLIA.—This is not strictly a bulbous-rooted, but tuberous-rooted plant, which requires treatment so analagous to that of some bulbs, that it seems more natural to treat of it in this connection.

The Dahlia prefers a deep, very rich, friable loam, one that is

not readily **affected** by drought, **nor** surcharged with **water.**
Varieties that **have** been in cultivation long enough to enable the
cultivator **to obtain** a stock of **tubers,** are usually sent out in **the
dormant or just** starting tuber, **but new and** scarce varieties
are received in the growing **state, in small pots.** Neither the
tubers nor the plants should **be set out** in the **open** ground until
all danger from frost is **past,** and as the stalk grows **it** should be
tied to a tall stake. They **will** give better satisfaction if planted
where they will be sheltered from very high winds, which often
injure the plants severely. After the autumn **frosts** have killed
the foliage, the stalk should be cut off **just above the ground,**
the tubers taken **up and removed to a dry, frost-proof cellar.**
Those who **have a green-house can keep them very well under**
the stage. **Two things are to be avoided, keeping them so dry**
and **warm that the tubers shrivel, and keeping them so cold and**
damp **that the stalk or** crown **rots. The eyes** or buds are **at** the
base **of the** stalk or on the neck **of the tuber,** and if these buds be
destroyed the Dahlia will not grow, **for** though the tuber be
ever so sound, there are no eyes or buds upon that, and it **has
no** means of growth. Hence it is important that the **part where**
these eyes are situate should be kept sound.

Dahlias are propagated by division **of the tuber,** taking care
that each piece has an **eye or** bud **upon it; also by** cuttings of
the young shoots, **which are taken off when an** inch or two in
length, **and rooted in bottom heat. As** soon as they are well
rooted they are **planted in small** pots, and kept in a frame or in
the green-house **until the** weather will admit of their being
planted in the **open ground.**

New **sorts are raised** from seed, usually sown in **pots in
spring,** and afterwards transplanted. Most of these will be likely
to prove worthless, yet in the **hands of** the skilful florist some
choice flowers are very sure to **be** produced, and for a time com-
mand a high price. As new flowers are, in this way, being con-
stantly produced, it is better that the intending purchaser should
make his selection from **the** lists that are offered in the cata-

logues of the florists, than be guided by any selection that the writer might now name.

The Dahlia is now produced in high perfection, quite unlike the single flowers, with yellow disk and dull scarlet rays, which it bore on its introduction to England, about the beginning of the present century. It is now most beautifully double, and of every color except blue, and with every conceivable variegation. The Pompone varieties produce much smaller flowers than the Dahlia proper, and are, therefore, more desirable for bouquets. All the Dahlias flower best in cool, moist seasons, and when the summers are hot, wait for the more favorable weather of September before they come perfect.

THE FRITILLARY.—*Fritillaria.*—We do not often see any other examples of this genus in our gardens than the Crown Imperials. The *Guinea-hen flower* is also a Fritillary, and though not so stately in its appearance, is a very interesting variety. They all flourish best in a deep, rich, well-drained, loamy soil, and when once planted should be seldom disturbed.

The *Crown Imperial* is perfectly hardy, grows to a height of two feet in favorable soil, bearing a tuft of leaves upon the top, beneath which are the flowers. There are a number of varieties, producing flowers of several shades of red and yellow, single and double, and with golden and silver variegated foliage. The bulbs should be planted in October, about six inches deep, and remain in the ground all the year.

The *English Fritillary*, or Guinea-hen flower, is of far less pretentious growth, and produces pretty pendant flowers, which are peculiarly marbled or tesselated. They are usually of a purple shade, some nearly red, or yellow and white. The bulbs are much smaller than those of the Crown Imperial, and should not be set more than half as deep. They flower in May. The dark-colored varieties seem to be more hardy than the light, and not so liable to perish.

GLADIOLUS.—Why it is that these beautiful flowers have not found their way more universally into the gardens of our people, it might be difficult to tell. Our climate is well suited to their growth and culture, much better in most of the Dominion than that of England or France, and they require no more care than a Potato. Indeed, we are inclined to believe, that with a covering

Fig. 63.

of leaves or strawy litter that would keep out the frost, where the winters are open, and with none at all where the snow keeps the ground from freezing, they could be wintered safely in the soil. Yet the better and safer method is to take them up in October, let the bulbs or corms dry for a day or two, and then put them away in a cool, dry place, free from frost. We are in the habit of packing them in perfectly dry sand, and find that they never fail to keep in fine condition.

To grow the Gladiolus in perfection, it is necessary to avoid all soils that are cold and wet, and that is uniformly the character of those that are badly drained. Care should also be taken in the use of manures, avoiding all that are fresh, partially fermented, or undecomposed; these tend to produce disease in the bulbs. The best manure for them is that which was also recommended for Hyacinths; old cow-dung, thoroughly rotted, or composted with rotten sods and ground bone. If the soil be a clayey loam, it will be of advantage to turn it up in the fall and leave it rough, that it may be well exposed to the action of the frost. After the weather has become settled in May, the ground should be dug over and the manure thoroughly mingled with the soil, and the bulbs planted out about ten inches apart each way, and five inches deep.

This is the whole secret of Gladiolus-raising save one, and that is this: our own amateurs might, with a little attention to selection and hybridization, raise much better new varieties from seed than are now raised for them in Europe, and which, when first sent out, cost from two to five dollars each bulb. So much better is our climate for the perfect development of the Gladiolus, that the seedlings which have been grown in America are much finer as a whole than any that can be imported. If the seed be gathered as soon as it is ripe, and sown the next spring in a frame or in pots, the young plants will grow finely, and will show bloom the third year. From these the finest may be selected, and the work of raising new and beautiful varieties be continued.

The varieties once obtained are increased by multiplication of the bulbs. After the bulb has become large enough to flower it will begin to multiply, and if the little tiny bulbs at the base of the old bulb are saved and kept out of ground for one season and then sown, they will all grow, increase in size, and the second year produce flowers.

The flowers are produced on tall spikes and are of a great variety of colors. They appear in the end of July and continue during August, and until early frosts. We name a few of the older sorts, which **can** be obtained at a reasonable price, partly to put our readers in the way of obtaining a pretty collection **of** choice varieties, and in part, **to give** them an idea of **the color and markings of the** flowers.

Aristotle.—Rose color, variegated with **red** and striped with carmine and purple.

Ceres.—Pure white, **with rose and violet** spots.

Flora.—White ground shaded with rosy lilac, and a distinct stain of deep rose on **each** petal.

Jeanne d'Arc.—White, very slightly tinted with rose, and striped and stained with violet.

Milton.—White, delicately **tinted with rose and broadly** flamed with red.

Mons Vinchon.—Light **salmon-red, variegated** and lined with white.

Norma.—**Pure** white, slightly blazed with lilac.

Peter Lawson.—Rosy lilac, with white satin shade.

Princess of Wales.—White, flamed with rose and blotched with dark carmine.

Raphael.—Red vermilion, centre lighted with **white and** shaded with purple.

Reine Victoria. — Pure white, with **large** carmine-violet **blotch.**

Rubens.—Very **bright** light vermilion. **Stains** striped with carmine on a whitish ground.

These will **be sufficient to** give an idea of their appearance. Those who **wish to go further** can consult the annual lists of dealers.

As cut flowers **they are** very useful, for if the stalk be cut just as the first **flowers** open, and put in water, all the **buds on the stalk** will open in succession. **On this account they are very** valuable **for** parlor or dining-room **decoration.**

IRIS.—The bulbous-rooted Iris have been sufficiently described at page **299.** Those known as the English, Spanish and Persian are the most easily obtained and the most desirable in our climate.

These may also be grown in the house in pots or in moss or sand, or in water, in the manner prescribed for Hyacinths.

THE LILY.—There is no need of any description of the beauty of this flower. In some of its varieties it is known to all; its loveliness has been spoken of by writers, sacred and profane, and pleasant emotions are awakened at the mere mention of its name.

Fortunately, nearly all the species known to us are sufficiently hardy to endure our climate, and thrive well in our gardens with but little attention. A collection of all these would be a treasure-house of beauty and enjoyment, rivalling even the Rose in queenly splendor and sweet perfume. Not one but has some attraction of its own, from the nodding Lily of our Canadian meadows to the amethystine spots and golden band of those from Japan. Nor are we at the end of the list; every year some new species rewards the searcher in new climes, and the Lilies of California are just being introduced for our admiration and delight.

In common with most bulbs, they grow best in well-drained, loamy soil, in which the sandy character predominates, and which is kept rich by the use of thoroughly-rotted manures. If the soil be naturally an adhesive clay, it will be necessary to remove some of the clay, and add enough sand to make it light; and if the subsoil be retentive, it will be a great improvement to remove some of the stiff clay and put in broken stone or gravel, with an under-drain leading from the bed to a convenient outlet.

It is very desirable that Lilies should be kept out of the ground as short a time as possible. Many of the imported Lilies fail altogether, or make but a feeble growth the first season, because the drying which the bulbs undergo while out of the ground weakens them. They should therefore be planted as soon as received, large bulbs requiring to be set six inches deep and small bulbs about four. The best season for transplanting most varieties is the month of October, when they are at rest.

Lilies are usually propagated by offsets—the small bulbs which form about the parent plant; and whenever the bed is becoming crowded it will be necessary to take them all up and separate them. Except for this cause, it will not be necessary to disturb them.

The following varieties are well worthy of cultivation, and without exception will winter safely in the ground.

Canadense.—This is the nodding Lily of our meadows, which gratefully responds to the care of garden cultivation, increasing in the size and number of its blooms.

Candidum.—For purity and fragrance this old favorite cannot be surpassed. Perfectly hardy, thriving in any garden, yet grateful for a little care, which it repays a hundred-fold, filling the air with its sweetness, and arrayed in snowy white, adorning alike the garden of the cottager or of the king. It is in bloom in July. There are varieties with golden and silver striped leaves, with spotted, and striped, and double flowers, but they are no improvement on the plain, single, pure white Lily.

Chalcedonicum.—Is very showy, the color being a very brilliant scarlet.

Excelsum.—Grows as tall as Candidum, the flowers are a Nankeen yellow.

Lancifolium.—There are several varieties of this species, but all are beautiful and very fragrant. They are delicately spotted with ruby-red or rose-colored dots, and when once established in good, loamy, well-drained soil, they will continue to increase in the number and beauty of their flowers.

Longiflorum.—The flowers are trumpet-shaped, from six to nine inches in length, white, and very fragrant. Where the winters are open, this species should be protected by a light covering of litter.

Superbum.—A very showy species, often producing twenty flowers on a stalk, which are of a handsome reddish-orange color.

Tigrinum.—The Tiger Lily has become almost as well-known as the White, and is a deserved favorite, being very hardy, and producing an abundance of showy orange-scarlet flowers, spotted with black. It produces little **bulbs** in the axils **of the leaves, and multiplies** very rapidly.

Those who desire to cultivate some of the green-house species cannot fail to be pleased with *Auratum*, the Golden-banded Lily from Japan, noted for its size, beauty, and fragrance; *Giganteum*, a very tall-growing white species from the Himalayas; *Thompsonianum*, from India, which produces rose-colored flowers; and *Concolor*, with brilliant red flowers, from China.

Lilium Brownii.—We have not tested the hardihood of this species, it is scarce and high-priced, but it is a most magnificent trumpet-shaped flower, of large size, white within and purple without, and very fragrant.

THE NARCISSUS.—The hardy species require the same treatment as that recommended for the Hyacinth. They thrive best in rich, sandy loam, and should remain in the ground until the increase of bulbs makes it necessary to divide them.

Poeticus.—One of the most beautiful of this class. There are double and semi-double varieties; all are perfectly hardy in well-drained soil. The flowers are snow-white with a cream-colored cup, the edge of which is delicately fringed with red.

Bulbicodium.—This is the hoop-petticoat Narcissus, producing large, bright yellow flowers. The leaves are small and rush-like. It thrives best in a somewhat sheltered position, and is the better, in open winters, for a slight covering.

Bicolor.—Perfectly hardy, but not very common. The flowers have a white cup and yellow crown.

Pseudo-Narcissus.—The Daffodil, so well known and generally admired for its double, golden-yellow flowers. Perfectly hardy in well-drained soil.

Jonquilla.—The Jonquil, much esteemed for its fragant, bright yellow flowers. Very hardy and free-flowering. Makes a fine window-plant for late winter blooming.

The POLIANTHUS NARCISSUS are not sufficiently hardy to endure our climate without careful protection, and the yearly taking up of the bulbs when the leaves die off, in order to prevent them from starting in the fall. But they are beautiful things for the house, blooming well with the same treatment as that laid down for the Hyacinth.

SNOWDROP.—*Galanthus.*—This delicate, frail-looking flower is our first harbinger of spring, telling us that winter is passing away. It hardly looks as though it could hold out against the rough blasts that toss it so rudely, but it struggles bravely on through all the adverse storms and snows, hiding its face until the storm be past, and looking up with a cheery smile when it is over. It is ever a favorite flower, simple yet pretty, lovely in itself, and for braving the storms, as if anxious to cheer us with sight of flowers after the long desolation of winter.

The Snowdrop is perfectly hardy, thrives well in any good garden soil, but better in a bed enriched with well-rotted cow manure, and if the soil be heavy, made light by the addition of sand. The bulbs should be planted in October, between two and three inches deep, in clusters of from twenty to thirty bulbs, leaving about an inch and a half of space between them. Here they should remain until they become so crowded that it is necessary to divide them. If some are planted on the south side of the house, or other sunny spot, they will bloom very early, and by planting another bed in some less favored exposure, they may be had in succession for a considerable time. They look well planted with the spring-flowering Crocus, contrasting finely with its more gaudy colors. There are two species in cultivation, the *G. Nivalis*, of which there are both single and double varieties; and *Plicatus*, a Russian variety, twice as large as the English, and with taller flower stems.

Another flower blooming later, called *Snowflake*, has been sometimes mistaken for the Snowdrop. It is the Leucojum. Two species of this are grown in our gardens. L. *Vernum*, a native of Germany and Italy, is somewhat tender, and thrives best in a peaty soil; L. *Œstivum*, a native of England, perfectly hardy, produces white flowers with bright green spots.

THE TIGER FLOWER.—*Tigridia.*—These bulbs are not hardy,

and require to be kept over winter in a dry place, free from frost, and out of the *reach of mice.* They should not be planted until the ground has become warm in spring, and then set about three inches deep in soil that is deep, light, and rich. They show to best advantage planted in clumps or masses. The flowers are very pretty and brilliant, each lasting only for a day, but renewed by a succession of blooms for several weeks. They appear in August and September. In October, when the frost has killed the foliage, the bulbs should be taken up, thoroughly dried, and stowed away in dry sand.

Pavonia.—The flowers of this species are of the richest scarlet, variegated with bright yellow and spotted with dark brown.

Conchiflora.—This species produces rich, orange-colored flowers, variegated with light yellow and spotted with black.

TUBEROSE.—*Polianthes Tuberosa.*—One of the most deliciously scented and lovely of all our flowers, blooming in the end of summer and throughout the autumn. It has but to be seen to be admired, and no one who has once enjoyed its exquisite perfume will ever willingly be deprived of it in its season. One flower will fill the whole room with its fragrance, and no bouquet, from August to Christmas, is complete without it. Being a native of India, it requires plenty of warmth, and will not endure frost, yet it is of simple culture when once its requirements are understood.

In the first place, the proper time to obtain the tubers is in October, before they have had time to become injured by improper treatment. Those grown in America are just as good as the imported, hence there is no necessity of looking to Europe any longer for a supply. Having procured the tubers, keep them dry and warm until they are wanted for planting. If they are kept in a temperature below 50° the flower germ will decay, and though the bulb may appear sound outwardly and throw out an abundance of leaves, it will never flower. Those who have greenhouses can keep them alongside the flue, those who have not must store them in some warm room where they will be kept at a temperature of twenty degrees above freezing, night or day. **It** is not enough **to keep** them, like Gladiolus, or Potatoes, free from frost. If thus kept they will remain sound, and there will be no difficulty in getting them to bloom.

If it is desired to have them **in** bloom early in August, it will be necessary to start them about the first of May, **either** in greenhouse, hot-bed, or warm **room.** The secret **of** flowering them well lies in keeping the **roots** well supplied with **food,** and as warm as possible. A soil composed of the same material as that recommended for Hyacinths, in which the **old** cow-manure is supplied even more liberally, and made quite **light** by the use of sand if needed, is just the thing in which **to** plant the Tuberose. If the hot-bed is used, **the** pots **in which the bulbs are planted** should be plunged **to** the rim, **and the temperature maintained** at about **seventy-five.** After they begin **to** grow they will require all the **sun and air** that can be given, having a care to keep the **temperature as** uniform as possible, **and** protecting well from **frosty nights** by a mat thrown over the sashes. As they increase their growth it will be necessary to increase the amount of watering, and when the summer is far enough advanced the sashes need be no longer used. Towards the end **of June they may** either be plunged or carefully turned out **into the** open border. For later flowering they do well **planted in the** ground about the tenth of **June, in warm,** rich, well **drained soil. If** wanted for the green-house or **window, in** November **or** December, they may be potted in **July and August, plunged in** a frame or in the open border where **they will** have all the sun-light and heat possible, and before the advent **of** the first frost brought into the house.

After the bulb **has** once flowered it is of no further use except to the propagator; it will **never flower again.** The offsets that are attached to it can be grown into flowering bulbs in a couple of years, but this is hardly worth the trouble **so** long as full-grown **flowering bulbs** can be obtained at such trifling cost from any of our nurserymen or florists.

There are two varieties, the single and the double flowering, both very desirable and equally fragrant, the single variety possessing the advantage of coming into bloom about a fortnight earlier than the double. In the neighborhood of the large cities of the United States a considerable trade is carried on in the flowers, which bring a dollar a hundred in the summer, and ten dollars in winter, and as each bulb will produce some twenty flowers, it will yield, if flowered at the time of high prices, many times its cost by the sale of the blossoms.

THE TULIP.—There is no need of any description of this much-admired flower, and now that the bulbs may be obtained at such very low prices, every one may indulge his fondness for their pretty blossoms by planting a bed of Tulips. And it is when massed in a bed that their full beauty is brought out. They are very hardy plants, requiring no very special care except in one particular, and that is that the ground be thoroughly drained, for they will not bear water in the soil. It is not necessary that the soil be very rich. Any good garden will grow them well. Nor is it important that the bulbs should be taken up every summer, although it is usually recommended, on the ground that if the bulbs remain in the earth for several years they "run out." But as every year brings some new additions to the list of Tulips, by the time those that we have planted run out, we are ready to set out a new bed of those of later introduction, and are quite willing to dispense with the old.

The *Duc Van Thol* are the earliest to bloom; they are both single and double. The double are red with a yellow border, the single of many colors, white, scarlet, crimson, yellow, etc. The plants are of dwarf habit, only growing about six inches high.

The *Tournesol* succeeds the foregoing in time of flowering. The blooms are red and yellow, or golden yellow, and very large and double. They keep in bloom for a long time and are very showy.

The *Early Single Tulips* of every shade of red, violet, purple, crimson, yellow, etc., striped, flaked and marbled, come next in order, and make a fine showy bed, which continues for a considerable length of time. Our Florists' catalogues abound with names of these, with markings more or less distinct, from which each may make selection according to his fancy, or the fulness of his purse.

The *Double Tulips* are great favorites with many. They are exceedingly beautiful, and may be had of various colors, which may be selected in the same way.

The *Parrot Tulips* are singularly formed, the petals being long and fringed. They are very attractive, from the singular appearance of the flower, and the striking combination of colors which they present.

The *Late Tulips* are divided into *Byblooms*, white ground marked with purple or lilac; *Roses*, white ground marked with scarlet, crimson or pink; and *Bizarres*, yellow ground, with markings of any color other than yellow.

These are the favorite florist's flowers, new and choice varieties commanding high prices. Here, too, selection can be made from hundreds of names, at prices ranging from five cents each to as many dollars as one may wish to give. Yet a very fine selection of a hundred bulbs can be made for five dollars, embracing as many as fifty sorts.

BEDDING PLANTS.

All the plants which are mentioned under this head are too tender to endure much frost. It is therefore necessary, either that they be allowed to perish on the approach of winter, or that they be removed to the green-house. Those who do not keep a green-house will find it to be much more satisfactory, and more economical, to purchase a new supply of bedding plants every spring, and enjoy their beauty and fragrance while the summer lasts. The keeping of a large number of plants in an ordinary dwelling house is not only attended with considerable inconvenience, but the plants seldom get through in good health. And when they do, they are not of a suitable age and size for bedding out.

Only the more useful and desirable of the plants which are used for this purpose are described, and such hints given, under each flower, as seem likely to prove useful to that great mass of cultivators who must content themselves with their summer culture.

THE VERBENA.—This flower is the most popular and generally planted of all the bedding plants. Beginning to flower when the plants are quite small, and even before the weather is warm enough for planting in the open air, it continues to bloom all the summer long, and even through the autumn, until severe frosts stop its growth. The flowers are of every color except yellow, some of them handsomely eyed, and others striped and mottled. They are borne in trusses, composed of many separate flowers, and these are so numerous as to cover the bed completely.

Young and healthy plants should be selected about the first of June, avoiding those with crumpled and misshapen foliage. For effective bedding display, those flowers are to be preferred which have not a large eye, and are not striped. Clear, bright, self-colors, when massed, are much more brilliant and showy.

The soil should be deep and rich, and free from all surplus moisture. The Verbena in its wild state grows on dry hills, and will not endure an excess of wet. If, however, this condition be granted, that is, the bed be thoroughly drained, the texture of the soil is of little consequence, it will grow in any, from light sand to quite strong clay. It is, however, important that it be well enriched; for this purpose all coarse, undecomposed and fermenting manures should be avoided, and that selected which has been thoroughly rotted. Having incorporated the manure thoroughly with the soil, and made the surface smooth and fine, the plants may be set out about eighteen inches apart each way. The various colors may be arranged to suit the taste of the planter.

It is desirable to plant in the latter part of the day, so that the plants will not suffer from the heat of the sun. After planting it is usually necessary to give them a thorough sprinkling through a fine rose, to settle the soil about the plants. Beyond this they will seldom require any attention other than to keep the ground free from weeds, and give it an occasional stirring and loosening around the plants. Inexperienced cultivators are very apt to give the Verbena too much water. If the soil be as rich as it should be, it is very seldom indeed that the Verbena bed will require water.

Those who wish to keep Verbenas over winter, either in the dwelling-house or in the green-house, should never take up the old plants that have been blooming all summer in the garden. They never do well, and will probably die before spring. In order to grow them in the house successfully they should obtain young plants. These may be obtained by selecting one or two plants of each variety it is desired to grow through the winter, and about the tenth of August cutting off all the flowers and seed vessels, and about six inches from the ends of the shoots. The object is to start the plant into a fresh and vigorous growth, hence whatever may tend to facilitate this may be done at this time, such as stirring the soil and adding a dressing of compost.

After the plants have started into a fresh growth, cuttings of the new and tender shoots, which will be sufficiently grown by the middle of September, may be taken from them and struck in a little pure sand with a gentle bottom heat. Cuttings of fresh growth only should be used, and as soon as rooted should be potted off in small pots. These plants will grow well during the winter, and will afford cuttings in March and April, from which plants may be struck for summer planting.

It is not necessary that any list of names should be given. Each one may select from the nurseryman's list such as please best ; all are beautiful, many are fragrant, and no one can fail of obtaining a bed of beautiful flowers that will be gay all the season. Besides, our florists are constantly producing new varieties from seed, and those that stand in the front rank to-day will soon be crowded out by new comers.

THE HELIOTROPE.—This plant is valued for the sweetness and delicacy of its perfume more than for the beauty of its flowers. It is of easy culture, growing freely in any rich and well drained garden soil. It should be planted in the open air after all fear of late frosts is over, and taken in before the early autumn frosts come on, for it is more tender than the Verbena, and apt to be injured by even a slight freezing.

The flowers vary from a very pale lilac to a deep purple, are individually small, but produced in close trusses or corymbs. They bloom profusely all the time they are in growth, and make excellent window plants if allowed plenty of room. Being sensitive under removals, it is important when they are taken out of the border that the transplanting should be done with care, disturbing the root as little as possible. They flourish best when they have plenty of pot room, or indeed, if in the green-house, they have a border in which the roots may ramble.

When a plant is taken up from the open border in autumn for window culture in winter, it should be pruned back so as to remove the soft wood and kept for some time in a cool room. Before the frosts become severe enough to penetrate the place where it was placed, it should be removed to a warm room. There its buds will soon break and the plant begin to grow, yielding an abundance of sweet-scented flowers.

It is propagated by cuttings of the soft wood, which strike freely in bottom heat. New varieties are raised from seed. The best now in cultivation are *The Gem* and *Voltaireanum*, with dark flowers; *Oculata*, violet with white centre; *Jersey Beauty* and *Jean Mesmer*, light blue; and *Garibaldi*, nearly white. *Pauline Pfitzer*, a new lilac-colored flower, is a splendid bedder, on account of the immense size of the truss and its profuseness of bloom.

THE COLEUS.—These are useful bedding plants in those parts of Canada where the summers are hot and the nights not chilly. Their beauty consists entirely in the color of the leaves and not in their flowers, and this is brought fully out only in

BEDDING PLANTS.

hot weather. They are not only sensitive to frost but to cool weather, requiring considerable heat to keep them in a vigorous growth. Hence they are not easily wintered in the dwelling-house, where there is a great variation between the night and day temperature, nor even in a cool green-house; the propagating-room or the stove is the best place for them.

The best and most showy bedding variety is *Verschaffeltii*; besides this, *Queen Victoria*, *Albert Victor*, *Her Majesty*, and *Princess Beatrice*, are beautiful plants. There are many other varieties, but the foregoing are quite sufficient for all our purposes.

THE BOUVARDIA.—But little has been done among us with this most lovely flower as a bedding plant, yet it is one of the most free flowering and beautiful plants we have, blooming when not more than three inches in height and naturally forming a nice bushy plant, which is covered all the season with blossoms. It is not easy to account for this want of attention, for among the beautiful things of the garden there is scarce anything more beautiful than a fine bed of the Bouvardia.

Fig. 69.

We have grown it in rich sandy loam, and know that it thrives well in such soil. We cannot say how well it will adapt itself to heavier soils, but those who desire to make the experiment must take care that the bed be perfectly underdrained, so that there shall be no excess of wet to render the soil cold and sour. Plants that have been shifted from "thumbs" into four inch pots, and pinched back, so as to be stout and bushy, are the best for bedding out.

Another and more common use made of the Bouvardia, by florists, is that of winter forcing for green-house decoration and the making of winter boquets. For this purpose it is without a rival, indeed quite indispensable. Nothing surpasses it, in its several varieties, in brilliancy of color; nor anything, save the Jessamine itself, in delicate purity and sweetness of perfume.

For pot culture it should be planted in rich, fibry loam, that is, rotted turf, made light by the admixture of sand, and rich with old, well-rotted manure. In potting, care should be used to secure perfect drainage, and if the plants are taken from the open border, they should be lifted with care, leaving a ball of earth about the roots if possible. After being potted they will require careful watering and shading until they recover from the shift. They must not be exposed to even a slight frost, but should have all the light and air possible before they go into winter quarters.

Plants intended for winter blooming should not be allowed to flower during the summer, but should be kept well pinched in. To make nice bushy plants the tops should be nipped every fortnight. Those that have been used as bedding plants should be taken up before frost, planted in a box of soil, and allowed to rest during the winter, storing them under the stage of the greenhouse. These may be again taken from the box and set out in the open bed on the return of summer.

Aurantiaca.—The flowers are of a bright orange color; the plant a very free summer bloomer.

Hogarth.—Produces splendid racemes of rich carmine flowers.

Elegans.—The flowers are light scarlet carmine, which are borne in very large trusses. Blooms finely in winter, and therefore well adapted for forcing.

Jasminoides.—A most abundant bloomer, flowers pure white, resembling a Jasmine in fragrance and appearance. A charming variety.

Leiantha.—The flowers are a dazzling scarlet. The **plant of** bushy habit, **very free** flowering and **healthy.**

Triphylla.—**Flowers** bright orange-scarlet, **very showy.** The plant is a free **summer** bloomer, **and is one of the best for bedding out.**

THE PETUNIA.—This is a **very popular bedding plant,** of very easy culture, and makes a very **showy bed.** It grows well in any rich garden soil, begins to **bloom in** June, **and** continues to grow and flower all through the summer, until checked by frost. It should be planted always in a bed devoted solely to Petunias, for the plants spread so rapidly, and often grow so luxuriantly, that they are apt to over-run and conceal other **plants. They** may be had of all colors, except blue and yellow, **and both single and double. Many are very** prettily striped, blotched, and spotted. **Some are also sweet-scented.** They **are not suitable** for bouquets, **wilting soon after being** cut, but they make a very showy bed, and should always **be grown** in masses, and not as **single plants.**

Varieties of any desired colors, and single or double, can always be obtained at very low prices of our florists, in the bedding season. Those who do not care for the choicest sorts can treat the Petunia as an annual, sow the seed in a **hot-bed** or cold frame, and transplant to the Petunia bed, setting the plants about eighteen inches apart. These will begin to bloom in July and continue until late **in the fall,** and though the plants will vary greatly **in the** color and markings of the flowers, yet many of them, doubtless, will be very fine, and all of them profuse bloomers.

We do not attempt a list of the named varieties. New kinds **are** being annually brought out, and each can select from the **tradesmen's** lists such as seem most desirable, without fear of **getting a** poor flower. The single **varieties** are the most profuse **blooming,** and to us the most satisfactory, but many prefer the double. All are propagated freely by cuttings.

THE LANTANA.—This very pretty and very free flowering plant has not been as much used among us for bedding purposes

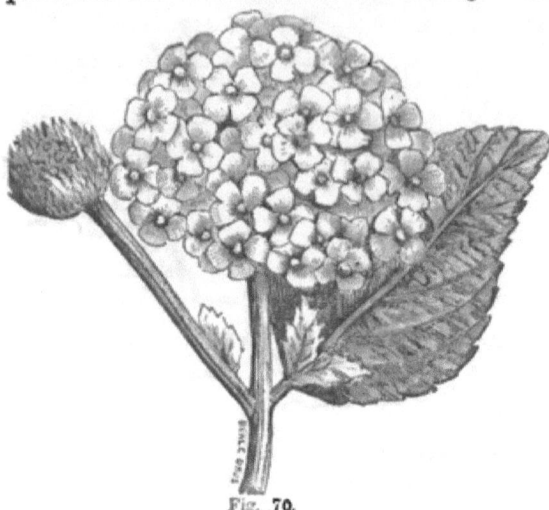

Fig. 70.

as its beauty deserves. It is of very easy culture, flourishes well in any garden soil, indeed, often growing too well, if planted in rich soil, running too much to wood in proportion to the bloom.

It is of a shrubby habit, beginning to flower when from four to six inches high, and continuing to increase in size and abundance of bloom until the frost comes. The flowers are of various colors, yellow, white, orange, lilac, rose, and purple, and these arranged in globular heads, each head, in many of the varieties, containing flowers of several colors. A bed, containing several varieties of the Lantana, is not to be easily surpassed in brilliancy of bloom or attractiveness of coloring.

Plants obtained at the same time with Verbenas may be planted in the open ground, as soon as danger from frost is over. They should be set in a bed by themselves, in not very rich, but well-drained soil, about two feet apart each way. As soon as the first frost blackens the leaves they should be taken up, cut well back, and with the roots in a pot or box of earth set under the green-house stage, or, if one has no green-house, in a warm dry cellar. The soil in the pot or box should be just kept from becoming entirely dry. In the spring they may be brought to the light and heat, watered more freely, started into growth, and when the frosts are over, planted again in the open ground, where they will continue to grow and bloom in all their former beauty. In the course of three or four years they will become too large to be easily handled, when small plants can be again had by striking soft wood cuttings in a gentle bottom heat. New varieties are raised from seed.

The following names are given as some of the most desirable now in cultivation, and by examining it our readers will be able to form some idea of the coloring of the flowers.

Alba Lutea Grandiflora.—White and yellow, dwarf habit.
Aurantiaca.—Varying from deep yellow to bright orange.
Clotilda.—Pink flowers, the centre yellow.
Eugenie.—Flowers rose and white.
Gustave Thomas.—Rose and orange **flowers**.
Monsieur Rougier.—**Crimson, scarlet, and yellow.**
Raphael.—**Purple, orange, and rose.**
Solfaterre.—**Golden yellow,** margined **straw color.**
Schlegelii.—Yellow, orange, and purple.
Victoria.—Pure white, with lemon eye.

THE LEMON-SCENTED VERBENA.—This favorite green-house shrub is grown for the delicous fragrance of its leaves. The flowers are small and unattractive, but a few sprigs of the leaves give a delightful fragrance to any bouquet, and they retain their **freshness** for a long time when placed in water. It may be planted in the open ground as soon as **freezing** nights are passed, when it will grow **rapidly in rich soil,** and form a handsome shrub. In the autumn, before the frosty nights return, it should be taken up with the **earth** adhering to the roots, set in a box or pot, and kept **over winter in** the cellar where it does not freeze. On the return of spring it should be pruned into shape, if **needed,** and again planted out. During the winter it should not be watered. It can be grown in a pot, and while in a growing state requires to be watered freely. It is propagated by cuttings **of the growing** shoots, which root freely in sand with a little **bottom heat.**

GERANIUMS.—These beautiful showy bedding plants are too

well known to need particular description, and are highly appreciated as summer ornaments of the flower garden. There is now a great variety. Some are grown almost exclusively on account of the many-colored variegation of the leaves, others because of the great brilliancy and abundance of the flowers. Some excel as plants for culture in pots, others are more particularly adapted for the open flower-bed, and yet others have a trailing habit that gives them great value for cultivation in hanging baskets and vases. They are all among the more hardy of our tender plants, enduring the chilly spring weather, if suitably prepared for it by gradual exposure, and not killed by the first autumnal frost. They are also patient under house treatment, and bear well the variations of temperature to which plants in the window are usually subjected.

Geraniums have been divided into many classes by florists, and in the endeavor to group those most nearly alike together, it is necessary that the names given to the several classes be somewhat arbitrary. Hence we term many Geraniums "Zonals" that have no zonal marking, but whose leaves are a plain green; and now, by the operations of the hybridist, the difference between the "Nosegay" section and the "Zonal" is fast disappearing. For these reasons we have grouped the several classes under four heads, the less to confuse the reader, and name them respectively Zonal and Nosegay, Variegated-leaved, Ivy-leaved, and Double.

The Zonal and Nosegay division comprises those most generally used for bedding out, though some from the Variegated-leaved and the Doubles are used for this purpose, with somewhat varying success. Of the Variegated-leaved varieties, those having a green leaf with silver markings answer best for bedding, while those known as "Tricolored" and "Gold and Bronze," have not seemed to be able to endure our hot summer suns. We say *seem*, because experiment with these has been limited, either because the little trial that has been made has not been encouraging, or because the taste of our cultivators has not been of that

BEDDING PLANTS. 341

artificial character which demands such gratification. A well-grown specimen **makes a** pretty **ornament** for the **window or** the green-**house,** giving a pleasing variety when **mingled with** the prevailing **green.** Yet the Variegated-leaved sorts are mostly slow growers, and make considerable **demands** upon our patience before they attain the size of fine specimen plants.

The doubles do not yet **take the place as bedders that they** may eventually be hoped **to fill. Thus far the plants have too** vigorous a style of growth in proportion to the number of trusses of bloom, and do not **make** that blaze in the bed which **we can** obtain with singles. **The** quality which they certainly possess of retaining the flowers longer, and the absence **of the unsightly** seed-pods, which **so soon disfigure the singles, give promise of** value as **bedders when the rampant habit of growth shall have been made to give way to** greater abundance of bloom. But **as pot plants they are beautiful additions to our floral wealth, blooming quite freely when once the pot has become filled with roots** and the over-luxuriance of growth checked for **want of** fuller root room.

The Ivy-leaved varieties have been much improved of late **years.** We now have some with beautiful silver or golden-edged **leaves** and pure white **flowers** borne in large trusses, **and some with the** thick-leaved habit of the class, but **producing** much **larger blossoms of a deep violet-rose color, or delicate** rosy pink. **These are particularly ornamental in vases and** hanging baskets, from their peculiar **trailing** habit of growth, or when treated as climbers and trained **upon some support.** They are of easy culture and patient **under varying treatment.**

All these varieties of Geranium are easily **propagated from** cuttings, which strike **readily** in sand without much **bottom heat. New** varieties are raised from seed, and the field is one of great **interest.** Canadian amateurs should produce as fine varieties as **any imported,** and they will, as **soon as** they give careful attention to selection and cross-fertilization.

The soil in which Geraniums are bedded should be made

friable and be well drained, but it is not necessary that it should be very rich. It may be too rich for the best display of bloom, inducing too great a growth of wood and foliage. The plants may be set out when the weather has become warm, and if they have been well hardened off no fears need be entertained because of a slight frost. When set as close together as the size of the plants will permit, and in considerable masses, they produce the best effect.

In autumn the plants may be taken up before the coming of hard frosts, and either potted singly or planted in boxes of earth. They can be kept over winter in a dry, frost-proof cellar, without being watered at all, unless they show signs of shrivelling from extreme dryness, and planted out in the late spring in the open bed. The branches will require to be cut back when they are planted out, so that they may retain a neat and compact head. If preferred, they may be wintered in the parlor window, but our experience teaches us that they will thrive better if, after being put into pots in autumn, they are allowed a couple of months of rest before being brought to the light and warmth.

ZONALE AND NOSEGAY GERANIUMS.—These give us our best bedders now, (1872), and many of them are extremely beautiful grown as specimens in pots. There is no end to the names; every year will give us new ones, some of which will doubtless be improvements on those now cultivated; yet we venture to give those of a few of the very best that we now have. These are all truly splendid sorts, that will not fail to give pleasure to the grower, until those that can excel them in beauty are produced.

Amy Hogg.—Bright **purplish rose.**
Black Dwarf.—Crimson **scarlet.**
Coleshill.—Bright scarlet.
Diana.—Clear glowing scarlet.
General Grant.—A splendid bedder; **scarlet.**
Gloire de Corbeny.—Salmon pink, margined with white.
Ianthe.—The nearest approach to blue yet grown; large rosy-purple flowers.

Jean Sisely.—Scarlet, with white eye.
Iago.—Bright crimson.
Lord Derby.—Intense scarlet.
Master Christine.—Bright rosy **pink**.
Orbiculata.—Glowing scarlet.
Richard Headly.—Clear **scarlet**.
Rose of Allandale.—Beautiful clear pink.
Sir Charles Napier.—Immense size; clear scarlet.
Surpasse Beaute de Surresnes.—Bright pink; enormous truss.
Sir John Moore.—Excellent bedder; scarlet.
Thomas Moore.—Another fine bedder; scarlet flowers.
Waltham Seedling.—Dark crimson.
Wellington.—Deep crimson scarlet.
White Princess.—Pure **white flowers**.

VARIEGATED–LEAVED GERANIUMS.—This division comprises those known as "Silver-edged," "Silver Tricolor," "Golden Tricolor," and "Gold and Bronze." They are all of slower growth than the foregoing, and, with the exception of the "Silver-edged," are better as pot plants than as bedders. The names given below are some of the very best:

Achievement.—Margined with gold **and zoned with bronze and** vermilion.
Albion Cliffs.—Broad edge of white.
Avalanche.—Silver edge and pure **white flowers**.
Black Douglas.—Broad dark zone with narrow gold margin.
Bijou.—Silvery white leaf margin.
Glen Eyre Beauty.—Bronze zone shaded with scarlet and margined with French white.
Imperatrice **Eugenie.**—Golden ground with bright chocolate zone.
Lady *Cullum.*—Bronze zone bordered with intense flame color.
Lucy *Grieve.*—Bronze ground suffused with lake and tinted with crimson.
Miss Burdett Coutts.—Bronze and scarlet zone with white leaf margin.

Mrs. Pollock.—Bronze zone belted with crimson and yellow margin.

Mrs. John Clutton.—Broad bright carmine zone, clear white margin.

Reine Victoria.—Yellow leaves, broad chestnut zone edged with deep golden yellow.

Sir Robert Napier.—Dark chocolate zone with scarlet vandyke blotches.

Waltham Bride.—White leaf edge, and large trusses of white flowers.

IVY-LEAVED GERANIUMS.—The following varieties are the best yet introduced, but they are capable of greater things than have yet been accomplished, and our readers may look for great improvements in the size and coloring of the flowers in the course of a few years.

Bridal Wreath.—Large trusses of pure white flowers.

Duke of Edinburgh.—Creamy-white leaf margin.

Gem of the Season.—Large trusses of bright rose-colored flowers.

Lady Edith.—Crimson flowers tinged with purple.

L'Elegante.—Leaves varigated with white, and pure white flowers.

Willsi Rosea.—Rich rose-colored flowers.

DOUBLE GERANIUMS.—The following are the cream of this division, but we look for varieties of finer habit and more abundant bloom, in the course of the next ten years.

Andrew Henderson.—Deep scarlet lake flowers.

Charles Glym.—Bright orange scarlet, dwarfish habit.

Crown Prince.—Flowers bright pink.

Gloire de Nancy.—Rosy scarlet flowers.

Le Vesuve.—Brilliant glowing scarlet.

Miss Evelyn.—Deep rose-pink flowers, with reddish crimson ground.

Madam Lemoine.—Clear bright rose color.

Princess Teck.—Rich carmine scarlet.

Victor Lemoine.—Bright scarlet, **very large flowers.**
Wilhelm Pfitzer.—Rich glowing **crimson.**

There is also a class of Geraniums which are grown on account of the fragrance of the leaves. These are of easy culture under the treatment already given for Geraniums. The flowers are not showy, but the foliage is more or less cut and is very serviceable in the formation of bouquets. They are known as *Apple-scented, Nutmeg-scented, Lemon-scented, Peppermint-scented,* and *Rose scented.* There is a variety of the Rose-scented with a cream-colored leaf margin, called *Lady Plymouth.* A well grown plant is very pretty.

PELARGONIUMS.—As popularly known, these have larger flowers than the Geranium, and of more varied coloring. Botanically speaking, those plants already described under the name of Geraniums, are Pelargoniums. An effort seems to be made of late to obliterate the name Geranium from our bedding plants, and use Pelargonium instead. But the name Geranium has been so long used to designate the particular section to which it is applied, and the name Pelargonium to denote the large-flowering varieties, that it is quite too late to unsettle long established public custom, and we have preferred to adhere to the popular habit.

The Pelargonium is not adapted for bedding purposes, but is strictly a conservatory plant. In the green-house or the window they are very showy when in bloom, and need no special care other than to keep down the green-fly or Aphis. The flowers are shaped much like those of a well-grown Pansy, and are exceedingly beautiful. The varieties are very numerous, new names are being constantly added to the list, and purchasers can best suit their taste by consulting the florists' catalogues.

ANNUALS.

By the term **Annuals** is meant that large class of plants which live but one season, coming up from seed, producing flowers and ripening seed in the course of the summer, and then perishing. We have endeavored to make a selection of those that will best repay care and culture in our Canadian climate. It is useless to grow everything. Not even everything that is pretty is worth the requisite labor, when compared with results just as easily obtained by a judicious selection.

The plants described under this head will flourish in any good well-tilled garden soil. Some of them are the better of being started in a frame and transplanted, like cabbage-plants, to their permanent place in the garden. Any special treatment that may be required, will be noticed under the several plants named. They all require cultivation and care, to be kept free from weeds, and to have the ground stirred occasionally, especially while the plants are small.

THE ASTER.—This flowers late in the summer and through the autumn. It flourishes best in a deep, rich soil. In our climate it is best to sow the seed in a cold frame, and get the plants started a little earlier than can be done in the open ground. It is possible to start them too early, by which means they are brought into flower while the sun is too powerful, and the flowers in consequence are scorched by the heat. When the plants are well grown, they should be transplanted into beds, setting the tall-growing kinds about a foot apart each way, and the dwarf varieties about half that distance.

Truffaut's Peonia-flowered Perfection is a very large-flowered variety, having long reflexed petals, and in various colors. The flower stalks grow about two feet high.

New Rose.—Grows to about the same height, the flowers are very double, of several colors, and the petals finely imbricated.

New Peonia-flowered Globe.—Is a very early flowering

variety, the blossoms are large, of various colors, and the plant of a stout branching habit.

Dwarf Chrysanthemum-flowered.—Grows about a foot high, the flowers are large, finely formed, of various colors, and very handsome.

Dwarf Pyramidal Boquet.—Presents a very pleasing appearance when in full bloom, producing a great profusion of flowers. The colors are various, and the plant only about a foot high.

THE BALSAM.—Requires a rich soil and good culture. The seed should be sown in a cold frame, and the young plants very carefully guarded from frost. Care must be taken not to let the plants be drawn up by overcrowding. This can be prevented by pricking them out when the second leaves have grown a little, and planting them in another frame, and by giving them plenty of air in **suitable weather.** When summer weather is established and frosty nights gone by, the plants may be set in the border, about a foot apart.

Camellia-flowered.—The German variety is very showy, producing very handsome double flowers, beautifully spotted with **white.**

Rose-flowered.—These flowers are perfectly double, and may be had of various colors.

Carnation.—The flowers are beautifully striped and perfectly double. A very pleasing variety.

THE CALLIOPSIS.—This is quite hardy, and the seed may be sown in the open border as soon as the weather has become settled. The flowers are exceedingly showy, of many shades of yellow, and orange, and brown, and are produced in great profusion. To produce the best effect they should be grown in a mass, not in single lines.

Burridgi.—The flowers **have a very rich** bronzy crimson **centre with an** orange yellow border.

Drummondii.—Produces yellow flowers with a crimson centre.

Cardaminifolia hybrida.—Has a compact pyramidal habit,

and is covered all the season with a great profusion of bright yellow flowers.

THE DRUMMOND PHLOX.—If there be any one annual of more beauty than another, beautiful in the variety and loveliness of the flowers, beautiful because of its long continuance in bloom, and beautiful in the durability and freshness of the cut flowers in water, this is the most beautiful of them all. The flowers are white, crimson, scarlet, purple, red, rose, pink, lilac, violet, and all of these colors with distinct eye of some other color. They vie with the Verbena in variety and intensity of coloring, and to be fully enjoyed should be grown in masses of distinct colors.

The seed may be sown in the open ground in May, though it is preferable to start it in a frame and get the plants on a little earlier. These may be set in the bed, about a foot apart each way, as soon as the weather becomes settled. They flourish in any good, rich, friable soil, though giving a preference to the lighter rather than the heavier. The plants begin to bloom while quite small, and continue to grow and bloom all summer and autumn; the abundance of bloom is improved by free cutting of the flowers, so as to lessen the amount of seed; if the plants are allowed to ripen a full crop of seed, it checks their growth, and injures the beauty of the bed.

If the seed of the several colors be kept and sown separate, a fine effect may be produced by planting the bed in ribbons of various colors. Being never out of bloom from June to November, and if the precaution in regard to the ripening of seed be observed, never sparsely supplied with flowers, it makes an excellent plant for such a purpose. But planted in any way, whether in separate masses of color, or in ribbons of distinct and various colors, or with all colors indiscriminately mingled, it is one of the lovliest flowers of the garden.

THE MARIGOLD.—Although useless in hand bouquets, on account of their strong disagreeable odor, the flowers of the French Marigold are exceedingly pretty. They have a very rich velvety appearance, are of a reddish-brown color, variously striped and variegated with yellow, and beautifully double. **The seed may** be sown in **a cold** frame, and if the **plants** are set out in rich soil, after frosts are over, they will grow to considerable size, **and continue** in bloom from July until sharp frosts destroy them.

THE MIGNONETTE.—This unpretending flower, with scarce coloring enough to distinguish the blossoms from the leaves, is known and loved by everybody for its sweetness. It will grow in any garden, and the seed may be sown at any time when the soil can be tilled, and anywhere. Yet it will repay a little care a thousand fold, and if spikes are cut so frequently that but little seed can ripen, it will continue to send forth fresh spikes of **bloom** throughout the season. If the bed be left undisturbed, self-sown plants will come up every summer, and the Mignonette bed **be** perpetuated **for many years.** Plants may be potted in the **fall,** and **will grow and** flower freely in the green-house or window.

PORTULACA.—**A valuable plant, of low** growth and creeping **habit,** blooming profusely, with **showy** flowers of all shades of **crimson, orange,** yellow, pink, **and** white, sometimes spotted and striped in curious fashion. **It is** just the thing for covering **a** bed of bulbs, or for carpeting the ground under taller plants that do not make much shade. It loves hot weather, and **grows luxuriantly** in heat and drouth. If the seed be sown in the open **ground it** will not come **up until the hot suns** of June have imparted considerable warmth to the soil, **but** the plants may be considerably forwarded by sowing in a frame and transplanting in June.

There are very **pretty** double varieties of various colors. When in full bloom, the ground looks as if carpeted with miniature **roses. The seed of** these is scarce, costing five times as much as the single, and not more than half the plants raised from a package of double seed will **come perfectly** double.

All **the** varieties are of easy **culture,** preferring a sandy soil, **and to be exposed** to the hottest suns, yet capable of growing in any warm, friable loam. When once planted and the bed left undisturbed, the self-sown seed will remain in the soil without injury through the winter, and the plants appear in it on the return of hot weather.

THE ROCKET LARKSPUR.—There are two varieties, the tall and the dwarf. The dwarf-growing variety, known by seedsmen as *Delphinium Ajacis Hyacinthiflorum*, produces the most showy flowers and most compact spikes. The flowers are of various shades of blue, pink, and white, and all these colors most strangely blended.

The seed should be sown in good friable soil in the fall, just before winter, where the plants are to remain. If they come up too thick they may be thinned out to about six inches apart. If the seed be not sown in the fall, it should be put in as early in the spring as possible, and sown where the plants are to remain. We have never succeeded in producing as fine a bloom when the plants were transplanted. If it must be done, they should be pricked out when quite small. A fine bed of these is a most beautiful sight, rivalling a bed of Hyacinths in everything except fragrance.

There is a new, dwarf, branching Larkspur, styled the Candelabra-flowered. It is very favorably noticed in the Horticultural magazines, but we have not yet flowered it.

THE SCABIOUS OR MOURNING BRIDE.—This probably received its name from the very dark color of some of the flowers, just relieved by a lacing of white. The seed may be sown in the open border very early in spring. The plants will do well in any good garden soil. The Double Dwarf is the most desirable variety. The flowers are of many colors, produced in great profusion, and continuing until after severe frosts.

THE SALPIGLOSSIS.—This beautiful plant seems to be but little known, so seldom is it seen in our flower gardens. Yet those who have once had a bed well filled with its rich and varied colors, will not willingly be without it afterward. The flowers are of the richest velvet-like texture, beautifully pencilled, and of scarlet, blue, purple, and yellow shades. The plants thrive best in a sandy loam. The seed may be sown in the open ground in spring, or the plants may be forwarded by sowing in a frame. They **may** be set out about six inches apart each way, in a bed devoted entirely to them. Planted in this way in a mass **they make a splendid** display, **flowering abundantly from August to October.**

THE TEN-WEEKS' STOCK.—**These** sweet-scented favorites are always welcome, and may **now** be had of every imaginable color. The seed may be sown in **a** frame in April, care being taken not to allow the plants to be drawn up by overcrowding or by being kept too close. If the young plants become drawn, the spikes of bloom will be very materially diminished in beauty. To prevent this, plenty of air must be given them while in the frame, and room given to each that **it may grow stocky.** The bed in **which** they are planted **out should be well enriched, and thoroughly** pulverized **to a good depth,. and the plants set about a foot apart** each **way.**

If seed be sown about the first **of July,** and the plants well **grown with a** stocky habit, they may be potted in the fall in rich loam, and will blossom finely in the house during the winter. Oftentimes they will continue to bloom, if set out in **the** open ground in the spring. The flowers are not all double, but **in a lot of** seedlings raised from good German seed, **more** than half will produce double flowers.

CLIMBING ANNUALS

IN every garden **there is a** suitable place for a few climbers, some screen to **be covered** with flowers, or fence or wall to be hid. We name **a few of** the Annuals most useful for such purposes.

THE CONVOLVULUS OR MORNING GLORY.—There is no occasion **to describe** this well known flower. Its rapid growth renders it a desirable and favorite climber. **It** will flourish in any good garden soil, and should be furnished with supports upon which to climb, as soon as it begins to run. The seed may be sown in the open border as soon as the weather becomes settled in spring. There are flowers of several shades of color, white striped with blue or violet, rose color, and lilac, and shades of bright and dark red.

THE DOLICHOS OR HYACINTH BEAN.—A very vigorous climber, attaining a height of twenty feet in a season. The flowers are purple, produced in spikes, and succeeded by shining purple pods. There is a white-flowered variety, but it is not as showy as the purple. It will not bear frosts, and the beans should not be planted before the ground gets warm.

THE GOURDS.—These are all tender Annuals, and require much the same treatment and soil as the Cucumber. Many of them are very ornamental. Some are yellow and green, striped with cream color; or half green and half yellow, striped with cream; or orange and red, or lemon-yellow, or orange-colored, &c., &c.

THE SWEET PEA.—If the seed be sown as soon as the ground can be worked in spring, this favorite climber will begin to bloom about the first of July. The seed should be sown about four inches deep in good soil, and the plants treated in the same manner as the common garden Pea. In order to keep up a profusion of bloom the pods should be gathered often, allowing only enough to ripen to supply seed for another year. The flowers are very fragrant, and of several colors, scarlet, scarlet striped with white, purple striped with white, rose and white, white and pink edged with blue, &c.

THE TROPEOLUM.—There are several varieties of the Tropeolum. They are all showy and profuse bloomers, producing flowers of several brilliant colors, as scarlet, dark orange, dark crimson, yellow, and some striped and spotted. *Tropeolum Majus*, and its varieties, grow well in rich sandy soil; the seed may be sown in the open ground when the weather becomes settled, or plants may be forwarded by sowing in a frame, and afterwards transplanted. *Tropeolum Peregrinum* is the well-known Canary Flower, producing an abundance of little canary-colored blossoms.

If the seed be planted in May, in light soil, the plants will grow rapidly, and bloom from July to October. *Tropeolum Lobbianum*, and its varieties, are not well adapted for out-door culture in our climate, but may be **grown as green-house climbers.**

EVERLASTING FLOWERS.

These are a special treasure to those who **do not** wish to undertake the care of **a** green-house, or who have no suitable exposure for window plants. They do not appear to any advantage in the garden when it is gay with summer flowers, but when wintry winds toss the seared leaves about the garden, or whirl the snows in blinding eddies above the flower beds, then the *Everlastings* play **an important part in the Christmas decorations,** and mingled with the ornamental grasses, make charming bouquets **of rare beauty.** Retaining both form and color, they may be **used for** the same purposes as fresh plucked flowers, but requiring no water to keep them fresh. They should be gathered just before they are fully expanded, tied loosely in small bunches—large bunches are apt to mildew—and hung up in the shade to **dry.** We have thought they retained their brightness **of color better** if laid away carefully in a drawer **as soon** as they are sufficiently dried, or hung in a dark closet.

ACROCLINIUM.—This is **one of the best.** There are pure white and bright rose-colored varieties. The seed may be sown in the open ground **after the** weather has become settled, and the plants **thinned** to about six or eight inches apart. The flowers should be cut just before they are fully expanded.

GOMPHRENA.—This is the Globe Amaranth or English Clover **of** many gardens. **The** seed grows best if started in a hot-bed, **or in a** box of fine earth in the kitchen. When the weather has **become** warm the plants may be set out about a foot apart in the **open** ground. The flowers of these should be allowed to remain on the plant until near the end of the summer, when they will have become fully developed. There are pure white, flesh-colored, dark purplish crimson, striped red and white, and orange-colored varieties.

Helichrysum.—The flowers are large and handsome, and should be cut just before they are fully expanded, and dried for winter use. The buds also are useful if preserved in the same way. The seed may be sown in the open border or in a cold frame, and the plants set out in June, about a foot apart. The *Helichrysum Monstrosum* produces larger flowers, and in its several varieties of double rose-colored, double red, double yellow, and double white, is the most desirable species.

Helipterum.—The species known as *Helipterum Sanfordii*, is exceedingly beautiful. The flowers are of a rich yellow color, produced in dense globular clusters, and make a very showy addition to our winter bouquets. It grows in any good garden soil, and the seed may be sown in the open border when the weather has become settled and warm. The flowers should be cut when at their best, and dried in the shade.

Rodanthe.—Another genus of Everlastings, producing most delicately beautiful flowers, which may be dried in the usual manner, and used in winter. The seed should be started in the house or a frame, and the plants set out after all danger of frost is over. It will grow best in a deep, rich soil.

Xeranthemum.—In order to have a few blue flowers to add to the winter's collection, it will be necessary to grow the *Xeranthemum Cœruleum*. The seed may be sown in a frame, or when the weather has become warm in the open border, and the plants set out eight or ten inches apart. They transplant easily, and grow in any light rich soil.

ORNAMENTAL GRASSES.

A few of these are very desirable to mingle with the Everlastings for winter decoration. Unfortunately, they will not retain their color, but nevertheless they are very beautiful. The following are among the most desirable.

Agrostis Nebulosa.—This is the most elegant variety, the panicles having a very graceful feathery appearance.

Briza Maxima.—A hardy shaking grass, very pretty. The seed may be sown as soon as the spring opens.

Erianthus Ravennæ.—A very pretty perennial grass, said to be hardy and well worth a trial. The spikes are silvery-white, plume-like, and graceful.

Pennisetum Longistilum and Fasciculatum.—Both of these are pretty and graceful, and help to give a pleasing variety to the collection.

Stipa Pennata.—Is truly magnificent. It does not flower until the second season, hence it must be carried through the winter before one can enjoy its beauty. We have not had good success in carrying it through the winter, and believe that our open winters are too severe for it. Probably it would thrive if it were well covered with snow through the winter.

WINDOW-GARDENING.

It is very pleasant to keep a few plants in the window, especially during the dreary months of winter, that one may have something bright and beautiful to look at, some pleasant reminder of sunny days and smiling blossoms. The following hints are written in the hope that they will help our friends in the pleasant task of caring for their window plants, and guide them to the selection of those that are best suited to such culture, and therefore more likely to afford them the pleasant gratification of healthy growth and abundance of bloom.

Plants will be most likely to thrive best in the south or east window. Our days are short, plants need light, and as we can give them at best only a few hours of light, it is important that there should be as much of brightness and warmth in it as can be furnished. If neither a south nor an east window can be had, then a west window is better than a north.

The room in which they are kept should be one which is not

subjected to great variations of temperature. If possible, the variation should be gradual, the atmosphere of the room becoming cooler as the daylight fades, and remaining cooler through the night, becoming warmer on the return of daylight, and warmest when the sun is shining in through the window. The night temperature should not be colder than 40° of Fahrenheit, and the thermometer should not be kept above 70° by day, except while the sun is shining into the room. It is better that the room should be one not usually occupied by the family in the evening, for at night we draw the curtains, stir up the fire, light the lamps or the gas, and usually increase the temperature several degrees above the average temperature of the day. But plants require that when the daylight fades the temperature should decline. Night is their time for rest, but they cannot rest if the temperature be kept as high or higher than it was during the day. The effect of such unnatural excitement upon plants is similar to that produced upon a human being by depriving him of his wonted sleep.

It is better that the room should be one that is not heated by a furnace. The air from furnaces is apt to be too dry and too hot. If it must be heated by a furnace, set a pail of water in the register, and at night shut off the heat so that the temperature may fall gradually to about 45° before morning.

Gas-lighted rooms are bad for plants. Enough gas escapes in the evening, unconsumed, though the flame may seem to be perfect, to kill delicate plants, and to injure materially the most robust. If they can not be kept out of such an atmosphere by closing a glazed door or sash, so as to shut them out from the air of the room, it would be better not to attempt their cultivation at all. In most houses the kitchen is the room in which plants will grow best. There they have a moist atmosphere, sufficient warmth by day, and cool temperature at night. Arrangements should be made for conveniently giving fresh air to the plants every day. The most convenient way is to have the upper sash moveable, and to let it down at the top when we wish to give fresh air, taking care that the plants are not allowed to stand in a draught of cold air. The quantity admitted at once should be proportioned to the weather outside; when it is very cold or frosty, admitting very little or none at all, but giving more when the weather is moderate, and **when the day is** very mild and bland, throwing the sash fully open. A plant confined in the house without fresh air, **will as** surely become sick and feeble as the child that is never suffered to run out-doors.

The leaves of plants need washing occasionally, in order to remove the dust that gathers on them and fills up the pores. In the open air this is done for them by the showers and rains, but in the house they get no showers from the skies, and we must in some way supply **their office. Geraniums and** other **plants** having **like soft** and hairy leaves, **are** best washed by taking them to the sink, **laying the pot on the** side, and syringing the foliage thoroughly through a fine rose. If you have not a garden syringe, the water may be poured upon them from a small watering pot with **a fine** sprinkler. Glossy-leaved plants, such as the Daphne, require to have the leaves cleaned off, one by one, with a moist sponge. The plants will thrive best if they get such a leaf-cleaning as often as once in each week. In all cases use soft water, rain water, or melted snow, and let it be lukewarm, not cold.

Watering house plants is very apt to be overdone. We deluge them in our kindness. **As a rule,** plants require more water when **they** are in bloom or growing rapidly that at any other time. **Of course,** aquatic plants, like the Calla, will thrive with abundant watering, while those that have their home in arid soils, like the Cactus, require almost none at all. Study, **then,** the natural habits of the plant you are growing, and **examine the** condition of the soil in the pot, and adapt your waterings to the requirements of **the plant.** It is not certain that it requires any water at **all,** merely because it is twenty-four hours since you last watered it. Therefore use your judgment as to whether water be needed, and act accordingly.

If you pot the plants yourself, be careful to secure perfect drainage. If purchased in pots from a gardener who understands his business, this matter will have been attended to by him. In potting yourself, use only clean pots; if your pots are not clean, let them first be thoroughly washed. Use only those that are porous, and avoid glazed and painted pots. If the unglazed pots are unsightly in your eyes, they may be set inside of a glazed or painted pot, leaving space for air between the inner and outer pot, or a pot screen may be set outside the pot. These screens may be had of our florists, of any desired color. In potting, first place a bit of broken pot over the hole in the bottom, then fill in an inch or so of potsherds, and cover these with a little moss; upon this fill in the soil and set the plant. The best soil is made of well-rotted turf, mixed with about one-third of old manure, and enough sharp sand to make it perfectly friable. Through such a soil the water percolates readily. If the pots stand in saucers, pour off the water that runs into them, and not allow it to be soaked up again into the pot.

It is a very common error in window gardening to attempt too much at once. Too many plants are crowded into the little space at command, so that it is impossible to give to each the air and light it ought to have. Besides this, plants of too diverse a character are sought to be grown in the same window. It is by no means uncommon to see inexperienced lovers of flowers attempting to grow, in the same window with plants from the temperate zone, those plants which require very high temperature, and possibly also Alpine plants, which require a very low temperature. It is simply impossible to make plants of such diverse habits thrive under such treatment, and there is no satisfaction in attempting what must end in failure. It is productive of much more pleasure to grow one plant well, to see it covered with healthy foliage and well-developed flowers, than to grow a windowful of sickly things.

The following list comprises the names of some of the most suitable plants for window culture. From among these a selection may be made of those that seem to be **desirable**. Do not undertake to grow them all, but choose those you like best, and give them plenty of room and the needed care.

The Daphne makes a charming window plant, and if any will thrive in a west window, **this** will. It **is** an evergreen shrub, producing bunches of sweetly fragrant **white** or pinkish flowers on the ends of the branches. The pot in which it is grown should be filled one-third full of broken crocks, so as to secure perfect drainage. The leaves should be kept perfectly clean. While the plant is growing it should be freely watered, and the temperature maintained at about seventy degrees by day, to about forty-five degrees by night.

The Heliotrope is a **very great favorite,** on account **of the profusion of bloom and the delicious fragrance of** its flowers. It should be encouraged to grow **large, by** giving it plenty of pot **room and plenty of** window room. It may be pruned and **trained into** any desired form.

Monthly Roses, especially the tea-scented, are beautiful window plants. They need rich soil, thorough drainage, frequent washing of the foliage with a fine rosed syringe, as even a temperature as possible, carefully guarding from draughts of cold air, and smoking with tobacco if the green **fly makes** its appearance. They should have the morning sun, but **be shaded** from the afternoon sun when it has become powerful.

A list of some of the best in this class will be found under the head of Monthly Roses, in that part of the book which treats of Roses.

Hyacinths **make beautiful** window plants grown either **in** pots filled with soil, or in moss, or in water. They should be kept in a dark cellar, free from frost, until well **rooted,** and then **placed in** the window to bloom. As soon as the flowers begin to expand, the plants will require abundant watering. If kept **in a low** temperature, say sixty-five degrees, the flowers will last much longer.

The Cyclamen is especially suited for window culture. The

bulbs should be planted in pots in November, in a rich loam, intermingled with a little pulverized charcoal, with the crown of the bulb just peeping through the surface of the soil. They should be kept in a cool atmosphere and close to the glass, until the leaves are well grown and the flower buds begin to appear; then they should be removed to a somewhat warmer atmosphere and a sunny window. The variety known as C. Persicum has white flowers tipped with rosy purple, and will bloom from January to March. When the bloom is over, water should be gradually withheld, and when the foliage dies off they may be stored away in the cellar, in some place where the mice will not get them, until next November.

THE IVY may be grown in any part of the room. The pots may be placed on the floor, and the plants so trained as to festoon a window or arch a door-way, or to wreath a picture-frame or mirror. They require to be watered often, yet the water must not be allowed to stand about the roots. There are varieties with golden and silver variegated leaves; others with lobed, or palmate, or heart-shaped leaves. All are pretty, grow rapidly, and endure the heat of our sitting-rooms, with their dust and extremes of temperature, and want of light, in a most astonishing manner.

VERBENAS.—If cuttings are taken off and struck in the last days of July, potting them first in "thumbs," and shifting into larger as soon as the roots have reached the sides, so as to keep the plants in vigorous growth, they may be made to bloom finely in the window all winter. After the cuttings are rooted, and during the summer and fall, until the flowers are wanted, every flower head should be nipped off as soon as it makes its appearance, and the leading shoots should be pinched in so as to give the plants a bushy form. They may be kept in the open air until severe frosts make it necessary to take them in. There is danger from over watering, and the Aphis, or Green-fly, is apt to become troublesome. A little attention in watering, and an occasional smoking with tobacco, will overcome these difficulties. The Verbena requires plenty of light and air.

ZONAL AND SCENTED-LEAVED GERANIUMS make good **window** plants, provided they can have plenty of light, plenty of air, and a moderate temperature. They **do not bear** crowding nor excess **of water.** They should be kept **as** near the glass as may be, and the plants frequently turned **so as to** expose all sides alike to the light. Some of the **very** finest varieties of recent introduction are mentioned in their proper place, under the head of Bedding Plants, and from **these** the cultivator may make selections of such colors of flower and foliage as may be preferred.

ROSES.

Fortunately it is **not our province** to tell of the beauty of **the** Rose. That has been told by more gifted votaries, both in song and story. **Ours is the humble duty to** tell how best to care for this Queen **of** Flowers, **how** her admiring attendants may win her brightest smiles, and see her come forth " with royal beauty bright."

Everybody admires the Rose, everybody grows the Rose, but **it is** not everyone that grows Roses. Perfect success in the cultivation of the Rose, is the outcome of a devotion that ever burns but never consumes. Down in the depths of the heart it glows **ever. Winter's** snows never **chill** it, clouds and storms never damp its ardor. With loving tenderness the true subject waits constantly upon his Queen, **never** remitting his attention even in the " sere and **yellow leaf," but** tending her as lovingly as when budding into **beauty, or** glowing in all the splendor of queenly majesty. Only they **who are** filled with such a spirit will grow Roses.

The Canadian cultivator **has his own peculiar soil and climate.** These **have** their influence upon **the work** of Rose-growing, but though **they** present some difficulties, they are by no means **insuperable.** A careful attention to the requirements of the Rose, **and a judicious** selection of those varieties best adapted to the peculiar conditions of our position, will enable us to achieve most gratifying results. It is hoped that the following hints, the results of some years of experience, will prove of value to those Canadian culturists who "have beautiful roses in their hearts."

In choosing a site for the Rose ground, it is very desirable that a place should be selected that is sheltered from the sweep of high winds. Yet in making such a selection, proximity to growing trees should be avoided, lest the tree-roots running into the Rose-ground rob the Roses of their proper nutriment. If possible, let groups of evergreens stand between the royal residence and the caves of Boreas, not necessarily in unbroken hedge, but rather in such form that the force of storms shall be broken, and the winds, tempered by sifting through the evergreen boughs, shall move among the Rose trees in gentle breezes.

The Rose grounds require to be open to the sun during the early part of the day, but such is the fierceness of his noon-day heat, in our climate, that the flowers, when exposed to its full power, very soon lose their freshness and become scorched and discolored. If the grounds can be selected where the shadows of buildings or tall trees will fall on them soon after mid-day, the flowers will continue much longer in their freshness and beauty. There is, however, a difficulty in doing this in our latitude, owing to the nearly vertical position of the noon-day sun. If the Rose trees be planted near enough to large evergreens or other trees, to be shaded by them at noon from a June or July sun, they will be so near as to be injuriously affected by their roots. Yet the remoter vicinity of such trees on the south-west and west will modify the heat somewhat, while a good thick mulch upon the surface of the ground will keep the roots moist and cool, and in this way preserve the flowers considerably by keeping up an abundant flow of sap. But the sun should never be wholly excluded. Better that the Roses have the sunshine all the day long than be kept in constant shadow. As the day declines, the trees that form the barrier to the sweep of westerly winds, will cast their lengthening shadows over the Rose beds, and give them some hours of repose before the night comes on. If possible, let the morning sun greet them with his earliest beams, and the shadows fall upon them as soon **as can be after** the meridian is passed.

The soil most congenial to the **Rose is** a well drained, clayey **loam,** and if abounding in lime, so much the **better.** It needs to **be** well enriched, indeed it can hardly be **made too rich. In such a soil** all the strong-growing Roses will **luxuriate.** The weaker-growing varieties will prefer a proportionably lighter soil, but a dry, gravelly soil, **or** a thin, sandy one, is a poor soil in which to grow fine Roses. Such soils require to be considerably improved by a very liberal mixture of **sods** from an old pasture, composted with an equal quantity of **manure. Clayey soils,** having a **yet more tenacious sub-soil, will require to be well** under-drained, by **putting down a few tile three to four feet below** the surface, **if** there be sufficient fall at the **outlet. A small bed** may be very cheaply under-drained, when one does not wish to under-drain the whole garden, by sinking a pit near the lower **side** of the Rose bed, and filling it with stone, into which the drain from the bed may be maded to empty. It will, of course, be necessary to dig the pit large enough and deep enough to **take all the** water that will run into it.

If the soil be very heavy and tenacious, **it may be** rendered more friable, and therefore better suited to the culture of anything, **by burning a portion of** it slowly and then returning it to the bed and thoroughly mixing it with the unburnt soil. By gathering a pile of small **sticks,** and intermingling with these some knotty bits or tough **roots** and stumps, and setting them on fire, and then covering the heap with the clay, so that the burning pile shall smoulder away slowly, the tenacious character **will be taken from** the clay, and it will be made an excellent fertilizer. The fire should not be allowed to burn fiercely, but clay added as **often as it** breaks out, and the whole kept in a state of slow combustion, after the manner of a charcoal pit. With this burnt clay may be added coarse barn-yard manure, until the soil becomes **loamy and friable. Where** snows do not keep out the frosts, these will do much towards rendering the ground mellow, if it be thrown up loose and rough in the autumn and exposed to their action.

Very light soils may be improved by the addition of clay. This is sometimes to be found within a spade's depth of the surface, and only needs to be turned up and mingled with the lighter earth to bring it to the desired texture. When it does not exist in the sub-soil, it may be brought from some convenient place and incorporated with the bed. If it can be had in the form of sods, and these composted with manure until the whole be thorougly rotted, it will be the very best material.

These are the extremes which will require to be ameliorated, but, in by far the greater number of our gardens there is only need of selecting a favorable spot, where the rough winds can not come with rude bluster, but where the breezes play gently with the flowers, and the sun shines brightly all the morning. There, with a little extra care in stirring the soil to a good depth, not mingling the bottom with the top unless required to improve the texture, and by adding a good supply of manures, a favorable bed may be formed in which to plant the Rose, and grow and bloom it in perfection.

The best manure for the Rose is that which, fortunately, is most accessible to all. It is that of the farm-yard, where the droppings from the stable are thrown out, mingled with the litter of the bedding, and the horned cattle trample it under foot, and the pigs work it over with their tireless rooting. If the soil be strong clay, with a somewhat too tenacious tendency, it may be well applied when about half-rotted, as the undecomposed straw helps to loosen the soil, and make it more porous and friable. If the soil be of a lighter tendency, the manure should be more thoroughly decomposed. In those parts of the Dominion where the winters are open and the ground often bare, it will be of great benefit to apply a liberal dressing to the surface in the fall, allowing it to remain as a mulch until spring, when it may be forked into the soil. This mulch will protect the roots from severe freezing, and the tops being able to draw upon the roots for moisture, to supply that which is evaporated from their surfaces by the frosty winds, suffer much less from extremes of cold than when the roots are held in frozen earth. Again, when the flower-buds are making themselves prominent, we are so often liable to suffer from insufficient rainfall and hot sunshine, that a good mulch of manure is exceedingly valuable in keeping the roots cool and moist, and supplying them with food at a time when it is much needed to perfect the nascent Roses. If such a mulch would be unsightly, it may be concealed by a covering of fresh mown grass. If the ground be not mulched, it should be kept loose and friable upon the surface, by frequent stirring with the pronged hoe.

Planting may be done either in the fall or spring, as may be most convenient. If it be done in the fall, the roots should be protected from frosts. If the snow cannot be depended on for this protection, the surface of the ground may be deeply mulched with a covering of strawy manure, sufficiently thick to exclude the frost. In addition to this a few evergreen branches may be laid over them, or the butts thrust into the ground around them, so as to shelter the stems and branches from the sun and drying winds, to the great benefit of the Rose trees. If done in the spring, the ground should be mulched in the same manner, to prevent the soil from becoming too dry in summer.

If the Rose trees are on their own roots, that is, not budded nor grafted, they should be planted so as to stand at the same depth in the ground as they did previously, when the newly disturbed soil has become settled to its place. But if the Roses are budded or grafted, they should be planted so that the place of union with the stock will be two or three inches below the surface. It is necessary in our climate to cover the point of union between the scion and stock deep enough in the soil to protect it from the hot, drying suns of summer, and severe frosts of winter.

In budding Roses the buds should be inserted as close to the ground as possible, so that, in order to cover the place of union, it may not be necessary to thrust the roots into the cold subsoil when they are transplanted. When the stock is so long, that in order to cover the place of union, it would be necessary to place the lower roots deep in the sub-soil, we prefer, if the root will at all admit of it, to cut off a portion of the lower part of the root, rather than to plant it so deep as to be below the reach of the requisite degree of warmth. The stock, when thus planted in the ground, will throw out roots throughout its entire length, and even the bud or graft will itself sometimes emit roots from the portion below the surface.

It sometimes happens, that by a combination of untoward circumstances, the Rose tree is killed back by the winter quite to the ground. If the point of union be above the ground, the Rose tree is wholly lost, for though sprouts may come up from the stock, the Roses it will give are not the Roses the cultivator wants; but if the place of union be a few inches below the surface, there is a probability that a sprout will be thrown up from the scion, and so the desired variety be preserved.

It is important that all sprouts which may come up from the stock should be promptly removed. If they are allowed to grow they will soon rob the scion of its proper nourishment, and in a short time choke it to death. The stock most commonly used for budding upon is the Manetti Rose, and the shoots may be readily distinguished from those of the scion by their peculiar reddish color, and the glossy green of the leaf. These sprouts should not be cut off at the surface of the ground, but carefully broken off from the stock. This may be done by loosening the soil a little, and crowding a forked or notched stick down upon the shoot until it is torn off from the stock. If cut off so that any part of the base of the shoot remains upon the stock, it will surely send up more sprouts from the same place.

The use of the Manetti is necessary in the case of new varieties, else, if recourse could not be had to budding, it would be a long time before we could hope to have the pleasure of seeing them **in our own** grounds. Besides this facility of **propagation and** dissemination, which is obtained by budding on the Manetti, there are some varieties which emit roots so feebly **that** they are grown with difficulty on their own roots, but when **worked on** Manetti stocks they grow luxuriantly, and bloom in profusion. Many varieties, **also, will produce** much finer flowers when grown on Manetti stocks than **on their own** roots. Yet, these advantages are at the cost of some care, lest shoots and suckers from the stock should be permitted to grow and choke out the Rose.

The further cultivation will consist chiefly in keeping the ground loose and friable, free from all grass and weeds, **and** protecting the roots from the severe frosts of winter and droughts of summer by **a suitable mulch.** If the summer mulch be three **or four inches of well-decomposed stable manure,** and the coarser mulch **of winter be worked into the soil** in spring, the Rose **ground will** be kept, **as it must be to** secure fine blooms, well **enriched.** Yet once in three or four years it will be found to **be of** great advantage to give the Rose grounds some fresh soil **formed** of well-rotted sods, which have **been** gathered and composted in the manner already mentioned. This may be spread on the surface, **to the depth of three or four inches, in the** spring, **and** forked in with the winter's mulch. **If it be** likely to raise the **bed too** high, a few shovelsful of the old soil may be removed as occasion **may require.**

Pruning **the Rose should never** be done in our climate in the fall. Somehow the wounds **of** the pruning-knife seem to open a door for the frost to enter; be that as it may, **experience** has taught us that Rose trees pruned in the fall are very sure to suffer from the winter, even while those that are unpruned **escape.** The best time to prune is early in the spring, after **severe** freezing weather is past, and before the sap is in active **circulation.** Pruning should be suited to the variety of Rose **under the knife.** Roses of very vigorous habit of growth should be moderately **pruned, for** if they are severely cut back they will rush into great **wood growth and give** but little bloom. On the contrary, those of feeble growth require to be cut back severely, in order that the root may be **able to** supply the remaining buds with sufficient sap to make them push vigorously, and cause the roses it does bear to be fully developed in size and form.

A little attention to the several varieties, and the peculiar **habits of each, will soon teach** the observing cultivator the pruning **requisite** in each case. There should be sufficient shortening in to proportion the quantity of bloom to the strength of the plant, so that the plant may not be weakened by excess of bloom, and so that the Roses may be all well developed. Beyond this, and a little thinning out occasionally of over-crowding branches, the Rose will not need much pruning to keep it in shape.

The form of Rose tree best suited to our climate is that of a low bush. Both the heat of summer and the cold of winter bear very injuriously upon tall standards. At best they are short-lived with us. By careful pruning they may be grown as pyramids, clothed with branches from the ground, like a well-formed Norway Spruce. The pruning necessary to form a pyramid is best done by pinching in the leader during the growing season, so as to develop the lower buds, cut back the following spring to four or five buds, train one as a leader, and the others horizontally; pinch the leader again, and the following season cut back as before, repeating this operation until the desired form and size are attained. But after all, the bush form is easier obtained, and is quite as satisfactory, besides being measurably exempt from the accidents which so often mar any attempts at more formal training. If the Rose trees are planted in a bed, the strongest and tallest growers may be planted in the centre, and those of shorter habit arranged in front and around them, in something like regular gradation, with the more dwarfish growths in the front rank. This will give the appearance of a bank of Roses.

There are a few insect enemies of the Rose that may require attention. In our own experience the Rose-slug has been the most annoying. It feeds upon the softer parts of the leaves, eating out all **the green** portion and leaving them skeletonized, thus giving **the** Rose trees a most unsightly appearance. **This** insect **usually** appears just as the flowers are beginning to open, **and when there is** a great number of them, the whole bush is **soon over-run, and** all the **leaves** destroyed. We have found **the use of white** hellebore, applied in the same manner as recommended **for the** Gooseberry **Saw-fly,** sure destruction to them. The hellebore was stirred into the water in the morning, allowed **to stand** until about sundown, and then applied with a sprinkler **from a** common watering-pot. This is a very convenient and cheap means of getting rid of these disgusting slugs.

In some seasons the Aphis or Green-fly become very numerous, completely covering the ends of the young shoots, and sucking out the **sap. They increase very** rapidly, and should not **be** neglected. **The little** Leaf-hopper also will appear in thousands sometimes, **and** feeding on the underside of the leaves, cause very **serious injury** by their operations. The Leaf-hopper that affects **the** Grape Vine is figured and described at page 112 of the **Report** of the Fruit Growers' Association of Ontario for 1870, **and** so similar are its habits to those of the Rose Leaf-hopper, **that** what is there said concerning that insect will apply equally **well to** this.

The best means with which to combat both the Aphis and the Leaf-hopper is, frequent syringing with strong tobacco water. This is sure destruction to the Aphis, and tolerably efficient upon the Leaf-hopper. **We** have been nearly exempt from the Leaf-hopper since we have used **the** white hellebore in water for the slugs, but, whether **their** decrease is owing to the hellebore or to one of **those** periodical diminutions in their number, arising from the **operation** of unknown **causes,** to which they **are** subject, we are **as yet unable** to say.

The Rose-bug is a small beetle **which feeds** upon the leaves. They are **very** destructive, and when suffered to live, soon become **very numerous,** and exceedingly troublesome. They will feed **not only upon the** Rose, **but** upon the Grape Vine, the Cherry tree, the **Plum and the Apple**. They laugh at whale-oil **soap** and decoctions of tobacco; **they get fat** upon all the applications hitherto made for **their destruction**. Whether they can **eat white hellebore with impunity we can not say**, not having made trial of their powers of digesting it. The only known **remedy is** that of picking **them** off and crushing **them**. Fortunately they are of a **sluggish habit**, and are easily caught.

And now we come to the Roses themselves. We shall **not weary our readers with long** disquisitions on classification. **Those who are curious on these points,** may read **some of the books in which this matter is fully** discussed, **but since hybridists have taken the Rose in hand, the old lines of distinction have been nearly obliterated. It is quite** enough for our purpose, **and that of our** readers, **to group** them under a few natural divisions. We **have therefore adopted the following,** as, on the whole, the **most convenient division, and group them under,** Climbing, Summer, **Autumnal, and Monthly Roses.**

CLIMBING ROSES.—In our climate, we must content ourselves with the hardy Prairie Roses, or those which have a large infusion of prairie blood. We can not grow Gloire de Dijon in the open air, nor climbing Devoniensis, nor, alas, **that glory of** Yellow Roses, Marechal **Niel,** when trained above the snow line. But the coarser Prairie Roses will **endure the climate in a large** part of the Dominion. They are strong, rapid growers, having luxuriant **foliage** and great abundance of bloom. The flowers are borne in large clusters, and **open in succession,** so that the plant is in **bloom** for a considerable **time.** The season of blooming is a little later than that of the great mass of our Roses, so that they **come into** full bloom just **as the other varieties** are passing away.

Queen of the Prairie.—This is probably the **best of** the family, being hardy and luxuriant. The color of the flowers is a bright **rosy-red, the** form, globular **and somewhat cupped,** of good size, and produced in great **profusion. They are** without scent, and their **beauty is not in the individual flowers, but in** the mass of **bloom.**

Baltimore Belle.—Not quite as hardy as the preceding, the extremities of the young shoots suffering in **extremely severe** winters, **but the** Roses, which it yields in great profusion, **are most** delicately beautiful. In color they are white, suffused with **a soft** tint of blush ; quite double, and borne in very full clusters.

Gem of the Prairies.—This is a new variety of much promise, and though it has not yet been widely disseminated, and consequently not yet submitted to a very thorough test in our climate, it seems, so far as it has been tried, to be as hardy **as** the Queen of the Prairie. It is claimed to be the product of cross fertilization, between that hardy climber and Madam Laffay, which **is** also a hardy **Rose.** The color of the flower is **a** light crimson, with occasionally **a white blotch ; it is of large** size, **perfectly** double, **and fragrant.**

These three are the most desirable varieties for cultivation in **our climate. Those of** the **Ayrshire** family will do very well to **run over a** bank, where they will get some protection from the snow, and by their proximity to the ground be somewhat sheltered. **The** best of these is the *Queen of the Belgians*, which is a pure white, and will flourish even in a poor soil.

SUMMER ROSES.—Under this head is grouped **all the Roses,** of whatever origin, which make no pretensions to being also autumnal bloomers. It contains some very beautiful roses, well **worthy of being retained in every garden.** The very best only are mentioned in the descriptions which follow, no one of which should **be left out of any general** collection.

Aureti.—This is a very dark medium-sized rose ; when newly opened **it is of a** blackish purple, with rich velvety petals. **It is** globular in form, **and** perfectly double.

Boule de Nanteuil.—A large crimson-purple flower, the centre sometimes fiery purple. It is a very handsome, showy Rose.

Cabbage, or, Common Provence.—Probably this is the oldest Rose in cultivation, the **Rose we have all** played with in childhood, the thought of which is fraught with many memories. And it is one of our prettiest Roses still, double as a hundred petals can make it, fair and fresh with the tint of blushes, lovely in itself and lovely in its **sweet and tender** associations.

Coupe de Hebe.—It is impossible to convey in words any just conception of the beautiful coloring **of this Rose.** In form it is most handsomely cupped, and **the bright glossy** pink coloring of the petals seems to be heightened by a **reflection from one petal to the other, as we look** down into the depths of **the flower.**

Charles Lawson.—A large, **showy** flower, very full, the color a clear vivid rose. **It blooms very** abundantly, **and makes a gorgeous** display.

Duchess of Buccleugh.—**An** exceedingly **beautiful Rose, of** large size and full form. Its color is a dark rose, with a **blush** margin.

Kean.—This **magnificent, rich,** velvety-purple flower, with **scarlet centre, is one of the very best** of the dark-colored Roses, **and makes a most delightful contrast with the** lighter colors.

Madam Plantier and Madam Hardy.—**It is not an easy task to make up one's mind to do without either of these. They are both white, and both beautiful. Madam Plantier blooms in** clusters, and in great profusion; Madam **Hardy has fewer** flowers, but they are larger. **Of** the two Madam Plantier is the more hardy plant, though neither can be called **tender.**

Paul Ricaut.—Is of **a beautiful, bright,** rosy crimson color, **of large size,** full, and deservedly ranks among our very best.

Persian Yellow.—**The best** of the Austrian Roses. The flowers are very **double,** of a deep golden yellow, not large, **but** full. It is among **the earliest in bloom.**

Vivid.—This Rose **is a very** vigorous grower, **and** makes a grand display when covered with its rich, **vivid** crimson flowers.

There is another Summer Rose, which looks more like a **striped** Carnation than a Rose, that has seemed, **in** the writer's experience **with it, to** lack vigor of constitution, but which is **worthy of attention, on account** of its being so beautifully **striped. It is** *Œillet Parfait.* There is a very distinct and very constant variegation of crimson and white stripes in the flower, which makes it exceedingly attractive.

MOSS ROSES.—Naturalists say that the Moss Rose is a sport from the common Provence Rose. Perhaps it is; but the following account by a German writer may help us to know how that sport was produced:

> "The Angel of the flowers one day
> Beneath a Rose-tree sleeping lay;
> That Spirit to whose charge is given
> To bathe young buds in dews from heaven:
> Awaking from his light repose,
> The Angel whispered to the Rose;
> 'O fondest object of my care,
> Still fairest found where all are fair
> For the sweet shade thou'st given to me,
> Ask what thou wilt, 'tis granted thee.
> 'Then,' said the Rose, with deepened glow,
> 'On me another grace bestow.'
> The Spirit paused in silent thought;
> What grace was there that flower had not?
> 'Twas but a moment;—o'er the Rose
> A veil of moss the Angel throws;
> And, robed in nature's simplest weed,
> Could there a flower that Rose exceed?"

The Moss Roses require the richest soil and most liberal culture possible, in order to have them in perfection.

Common Moss.—The oldest and the best of them all. The flowers are large, full, clear rose, and the half-opened buds beautifully covered with moss.

Crested.—The Calyx of this Rose is most singularly edged with a mossy fringe, which gives the buds a very pleasing appearance. Beyond this it has no mossy covering. The flowers resemble in form and color the common Provence.

Glory of the Mosses.—The flower-buds are very mossy. The Roses are of a deep blush, very large and full.

Laneii.—The flowers are of a brilliant, rosy-crimson color, and very handsomely formed. The plant is a vigorous, healthy grower, with fine, clear foliage.

Luxembourg.—A large, purplish-crimson flower; the plant of a very luxuriant habit of growth, yet blooming freely.

Nuits de Young.—A very dark, velvety-purple flower, quite different from any other of the Moss Roses, and a very desirable variety.

AUTUMNAL ROSES.—These are also known as *Remontants* or *Hybrid Perpetuals.* Their distinctive character should be, that they give an autumnal bloom in addition to the midsummer flowering, but many that are placed in this class yield very few autumn flowers. It is a difficult matter to give a selection of the very best out of such an endless number. Yet the following names are given, having reference to variety of coloring, as comprising the most valuable of those in general cultivation. In making this selection, reference is also had to the constitutional vigor and hardihood, and preference given rather to those that make a fine garden display, than those that are best suited for exhibition. We have not yet attained to that general enthusiasm in the cultivation of the Rose that demands a Provincial Rose Show, where each flower is most critically examined. Yet, some of these names have won distinguished laurels in more than one well contested trial; and those who have opportunity to exhibit, can make selection from among these of those that, if well grown, it will be hard to beat.

In order to obtain an abundant autumnal bloom, it will be necessary to cut off a part of the summer bloom as soon as the flower-buds form. By taking off half of the summer flowers, and cutting back the branches to three or four buds, as soon as the flowers fade, the plant will start into a new growth, and the autumn bloom be much increased.

But in our climate this second growth, thus induced, does not always ripen well enough to endure our winters, and in consequence, the plant is often severely killed back by the cold. Hence, the forcing out of a full autumnal display may be dangerous to the life of the plant.

But above all must it be borne in mind, that in order to

grow these **Roses in** perfection, they must have the very **highest** and most liberal culture. True, most of them will show **something of beauty** under a tolerable **measure of care, but our flower Queen** puts on her royal robes only in response to loving **care,** and if we would grow Roses that will challenge the attention of every passer-by, and compel **him to** pause and admire, we must cultivate them thoroughly.

Achille Gonod.—Bright reddish-carmine, very large and full. Gives a very fine mid-summer bloom.

Baron Haussman.—Bright dark-red; fine form, large and full, one of the very best.

Boule de Neige.—Pure white; fine form, good habit, hardy and free bloomer **in the autumn.**

Comtesse de Chabrilliant.—Beautifully cupped; large, **full, very sweet, pink color; blooms** finely in midsummer.

Charles Lefebvre.—Bright crimson; large, **very double; one of the best** for exhibition.

Charles Verdier.—Rose bordered with white, very full and large, fine form and good habit.

Dr. Lindley.—Crimson, with black centre, very large and full, exceedingly showy.

Duchesse de Caylus.—Brilliant carmine, large, full, perfect in form, makes a fine display in the garden.

Duke of Edinburgh.—Brilliant scarlet crimson, shaded with maroon, large and full; a most gorgeous flower.

Fisher Holmes.—Reddish scarlet, shaded with deep velvety crimson, large and very brilliant.

Felix Genero.—Beautiful violet Rose, large, of good form and very showy **in the** garden.

Gloire de Ducher.—Purple, illuminated with crimson and scarlet, extra large, blooming well in autumn; one of the best.

John Hopper.—Rosy crimson, **large and** full, color deeper in **the centre,** very attractive.

Lord Macaulay.—Rich clouded crimson, large and full, petals of great substance.

Le Rhone.—Dark vermilion, rich and brilliant, large, **full**, and of good form; **one** of the best.

Marechal Vaillant.—Vivid red, **with** a shade of purple, large, full, and showy.

Maurice Bernardine.—Clear vermilion, petals handsomely **imbricated**, flowers large and showy.

Madam Fillion.—Fine salmon rose **color, large, finely** formed, one of the best.

Madam Rival.—Beautiful clear satin Rose, **large**, handsomely cupped, blooming well **in** the autumn.

Monsieur de Pontbriant.—Dark crimson, **shaded with** carmine, very large and full, **plant vigorous.**

Madame Alfred de Rougemont.—Pure white, **delicately** shaded with rose, medium size. A charming flower, blooms **well** in the fall.

Madame la Baronne de Rothschild.—Clear pale rose, shaded **with white,** very large, a fine exhibition **flower,** one of the best of its color.

Madame Marie Cirodde.—Beautiful rosy pink, **large, full, handsomely imbricated, one of the best.**

Mademoiselle Annie Wood.—Fine, clear red, large flower, and abundant autumn bloomer.

Prince Camille de Rohan.—Dark crimson maroon, very rich, velvety petals, blooms best at midsummer.

Pierre Notting.—Very dark red, shaded with violet, very large, full, **blooming** well in the fall; one of the best.

Pitord.—Fiery red, velvety, large and full; a fine autumnal bloomer.

Prince de **Porcia.**—**Bright** vermilion, large, fine form, showy and beautiful; one of the best.

Prince Humbert.—A very dark violet red, velvety appearance, large, and of fine form and good habit.

Senateur Vaisse.—One of the most superb, color brilliant red, large and showy.

Souvenir de Dr. Jamin.—**Fine bluish** violet, large, of fine form, and free fall flowering.

Souvenir de Ponsard.—Metallic rose, flamed **with scarlet**, large **and full; one** of the best.

Souvenir de William Wood.—**Dark maroon**, shaded **with scarlet, large** and very showy; a good autumnal bloomer.

Thorin.—Deep dark rose, large, full, and of fine form; very showy in the garden.

William Griffith.—Rosy **lilac, large size, vigorous** habit, a good autumn bloomer.

Xavier Olibo.—Velvety black, shaded with amaranth, large and full, blooms freely in the fall; one of the best.

We have limited the number to three **dozen,** and in doing so have been obliged **to** leave out many good Roses, because, for one reason and another, those **named were to be preferred.** Géant des batailles is subject to mildew, General Jacqueminot loose **and** open, La Reine does not always expand well; and yet **those who** have room for them will grow them with pleasure.

Some attempts have been made to obtain Moss Roses yielding **an** autumnal bloom, but thus far without any marked success. The best of the Autumnal Mosses are *Madame Edouard Ory,* bright rosy carmine; and *Salet,* bright rose, large and full.

Monthly Roses.—These Roses are all too tender to endure exposure to our winters, but they can be grown in the garden in summer, taken up on the approach of winter, the roots buried in a box of earth, and then placed in a **cool** cellar until the return of spring. Or, they may be grown in pots in the greenhouse or **in the window.** They bloom almost continuously, and it is owing to the infusion of the blood of some of these with the hardy Roses, that we now have the autumnal blooming **section.** Under this title we group those known as Bourbons, **Teas,** Noisettes, &c., merely denoting them in the **list by the initial letter** of the family to which they are supposed to belong.

Alba Rosea, T.—White with rose-colored centre, flower large **and full,** and very sweet scented.

Archimede, T.—A large full Rose, **of** a light blush color, **with** a salmon shade, very fragrant

Bougere, T.—A fine Rose for pot culture, very large and full, color deep rosy bronze.

Devoniensis, T.—Pale yellow, centre a deeper shade, of very large size, full; a good pot rose.

Emotion, B.—A very pretty, exceedingly free flowering Rose, white, delicately tinted with rose, form perfect.

Gloire de Dijon, T.—Yellow, shaded with **salmon**, very large and full, vigorous habit.

Marechal Niel, T.—The most beautiful deep yellow Rose, large and full, globular in form, very sweet scented. It has a rambling habit, and should not be very closely pruned; makes a fine green-house climber.

Lamarque, N.—A beautiful pale yellow flower, very large and full, grows well in a pot, or as a green-house climber.

Madame Villermoz, T.—An excellent Rose for pot culture, of free growth, white, with salmon centre, large and full.

Modele de Perfection, B.—A very pretty flower, of a lively pink color, blooms freely, and thrives well in a pot.

Madame Margottin, T.—A large dark citron yellow Rose, with a deeper shade in the centre, large and globular, and a free bloomer.

Niphetos, T.—A very large full Rose, of a very pale lemon color, sometimes white, grows well in pots.

President, T.—This has given great satisfaction in pot culture, blooming almost constantly. The flowers are large, rose color, shaded with salmon, and of fine form.

Rev. H. Dombrain, B.—A large carmine Rose, handsomely cupped, and blooming very freely.

Souvenir d' Elise Vardon, T.—Excellent for pot culture, very large, creamy white, with a yellowish centre.

Souvenir de Malmaison, B.—A very large, full and beautiful Rose, of a clear flesh color, with a shade of fawn, does well in a pot.

Souvenir d' un Ami, T.—A favorite flower, much like President in color, but with a deeper salmon tint; large and full, excellent for pot culture.

Triomphe de Guillot Fils, T.—One of the best, sweet scented, very large and full, color white, delicately shaded with rose and salmon.

The foregoing are, perhaps, the best we have; newer sorts, as *Adrienne Christophle, Belle Lyonnaise, Madame Levet,* &c., have not yet been sufficiently tested here to speak confidently of their merits.

CLIMATIC VARIATIONS.

There is a great variety of climate within the boundaries of our Dominion, which necessarily affects the cultivation of Fruits, and places certain limitations upon the variety of ornamental plants that may be used in the adornment of grounds, and of vegetables wherewith to supply the table. In addition to what has already been said upon the hardihood of the several varieties, it may be profitable to take a general survey of the variations in climate which obtain in the several Provinces, and of their effect upon horticulture.

In the Province of Ontario, there is a strip of land lying between Lakes Erie and Ontario, and along the northern shore of Lake Erie and the southern shore of Lake Huron, where the Peach can be successfully grown in the open air. This is owing to the influence which those large bodies of water exert upon the temperature. It follows that all other plants as hardy as the Peach can be grown within these limits, hence we find here the Heart and Bigarreau Cherries, and a large variety of Pears and Grapes, and nearly every valuable variety of Apple. There is also a strip bordering upon the north shore of Lake Ontario, and along the St. Lawrence, and upon the Georgian Bay, where the like ameliorating influence is exhibited, but not in a degree sufficient to admit of the successful open air culture of the Peach. Yet its influence is seen in the number of varieties of Apple and Pear that can be grown in perfection near the water, as compared with the number that will succeed a few miles inland, though in the same degree of latitude. As soon as we pass beyond the influence of the water, a marked change of climate is noticeable. In the northern interior parts of Ontario only the hardy Morello Cherries can be grown, the Hearts and Bigarreaus disappearing altogether; many of the choice varieties of the Pear fail, and some of the Apples prove too tender. Yet again, in some of the small fruits and the smaller growing ornamental shrubs, the protection afforded by continuous deep winter snows more than counterbalances the change of atmospheric temperature. Hence it is that in northern Ontario and in the Province of Quebec, all varieties of Raspberry and Blackbery are hardy, and many other plants and shrubs that perish or suffer severely where the winters are open, are there so completely shielded by the snow, that they pass the winter safely, and are cultivated without difficulty.

In the Province of Quebec, only the hardier varieties of Apple can be grown, a limited number of Pears, and only the Morello Cherries, while the Peach wholly fails, and the Plum must be substituted in its stead. In the vicinity of Montreal, such Apples as the Early Joe, Fameuse, St. Lawrence, Pomme Grise, Alexander, Duchess of Oldenburg, Red Astracan, Borassa, and Ribston Pippin thrive well; and with them such Pears as St. Ghislain, Flemish Beauty, Oswego Beurre, White Doyenne, Osband's Summer, Napoleon, Tyson, Belle Lucrative, Doyenne d' Eté, Lawrence, Beurre d'Amalis, Beurre Hardy, Duchesse d'Orleans, Beurre d'Anjou, Louise Bonne de Jersey, Dana's Hovey, and Winter Nelis.

In that climate, the Pear tree may be easily made so tender by manuring, as to be seriously injured, and oftentimes killed outright by the cold of winter, while, if they are allowed to grow more slowly, without the application of stimulating manures, they produce a better ripened wood, more capable of enduring the severity of winter.

So common is the error of stimulating the trees into a too luxuriant growth, that an intelligent observer writes to us that ninety per cent. of all the Pear trees which are planted and grow are killed by manuring. If planted in well-drained ground, which has been enriched only by the rain, snow, decayed foliage, and air, and as they arrive at bearing age top-dressed with lime, wood ashes, and bone-dust, increasing the quantity as the trees come more fully into bearing, they would make a short, stocky growth, ripen their wood, live, and bear fruit. These suggestions are applicable not only to the Pear tree, but to every other fruit tree. Beyond doubt, with such treatment, many varieties now considered too tender, would be found valuable additions to the list of those that succeed well.

In Nova Scotia, the rules that apply in Ontario seem to be in some measure reversed, for there the best fruit is not grown near the sea, but where the range of hills, known as the North Mountain, shuts out the cold winds and sea fogs of the Bay of Fundy, and in other interior portions that are sheltered from the sea. There none of the varieties of Apple are discarded as being *too tender.* Some do not bring their fruit to its full perfection of coloring and flavor, and hence are not suited to that climate, though the tree is vigorous, healthy, and productive. Among the leading sorts that are cultivated there, we find the Alexander, Baldwin, Esopus Spitzenberg, Gravenstein, Golden Russet, Hubbardston Nonsuch, King of Tompkins County, Pomme Grise, Ribston Pippin, Rhode Island Greening, Snow Apple, and Talman Sweet.

Among Pears, we find the Bartlet, Beurre Bosc, Seckel, Swan's Orange, Flemish Beauty, Vicar of Winkfield, Winter Nelis, Duchesse d'Angouleme, Louise Bonne de Jersey and Bloodgood. Plums of all kinds do well, even such late ripening sorts as Coe's Golden Drop, and Reine Claude de Bavay, coming to maturity. Many varieties of the Heart and Bigarreau Cherries also thrive there, such as Black Heart, Black Tartarian, Yellow Spanish, and Downer's Late.

The Quince thrives in deep, moist soils; and even Peaches and Nectarines, when trained against a wall. But on comparing the meteorological tables for *Wolfville,* N.S., with those for

Toronto, Ont., it is found that the difference of temperature in the two places is not very great. The observations from Wolfville, extending over a period of ten years, give the average mean temperature of the year to be 44°.46, while that of Toronto, extending over a period of thirty years, is 44°.10. The warmest month, both at Toronto and Wolfville, is July, and the average mean temperature of that month, for ten years, at Wolfville, is 66°.50; for thirty years, at Toronto, is 67°.33. The coldest month at Wolfville is January; at Toronto, is February; the average mean temperature of January at Wolfville, for ten years, being 23°.05, and of February, at Toronto, for thirty years, being 23°.02. It might then be expected, that so far as the range of temperature affects the cultivation of fruit, vegetables, and flowers, these parts of Nova Scotia would produce the same varieties as those that are grown in the vicinity of Toronto.

In New Brunswick, it seems to be quite impossible to grow fruit trees of any kind on the east and south side of the Province, with the exception of the Siberian Crabs, and the Plum, owing to the prevalence of dense sea fogs. As far inland as the fog reaches, the Plum tree is free from the Black-knot, while beyond the influence of the fog the trees are very badly affected. In the interior of the Province there are some good apple orchards, and some varieties of Grape thrive well, that part being beyond the influence of the fogs. But little, however, seems yet to have been done in that Province, in the cultivation of fruits, and very little reliable information can be had in regard to the varieties that do succeed, on account of the confusion that seems to exist with regard to the names of those that are in cultivation.

It is a noticeable fact, that in those parts of the maritime Provinces where the sea-fogs prevail, so that scarcely any fruit trees can be grown, there the English Gooseberry thrives in perfection, being exempt from the mildew that attacks it so persistently in nearly all the other parts of the Dominion.

Thus it is, that even in the most unfavorable localities there seem to be some compensating benefits. In the milder climates, where the sweeter Cherries and the Peach tree flourish, the winters are so open, that oftentimes the Strawberry and Raspberry crops suffer severely, and many herbaceous plants are unable to endure the winter without protection. But where the winters are too cold to admit of the cultivation of these trees, there the winter snows completely protect the canes of the most tender Raspberries, and without any care from the cultivator, the small fruits and herbaceous plants and dwarfer shrubs pass the winter in safety. By taking advantage of all these varying peculiarities, each may grow those fruits which are most readily produced in his own locality, supplying his table during the summer and autumn, at least with the smaller fruits, from his own garden, while he **obtains his winter stores** from those regions where **the** long-keeping **fruits are more easily** grown.

HARDY EVERGREENS.

The following list of hardy Evergreens may be useful, as a **guide** to those who desire to plant these trees, either for ornament or shelter. The brief description given of each will convey some idea of the peculiar character of the tree, and of its adaptation to particular purposes. The Canadian has need, **if any one, to** plant these, not only for the sake of ornamenting the grounds about his buildings, but for the **shelter** from the chilly blasts of winter, **which they** afford. **From this list, he** will be able to make a selection **which he can plant** with confidence that they will thrive in our **climate. They should** be transplanted in the spring.

AMERICAN **ARBOR VITÆ.**—*Thuja Occidentalis*—This **is a** very common native tree, abounding in moist situations, throughout the Dominion. It is frequently called White Cedar, and in **this way is** confounded with **a very** different tree, the *Cupressus thyoides*, which is the **true White Cedar.** It is exceedingly **hardy,** of very rapid growth, attaining a height of from twenty-**five to fifty** feet, and as it bears clipping well, is one of **our most** useful trees for making evergreen screens and hedges.

There are some very fine dwarf-growing varieties which make very pretty low hedges or bordering for walks, and are an excellent substitute for the Dwarf Box. Those known as Booth's and Parson's Dwarf Arbor Vitæ, are among the best of this class.

AMERICAN YEW.—*Taxus Baccata, var.* **Canadensis.**—This also is a native, and the only Yew that we know to be sufficiently hardy to endure perfectly the severity of our climate. It forms a low spreading shrub, of about three feet in height, naturally somewhat straggling, but very patient under the knife, and can be pruned into any desired form. The foliage is of a deep and somewhat sombre green. The seed is surrounded by a pulpy, cup-shaped disc, of a pretty coral-red color. It is sometimes called Ground Hemlock.

AUSTRIAN PINE.—*Pinus Austriaca.*—This is one of the most popular Pines for ornamental planting. Introduced from the mountains of Austria, it seems to be quite at home in our Canadian climate. It has a rough, shaggy appearance, is of rapid growth, and valuable as a strong, hardy tree, that will produce a speedy effect on the lawn, or be serviceable in breaking the force of sweeping winds.

BALSAM FIR.—*Abies* **Balsamea.**—Another hardy native tree, of a very regular conical outline, attaining a height of some thirty feet or more. It is a beautiful tree when young, but as it acquires age, the lower branches begin to decay, marring sadly the beauty of its earlier years.

COMMON JUNIPER.—*Juniperus Communis.*—Is common to North America, Europe, and Asia. It seldom rises above eight or ten feet in height, and makes a valuable variety for small grounds. It is not suitable for hedges, for which it is sometimes used, the branches frequently dying out, and destroying the appearance of the hedge. It bears pruning well, and may be trimmed into a very neat and compact form.

EASTERN SPRUCE.—*Abies Orientalis.*—One of the most compact growing evergreen trees, attaining a height of about seventy-five feet, of a most beautiful and regularly conical form, branching to the ground. It is as hardy as the Norway Spruce, and makes a very handsome ornamental tree.

HEMLOCK SPRUCE.—*Abies Canadensis.*—A tree of the North, enduring the cold and the storm, yet of most graceful form and foliage, rivalling, nay, surpassing in beauty and elegance most of the evergreens introduced from foreign lands. It is in moist, loamy, and deep soils that it thrives best, there its gracefulness and beauty of form and foliage are fully developed, but in very dry or very wet soils it does not thrive well. When grown in clumps, or crowded with other trees, the lower limbs die out, but standing singly, the branches continue, clothing the tree to the very ground.

LAMBERT'S PINE.—*Pinus Lambertiana.*—This noble tree bears considerable resemblance to our White Pine while it is young, but it attains to a much larger size, rising in its native habitat, on the California coast, to a height of over two hundred feet. It is perfectly hardy in our climate, and makes a valuable addition to the group of Pines.

NORWAY SPRUCE.—*Abies Excelsa.*—Probably the best known and most generally planted of all the evergreens. None surpass it in general utility, for it is hardy, adapts itself to a great variety of soils, grows rapidly, makes a handsome specimen tree when standing singly, and splendid screens or wind-breaks when planted in groups or in more formal hedge-rows.

NORDMANN'S FIR.—*Abies Nordmanniana.*—A native of the Crimean mountains, that deserves a place with us on account of its beauty and hardihood. The specimens we have seen have been perfect models in form and outline, the foliage retaining its freshness in all temperatures, and the growth sturdy and vigorous.

RED CEDAR.—*Juniperus Virginiana.*—Planted in groups, not too closely, this tree may be used as a screen to break the force of our wintry winds, but it is not suitable for hedges, on account of the tendency of the branches to die out when overcrowded. It is extremely variable in its habit of growth, and becomes a very useful tree in the hands of the landscape gardener,.

for the embellishment of rugged spots, or to take a place in picturesque planting.

SCOTCH PINE.—*Pinus Silvestris.*—This well known tree thrives best in cool, well drained subsoils, yet can adapt itself to a great variety of situations, and bear unharmed the rigors of our coldest winters. Somewhat akin to the Austrian Pine in appearance, it is, nevertheless, sufficiently distinct to add to the variety in a collection, and, planted with others for shelter, helps to relieve the monotony which must exist when the planter confines himself to but one or two varieties.

SIBERIAN SILVER FIR.—*Abies Pichta.*—A very handsome small-sized tree, of dense, compact habit, yet graceful outline, and foliage of a peculiarly dark and somewhat sombre hue. It is found in the mountains of Siberia, but thrives well in our climate, and readily adapts itself to a great variety of soils. Owing to its small size, it should be planted in front of its fellows; in such situations it will form a most pleasing contrast to the foliage of other varieties.

SIBERIAN ARBOR VITÆ.—*Thuja Occidentalis, var. Sibirica.*—This variety is exceedingly hardy, and is distinguished from the American Arbor Vitæ by its conical form, and its very dense and fine, dark-green foliage. It is a most beautiful hedge plant.

SWEEDISH JUNIPER.—*Juniperus communis, var. Suecica.*—A very hardy and useful Juniper, from the north of Europe. It has a more fastigiate habit of growth than the common Juniper, with lighter yellowish-green foliage, and larger berries.

TARTARIAN ARBOR VITÆ.—*Biota Orientalis, var. Tartarica.* This is quite hardy. The leaves are of a dark, glossy-green, and the tree has a very pleasing appearance. It makes beautiful evergreen screens and hedges, and a very suitable tree for cemeteries.

WHITE PINE.—*Pinus Strobus.*—A well known native tree, that in the crowded forest is tall and naked, but grown singly, forms a handsome head. It thrives best on dry, gravelly or sandy soils, and refuses to display its perfection of form and beauty of outline when planted on a wet soil. It is perfectly hardy throughout the Dominion, and contrasts finely with the darker leaved Evergreens.

WHITE SPRUCE.—*Abies Alba.*—Another of our beautiful native evergreens, hardy everywhere, growing rapidly, with a fine compact habit, and handsome, regular outline. It thrives well in damp grounds and moist places. It should be planted in the foreground, where its beautiful glaucous-green leaves may be brought into contrast with those of darker shades behind.

WHITE CEDAR.—*Cupressus thyoides.*—This tree is found upon the borders of the great lakes, but is most plentiful in the middle United States. It is a different tree from the American Arbor Vitæ, which is so commonly called White Cedar with us, and seems to be a connecting link between the Arbor Vitæ and the Cypress. It thrives in low, swampy places, and will make a very pretty screen.

LAWSON'S CYPRESS.—*Cupressus Lawsoniana.*—We can not refrain from mentioning this most beautiful Evergreen Cypress, believing that it will be found sufficiently hardy to endure the climate of a considerable part of Ontario, and possibly of some parts of the Maritime Provinces. There is nothing we have yet seen that equals the gracefulness, elegance and beauty, of this tree. Its plume-like branches have a charming, airy lightness, the foliage has the most delicate tints of bluish-green, and the whole contour of the tree has such a fern-like character, that one can only gaze upon it with delight. In planting it, we advise that the ground be not enriched with any stimulating fertilizers, and that the location be free from excess of moisture. A late autumn growth is to be avoided as much as possible, as such growth is very apt to suffer from the frosts of winter.

CONCLUSION.

There may be "no royal road to learning," but there is a royal road to success in the cultivation of fruits, vegetables and flowers in Canada. It is a road that none but those who have royal blood in their veins may travel. It is for those who, though they boast not their descent from regal sires, are nature's noblemen; men of earnest purpose, who, with head and heart devoted to the culture of the garden, have learned "to labor and to wait."

"Knowledge is power," as truly in the cultivation of the soil as in anything else. It was quaintly replied by a successful cultivator, when asked what fertilizer he used to obtain such splendid results: "Brains, sir, brains; I manure my grounds with brains!"

Use, then, your brains. Study your business. Bring all the activities of your mind to bear upon your gardening. Enlarge your powers of thought and observation by studying the opinions and doings of others; follow nothing blindly, but bring all to the test of your own common sense. Keep your eyes open to the operations of nature, and let the experience of each year teach you how to remedy the defects of the past, and place you on vantage ground for the operations of the future.

In the hope that the hints contained in these pages, drawn mainly from the writer's own experience and observation, may contribute something to the reader's progress, and stimulate to increased thoughtfulness and zeal in the cultivation of the garden, we bid you

"Study culture, and with artful toil,
Meliorate and tame the stubborn soil."

ACKNOWLEDGMENTS.

To those gentlemen who have so kindly placed at the author's disposal their valuable stores of information, the results of many years of experience and toil, the thanks not only of the writer are due, but of all who take an interest in the cultivation of fruits, flowers, and vegetables throughout the Dominion.

From R. W. Starr, Esq., of Port Williams, Nova Scotia, very full and important information has been received concerning the several kinds and varieties of fruit usually cultivated in that Province; and from Herbert Harris, Esq., of the Halifax Nurseries, equally valuable data have been obtained with regard to the ornamental trees, shrubs, roses, and flowering plants that flourish in Nova Scotia.

To Thomas Miller, Esq., of St. Johns, we are under obligations for much valuable information concerning the fruits; and to Mr. John Fisher, Florist, of the same place, for notes of fruits, flowers, and vegetables grown in New Brunswick. Our thanks are also due to Richard Thompson, Esq., of St. Johns, for like favors.

With reference to the Province of Quebec, we have been greatly aided by the perusal of very full and very valuable notes, embracing the experience of a long series of years, kindly placed at our disposal by James H. Springle, Esq., of Montreal.

To each of these gentlemen, and to all who have kindly contributed of their valuable stores of knowledge, we desire to express our most hearty thanks, though we well know they themselves feel amply repaid for any trouble they have taken, by the hope that they may have in this way done something to lighten the labors of some toiling brother.

One request the writer would make of all those who may do him the honor to examine this first attempt to prepare a Canadian work of this kind; it is, that they would kindly note down any omissions they may discover, or any fuller information they may have in their possession upon any of the varieties of fruits, flowers, or vegetables that are cultivated in their vicinity, and communicate the same to the author. It will be his endeavor to use such information for the benefit of the whole Dominion, through the columns of the *Canada Farmer*, and in such other manner as he may find possible.

www.ingramcontent.com/pod-product-compliance
Lightning Source LLC
Chambersburg PA
CBHW030554300426
44111CB00009B/977